GLOBAL POPULAR MUSIC

Global Popular Music: A Research and Information Guide offers an essential annotated bibliography of scholarship on popular music around the world in a two-volume set. Featuring a broad range of subjects, people, cultures, and geographic areas, and spanning musical genres such as traditional, folk, jazz, rock, reggae, samba, rai, punk, hip-hop, and many more, this guide highlights different approaches and discussions within global popular music research. This research guide is comprehensive in scope, providing a vital resource for scholars and students approaching the vast amount of publications on popular music studies and popular music traditions around the world. Thorough cross-referencing and robust indexes of genres, places, names, and subjects make the guide easy to use.

Volume 1, *Global Perspectives in Popular Music Studies*, situates popular music studies within global perspectives and geocultural settings at large. It offers over nine hundred in-depth annotated bibliographic entries of interdisciplinary research and several topical categories that include analytical, critical, and historical studies; theory, methodology, and musicianship studies; annotations of in-depth special issues published in scholarly journals on different topics, issues, trends, and music genres in popular music studies that relate to the contributions of numerous musicians, artists, bands, and music groups; and annotations of selected reference works.

Clarence Bernard Henry, author of Routledge titles *Global Jazz: A Research and Information Guide* (2021), *Miles Davis: A Research and Information Guide* (2017), and *Quincy Jones: A Research and Information Guide* (2014), is an independent scholar.

ROUTLEDGE MUSIC BIBLIOGRAPHIES

RECENT TITLES

COMPOSERS

John Adams (2020)
Alexander Sanchez-Behar

Isaac Albéniz, 2nd Edition (2015)
Walter A. Clark

William Alwyn (2013)
John C. Dressler

Samuel Barber, 2nd Edition (2012)
Wayne C. Wentzel

Béla Bartók, 3rd Edition (2011)
Elliott Antokoletz and Paolo
Susanni

Alban Berg, 3rd Edition (2018)
Bryan R. Simms

Leonard Bernstein, 2nd Edition
(2015)
Paul R. Laird and Hsun Lin

Johannes Brahms, 2nd Edition
(2011)
Heather Platt

William Byrd, 3rd Edition (2012)
Richard Turbet

John Cage (2017)
Sara Haefeli

Frédéric Chopin, 2nd Edition (2015)
William Smialek and Maja
Trochimczyk

Miles Davis (2017)
Clarence Bernard Henry

John Dowland (2019)
K. Dawn Grapes

Edward Elgar, 2nd Edition (2013)
Christopher Kent

Gabriel Fauré, 2nd Edition (2011)
Edward R. Phillips

Alberto Ginastera (2011)
Deborah Schwartz-Kates

Fanny Hensel (2019)
Laura K.T. Stokes

Gustav Holst (2011)
Mary Christison Huismann

Charles Ives, 2nd Edition (2010)
Gayle Sherwood Magee

Quincy Jones (2014)
Clarence Bernard Henry

*Alma Mahler and Her
Contemporaries* (2017)
Susan M. Filler

Bohuslav Martinů (2014)
Robert Simon

*Felix Mendelssohn Bartholdy, 2nd
Edition* (2011)
John Michael Cooper with
Angela R. Mace

Olivier Messiaen, 2nd Edition
(2017)
Vincent P. Benitez

Claudio Monteverdi (2018)
Susan Lewis and Maria Virginia
Acuña

*Nikolay Andreevich Rimsky-
Korsakov, 2nd Edition* (2015)
Gerald R. Seaman

Joaquín Rodrigo (2021)
Walter A. Clark

Gioachino Rossini, 2nd Edition
(2010)
Denise P. Gallo

Pëtr Il'ich Tchaikovsky (2019)
Gerald R. Seaman

Ralph Vaughan Williams (2016)
Ryan Ross

Giuseppe Verdi, 2nd Edition (2012)
Gregory W. Harwood

Richard Wagner, 2nd Edition
(2010)
Michael Saffle

Anton Webern (2017)
Darin Hoskisson

GENRES

*Blues, Funk, R&B, Soul, Hip Hop,
and Rap* (2010)
Eddie S. Meadows

Chamber Music, 3rd Edition (2010)
John H. Baron

Choral Music, 3rd Edition (2019)
James Michael Floyd

*Church and Worship Music in the
United States, 2nd Edition* (2017)
Avery T. Sharp and James
Michael Floyd

Ethnomusicology, 2nd Edition (2013)
Jennifer C. Post

*Film Music in the Sound Era,
Volumes 1 & 2* (2020)
Jonathan Rhodes Lee

Free Jazz (2018)
Jeffrey Schwartz

Global Jazz (2021)
Clarence Bernard Henry

The Madrigal (2012)
Susan Lewis Hammond

The Musical, 2nd Edition (2011)
William A. Everett

North American Fiddle Music (2011)
Drew Beisswenger

*Popular Music Theory and
Analysis* (2017)
Thomas Robinson

The Recorder, 3rd Edition (2012)
Richard Griscom and David Lasocki

String Quartets, 2nd Edition (2011)
Mara E. Parker

Women in Music, 2nd Edition (2011)
Karin Pendle and Melinda Boyd

*Global Popular Music: A Research
and Information Guide, Volumes
1 & 2*
Clarence Bernard Henry

GLOBAL POPULAR MUSIC
A Research and Information Guide

VOLUME 1: GLOBAL PERSPECTIVES IN POPULAR MUSIC STUDIES

CLARENCE BERNARD HENRY

ROUTLEDGE MUSIC BIBLIOGRAPHIES

NEW YORK AND LONDON

First published 2025
by Routledge
605 Third Avenue, New York, NY 10158

and by Routledge
4 Park Square, Milton Park, Abingdon, Oxon, OX14 4RN

Routledge is an imprint of the Taylor & Francis Group, an informa business

© 2025 Clarence Bernard Henry

Library of Congress Cataloging-in-Publication Data
Names: Henry, Clarence Bernard, author.
Title: Global popular music : a research and information guide / Clarence Bernard Henry.
Description: New York, NY : Routledge, 2024. | Series: Routledge music bibliographies |
    Includes bibliographical references and index.
Contents: Volume 1. Global perspectives in popular music studies
Identifiers: LCCN 2024025558 (print) | LCCN 2024025559 (ebook) | ISBN 9781032830186
    (hardback) | ISBN 9781032830223 (paperback) | ISBN 9781003507345 (ebook)
Subjects: LCSH: Popular music—Bibliography. | World music—Bibliography.
Classification: LCC ML128.P63 H46 2024 (print) | LCC ML128.P63 (ebook) |
    DDC 016.78242164—dc23/eng/20240611
LC record available at https://lccn.loc.gov/2024025558
LC ebook record available at https://lccn.loc.gov/2024025559

ISBN: 978-1-032-86573-7 (hbk set)
ISBN: 978-1-032-86576-8 (pbk set)

ISBN: 978-1-032-83018-6 (hbk)
ISBN: 978-1-032-83022-3 (pbk)
ISBN: 978-1-003-50734-5 (ebk)

DOI: 10.4324/9781003507345

Typeset in Minion
by Apex CoVantage, LLC

Contents

Preface

GLOBAL POPULAR MUSIC AND SCHOLARLY DISCOURSE

Global popular music reflects the processes of globalization, transmusical and transnational experiences, and transcultural flows of musical ideologies, aesthetic behavior, and the stylistic influences from popular music genres as jazz, rock, blues, rhythm and blues (R&B), soul, country, punk, metal, techno, house, zydeco, hip-hop, reggae, samba, flamenco, krautrock, K-pop, Eurobeat, Afrobeat, and many others that have become part of diverse musical and artistic lexicons in the world and in geocultural constructs at large. Thus, a focus on global popular music within the rubrics of scholarly discourses of popular music, popular music studies, and world music studies offers appropriate areas for the construction of a research and information guide that displays annotations of selected publications on global popular music. Furthermore, such scholarly discourses on global popular music and the influences of world music in societies and cultural settings offer a variety of approaches, issues, and perspectives.

Global Popular Music: A Research and Information Guide comprises two volumes of scholarly research designed to appeal widely to international audiences and researchers. It serves as a comprehensive resource for navigating extensive publications on popular music studies and traditions worldwide. The body of scholarly works covering global popular music is massive, evident by the many publications of books, book series, book chapters, scholarly journal essays, scholarly journal special issues, conference proceedings, reference works, trade magazines, online databases, website information, recording compilations, films and documentaries, and others. Therefore, it is opined that no single volume can inform the entire massive amounts of materials published on global popular music or popular music studies in general. Thus, one of the reasons for completing a tailored research and information guide on global popular music is to provide a compendium of global popular music as part of academic discourse in popular music studies covering issues of research, theory, methodology, interdisciplinary studies, and others to demonstrate how scholars have attempted to expand the study of popular music in research, scholarship, and curricula design beyond the grounded principles of the academic canon positioned solely in the study of Western art music.

The two-volume set of *Global Popular Music: A Research and Information Guide* features annotated entries covering bodies of extensive research that extend beyond the borders of the United States. Furthermore, because of its interdisciplinary scope, this research and information guide can be used to complement and enhance the topic of global popular music and inform combinations of new millennium discourses from a variety of perspectives. It should be noted that this research and information guide is not intended to be an exhaustive resource that contains every published scholarly work on global popular music. But this research and information guide is comprehensive in scope and offers a representative body of selected annotated entries contained therein from the massive amounts of materials that contribute to global, local, and regional studies on issues and topics on popular music, popular music studies, and popular music research as part of interdisciplinary and academic discourses.

Many of the selected scholarly works, which detail information on artists, musicians, bands, and so forth, contribute to geo-musical constructs within popular music or what can be described as global popular music research where the subject of "popular music," drawn from a worldview perspective, is approached broadly and designed to encompass diverse research on musical genres such as traditional, folk, classical, jazz, rock, reggae, samba, rai, punk, hip-hop, and others from around the world that can be identified and linked with popular music studies. The resources of materials gathered for the annotated entries were carefully selected to represent a breadth, scope, and thoroughness of various topics covering scholarly writings concerning popular music traditions, histories, genres, trends, and musicians from a global perspective.

Many of the scholarly works were selected because they also incorporate a vast amount of additional bibliographic sources that can further benefit users of this research and information guide and expand research in global popular music. This research and information guide and the selected annotations are also intended to highlight different approaches and discussions of popular music, trends, and genres that focus on particular bands, musical groups, and artists such as Beyoncé, Jay-Z, Michael Jackson, Bruce Springsteen, Lady Gaga, Taylor Swift, Dolly Parton, Madonna, the Rolling Stones, the Beatles, Prince, James Brown, Quincy Jones, Joni Mitchell, Paul Simon, David Bowie, Pink Floyd, Aretha Franklin, BTS, Lin-Manuel Miranda (*Hamilton* and *In the Heights*), and many others from around the world that inform the extension of popular music studies within paradigms of analytical, critical, historical, musicological, sociocultural, political, theoretical, and other types of scholarly discourses.

VOLUME 1: THE CHAPTERS AND ANNOTATED ENTRIES

Volume 1, titled *Global Perspectives in Popular Music Studies*, offers in-depth annotated entries that feature several topical categories—analytical, critical, and historical studies; theory, methodology, and musicianship studies; annotations to in-depth special issues published in scholarly journals on different topics, issues, trends, and music genres in popular music studies that relate to the contributions of numerous musicians, artists, bands, and music groups; and annotations of selected reference works, edited companions, dictionaries, encyclopedias, handbooks, and other resources. Volume 1 includes over nine hundred annotated entries and is comprised of chapters one through four that feature interdisciplinary research topics and issues on global perspectives in popular music studies.

Chapter one provides selected annotations of analytical, critical, and historical studies that includes many annotated entries of case studies from different parts of the world that examine or define aspects of globalization in popular music. For example, included in this chapter is the annotation of the edited volume *Geographically Isolated and Peripheral Music Scenes: Global Insights and Perspectives* (Ballico 2021), which explores the connection between music and the social production of remote places. Compiled essays in this volume provide case studies from around the world and lay out the challenges of peripheral locales and how musical activities emerge because they take place in the periphery, not just because of their relative isolation. Another edited volume, *Living Metal: Metal Scenes Around the World* (Bardine & Steuart 2022), explores metal scenes throughout the world and presents a portrayal of how these scenes developed, are experienced by fans, and are influenced by the contexts in which they are embedded. Essays compiled in this edited volume also connect metal to other disciplines in the field of music. Chapter one also includes annotations to edited volumes such as *DIY Cultures and Underground Music Scenes* (Bennett & Guerra 2019), a compilation of essays that examine the global influence and impact of DIY cultural practices, as these inform the production, performance, and consumption of underground in different parts of the world. This volume compiles a series of essays from original studies of do-it-yourself (DIY) musical activities in Europe, North and South America, Asia, and Oceania (e.g., Bucharest, France, Northern Germany, the Basque Country, Aotearoa/New Zealand, Finland, Indonesia, Brazil, Berlin, Hungary, Scotland, Britain, and Bulgaria).

Chapter two provides a series of annotated entries of scholarly research that focus on popular music studies in terms of theory, methodology, and musicianship. For example, included in this chapter are studies such as *Groove Theory: The Blues Foundation of Funk* (Bolden 2020), a book that presents an innovative history of funk music focused on the performers as intellectuals who fashioned a new aesthetic that utilizes musicology, literary studies, performance studies, and African American intellectual history to explore what it means for music or as a cultural artifact to be funky. The author undertakes a theoretical examination of the development of funk and the historical conditions in which Black artists reimagined their music and provides historical and biographical studies of key funk artists who transfigured elements of blues tradition into new styles and visions. In the book *Interpreting Popular Music* (Brackett 1995), the author focuses on how we analyze the effects of popular music and its meaning. Brackett draws from the disciplines of cultural studies and music theory to demonstrate how listeners form opinions about popular songs and come to attribute a rich variety of meanings to them. The author also explores several genres of popular music through recordings of Hank Williams, James Brown, Billie Holiday, Bing Crosby, and Elvis Costello and develops a set of tools for looking at both formal and cultural dimensions of popular music of all kinds.

In a pedagogical study titled "Music Theory as Social Justice: Pedagogical Applications of Kendrick Lamar's *To Pimp a Butterfly*," (Attas 2019), the author employs the use of American rapper and Pulitzer Prize winner Kendrick Lamar's album, *To Pimp a Butterfly* ("*Butterfly*"), as a case study to demonstrate possible ways that music theorists can integrate their discipline with the world at large. The author suggests that the album draws attention to the genre of hip-hop and its political history, incorporating Lamar's rich and unique musical language, and discusses issues of race and racism in the United States in a compelling way. The author's intention is to demonstrate how *Butterfly* can offer several methods for bringing social justice into the music theory classroom, but also discusses how many hip-hop albums can be used to teach standard core theory topics with the social justice agenda left implicit.

Chapter three provides annotations to many in-depth special issues published in scholarly journals on different topics, issues, trends, and music genres in popular music studies that relate to the contributions of numerous musicians, artists, bands, and music groups. Some of the topics of selected special journal issues include popular music and populism; regional and rural popular music scenes; popular music, cultural memory, and heritage; perspectives on popular music and sound recording; popular music and canonization; popular music and labor; autoethnographic and qualitative research on popular music; gender and sexuality; popular music and music education; women in popular music; reflections on the past, present, and future of popular music scholarship; the pandemic (popular music and COVID-19); popular music and aging, popular music and disability; popular music and dance; forum on religion, popular music, and globalization; the politics and aesthetics of world music; progressive rock; hip-hop studies; and many others. In addition, this chapter also presents special journal issues dedicated to scholarly discourses on the contributions of iconic popular musicians and bands such as the Beatles, Rolling Stones, Sex Pistols, Velvet Underground, Michael Jackson, Prince, Beyoncé, Taylor Swift, Steely Dan, Chuck Berry, Bob Dylan, and many others. For further research, the selected special journal issues also include a series of book, record and audio, and film reviews.

Chapter four includes annotations of selected reference works, annotated bibliographies, edited companions, dictionaries, encyclopedias, handbooks, and others that provide a wealth of information and can be incorporated as part of interdisciplinary popular music studies research. For example, the edited volume *The Routledge Companion to Popular Music and Humor* (Baxter-Moore & Kitts 2019) compiles essays that draw on scholarship exploring how the element of humor interacts with the artistic and social aspects of the musical experience and discusses humor in popular music in a global perspective. *The Bloomsbury Handbook of Popular Music and Youth Culture* (Bennett 2022) provides a comprehensive overview of key themes and debates relating to the academic study of popular music and youth culture. The essays in this compilation cover a range of topics such as historical perspectives, genres, audiences, media, globalization, aging, and generation. *The Bloomsbury Handbook of Popular Music Video Analysis* (Burns & Hawkins 2019) covers a wide range of current research on music video and audiovisual elements in popular music, multimodality and transmedia practice in popular music, palimpsestic pop music video, and more.

Additional annotated sources provided in chapter four feature *The Routledge Research Companion to Electronic Music: Reaching Out With Technology* (Emmerson 2018), a series of essays with the themes of connectivity and the global reach of electroacoustic music and sonic arts made with technology that emphasize the trends of the field in the last thirty years, including the definition of the field as broadening no clear boundary between electronic music and "sound art" and the simple divide between "art" and "popular" practice with many histories including world music traditions. *The Cambridge Companion to Pop and Rock* (Firth, Straw & Street 2011), an edited volume, maps the world of pop and rock covering topics such as technology and popular music, the pop music industry, consumption, interpretations of pop, rock, gender, sexuality, and race, and local and global perspectives in popular music. *The Bloomsbury Handbook of Religion and Popular Music* (Partridge & Moberg 2017) explores the principal areas of inquiry, suggests new directions for scholarship, and covers religious traditions such as

Christianity, Islam, Judaism, Hinduism, Buddhism, Paganism, Occultism, and popular music genres that range from heavy metal and hip-hop to country music and film and television music.

The resources mentioned are just a few examples of the extensive research on global perspectives within popular music studies, compiled as selected annotated entries in Volume 1. The entries cover a diverse range of domestic and international books, book series, chapters, edited volumes, biographies, biographical profiles, reference and scholarly essays, conference and symposium papers, annotated bibliographies, companions, dictionaries, encyclopedias, handbooks, reference sources, dissertations and theses, peer-reviewed journal articles (print, electronic resource, and online materials), discographies, and film documentaries and special programming. The research is generated from a variety of organizations and sources that include World Catalog, Library of Congress Catalog, The New York Public Library for the Performing Arts, Dorothy and Lewis B. Cullman Center, Music Index, RILM: Abstracts of Music Literature, Oxford and Grove Music Online, ProQuest, Academic Search Primer, JSTOR, Project Muse, International Index to Music Periodicals, dissertation and theses abstracts, and others.

The citations of selected annotated entries presented in each chapter and section are arranged alphabetically by names of authors and editors and are also arranged in numerical order. The entries include publication dates, titles, publisher information, names of academic institutions, academic degrees (for dissertations and theses information), series titles, volume numbers, page numbers, International Standard Book Numbers (ISBN), International Serial Numbers (ISSN), and/or OCLC Numbers. When appropriate, specific languages of a publication other than English are also indicated within the citation as well as the indication of an English abstract, summary, or language translation. Also, a brief description is provided of special features that accompany the publication such as the inclusion of a bibliography, index, filmography, discography, music examples, compact discs, DVDs, illustrations, maps, facsimiles, portraits, and photographs. A summary of the publication's contents is also presented within each annotated entry.

VOLUME 1: THE INDEXES

Volume 1 of this research and information guide includes four comprehensive indexes that are arranged and integrated with the appropriate number of each annotated entry. The "Index of Global Popular Music Genres" offers an alphabetical a listing of music genres from around the world that are included in this guide. The "Index of Continents, Countries, Cities, Regions, and Localities" provides an alphabetical listing of the many geographical areas included. The "Index of Names" provides an alphabetical listing of covered authors, musicians, bands, venues, organizations, and so on. In addition, researchers are encouraged to explore the annotated entries to reference sources such as *International Who's Who in Popular Music* (Europa Publications 2024a) and *International Who's Who in Classical Music* (Europa Publications 2024b), which provide additional biographical and contact information of thousands of influential musicians, artists, singers, instrumentalists, composers, conductors, managers, and others from the world of global popular music.

The "Index of Subjects" is arranged in alphabetical order of subjects and topics covered throughout the guide. The subjects and topics include Aboriginal, Indigenous, and Native American Studies; African American, Africana, and Black Studies; Aging and Disability Studies; Analytical, Critical, and Historical Studies; Annotated Bibliographies, Companions, Dictionaries, Discographies, Encyclopedias, Handbooks, Reference Works, Research Guides; Arab, Muslim, and Islamic Identities in Popular Music; Audience and Fandom Studies; Classical, Western Art Music, and Popular Music; Continental and Regional Studies; Dance and Electronic Dance Music Culture (EDMC) Studies; Digital, Social Media, and Technology Studies; Documentary Films and Special Programming; Extreme, Protest, Violence, Trauma Popular Music Studies; Film and Popular Music Studies; Folk Music and Popular Music Studies; Gender, Identity, and Sexuality Studies; General Studies and Additional Reference Works; Global and Globalization Discourses in Popular Music Studies; Jews and Jewish Studies; Latinx, Latino/a, Chicano Studies; Music Festivals and Popular Music Studies; Music Industry, Music Business; Musical Theater; Pandemics, Community Health, and Popular Music Studies; Popular Music and Ethnomusicological Studies; Popular Music and Interdisciplinary Studies; Popular Music, Archival, Cultural Heritage, and Museum Studies; Popular Music, Artistic Expressions, Social, Sociocultural, and Political Discourses; Popular Music, Criticism, and Journalism; Popular Music, Education, and Pedagogy; Popular Music, Language, Linguistic, and Literary Studies; Popular Music, Lyrics and Lyrical Texts Studies; Queer, LGBTQ, and Trans Studies; Regional and Local Perspectives in Popular Music Studies; Religion and Popular Music Studies; Sonic and Sound Studies; Special Journal Issues; Theory, Methodology, and Musicianship Studies; Transmusical, Transcultural, Transnational, Cross-Cultural Studies; Women Studies; and World Music.

REFERENCES

Attas, Robin. 2019. "Music Theory as Social Justice: Pedagogical Applications of Kendrick Lamar's *To Pimp a Butterfly*." *Music Theory Online* 25(1): 1–13.

Ballico, Christina, ed. 2021. *Geographically Isolated and Peripheral Music Scenes: Global Insights and Perspectives*. Singapore: Palgrave MacMillan.

Bardine, Bryan A., and Jerome Stueart, eds. 2022. *Living Metal: Metal Scenes around the World*. Bristol: Intellect Books.

Baxter-Moore, Nicolas, and Thomas M. Kitts, eds. 2019. *The Routledge Companion to Popular Music and Humor*. Abingdon, Oxon & New York: Routledge.

Bennett, Andy, ed. 2022. *The Bloomsbury Handbook of Popular Music and Youth Culture*. New York: Bloomsbury.

Bennett, Andy, and Paula Guerra, eds. 2019. *DIY Cultures and Underground Music Scenes*. Abingdon, Oxon & New York: Routledge.

Bolden, Tony. 2020. *Groove Theory: The Blues Foundation of Funk*. Jackson: University of Mississippi Press.

Brackett, David. 1995. *Interpreting Popular Music*. Cambridge & New York: Cambridge University Press.

Burns, Lori, and Stan Hawkins, eds. 2019. *The Bloomsbury Handbook of Popular Music Video Analysis*. New York: Bloomsbury.

Emmerson, Simon, ed. 2018. *The Routledge Research Companion to Electronic Music: Reaching Out with Technology*. Abingdon, Oxon: Routledge.

Europa Publications, ed. 2024a. *International Who's Who in Popular Music, 26th ed*. London: Routledge.

Europa Publications, ed. 2024b. *International Who's Who in Classical Music, 40th ed*. New York: Routledge.

Firth, Simon, WillStraw, and John Street, eds. 2011. *The Cambridge Companion to Pop and Rock*. Cambridge: Cambridge University Press.

Partridge, Christopher, and Marcus Moberg. 2017. *The Bloomsbury Handbook of Religion and Popular Music*. London & New York: Bloomsbury.

1

Analytical, Critical, and Historical Studies

1. **Adorno, Theodor**. 2002. "On Popular Music." In *Essays on Music*, Richard Leppert, ed., and Susan H. Gillespie, translator. xvii, 743 p. Bibliography and Index. ISBN: 9-780-52023-159-7.

    Focuses on the works and writings on Theodor Adorno, a principal figure of the Frankfurt School, and his writing on music. Distinguishes between "popular" and "serious" music. Argues that the hallmark of popular music is standardization across different genres. The essay offers a critical reading and is divided into several sections where Adorno further explicates notions about the influences of music in popular culture.

2. **Agamennone, Maurizio, Daniele Palma, and Giulia Sarno, eds**. 2023. *Sounds of the Pandemic: Accounts, Experiences, Perspective in Time of COVID-19*. Abingdon, Oxon: Routledge. xiii, 195 p. Illustrations, Bibliography, and Index. ISBN: 9-781-03206-023-1.

    Offers a critical analysis of the changes in sonic environments, artistic practice, and listening behavior caused by the coronavirus outbreak. Compiled essays provide detailed picture of a wide array of phenomena related to sound and music including soundscapes, music production, music performance, and mediatization processes in the context of COVID-19.

3. **Alim, H. Samy, Ibrahim Awad, and Alistair Pennycock, eds**. 2009. *Global Linguistic Flows: Hip-Hop Cultures, Youth Identities, and the Politics of Language*. New York: Routledge. xi, 260 p. Illustrations, Bibliography, and Index. ISBN: 9-780-20389-278-7.

DOI: 10.4324/9781003507345-1

An edited volume of essays that inform the intersection of sociolinguistics and hip-hop studies. Compiled essays integrate research from an international group of scholars who study hip-hop textually, ethnographically, socially, aesthetically, and linguistically. Compiled essays also fill the gap in hip-hop literature and provide in-depth analysis of the very medium that is used to express and perform hip-hop. Geographical areas covered include Africa, Australia, Asia, the Americas, and the European Union and hip-hop manifestation in places such as Brazil, Tanzania, Canada (Quebec), Hong Kong, and Japan.

4. **Alim, H. Samy, Jeff Chang, and Casey P. Wong, eds**. 2023. *Freedom Moves: Hip-Hop Knowledges, Pedagogies, and Futures*. Series: *California Series in Hip-Hop Studies, 3*. Oakland: University of California Press. 478 p. Illustrations, Bibliography, and Index. ISBN: 9-780-52038-280-0.

A collection of essays that examine how hip-hop continues to be one of the most profound and transformative social, cultural, and political movements of the late twentieth and early twenty-first centuries. Engages dialogically with innovative and provocative hip-hop artists and intellectuals as they collectively rethink the relationships between hip-hop knowledges, pedagogies, and futures. Constructed to present globally diverse groups of Black, Latinx, Asian American, Arab European, North African, and South African artists, activists, and thinkers who view hip-hop to move freedom forward.

5. **Allison, Adrian, and Jacqueline Warwick, eds**. 2016. *Voicing Girlhood in Popular Music: Performance, Authority, Authenticity*. Series: *Routledge Studies in Popular Music, 13*. New York: Routledge. x, 300 p. Illustrations, Bibliography, and Index. ISBN: 9-781-31742-460-4.

An interdisciplinary volume of essays that explores the girl's voice and the construction of girlhood in contemporary music, focusing on girls as musicians, artists, and performers. Essay topics range from female voice development during adolescence to girls' online media culture. Essays consider girl performers, such as Jackie Evancho and Lorde, and all-girl bands such as Sleater-Kinney, The Slits, and Warpaint, as well as performative "girlishness" in the voices of female vocalists such as Joni Mitchell, Beyoncé, Miley Cyrus, Taylor Swift, Kathleen Hanna, and Rebecca Black.

6. **Anderton, Chris, and Martin James, eds**. 2022. *Media Narratives in Popular Music*. New York: Bloomsbury. 257 p. Bibliography and Index. ISBN: 9-781-50135-727-5.

Examines various publications and questions about how and why media narratives are constructed. Considers the typically linear narratives that are based on simplifications, exaggerations, and omissions and the histories they construct. Examines and questions the basis on which these mediated histories are constructed. Topics include consumerism, the production pressure behind documentaries, punk fanzines, *Rolling Stone* covers, feminist music press, discourse in electronic dance music, media narratives of hip-hop, narratives of progressive rock, pre-punk history, and Britpop counter-narratives.

7. **Andrews, Gavin J., Paul Kingsbury, and Robin Kearns, eds**. 2016. *Soundscapes of Wellbeing in Popular Music*. Series: *Ashgate's Geographies of Health Series*. London & New York. Previously published, Farnham & Burlington: Ashgate, 2014. xvi, 340 p. Illustrations, Bibliography, and Index. ISBN: 9-781-13826-924-8.

    A compilation of essays that explore musical soundscapes of health, ranging from activism and international charity to therapeutic treatments and how wellbeing is sought after and attained in contexts of music. Compiled essays draw on critical social theories of the production, circulation, and consumption of popular music that integrate diverse insights from geographers and musicologists. Essays also demonstrate how popular music has become increasingly embedded in complex and often contradictory discourses of wellbeing.

8. **Appadurai, Arjun**. 1996. *Modernity at Large: Cultural Dimensions of Globalization*. Series: *Public Worlds, Volume 1*. Minneapolis: University of Minnesota Press. xi, 229 p. Bibliography and Index. ISBN: 0-81662-792-4.

    Offers a new framework for the cultural study of globalization. Demonstrates how the imagination works as a social force for identity and energies for creating alternatives to the nation-state, whose era some see as coming to an end. Examines the current epoch of globalization, which is characterized by migration, electronic mediation, and so on. Considers the way images—lifestyles, popular culture, and self-representation—circulate internationally through the media and are often borrowed in surprising and innovative ways.

9. **Appen, Ralf von, André Doehring, and Allan Moore, eds**. 2016. *Song Interpretation in 21st Century Pop Music*. Series: *Ashgate Popular and Folk Music Series*. London & New York: Routledge. 304 p. Bibliography and Index. ISBN: 9-781-13863-050-5.

    A compilation of essays that compare and discuss the ways in which to make sense of specific songs. Essays provide analysis of songs from the twenty-first century and offer insight on how million sellers work. Essays highlight mainstream pop (Lady Gaga, Kesha, Lucenzo, Amy McDonald); indie styles (Fleet Foxes, Death Cab for Cutie, PJ Harvey); R&B (Destiny's Child, Janelle Monae); popular hard rock (Kings of Leon, Rammstein); and current electronic music (Andrés, Björk).

10. **Archer, William K. ed**. 1964. *The Presentation of Traditional Forms of the Learned and Popular Music of the Orient and the Occidental*. Urbana: Center for Comparative Psycholinguistics; Institute of Communications Research; University of Illinois. English and French texts. vii, 324 p. OCLC Number: 1-7463-9.

    A compilation of papers that demonstrate an early example of the focus in the 1960s and treatment of scholarly research on popular music studies. Compilation of papers stem from part of the International Counsel, UNESCO, Paris, and International Congress held in Tehran, Iran, in April 1964.

11. **Archer-Capuzzo, Sonia**. 2021. "Mining for Metal: Heavy Metal and the Music Library." *Notes* 78(1): 1–21. ISSN: 0027-4380.

Provides a basic introduction to heavy metal music and materials and some suggested best practices for working with these materials in a library or archival setting. Argues that heavy metal, once considered an outlier among the popular music genres by music critics and scholars, has enjoyed a large and dedicated fan base. Moreover, in the twenty-first century it has become an increasingly popular subject of music scholarship, which has led to an increase in the number and variety of metal resources available to and collected by librarians.

12. **Atkins, Paul**. 2020. *Amplified: A Design of the Electric Guitar*. London: Reaktion Books. 297 p. Illustrations, Bibliography, and Index. ISBN: 9-781-78914-274-7.

Examines the invention and development of the electric guitar. Explores how the electric guitar's design has changed and what its design over the years has meant for its sound. Reveals how the electric guitar has evolved through the experiments of amateur makers and others. Features interviews with makers and players.

13. **Attias, Bernardo A., Anna Gavanas, and Hillegonda C. Rietveld, eds.** 2013. *DJ Culture in the Mix: Power, Technology, and Social Change in Electronic Dance Music*. New York: Bloomsbury. x, 331 p. Bibliography and Index. ISBN: 9-781-62356-690-8.

A compilation of essays that integrate an international collaboration among academics in the study of electronic dance music. Compiled essays examine how in many ways DJs have pushed forward music techniques and technological developments. Topics covered include phonography, digitality, and fidelity; social networks and gendered trajectories in European DJ culture; the commercial club scene in Sydney (Australia); and the mixing work of São Paulo's (Brazil) peripheral DJs.

14. **Aubert, Laurent**. 2017. *The Music of the Other: New Challenges for Ethnomusicology in a Global Age*. Translated by Carla Ribeiro. Foreword by Anthony Seeger. Previously published, Aldershot & Burlington, 2007: Ashgate. London: Routledge. xii, 96 p. Bibliography and Index. ISBN: 9-780-75465-343-1.

Traces the dimensions of new musical encounters and considers the impact of world music on values, habits, and cultural practices. Offers discussions of key questions about contemporary music culture that widens conventional ethnomusicological perspectives and considers not only the nature of Western society as a "global village" but also the impact of current Western demands on the future of world musics and their practitioners.

15. **Auslander, Philip**. 2004. "Performance Analysis and Popular Music: A Manifesto." *Contemporary Theatre Review* 14(1): 1–13. ISSN: 1048-6801.

Offers concerns that performance studies and the academic disciplines say little about musical performances. Finds that primary journals in the field seldom publish articles about music as performance or musicians as performers, and only a small number of papers on these topics are presented at conferences. Examines the general absence of music-based performance genres from the purview of theater and performance studies. Proposes an approach to performance analysis that focuses primarily on popular musicians. Concentrates more on defining the approach than applying it to cases.

16. **Auslander, Philip**. 2006. *Performing Glam Rock: Gender and Theatricality in Popular Music*. Ann Arbor: University of Michigan Press. 259 p. Illustrations, Bibliography, and Index. ISBN: 9-780-42709-868-2.

Explores the many ways glam rock that was personified by performers such as Marc Bolan, David Bowie, Bryan Ferry, and Suzi Quatro, who paved the way for new explorations of identity in terms of gender, sexuality, and performance. Positions glam historically and examines it as a set of performance strategies and the ways in which glam rock, while celebrating the showmanship of 1950s rock 'n' roll, began to undermine rock's adherence to the ideology of authenticity in the late 1960s.

17. **Auslander, Philip**. 2021. *In Concert: Performing Musical Persona*. Ann Arbor: University of Michigan Press. x, 293 p. Illustrations, Photographs, Bibliography, and Index. ISBN: 9-780-47207-471-6.

Argues that the conventional way of understanding what musicians do as performers is to treat them as producers of sound and that some also think that it is unnecessary to see musicians in performance as long as one can hear them. Addresses not only the visual means by which musicians engage their audiences through costume and physical gesture but also spectacular aspects of performance as light shows. Suggests that although musicians do not usually enact fictional characters on stage, they nevertheless present themselves to audiences in ways specific to the performance situation. Employs the *musical persona* to denote musicians' presence before the audience through discussion of the Beatles, Miles Davis, Keith Urban, Lady Gaga, Nicki Minaj, Frank Zappa, B. B. King, Jefferson Airplane, Virgil Fox, Keith Jarrett, Glen Gould, and Laurie Anderson.

18. **Baker, Hugh, and Yuval Taylor**. 2007. *Faking It: The Quest for Authenticity in Popular Music*. New York: W. W. Norton. xiii, 375 p. Illustrations, Bibliography, and Index. ISBN: 0-39306-078-0.

Examines why so many musicians base their approach on being authentic. Employs examples of Elvis Presley, John Lennon, Kurt Cobain, Jimmie Rogers, Donna Summer, Leadbelly, Neil Young, Moby, and others. Considers what makes popular work and discusses the segregation of music, aspects of rockabilly, disco, and other topics.

19. **Baker, Sarah, Andy Bennett, and Jodie Taylor, eds**. 2013. *Redefining Mainstream Popular Music*. New York: Routledge. xiv, 222 p. Illustrations, Bibliography, and Index. ISBN: 9-780-41580-780-7.

A collection of essays that critically examine the idea of the "mainstream" in and across a variety of popular music styles and contexts. Considers how notions of what is popular vary across generations and cultures and what may have been considered alternative to one group may be perceived as mainstream to another. Compiled essays incorporate a wide range of popular music texts, genres, scenes, practices, and technology from the United Kingdom, North America, Australia, and New Zealand. Essays also theoretically challenge and augment notions of mainstream popular music.

20. **Baker, Sarah, ed**. 2015. *Preserving Popular Music Heritage: Do-It-Yourself, Do-It-Together*. Series: *Routledge Research in Music*. New York: Routledge. 266 p. Bibliography and Index. ISBN: 9-781-31576-988-2.

An edited volume of essays constructed around the growing awareness of the need to archive the material remnants of popular music to safeguard the national and local histories of this cultural form. The essays are also constructed around current research that suggest that in the past twenty years or so there has been an expansion of DIY heritage practice with the founding of numerous DIY music institutions, archives, and museums around the world. The essays in this volume seek to explore the role of the DIY or professional-amateur (pro-am) practitioners of popular music archiving and preservation.

21. **Baker, Sarah, Lauren Isvandity, and Raphael Nowak, eds**. 2019. *Curating Pop: Exhibiting Popular Music in the Museum*. New York: Bloomsbury. x, 179 p. Bibliography and Index. ISBN: 9-781-50134-357-5.

A collection of essays that addresses the rapidly growing interest in the study of popular music exhibitions, which has occurred alongside the increasing number of popular museums in operation across the world. Essays focus on curational practices and processes drawn from interviews with museum works and curators from nineteen museums globally, including the Country Music Hall of Fame in Nashville, the Museum of Pop Culture in Seattle, and the Pop Museum in Prague. Considers the subjective experiences of curators involved in the exhibition of popular music in museums in a wide range of geographical locations and compares institutional practices and the way in which popular music history is presented to visitors in a wider sense.

22. **Baker, Sarah**. 2018. *Community Custodians of Popular Music's Past: A DIY Approach to Heritage*. Series: *Routledge Research in Music*. Abingdon, Oxon: Routledge. xii, 198 p. Bibliography and Index. ISBN: 9-780-36787-533-6.

Examines the do-it-yourself approach to the collection, preservation, and display of popular music heritage being undertaken by volunteers in community archives, museums, and halls of fame globally. Draws on interviews and observations with founders, volunteers, and heritage workers in several institutions in North America, Europe, and Australia. Offer highlights of the possibilities of bottom-up community-based interventions into the archiving and preservation of popular music's heritage.

23. **Baldacchino, Godfrey**. 2011. *Island Songs: A Global Repertoire*. Lanham: Scarecrow Press. xli, 297 p. Bibliography and Index. ISBN: 9-780-81088-178-5.

Illuminates how song performs island life. Incorporates a series of case studies on islands in the Caribbean, North Atlantic, Mediterranean, Baltic, and the South Pacific. Includes essays by an interdisciplinary group of scholars, artists, and performing musicians to examine songs and singing on selected islands around the world. Specific geographic areas covered include the English, French, and Spanish Caribbean, Cape Breton Island and Newfoundland, the Hebrides and Jersey, Fiji, Chiloe, Papua New Guinea, Ibiza, and Gotland.

24. **Ballam-Cross, Paul**. 2021. "Reconstructed Nostalgia: Aesthetic Commonalities and Self-Soothing in Chillwave, Synthwave, and Vaporwave." *Journal of Popular Music Studies* 33(1): 70–93. ISSN: 1533-1598.

Posits that in chillwave, synthwave, and vaporwave and their respective subgenres, a common element is the thread of nostalgia constant in each. Argues that the reinterpretation of cultural memory is an important structural feature in chillwave, synthwave, and vaporwave and such vaporwave subgenres as mallsoft and the associated Japanese "city pop" revival. Offers a discussion of the visual and musical connections that draw these genres together with an exploration of the concepts of nostalgia in music, as well as the related concept of reconstructed nostalgia.

25. **Ballico, Christina, and Allan Watson, eds**. 2020. *Music Cities: Evaluating a Global Cultural Policy Concept*. Series: *New Directions in Cultural Policy Research*. Cham: Palgrave Macmillan. xiii, 194 p. Bibliography and Index. ISBN: 9-783-03035-872-3.

A collection of essays that provide a critical academic evaluation of the "Music City," as a form of urban cultural policy that has been keenly adopted in policy circles across the global but which has only been subject to limited empirical and conceptual interrogation. Essays examine music cities as diverse as San Francisco, Liverpool, Chennai, San Juan, Birmingham, and South Hampton.

26. **Ballico, Christina, ed**. 2021. *Geographically Isolated and Peripheral Music Scenes: Global Insights and Perspectives*. Singapore: Palgrave MacMillan. xii, 210 p. Bibliography and Index. ISBN: 9-789-81164-580-8.

An edited volume that explores the connection between music and the social production of remote places. Compiled essays provide case studies from around the world and lay out the challenges of peripheral locales and how musical activities emerge because they take place in the periphery, not just because of their relative isolation. Topics include Dublin's popular music; the contemporary music scene in Perth, Western Australia; Icelandic and Faroese music festivals; the Dawson City, Yukon (Canada), Music Festival; Chile's indie music scene; diversity and impact on popular music in Papua New Guinea; the formation of an independent music scene in Montreal; Thunder Bay's Crock N Rolls and a stretch of Canadian Highway; and Austin's (Texas) round trip journey from the periphery to the center of the earth.

27. **Bardine, Bryan A., and Jerome Stueart, eds**. 2022. *Living Metal: Metal Scenes Around the World*. Series: *Advances in Metal Music and Culture*. Bristol: Intellect Books. xii, 296 p. Illustrations, Music Examples, Maps, Bibliography, and Index. ISBN: 9-781-78938-400-0.

A collection of essays that explore metal scenes throughout the world from Dayton to Hull, from Copenhagen to Osaka. Essays present a portrayal of how these scenes developed, are experienced by fans, and are influenced by the contexts in which they are embedded. Essays also connect metal to other disciplines in the field of music. A foreword is included by Henkka Seppälä, former bassist with the Finnish metal band Children of Bodom.

28. **Barratt-Peacock, Ruth, and Ross Hagen, eds**. 2019. *Medievalism and Metal Music Studies: Throwing Down the Gauntlet*. Series: *Emerald Studies in Metal Music and Culture*. Bingley: Emerald. xx, 189 p. Illustrations, Bibliography, and Index. ISBN: 9-781-78756-396-4.

A compilation of essays that investigate metal music's enduring fascination with the medieval period from a variety of critical perspectives. Compiled essays explore how metal musicians and fans use the medieval period as a foundation of creativity and critique.

29. **Basu, Dipannita, and Sidney J. Lemelle, eds**. 2006. *The Vinyl Ain't Final: Hip-Hop and the Globalization of Black Culture*. London: Pluto. xvii, 268 p. Illustrations, Bibliography, and Index. ISBN: 0-74531-941-6.

A combination of essays that results in a unique and critical insight into the implications of hip-hop globally and locally. Essay topics include rap and hip-hop in the United States, For the People, Tribute and Redbone; rap and hip-hop homeland security; evolution of global consciousness in Bay Area hip-hop; hip-hop and a Hawaiian nation; hip-hop and the Afro-Asian Atlantic; rap and hip-hop groove globally; the nation question; Americanization and hip-hop in Germany; Africa rap, Blackness an citizenship in France; Cuban hip-hop; hip-hop in the Samoan diaspora; negotiating ethnicity and authenticity in Tokyo's Club Harlem; globalization and gangsta rap; hip-hop in the post-apartheid; and hip-hop culture and the children of Arusha (Tanzania).

30. **Bates, Eliot**. 2020. "Resource Ecologies, Political Economies and the Ethics of Audio Technologies in the Anthropocene." *Popular Music* 39(1): 66–87. ISSN: 0261-1430.

Deals with popular music and innovations in audio technologies. Seeks to understand how recorded and amplified stage musics contributed to producing the Anthropocene, which necessitates attending to complex transnational flows of material, capital, and labor and how they coalesce into technological objects. Provides a partial account of an early 2000 mic preamp, a mundane but fetishized recording studio technological object. Focuses on two metals, tin and tantalum, that are primarily extracted for electronic manufacturing and two building blocks of electronics, solder and capacitors, which are essential for making contemporary electronics.

31.   **Bayer, Gerd, ed**. 2019. *Heavy Metal at the Movies*. Series: *Ashgate Screen Music Series*. Abingdon, Oxon: Routledge. 216 p. Bibliography and Index. ISBN: 9-780-36766-238-7.

Compiled essays inform about the area of interaction between film studies and heavy metal research, highlighting how the audiovisual medium of film relates to, builds on, and shapes metal culture. Essays consider how metal music serves as a form of ambient background in horror films, which creates an intense and somewhat threatening atmosphere and high spectacle, and how the recent and ongoing wave of metal documentaries relies on either satire or hagiography.

32.   **Baym, Nancy K**. 2018. *Playing to the Crowd: Musicians, Audiences, and the Intimate Work of Connection*. Series: *Postmillennial Pop*. New York: New York University Press. 253 p. Illustrations, Bibliography, and Index. ISBN: 9-781-47981-535-7.

Explores and explains how the rise of digital communication platforms has transformed the artist-fan relationship into something more intimate. Incorporates in-depth interviews with musicians such as the Cure, UB40, and Throwing Muses and reveals how media has facilitated connections through the active participation of both the artists and their devoted digital fan base.

33.   **Bayton, Mavis**. 1999. *Frock Rock: Women Performing Popular Music*. New York: Oxford University Press. xii, 246 p. Illustrations, Discography, Bibliography, and Index. ISBN: 01-98166-515-X.

Covers the period from the late 1970s to the mid-1990s and focuses on women instrumentalists in female and mixed bands. Includes interviews with Skin from Skunk Anasie, Debbie Smith from Echoberry, Candida Doyle from Pulp, Gail Greenwood from Belly, Natasha Atlas from Transglobal Underground, and Vi Subversa from Poison Girls. Explores the everyday worlds of women music making from bands just starting up to the professional stage.

34.   **Beadle, Jeremy J**. 1993. *Will Pop Eat Itself? Pop Music in the Soundbite Era*. London: Farber & Farber. 269 p. Discography and Index. ISBN: 0-57116-241-X.

Explores the advent of modernism in popular music in contemporary times and "high art" earlier in the twentieth century. Central to the arguments is a musical instrument called the "sampler," which uses existing recordings and original materials to make a new patchwork of sound. Examines the 1980s as an unappreciated oddity. Examples show how the sample started a morbid music through the work of The KLF and Pump Up the Volume. Describes the practice and repercussions of sampling and traces the history of the popular music producer.

35.   **Beebe, Roger, Denise Fulbrook, and Ben Sounders, eds**. 2002. *Rock Over the Edge: Transformations in Popular Music Culture*. Durham: Duke University Press. 392 p. Illustrations, Bibliography, and Index. ISBN: 0-82232-900-X.

A collection of interdisciplinary essays that examine the changing communities and discussions connected to American popular music. Topics include reflections on a disappointed popular music scholar; musicology and popular music studies at the twilight of the canon; rock historiography and the construction of a race-based dialectic; cover songs, race, and postwar marketing; country music and youth culture; Asian music videos and transnational gender; the feminization of rock; rock's Reconquista; a fan's note; Kurt Cobain, Tupac Shakur, and the waning of affect; DC punk and the production of authenticity; and queer theory notes on the Pet Shop Boys.

36.   **Bennett, Andy, and Jodie Taylor**. 2012. "Popular Music and the Aesthetics of Ageing." *Popular Music* 31(2) [Special Issue: *As Time Goes By: Music, Dance and Ageing*]: 231–243. ISSN: 0261-1430.

Posits that a post-structural landscape and social identities must increasingly be regarded as reflexively derived performative assemblages that incorporate elements of the local vernacular and global popular culture. Builds on the reinterpretation of social identity and takes as its central premise the notion that in addition to its well-mapped cultural importance for youth, popular music retains a critical currency for the aging audience as a key cultural resource of post-youth identification, lifestyle, and associated cultural practices. Examines the relationships between popular music, aging, and identity using illustrative examples drawn from ethnographic data collected between 2002 and 2009 in Australia and the United Kingdom.

37.   **Bennett, Andy, and Paula Guerra, eds**. 2019. *DIY Cultures and Underground Music Scenes*. Series: *Routledge Advances in Sociology*. Abingdon, Oxon & New York: Routledge. xiv, 266 p. Illustrations, Bibliography, and Index. ISBN: 9-780-36766-451-0.

A compilation of essays that examine the global influence and impact of DIY cultural practices as this informs the production, performance, and consumption of underground in different parts of the world. Compiles a series of essays of original studies of DIY musical activities in Europe, North and South America, Asia, and Oceania (e.g., Bucharest, France, Northern Germany, the Basque Country, New Zealand, Finland, Indonesia, Brazil, Berlin, Hungary, Scotland, Britain, and Bulgaria). Combines insights from established academic writers with the work of younger scholars, some of whom are directly engaged in contemporary underground music scenes. Revaluates key theses and issues that have been used in studying the cultural meaning of alternative and underground music scenes, space, place, identity, the political economy of DIY cultural practice, and others. Compilation is divided into four parts: I. Underground Music Scenes Between the Local and the Translocal; II. Music and DIY Cultures: DIY or Die!; III. Art,

Music and Technological Changes; and IV. Music, Scenes, Memory, and Emotional Geographies.

38.　**Bennett, Andy, and Richard A. Peterson**. 2004. *Music Scenes: Local, Translocal and Virtual.* Nashville: Vanderbilt University. xvi, 264 p. Illustration, Bibliography, and Index. ISBN: 0-82651-450-2.

Integrates a compilation of essays that focus on the world of music scenes, which are inconspicuous sites where clusters, musicians, producers, and fans explore their common musical taste and distinctive lifestyle choice. Argues that although most music scenes come and go with barely a trace, they give immense satisfaction to their participants, and a few such as New York bebop jazz, Merseybeat, Memphis rockabilly, London punk, and Bronx hip-hop achieve fame and spur musical innovations. Focuses on music scenes and how individuals construct and negotiate scenes to the various activities. Topics include Chicago blues, rave, karaoke, London salsa, music festivals, womyn's music, skatepunk, anarcho-punk, Canterbury, post-rock, and others.

39.　**Bennett, Andy, Barry Shank, and Jason Toynbee, eds**. 2006. *The Popular Music Studies Reader.* London & New York: Routledge. xxii, 408 p. Bibliography and Index. ISBN: 9-780-41530-710-9.

Maps the changing nature of popular music over the last decade and considers how popular music studies has expanded and developed to deal with these changes. Essays in the volume stem from international scholars, place popular music in its cultural contexts, look at the significance of popular music in our everyday lives, and examine the global nature of the popular music industry. Parts and topical sections include Music as Sound, Music as Text; Making Music; Popular Music Scenes; Popular Music and Everyday Life; Music, Diaspora, and Social Movements; Music Industry; Popular Music and Technology; Popular Music and Media; and Popular Music, Gender, and Sexuality.

40.　**Bennett, Andy, David Cashman, Ben Green, and Natalie Lewandowski, eds**. 2023. *Popular Music Scenes: Regional and Rural Perspectives.* Series: *Pop Music, Culture, and Identity.* Cham: Palgrave Macmillan. xxxi, 253 p. Illustrations and Bibliography. ISBN: 9-783-03108-615-1.

An edited volume of essays that represent a full-length study of regional and rural music scenes across the globe. Essays explore how globalization influences development of translocal connections between music scenes. Essays are intended to provide insight on understudied music scenes in towns and small cities across the world.

41.　**Bennett, Andy**. 2001. *Cultures of Popular Music.* Buckingham & Philadelphia: Open University Press. ix, 194 p. Bibliography and Index. ISBN: 0-33520-251-9.

Presents a comprehensive cultural, social, and historical overview of postwar popular music genres from rock 'n' roll and psychedelic pop, through punk and heavy metal, to rap, rave, and techno. Examines the style-based youth cultures from which such genres rise. Considers the cultural significance of respective postwar music genres for young audiences with reference to such issues as space and place, ethnicity, gender, creativity, education, and leisure. Incorporates studies conducted in Britain, the United States, Germany, Netherlands (Holland), Sweden, Israel, Australia, New Zealand, Mexico, Japan, Russia, and Hungary.

42.   **Bennett, Andy**. 2022. *Popular Music Heritage Places, Objects, Images, and Texts.* Cham: Palgrave. xi, 181 p. Bibliography and Index. ISBN: 9-783-03108-296-2.

Discusses the significance of popular music heritage as a means of remembering and representing rock and pop artists and their music and place in the culture of contemporary society. Examines how since the mid-1990s the contribution of popular music to the shaping of contemporary history, and heritage, has been increasingly acknowledged in exhibitions of popular music, museums, related artifacts, and others.

43.   **Bennett, Samantha, and Eliot Bates, eds**. 2018. *Critical Approaches to the Production of Music and Sound.* New York: Bloomsbury. x, 274 p. Illustrations, Bibliography, and Index. ISBN: 9-781-50133-205-0.

A compilation of essays that consider the production of music and sound in the twenty-first century that converges with multimedia. Compiled essays represent the research of scholars around the world revisiting established themes such as record production and the construction of genre with new perspectives and issues in cultural and virtual production. Topics and themes covered include who produces sound and music and sound and music in what localities and contexts.

44.   **Bennett, Samantha**. 2019. *Modern Records, Maverick Methods: Technology and Process in Popular Music Record Production, 1978–2000.* New York: Bloomsbury. 264 p. Discography, Filmography, Bibliography, and Index. ISBN: 9-781-50134-409-1.

Covers technologies from Fairlight CMI through MIDI to the digital audio workspace at the turn of the millennium. Examines a critical period in commercial popular music record production and the transformative digital age form the late 1970s to 2000. Draws on a discography of more than three thousand recordings from pop, rock, hip-hop, dance, and alternative music from artists such as the Beastie Boys, Madonna, U2, Fatboy Slim, and others.

45.   **Bennett, Tony, and Simon Firth, eds**. 2005. *Rock and Popular Music.* Originally published in 1993. Series: *Culture: Policy and Politics.* London: Routledge. xiv, 306 p. Bibliography and Index. ISBN: 9-780-41506-369-2.

A compilation of essays that examine the relations between policies and institutions that regulate contemporary popular music and the political debates, contradictions, and struggles in which those musics are involved. Essays compiled are international in scope and explore the reasons for and ways in which governments have sought to either support or prohibit popular music in Australia,

Canada, and Europe, as well as the impact of broadcasting policies in forming and shaping different musical communities.

46. **Berger, Harris, and Michael T. Carroll**. 2003. *Global Pop, Local Language*. Jackson: University Press of Mississippi. 352 p. Bibliography and Index. ISBN: 9-781-57806-536-3.

A compilation of essays that examine how performers and audiences from a wide range of cultures deal with the issue of language choice and dialect in popular music. Deals with related issues that confront performers in Latin music in the United States and traditional MCs in Toronto, Canada, rappers, rockers, and traditional folksingers from England and Ireland to France, Germany, Belarus, Nepal, China, New Zealand, Hawaii, and beyond. Addresses broad issues that include the globalization of the music industry, the problems of authenticity in popular culture, the politics of identity, multiculturalism, and the emergence of English as a dominant world language.

47. **Berger, Monica**. 2007. "Playing With a Different Sex: Academic Writing on Women in Rock and Pop." In *Singing for Themselves: Essays on Women in Popular Music*, Patricia S. Rudden, ed. Newcastle: Cambridge Scholars. ix, 280 p. Bibliography. ISBN: 9-781-84718-345-3.

Provides an annotated bibliography of academic writing on women in rock and pop that offers an overview of most of the scholarly literature on the topic and reflects the author's personal interest in methodology. Annotated bibliographic information is divided into several categories: specific performers; special genres, topics, related subcultures; and/or women as fans or as listeners. Also covers more general and theoretical matters that touch on multiple performers and topics.

48. **Bestley, Russ, Michael Dines, Alastair Gordon, and Paula Guerra, eds**. 2021. *Trans-Global Punk Scenes: The Punk Reader, Volume 2*. Series: *Global Punk Series*. Bristol: Intellect. 340 p. Illustrations, Bibliography, and Index. ISBN: 9-781-78938-337-9.

Critically engages with local, national, and transglobal contemporary punk scenes across countries and regions including New Zealand, Indonesia, South Africa, Siberia, and the Philippines. Includes thematic discussion on the evolution and adaptation of subcultural styles, punk demographics, and the notion of punk identity. Compiled essays present interdisciplinary perspectives from cultural studies, musicology, ethnography, art and design, history, and the social sciences.

49. **Bestley, Russ, Michael Dines, Alastair Gordon, and Paula Guerra, eds**. 2019. *The Punk Reader: Research Transmission From the Local and the Global*. Series: *Global Punk Series*. Bristol: Intellect. 324 p. Illustrations, Maps, Discography, Filmography, Bibliography, and Index. ISBN: 9-781-78938-129-0.

Explores and critically interrogates punk culture in relation to contemporary radicalized globalization. Compiled essays document disparate international punk scenes in Mexico, China, Malaysia, Iran, Brazil, United Kingdom, United States, Netherlands, Portugal, Spain, and Canada and seek to inform more about the globalized influence of punk beyond the 1970s.

50.   **Bickford, Tyler**. 2020. *Tween Pop: Children's Music and Public Culture*. Durham: Duke University Press. x, 229 p. Illustrations, Bibliography, and Index. ISBN: 9-781-47800-685-5.

Concentrates on the creation of the "tween" in the early 2000s as a gendered and raced consumer audience. Argues that this narrow market grew broadly to include four- to fifteen-year-olds with producers and markets pulling upward and downward by creating material that would attract younger viewers and teenagers. Suggests that the key to this expansion was popular music, as it provided an intensity of experience that mirrored childhood in its investments in emotional authenticity, cultural value, and relational intimacies.

51.   **Bidder, Sean**. 2001. *Pump Up the Volume: A History of House*. London: Channel 4 Books. v, 250 p. Illustrations and Index. ISBN: 0-75221-986-3.

Documents the history of the social and cultural explosion that was house music, tracing its roots back to where it emerged from disco. Examines how house music has become the soundtrack of fashion shows, after-show parties, premieres, and club openings around the world. Examines how house music is used by many of the leading mainstream music stars, including Madonna, Kylie Minogue, U2, and Boy George to break new markets and update their sound, and has influenced more people than any style since rock 'n' roll. Includes discussion of the development of house music in Chicago, New York, Ibiza, Britain, and others.

52.   **Biddle, Ian, and Vanessa Knights, eds**. 2016. *Music, National Identity, and the Politics of Location: Between the Global and the Local*. Series: *Ashgate Popular and Folk Music Series*. London & New York: Routledge. xii, 251 p. Illustrations, Bibliography, and Index. ISBN: 9-781-31709-160-8.

A collection of essays that brings together several scholars working on world musics, many of whom attended the conference "Popular Music and National Identities," held at the University of Newcastle in 2000. The essays consider how national identities are constructed through music. Argues that popular music identity has long been associated with political dissent and that the nation-state has consistently demonstrated a determination to seek out and procure for itself a stake in the management of its popular music. Essay topics include Afro-pop, Spanish/Moroccan rai, banda songs in Los Angeles, identities in contemporary France, Uyghur popular song, voice of Brazil, popular music and Serbian nationalism, and Norwegian club music.

53.   **Binas, Susanne**. 2001. "Sampling the Didjeridoo." In *Global Repertoires: Popular Music Within and Beyond the Transnational Music Industry*, Alfred Smudits, and Andreas Gebesmair, eds. Series: *Ashgate Popular and Folk Music Series*.

Aldershot, Hants & Burlington: Ashgate. xi, 176 p. Illustrations, Music Examples, Bibliography, and Index. ISBN: 0-754-60526-4.

Argues that the various forms of popular music are the results of a profound technological and social modernization process starting from North American and Europe and that have cultural constellations worldwide. Furthermore, styles such as world music, tribal dance, and sample beats consisting of indigenous sound patterns seem to be a suitable area of investigation that deal with musical globalization or localization. Examines the modernization of the didgeridoo, one of the oldest instruments in the world. Examines sound that introduces the track and is a digital sample that can be used and tuned electronically.

54. **Biron, Dean**. 2011. "Towards a Popular Music Criticism of Replenishment." *Popular Music and Society* 34(5): 661–682. ISSN: 0300-7766.

Analyzes the attitudes of popular music critics to identify the various exhaustion narratives that have arisen in the wake of the post-Beatles dissolution of rock and popular music into a multitude of genres and subgenres. Argues that criticism might better serve audiences by focusing less on narrow, nostalgic treatments of canonical rock music and more on a narrative of replenishment of the contemporary musical landscape.

55. **Birosik, Patti J**. 1989. *The New Age Guide: Profiles and Recordings of 500 Top New Age Musicians*. New York: Collier Books & London: Macmillan. xxii, 218 p. ISBN: 0-02041-640-7.

Presents profiles and discographies of five hundred artists and their recordings who are creating the genre of new age music. Information on artists and their recordings is divided into several sections: East-West; Electronic Computer Music; Environmental Nature Sounds; Folk Music; Jazz Fusion; Meditation Music; Native American-Indigenous Music; Pop Music; Progressive Music; Related Artists of Interest; Solo Instrumental Music; Sound Health Music; Traditional Music; Vocal Music; and World Music.

56. **Bishop, Jack**. 2005. "Building the International Empire of Sound: Concentrations of Power and Property in the 'Global' Music Market." *Popular Music and Society* 28(4): 443–471. ISSN: 0300-7766.

Argues that the merger of the recorded music divisions of Sony and BMG finalized on August 5, 2004, created the world's largest music company while reducing the "Big Five" labels to the "Big Four." Furthermore, the new Sony BMG Music Entertainment will now control over thirty percent of the global music market. Argues that as power and resources were being consolidated in the music industry, regular amendments to the length of copyright terms were extending private ownership of creative works, delaying their passage into the public domain. Presents an analysis of how the world's media giants use their power and property to influence national and international laws to lock down culture and control creativity.

57. **Blacking, John, and Joann M. Kealiinohomoku, eds**. 1979. *The Performing Arts: Music and Dance*. The Hague & New York: Mouton. xxii, 344 p. Illustrations, Music Examples, Bibliography, and Index. ISBN: 9-783-11080-069-2.

A compilation of papers that were presented at the International Congress of Anthropological and Ethnological Sciences held in Chicago, August–September 1973. A number of papers integrate a focus on traditional and popular music. Topics covered include music and dance in society; case studies in dance; cross-cultural studies of the performing arts; case studies in folklore from Asia and Eastern Europe; aspects of the musical process; and music and dance in Africa and the new world.

58. **Boedt, Steve**. 2014. *Zumba Global Burst: Cardio Interval*. [United States]: Zumba Fitness. DVD. 29 Minutes. OCLC Number: 9-0322-706-8.

A special video programming that may inform popular music studies by showing how global popular music is often employed in physical activities. Provides an example of aerobic dancing trends that incorporates global popular music with cardio burst intervals and dance employing global popular music such as jazz, hip-hop, African, bhangra, Ashe, and others.

59. **Boomkens, René**. 2004. "Global Sounds and Local Audiences: The Coming of Age of Pop Music." *European Journal of Cultural Studies* 7(1): 5–7. ISSN: 1367-5494.

Concentrates on scholarly articles on the evolution of popular music. Incorporates a study of the largely overlooked underground phenomenon of "ground turntablism" by Juliana Snapper, an exploration of the images of America as they are produced by music videos by Jaap Kooijman, and Simon Firth's analysis of the supposedly unique and exceptional status of British pop since the success of the Beatles. Also examines the musical career of Elvis Costello as an example of the growing national and international self-confidence of popular music scenes.

60. **Born, Georgina, ed**. 2022. *Music and Digital Media: A Planetary Anthropology*. London: UCL Press. xvi, 527 p. Bibliography and Index. ISBN: 9-781-80008-243-4.

An edited volume that encompasses an ethnographic study of the impact of digital media on music worldwide. Essays offer a theoretical framework for understanding digital media through music and provide research on popular music folk music, art, and crossover musics from the Global South and North. Some of the geographic areas discussed are Kenya (Nairobi), Argentina (Buenos Aires), North India, and Canada (Montreal).

61. **Borschke, Margie**. 2017. *This Is Not a Remix: Piracy, Authentication, and Popular Music*. New York: Bloomsbury. vi, 186 p. Bibliography and Index. ISBN: 9-781-50131-891-7.

Uncovers the analog roots of digital practices and brings the extensive history of copies and piracy into contact with contemporary controversies about the reproduction, use, and circulation of recordings on the Internet. Examines the innovations that have sprung from the use of recording formats in grassroots music scenes from vinyl, tape, and acetate that early disco DJs used to create remixes to the mp3 blogs and vinyl revivalists of the twenty-first century. Focuses on questions about the materiality of media, its use, and the aesthetic dimensions of reproduction and circulation in digital networks.

62.   **Bottà, Giacomo, ed**. 2016. *Unsichtbare Landschaften Populäre Musik und Räumlichkeit* (*Invisible Landscape: Popular Music and Spatiality*). Series: *Populäre Kulter und Musik*. German and English texts. 201 p. Bibliography and Index. ISBN: 9-783-83093-039-6.

A collection of essays that stem from a seminar on the city experience in popular music held at the University of Freiburg. Compiled essays are in both German and English texts by scholars of various nationalities. Essay topics focus on various genres and touch upon matters such as national identities, urban development, scene formation, multiculturalism, and political issues. Essays present transdisciplinary perspectives on musical spatiality that is rooted in popular music studies but also draw from views and methods of cultural studies, urban studies, and ethnomusicology.

63.   **Bottà, Giacomo**. 2015. "Dead Industrial Atmosphere: Popular Music, Cultural Heritage, and Industrial Cities." *Journal of Urban Cultural Studies* 2(1–2): 107–119. ISSN: 2050-9790.

Argues that economic crisis and popular music have often been put in synergic relation to each other, particularly in the context of industrial cities with disparate genres conceived there, such as hardcorepunk, house, post-punk, and heavy metal. Addresses these issues and considers the relation between industrial soundscapes and landscapes, symbolic representations of material changes, and crisis in the context of 1980s European cities.

64.   **Boulton, Andrew**. 2008. "The Popular Geopolitical Wor(l)ds of Post-9/11 Country Music." *Popular Music and Society* 31(3): 373–387. ISSN: 0300-7766.

Explores the ways in which country music has engaged with geopolitical issues surrounding the War on Terror. Employs and considers the idea of "political geopolitics" as its theoretical point of departure, the intertext between the attitudes, and understandings articulated in a body of patriotic post-9/11 country music hits and those expressed in broader geopolitical discourse.

65.   **Brabazon, Tara**. 2012. *Popular Music: Topics, Trends & Trajectories*. Los Angeles: Sage. vi, 287 p. Discographies, Bibliography, and Index. ISBN: 9-781-44625-420-2.

Examines key approaches to understanding popular music, the main settings of exchange and consumption, the role of technology in the production of popular music, the main genres of popular music, and the debates of contemporary times. Provides a network to the core library of concepts and issues in the field. Topics include music and dancing; city music and urban spaces; soundtracks and filmic spaces; MP3; instruments—guitar culture, keyboard culture, drumming, and percussion; voice, turntablism; iPod; genre and community; country, folk, blues, rock 'n' roll, soul, reggae, ska, salsa, metal, punk, indie, hip-hop, disco, house, and world music; boy bands; and bisexual, lesbian, and transgender music.

66.   **Bramley, Charlie**. 2017. "Beyond the Boundaries of Professionalism: Introducing Anarcho-Pop Into the Lexicon of Popular Music Studies and Education." *Lied und Populäre kultur/Song and Popular Culture* 62: 13–32. German and English texts. ISSN: 1619-0548.

Critically explores the role of professionalism within popular music culture and the legitimacy of its boundaries as a precursor for music education. Introduces the concept of anarcho-pop in order to demonstrate an alternative, improvised approach to making popular music that seeks to move beyond the boundaries of professionalism. Presents ethnographic accounts of music making to create an image of music that is fully accessible.

67.   **Bratus, Alessandro**. 2019. *Mediatization in Popular Music Recorded Artifacts: Performance on Record and on Screen*. Lanham: Lexington Books. xii, 265 p. Illustrations, Music Examples, Bibliography, and Index. ISBN: 9-781-49855-632-3.

A study of the relationship between performance, technological mediation, and the sense of live presence through a series of case studies related to popular music. Explores technological mediation as a process of authentication that involves a chain of interconnected instances that have their roots in the cultural context in which the media products are designed to be marketed and that also shape its recording technique and post-production. Covers musicians and trends such as Jimi Hendrix, Johnny Cash, Tupac Shakur, electric dance music (EDM), and so forth.

68.   **Bretthauer, Brook, Toni S. Zimmerman, and James H. Banning**. 2007. "A Feminist Analysis of Popular Music: Power Over, Objectification of, and Violence Against Women." *Journal of Feminist Family Therapy* 18(4): 29–51. ISSN: 1540-4099.

Discusses and integrates qualitative content analysis that was conducted on lyrics to identify predominant themes in popular music of songs for analysis. Analyzes popular music songs from "The Hot 100" list generated by *Billboard* Chart Research Services. Applies feminist and cognitive social learning theories as a foundation to identify themes. Results found that power over, objectification of, and violence against women were the overall frameworks that emerged from the lyrics. Also found within this framework were six themes: men and power; sex as top priority for males; objectification of women; sexual violence; women defined as having a man; and women as not valuing themselves. Also found that these themes are used in gender relationship messages to music listeners who are predominately adolescents.

69. **Brewster, Bill, and Frank Broughton**. 2014. *Last Night a DJ Saved My Life: A History of the Disc Jockey*. New York: Grove Press. Originally published, London: Headline Book Publishing, 1999. 606 p. Illustrations. ISBN: 9-780-80214-610-6.

Comprehensive history of the disc jockey, a figure who has become a powerful force in shaping the popular music industry. Examines different social, cultural, and artistic aspects of the DJ in terms of influencing innovative trends in the popular music industry. Provides examples of DJ culture from the first record played over airwaves to house, hip-hop, techno, and beyond.

70. **Bridge, Simone K**. 2018. *Trajectories and Themes in World Popular Music, Globalization, Capitalism, Identity*. Sheffield & Bristol: Equinox Publishing. xi, 298 p. Bibliography and Index. ISBN: 9-781-78179-621-4.

Traces the trajectories of modern globalization since the late nineteenth century. Considers hegemonic cultural beliefs and practices during the phases of the history of capitalism. Offers a way to study world popular music from the perspective of critical social theory. Also adopts three phases in history of capitalist hegemony since the nineteenth century—liberal, organized, and neoliberal—to consider world popular music in each of these contexts.

71. **Brooks, Jeanice, Matthew Stephens, and Wiebke Thormählen, eds**. 2022. *Sound Heritage: Making Music Matter in Historic Houses*. Series: *Routledge Studies in Popular Music*. Abingdon, Oxon & New York: Routledge. xx, 363 p. Illustrations, Bibliography, and Index. ISBN: 9-780-36723-716-5.

A compilation of essays that focus on the study of music in the historic house museums. Features essays from both music and heritage scholars and professionals in a richly interdisciplinary approach to central issues. Essays examine how music materials can be used to create narratives about past inhabitants and their surroundings, including aspects of social and cultural life beyond the activity of music making itself. Provides a study that intersects music with museum and heritage studies that is appropriate for scholars and researchers of music history, popular music, performance studies, and material culture.

72. **Brouillette, Liane, and Stephanie Feder**. 2010. "Tracing Cultural Migration Through Music: An Inquiry Approach to Enhancing Global Understanding." *Ohio Social Studies Review* 46(1): 11–18. ISSN: 1050-2130.

Focuses on how enhanced global awareness develops naturally through adopting a discovery approach to world geography and offers information on "Mapping the Beat," an innovative curriculum funded by the periodical *National Geographic*, which builds on the interest of students in popular music to initiate a process of geographic discovery. Discusses the evolution of African American musical traditions from sorrow songs sung in the fields to rap music at the top of the music charts. Argues that the Mapping the Beat curriculum provides a stronger and more immediate connection with world cultures and geography rather than the study of textbook alone as it provides students an opportunity to explore varied cultural perspectives.

73.   **Brøvig-Hanssen, Ragnhild, and Anne Danielsen**. 2016. *Digital Signatures: The Impact of Digitization on Popular Music Sound.* Cambridge: MIT Press. ix, 188 p. Illustrations, Bibliography, and Index. ISBN: 9-780-26203-414-2.

Sheds light on some of the processes that mediate between the intervention of music and what is presented to listeners. Enhances the growing number of studies that address music technologies and its mediations. Provides a series of case studies that demonstrate how to bring digital sound manipulation within the orbit of music analysis, insisting that it is the musical effects of the use of technology that matters. Suggests that issues of musical meaning are what draws listeners to the music in the first place.

74.   **Brown, Andy R., Karl Spracklen, Keith Kahn-Harris, and Niall Scott**. 2016. *Global Metal Music and Culture-Current Directions in Metal Studies.* Series: *Routledge Studies in Popular Music, 12.* New York & London: Routledge. xv, 369 p. Illustrations, Diagrams, Bibliography, and Index.

Defines the key ideas, scholarly debates, and research activities that have contributed to the formation of the international and interdisciplinary field of metal studies. Offers new and innovative research on metal musicology, local and global scene studies, fandom, gender and metal identity, metal media, and commerce. Also offers a wide range of topics that explore riff-based songwriting of classic heavy metal, aesthetics of grindcore, doom metal, death metal, and progressive metal.

75.   **Brown, Andy**. 2008. "Popular Music Cultures, Media and Youth Consumption: Towards an Integration of Structure, Culture, and Agency." *Sociology Compass* 2(2): 388–408. ISSN: 1468-4446.

Argues that youth, media, and popular music studies have developed in separate fields of research that has resulted in a lack of integration of key ideas of inquiry, such as the relationship between the cultural and structural in youth music consumption and the role of the media industries in framing such a process. Provides an overview of three frameworks: the production of consumption; production of culture/cultures of production; and cultures of consumption evaluating their contribution to a more integrated understanding of how youth consume music as a structurally and culturally mediated process. Also considers the global music industry and its impact on youth consumption.

76.   **Bruenger, David**. 2019. *Create, Produce, Consume: New Models for Understanding Music Business.* Oakland: University of California Press. 414 p. Illustrations, [8 p.] of plates, Charts, Bibliography, and Index. ISBN: 9-780-52030-350-8.

Considers musical creation as a given and focuses on what comes after shared musical experience, what makes it happen, and the form of value it can generate. Suggests that all forms of music production provide access to musical experience regardless of venue or technological medium and access to music and musicians is what brings music commerce, community, and culture to life.

77. **Brunt, Shelley, and Liz Giuffre**. 2023. *Popular Music and Parenting*. New York: Routledge. 168 p. Illustrations, Bibliography, and Index. ISBN: 9-780-36736-713-8.

Explores the culture of popular music as a shared experience between parents, careers, and young children. Offers a critical overview from a popular music studies perspective. Expands on assumptions about how young audiences and caregivers engage with music together. Examines through case studies and participation between children and parents in both domestic and public settings ranging across children's music media, digital streaming, live concerts, formal and informal popular music education, music merchandizing, and song lyrics.

78. **Burghart, Devin, ed**. 1999. *Soundtracks to the White Revolution: White Supremacist Assaults on Youth Music Subcultures*. Chicago: Center for New Community. 107 p. Bibliography and Index. ISBN: 9-780-96770-040-3.

Details the growth of the White power music scene, which became an international multimillion-dollar-a-year industry. Examines entries into new subcultures such as the national social black metal underground, the fascist experimental, and the apocalyptic folk scene. Also highlights music's power as a recruitment tool and to create bigotry. Points out that White power music has also worked to raise millions of dollars for White supremacists and so forth.

79. **Burkhart, Patrick**. 2005. "Loose Integration in the Popular Music Industry." *Popular Music and Society* 28(4): 489–500. ISSN: 030-7766.

A study that deals with record labels, recording industry, online music, digital music, ownership, mergers, and future trends in popular music. Argues that despite consolidation in the record music sector, the industry is more loosely integrated than the rest of the entertainment industry than it was under the Big Five record labels that later became integrated as part of the Big Four. Moreover, as the sector concentrated it also differentiated into ownership class. Also argues that the Big Four is now constructed as music oligopoly practices for cultural gate-keeping for global markets. Suggests that the interaction of the groups in online music markets may divulge coordinated rules for CD (compact disc) pricing and controlling over access to digital catalogs.

80. **Burnett, Robert**. 1996. *The Global Jukebox: The International Music Industry*. Series: *Communication and Society (Routledge)*. London: Routledge. 188 p. Illustrations, Appendix, Bibliography, and Internet WWW music sites. ISBN: 9-780-41509-276-0.

Offers a comprehensive study of the international music industry at a time of great change as the entertainment industry acknowledges its ever-growing global audience. Provides an international overview of the music business and its prospects in the United Kingdom, Northern, Europe, the United States, and Canada.

Examines the relationship between local and global cultures and between con-
centration of ownership (e.g., Sony, Warner, and the rest of the "big six") and the
diversity of music production and consumption.

81.   **Burns, Gary**. 1997. "*Popular Music and Society* and the Evolving Discipline
      of Popular Music Studies." *Popular Music and Society* 21(1): 123–131. ISSN:
      0030-7766.

      Documents the historical and critical significance of the journal *Popular Music
      and Society* and its focus on integrating popular music studies as a discipline.
      Suggests that if there is such as a discipline as popular music studies it probably
      began not coincidentally at about the same time as the beginning of the journal.
      Discusses the need for a journal that focused on popular music. Also discusses
      aspects of academic issues in research and coursework in popular music.

82.   **Burns, Lori, and Mélisse Lafrance, eds**. 2013. *Disruptive Divas: Feminism, Iden-
      tity, and Popular Music*. Series: *Studies in Contemporary Music and Culture*. New
      York & London: Routledge. xix, 28 p. Illustrations, Bibliography, and Index. ISBN:
      0-81533-553-9.

      Examines how four "disruptive divas"—Tori Amos, Courtney Love, Meshell Nde-
      geocello, and PJ Harvey—have expanded and upset the boundaries of acceptable
      female musicianship. Examines how these four women have challenged the sense
      of what a female popular music should be and have disrupted a dominant dis-
      course that includes ideas of femininity, sexuality, desire, and the social relations
      of domination and subordination. Provides an analysis of these four women and
      their songs from both cultural and musicological perspectives and discusses how
      a woman/musician/icon can disturb the very logic of her own personality.

83.   **Burton, Justin D., and Ali Colleene Neff**. 2015. "Sounding Global Southern-
      ness." *Journal of Popular Music Studies* 27(4): 381–386. ISSN: 1524-2226.

      Offers information on the emerging lexicon used by famous music scholars in
      the invention and representation of music during the digital globalization age.
      Topics include the complexity of the popular music binary, the genealogy of the
      scholarship of popular music, and the globalization of hip-hop music.

84.   **Butler, Mark, ed**. 2012. *Electronica, Dance and Club Music*. Series: *The
      Library of Essayson Popular Music*. Farnham, Surrey & Burlington: Ashgate.
      xxxii, 536 p. Illustrations, Music Examples, Bibliography, and Index. ISBN:
      9-780-75462-965-8.

      Presents an array of scholarship that has sprung up in response to discos, clubs,
      and raves and the development of new, distinctive musical and cultural prac-
      tices over the past four decades. Offers a broad range of perspectives from aca-
      demic disciplines. Essays cover topics that include aesthetics, agency, the body
      in dance, movement, space, composition, identity (gender, sexuality, race, and
      other constructs), musical design, place, pleasure, policing and moral panics,
      production techniques (sampling, spirituality, and religion), subcultural affilia-
      tions and distinctions, and technology.

85. **Butler, Mark**. 2005. *Unlocking the Groove: Rhythm, Meter, and Musical Design in Electronic Dance Music*. Series: *Profiles in Popular Music*. Bloomington: Indiana University Press. xi, 346 p. Illustrations, Music Examples, Compact Disc, Discography, Bibliography, and Index. ISBN: 0-25334-662-2.

   Analyzes electronic dance music and interweaves traditional and non-traditional musical analysis with consideration of the generic history and social significance. Deconstructs several examples of EDM and focuses on the interaction of beat and rhythmic structure in creating an overall music design. Incorporates interview with DJs, listeners, and producers that provide insight into the perception and performance world of EDM and the musical artists of EDM and DJs.

86. **Byrne, Kevin, and Emily Fuchs**. 2022. *The Jukebox Musical: An Interpretative History*. New York: Routledge. 148 p. Bibliography and Index. ISBN: 9-780-36764-892-3.

   A comprehensive guide to the genre of the jukebox musical and its history to explain why it has become loved for multiple generations of theatergoers and practitioners. Explores three main categories of the jukebox musical: biographies, genre-specific, and artist catalog.

87. **Calvo-Sotelo, Javier C**. 2019. "Apocalypse as Critical Dystopia in Modern Popular Music." *Journal of Religion, Film & Media* 5(2): 69–94. ISSN: 2414-0201.

   Argues that in the realm of popular music, the apocalypse has been embraced as synonymous with imminent catastrophe, generating a dystopian discourse. Examines how as a tool for analysis the concept of "critical dystopia" has built a usefulness of connecting apocalyptic menaces, re-enchantment of the world, and social protest. Also examines how at the same time authenticity is a sacred dimension within rock, an antidote to commercialism and a key notion of doomsday scenarios. Presents a conceptual review of the state of the questions and debate involved and an exposition of selected songs with a summary of their main traits.

88. **Carter, James**. 2020. "Campus Rock: Rock Music Culture on the College Campus During the Counterculture Sixties, 1967–1968." *Journal of Popular Music Studies* 32(3): 51–72. ISSN: 1533-1598.

   Explores the relationship between the growth of rock culture, the college campus, and the broader sixties experiences. Contends that the college campus was crucial in the development of rock music as student tastes determined "rock culture." Further argues that folk, pop, soul, rhythm and blues, folk rock, hard rock, and psychedelic/acid rock thrived simultaneously on the college campus from 1967 to 1970 during the period of significant changes in popular music.

89. **Case, George**. 2021. *Takin' Care of Business: A History of Working People's Rock 'n' Roll*. New York: Oxford University Press. 203 p. Bibliography and Index. ISBN: 9-780-19754-884-4.

   Examines rock from the late 1960s onward to regular working-class fans. Focuses on Creedence Clearwater Revival to Bruce Springsteen, from Lynyrd Skynyrd to

AC/DC, and from Judas Priest to Ted Nugent. Discusses how the music provided the anthems of an increasingly distinct and vulnerable demographic that since has become a key influence on political culture around the world.

90.   **Cashman, David, and Philip Hayward**. 2020. *Cruisicology: The Music Culture of Cruise Ships*. Series: *Critical Perspectives on Music and Society*. London: Lexington Books. 104 p. Bibliography and Index. ISBN: 9-781-79360-202-2.

Provides an account of the culture and the industrial determinants of cruise ships. Integrates how music is organized and made on board a cruise ship. Offers a study of the working life, why, and how corporate shipping lines include music on board their vessels, the history of musicians on passenger shipping, and the likely future directions of musical entertainment within the industry.

91.   **Cashman, David, and Waldo Garrido, eds**. 2020. *Performing Popular Music: The Art of Creating Memorable and Successful Performances*. New York: Routledge. 208 p. Illustrations, Bibliography, and Index. ISBN: 9-781-13858-506-5.

A compilation of essays that explore the fundamentals of popular music performance for students in contemporary music instruction. Draws on the insights of performance practice research and discusses the unwritten rules of performances in popular music, what it takes to create a memorable performance, and live popular music as a creative industry. Offers a practical view of topics ranging from rehearsals to stagecraft and what to do when things go wrong, promotion, recordings, and how the music industry places performance in the context of building a career. Introduces aspiring musicians to the elements of crafting compelling performances and succeeding in the world of today's pop music.

92.   **Cateforis, Theo, ed**. 2019. *The Rock History Reader, 3rd ed*. New York: Routledge. xv, 463 p. Bibliography and Index. ISBN: 9-781-13822-771-2.

An edited volume that tells the story of rock as it has been received and explained as a social and musical practice throughout its six-decade history. Includes new readings with added material on the early origins of rock 'n' roll as well as coverage of recent developments, including the changing shape of the music industry in the twenty-first century. Many of the compiled essays delve into issues such as censorship, copyright, race relations, feminism, youth subcultures, and the meaning of musical value.

93.   **Cateforis, Theo**. 2018. "'Total Trash': Analysis and Post-Punk Music." *Journal of Popular Music Studies* 30(4): 95–112. ISSN: 1533-1598.

Examines how music may bring the analyst's dependence upon lyrical and music-notational devices into question. Provides a discussion centered on the issues of sound that complicates analytical efforts to control a particular generic type of post-punk music. Defines the term post-punk as music that expands on punk's noticeable stylistic traits.

94.   **Chapman, Ian, and Henry M. Johnson, eds**. 2019. *Global Glam and Popular Music: Style and Spectacle From the 1970s to the 2000s*. Series: *Routledge Studies*

in Popular Music. London & New York: Routledge. viii, 300 p. Illustrations, Bibliography, and Index. ISBN: 9-780-36787-122-2.

Explores styles and spectacle in glam popular music performance from the 1970s to the present day and from an international perspective. Focuses on several representative artists, bands, and movements as well as national, regional, and cultural contexts from around the world. Approaches glam music performance and style broadly employing glam/glitter rock genre of the early 1970s as a foundation for case studies and comparisons. Engages subjects that help in defining the glam/glitter phenomenon—David Bowie, T Rex, Slade, Roxy Music, Alice Cooper, Suzi Quarto, the New York Dolls, Kiss, and many others. Situates the study of glam rock at the intersection of other styles such as punk, metal, disco, and goth.

95. **Chen, Stephen, Shane Homan, Tracey Redhead, and Richard Vella**. 2021. *The Music Export Business: Born Global*. Series: *Routledge Research in the Creative and Cultural Industries*. Abingdon, Oxon: Routledge. ix, 217 p. Illustrations, Bibliography, and Index. ISBN: 9-780-36774-463-2.

Assesses global trends in the music industry business models including streaming and national export policies. Incorporates interviews with industry insiders, musicians, managers, record labels, and government stakeholders employing case studies that highlight cultural and economic value creation in a global value chain. Also reassesses the "born global" phenomenon.

96. **Choi, Grace Y**. 2017. "'Who Run the Music? Girls!': Examining the Construction of Female Digital Musicians' Online Presence." *Popular Music and Society* 40(4): 474–487. ISSN: 0300-7766.

Argues that female digital musicians who are self-taught are making their presence known online by using digital technologies, especially social media. Provides research from one-on-one interviews conducted with an international sample of seventeen female digital musicians who create content on YouTube, SoundCloud, and Vine. Interviews indicate that these women musicians were self-motivated to acquire the necessary skills to become efficient social media users and to construct their online presence. Also finds that these women musicians were able to incorporate online comments negotiating their position as women and musicians. Concludes that overall female digital musicians illustrate how the music audience has the ability and power to create its own culture in today's music industry.

97. **Cicchelli, Vincenzo, Sylvie Octobre, and Viviane Riegel, eds**. 2020. *Aesthetic Cosmopolitanism and Global Culture*. Series: *Youth in a Globalizing World*. Leiden & Boston: Brill. xxvii, 361 p. Bibliography and Index. ISBN: 9-789-00437-501-7 and ISSN: 2212-9383.

A compilation of essays that consider aesthetic cosmopolitanism as a tool to understand how individuals and social groups appropriate the sphere of culture in a global world. Compiled essays are based on the discussion of theoretical perspectives and empirically grounded research conducted in many countries. Topics are varied and include rock music, K-pop, samba, tourism museums, TV series, movies, food, and architecture. Essays also provide resources for making sense of preferences in a global perspective.

98. **Clarke, Paul**. 1983. "'A Magic Science': Rock Music as a Recorded Art." *Popular Music* 3 [Special Issue: *Producers and Markets*]: 195–213. ISSN: 0261-1430.

Contends that modes of inquiry developed for the analysis of Western art music focusing on the text and the musical score are inappropriate for the analysis of rock music. Moreover, rock analysis inappropriately attempts to fit the music within a narrowly established template. Suggests a more informed approach would offer an evaluation of the music not on any one aural strand (e.g., lyrical, musical, or vocal) but on the complex created relationships between sounds as they act through time.

99. **Clifford-Napoleone, Amber R**. 2015. *Queerness in Heavy Metal: Metal Bent.* Series: *Routledge Studies in Popular Music*. Abingdon, Oxon & New York: Rout-ledge. xiv, 180 p. Illustrations, Bibliography, and Index. ISBN: 9-780-81536-558-7.

Focuses on queer fans, performers, and spaces within the heavy metal sphere and demonstrates the importance, pervasiveness, and subcultural significance of queerness to the heavy metal ethos. Queers heavy metal studies by bringing discussions of gender and sexuality in heavy metal out of a theorizing dichot-omy. Connects new and existing scholarship with a strong ethnographic study of heavy metal's self-identified queer performance fans in their own words, giving them a voice and offering an original and groundbreaking addition to scholar-ship in popular music, rock, and queer studies.

100. **Cloonan, Martin, and Reebee Garofalo, eds**. 2003. *Policing Pop.* Philadelphia: Temple University Press. x, 241 p. Illustrations, Bibliography, and Index. ISBN: 9-781-43990-138-0.

Posits that fans and detractors of popular music tend to agree that popular music is a bellwether of an individual's political and cultural values, and in virtually every country in the world some group identifies popular music as a source of potential danger and desires to regulate it. Compiled essays examine the many ways in which popular music and artists around the world are subjected to cen-sorship ranging from state control to the efforts of special interest or religious groups.

101. **Cloonan, Martin**. 2005. "What Is Popular Music Studies? Some Observations." *British Journal of Music Education* 22(1): 77–93. ISSN: 0265-0517.

Considers how popular music studies is now taught in over twenty higher edu-cation institutions in the United Kingdom and in numerous others across the world. Provides an outline of the constituent parts of popular music studies in the United Kingdom and questions its status as a discipline. Concludes by argu-ing that having established itself, popular music studies will need to deal with two key pressures in modern academic life: those of conducting research and widening participation. Offers suggestions that in conducting research within popular music studies, pragmatism may be necessary, and expanding participation holds potential for radicalism.

102.   **Coggins, Owen**. 2018. *Mysticism, Ritual, and Religion in Drone Metal.* Series: *Bloomsbury Studies in Religion and Popular Music.* New York: Bloomsbury. 125 p. Bibliography and Index. ISBN: 9-781-35002-511-0.

Offers an extensive study of drone metal music and its religious associations. Draws on five years of ethnographic research and observation from numerous performers, interviews and surveys, analysis of sound recordings, artwork, and discourse about music. Demonstrates that while many drone metal listeners identify as non-religious, their ways of engaging with and talking about drone metal are informed by mysticism, ritual, and religion.

103.   **Cohen, Sara, Robert Knifton, Marion Leonard, and Les Roberts, eds**. 2015. *Sites of Popular Music Heritage: Memories, Histories, Places.* Series: *Studies in Popular Music.* New York: Routledge. vi, 267 p. Bibliography and Index. ISBN: 9-780-41582-450-7.

An interdisciplinary compilation of essays that examine the location of memories and histories of popular music and its multiple pasts. Explores the different places in which popular music can be situated, including the local physical site, the museum storeroom, and exhibition space, as well as the digitized archive and display spaces made possible by the Internet. Offers a re-evaluation of such sites and reinserts them into the function and significance within the production of popular music heritage. Integrates research based on extensive fieldwork from scholars of popular music studies, cultural sociology, and museum studies alongside the new insights of practice-based consideration of current practitioners within the field of popular music heritage.

104.   **Cohen, Sara**. 1993. "Ethnography and Popular Music Studies." *Popular Music* 12(2): 123–138. ISSN: 0261-1430.

A response and critical evaluation that relates to ethnography and popular music studies. Offers a response to Simon Firth (1982), who bemoaned that fact that students would rather sit in the library and study popular music (mainly punk) in terms of the appropriate critical theory rather than conduct ethnographic research that would treat popular music as social practice and process. Observes that ten years later the literature on popular music is still lacking ethnography.

105.   **Collins, Karen**. 2017. *From Pac Man to Pop Music: Interactive Audio Games and New Media.* Previously published, Aldershot, Hampshire, & Burlington: Ashgate, 2008. Series: *Ashgate Popular and Folk Music Series.* London: Routledge. xv, 207 p. Illustrations, Bibliography, and Index. ISBN: 9-781-40942-903-6.

Presents the research of academics, composers, and music programmers to introduce the topic of the digital interactive audio as the future of audio media.

Provides a supplementary text for music and multimedia course instruction. Covers practical and theoretical approaches including historical perspectives, emerging theories, sociocultural approaches to fandom, semiotic analysis, reception theory, and case studies analysis.

106.   Collins, Mathew. 2015. *Pop Grenade: From Public Enemy to Pussy Riot: Dispatches From Music Frontlines.* Winchester & Washington, D.C.: Zero Books. vi, 249 p. Bibliography. ISBN: 9-781-78279-831-6.

Covers some of the cultural flashpoints of the past few decades and celebrates the power of music as a force for change. Provides a firsthand reportage from raves, riots, and rebellions. Explores how music has been used as a weapon in struggles for liberation and attempts to create temporary paradises.

107.   Collins, Mathew. 2018. *Rave On: Global Adventures in Electronic Dance Music.* Chicago: University of Chicago Press. 378 p. Illustrations, Music Examples, Bibliography, and Index. ISBN: 9-780-22659-548-1.

Investigates and inquires into the world to experience firsthand the unique scenes of electronic dance music, interview the key players, and relate the narratives of how dance went global. Discusses aspects of how electronic dance music was once the utopian frontier of pop culture but after over three decades after acid house "Summer of Love," it has gone from subculture to the global mainstream. Examines closely the pleasure palaces in Ibiza and Las Vegas to the new frontiers in Shanghai (China) and Dubai (United Arab Emirates) and how raving is now a multimillion-dollar business.

108.   Collins, Nicolas. 2020. *Handmade Electronic Music: The Art of Hardware Hacking, 3rd ed.* New York: Routledge. 452 p. CD-ROM, Bibliography, and Index. ISBN: 9-780-36721-010-6.

Introduces the craft of making as well as creatively cannibalizing electronic circuits for artistic purposes. Offers insight into core technology of early live electronic music as well as developments at the hands of emerging artists. Demystifies the process of crafting on instruments and enables musicians, composers, artists, and anyone interested in music technology to draw on the creative potential of hardware hacking.

109.   Connell, John, and Chris Gibson, eds. 2003. *Soundtracks: Popular Music, Identity, and Place.* Series: *Critical Geographies.* London & New York: Routledge. xii, 320 p. Illustrations, Bibliography, and Index. ISBN: 9-780-41517-028-4.

Presents a new geography of popular music, examining the complex links between places, music, and cultural identities. Provides an interdisciplinary perspective on local, national, and global scenes from the "Mersey" and "Icelandic" sounds to "world music." Explores the diverse meanings of music in a range of regional contexts. Develops a new perspective on such issues as globalization, links between space, music and industry, place and credibility of music, originality, tradition, and marketing devices.

110. **Cook, Susan C., and Sherrill Dodds, eds**. 2016. *Bodies of Sound: Studies Across Popular Music and Dance*. Previously published, Burlington: Ashgate, 2013. Series: *Ashgate Popular and Folk Music Series*. London & New York: Routledge. xviii, 237 p. Illustrations, Music Examples, Bibliography, and Index. ISBN: 9-781-31556-960-4.

A collection of essays that reveal the intimate connections between the corporeal and the sonic in the creation, transmission, and reception of popular music and dance which is imagined as "bodies of sound." Compiled essays provoke a wide-ranging interdisciplinary scholarship from Asia, Europe, and the United States that explores topics from the nineteenth century to the present day and engages with practices of local, national, and international levels.

111. **Cooper, B. Lee**. 2008. "Women's Studies and Popular Music Stereotypes." *Popular Music and Society* 23(4): 31–43. ISSN: 0300-766.

A study that focuses on women's images in popular music lyrics. Argues that analyzing women's images in popular lyrics calls for measured subtlety rather than forced choices. Further argues that too often well-intentioned ideologues have selected songs such as "Born a Woman" or "Under My Thumb" to illustrate lyrics based on gender dichotomies and cultural hierarchies. Suggests that a healthier perspective lyric imagery requires consideration of entire spectrums of gendered-related behavior, different images, and stereotypes of women in popular music.

112. **Corbett, John**. 2015. *Micro-Groove: Forays Into Other Music*. Durham: Duke University Press. xxi, 468 p. Illustrations, Bibliography, and Index. ISBN: 9-780-82235-900-5.

An exploration of diverse music with essays, interviews, commentaries, and musician profiles that focus on jazz, improvised music, contemporary classical, rock, folk, post-punk, and cartoon music. Advocates for the relevance of the "little" music, which despite its smaller audience is of enormous significance. Discusses musicians such as Sun Ra, PJ Harvey, KoKo Taylor, Steve Lacey, Helmut Lachenmann, and others.

113. **Cornelius, Steven, and Mary Natvig**. 2022. *Music: A Social Experience, 3rd ed*. London: Routledge. 408 p. Illustrations, Bibliography, and Index. ISBN: 9-780-36774-033-7.

A teaching resource that takes a thematic approach to the study of music appreciation and demonstrates how music reflects and deepens both individual and cultural understandings. Includes music examples within universally experienced social frameworks of ethnicity, gender, spirituality, love, and so forth, to aid students in understanding how music reflects and advances human experience. Engages with multiple genres—Western art music, popular music, and world music—through integrative narratives and innovative activities.

114. **Covach, John, and Mark Spicer, eds**. 2013. *Sounding Out Pop: Analytical Essays in Popular Music*. Series: *Tracking Pop*. Ann Arbor: University of Michigan Press. xiv, 265 p. Illustrations, Bibliography, and Index. ISBN: 9-780-47211-505-1.

A collection of essays that explore a broad spectrum of popular music. Compiled essays work together to map the myriad styles and genres of the pop-rock idiom through a series of case studies. Topics include Lieber and Stoller, the Coasters, and the dramatic AABA form; Roy Orbison's sweetheart Texas style; artistic interaction between Bob Dylan and Roger McGuinn; Marvin Gaye as a vocal composer; the mid-1970s music of Genesis; style in the music of the Police; musical narrative strategies in the female pop-rock artists, 1993–1995; the past and future of sampling; and the vanishing subject in Radiohead's Kid A.

115. **Cox, Christoph, and Daniel Warner, eds**. 2017. *Audio Culture: Readings in Modern Music, revised ed*. New York: Bloomsbury. xviii, 646 p. Bibliography and Index. ISBN: 9-781-50131-835-1.

Attempts to map the aural and discursive terrain of vanguard musical culture. Traces the genealogy of lines of contemporary musical practices and theoretical concerns, drawing lines of connection between recent musical practices and earlier moments of sonic experimentation. Explores the interconnection among such forms as minimalism, the classical avant-garde, *musique concreté*, improvised music, dub reggae, ambient music, hip-hop, and techno. Includes essays by Jacques Attali, John Cage, Simon Reynolds, Brian Eco, Glen Gould, Umberto Eco, Michael Nyman, Ornette Coleman, Karl Stockhausen, and many others.

116. **Croland, Michael**. 2016. *Oy Oy Oy Gevalt!: Jews and Punk*. Santa Barbara: ABC-CLIO. xxviii, 181 p. Glossary, Appendix, Bibliography, and Index. ISBN: 9-781-44083-219-2.

Examines the world of Jews who relate to their Jewishness through the vehicle of punk to musicians who put their Jewish identity front and center. Explores alternative expressions of Jewish identity as seen in music documentary, young adult novels, and much more. Also demonstrates the prominent role of Jewish individuals in the history of punk, including in such bands as the Ramones, the Dictators, the Clash, Bad Religion, and NOFX, as well as Malcolm McLaren, the manager of the Sex Pistols.

117. **Cvetkovski, Trajce**. 2015. *The Pop Music Idol and the Spirt of Charisma: Reality Television Talent Shows in the Digital Economy of Hope*. Series: *Pop Music, Culture and Identity*. Houndmills, Basingstoke, Hampshire & New York: Palgrave Macmillan. xiii, 225 p. Illustrations, Bibliography, and Index. ISBN: 9-781-13749-445-0.

Considers the political economy of the music industry and the sale of recorded music that resides in a contestable digital landscape, as the centralized industry organizational model is no longer viable. Examines the influence of music reality TV and music contests, such as *Idol, X Factor*, and *The Voice*, that have become dream machines in a pop cultural marketplace.

118. **Dale, Pete**. 2016. *Popular Music and the Politics of Novelty*. New York: Blooms-
      bury. 225 p. Bibliography and Index. ISBN: 9-781-50130-704-1.

      Demonstrates that the utilization of popular music to promote political cause
      and the expression of dissent through the medium of "popular song" remain
      widely in practice in contemporary times. Examines actual usages of popular
      music in political processes as well as expressions of political feeling through
      song. Argues that there is much to think about that the demand for radical
      change remain in circulation. Considers how necessary it is for politically moti-
      vated popular music to offer aesthetic novelty.

119. **Danielsen, Anne, ed**. 2010. *Musical Rhythm in the Age of Digital Reproduction*.
      Series: *Ashgate Popular Music and Folk Music Series*. London: Routledge. xiii,
      252 p. Illustrations, Bibliography, and Index. ISBN: 9-781-40940-931-1.

      Presents new insights into the study of musical rhythm through the investiga-
      tion of the micro-rhythm design groove-based music. Investigates how techno-
      logical mediation in the age of digital music production tool has influenced the
      design of rhythm at the micro level. Compiled essays integrate close readings
      of technology-driven popular music genres such as contemporary rhythm and
      blues, hip-hop, trip-hop, electro-pop, electronica, house, and techno, as well as
      played folk music styles.

120. **Davis, James A., and Christopher Lynch, eds**. 2002. *Listening Across Borders:
      Musicology in the Global Classroom*. Series: *Modern Musicology and the Col-
      lege Classroom*. New York: Routledge. vi, 171 p. Bibliography and Index. ISBN:
      9-780-36713-567-6.

      An edited volume that informs popular music studies, research, and teaching
      from a global perspective. Essays provide concrete examples of how a global
      approach to music history can be integrated into modern curriculum within the
      framework of the roots, challenges, and benefits of internationalization. Essays
      suggest approaches and strategies that are applicable in a variety of teaching sit-
      uations and aim to promote internalized teaching approaches to teachers all over
      the world. Essays are divided into several parts that include Part I—Creating
      Global Citizens; Part II—Teaching With Case Studies of Intercultural Encoun-
      ters; and Part III—Challenges and Opportunities. Geographical areas of case
      studies include Taiwan, North India, Canada, China, South India, Brazil, Jordan,
      and South Africa.

121. **De Boise, Sam**. 2020. "Music and Misogyny: A Context Analysis of Misogynis-
      tic, Antifeminist Forums." *Popular Music* 39(3–4): 459–481. ISSN: 0261-1430.

      Considers how music is discussed among those who espouse misogynistic
      views. Examines content analysis of 1,173 posts from six misogynistic antifem-
      inist movement (MAM) forums. Demonstrates that while hip-hop, rap, and
      metal genres and artists are the more commonly mentioned, there is also signif-
      icant variation in terms of musical preferences and justifications. Also demon-
      strates how MAM communities' musical judgments are a confluence of sonic

and extramusical discourses that are shaped and amplified within these online communities.

122.   **De Bruin, Leon, and Jane Southcott, eds**. 2023. *Musical Ecologies: Instrumental Music Ensembles Around the World*. Abingdon, Oxon: Routledge. xiii, 241 p. Illustrations, Map, Bibliography, and Index. ISBN: 9-781-03218-433-3.

Explores the role community music plays around the world and how various instrumentally based music-making communities operate ecologies that allow notions of social, political, and cultural agency, and identities. Explores community music as local, glocal, global phenomenon by critically discussing the redefinition of community music and what music making means to people in the twenty-first century. Reveals the complexity of social ways people come together to make music and that making music is central to this sociality.

123.   **Demont-Heinrich, Christof**. 2011. "Cultural Imperialism Versus Globalization of Culture: Riding the Structure-Agency Dialectic in Global Communications and Media Studies." *Sociology Compass* 5(8): 666–678. ISSN: 1751-9020.

Discusses and analyzes the dialectic between so-called cultural imperialism and globalization of culture perspectives in global communication and media studies. Situates a paradigm of cultural imperialism within the framework of an international extension of the long-discredited hypodermic needle theory, which views cultural consumers as passive automatons. Discusses how there has been a growing trend among many global communication and media scholars to locate a productive middle ground between cultural imperialism and globalization of culture.

124.   **Denning, Michael**. 2015. *Noise Uprising: The Audiopolitics of a World Musical Revolution*. New York & London: Verso. 306 p. Bibliography and Index. ISBN: 9-781-78168-856-4.

Argues that the early recording industry unleashed a worldwide sonic revolution. Focuses on the five-year period that was inaugurated by the invention of electric recording technology in 1925 and analyzes the recording boom that played out in port cities throughout the world. Borrows Beatriz Sarlo's concept of "peripheral modernity" to emphasize that the genres that emerged in ports— tango, samba, jazz, calypso, son, palm wine, and others—were a long way from folk.

125.   **Denning, Michael**. 2016. "Decolonizing the Ear: The Transcolonial Reverberations of Vernacular Phonograph Music." In *Audible Empire: Music, Global Politics, Critique*. Series: *Refiguring American Music*, Ronaldo Radano and Tejumola Olaniyan, eds. xi, 418 p. Illustrations, Bibliography, and Index. ISBN: 9-780-82235-986-9.

Explores the relations between worldwide circulations of vernacular phonograph music in the late 1920s and the dialectic of colonization and decolonization. Explores the boom in recorded vernacular music from son to jazz, samba to

krongcong, marabi to beguine that took place between the development of electrical recording in the mid-1920s and 1930s that coincided with the first stirrings
of anti-colonial activist thought. Also considers the contradictory meanings and
appropriations of vernacular gramophone. Draws examples from Hawaii to
Cuba, India to North Africa.

126. **De Quadros, Andre**. 2019. *Focus: Choral Music in Global Perspective*. Series:
Focus on World Music. New York: Routledge. xxvii, 228 p. Illustrations, Map,
Bibliography, and Index. ISBN: 9-780-41589-654-2.

Introduces traditions and repertoires of the world's choral diversity from prison
choirs in Thailand and gay and lesbian choruses of the Western world to community choruses in the Middle East and youth choirs in the United States.
Weaves together the stories of diverse individuals and organizations, examining
their musical and pedagogical practices while presenting research on how choral
cultures around the world interact with societies and transform lives of their
members.

127. **Devine, Kyle**. 2015. "Decomposed: A Political Ecology of Music." *Popular Music*
34(3): 367–389. ISSN: 0261-1430.

Concerns what recordings are made of and about what happens to those recordings when they are disposed of. Inscribes a history of recorded music in three main
materials: shellac, plastic, and data. Forges a political economy of the evolving
relationship between popular music and sound technology that accounts for not
only human production and consumption but also material manufacture disposal.
Contends that such an orientation is useful for developing an analytical framework
that is adequate to the complexities of the global material-cultural flows in which
the recorded music commodity is constituted and de-constituted. It also strives
towards a more responsible way of thinking about the relationship between popular music and cultural and economic value and its environmental costs.

128. **Diallo, David**. 2019. *Collective Participation and Audience Engagement in Rap
Music*. Series: *Pop Music, Culture, and Identity*. Cham: Palgrave Macmillan. xi,
150 p. Illustrations, Bibliography, and Index. ISBN: 9-783-03025-376-9.

Examines the compositional practice of rap lyricists. Argues that whether
through the privileging of chanted call-and-response phrases or through rhetorical strategies meant to assist in getting one's listening audience open, the focus
on the first rap MCs is on community building, and successful records with lyrics and production techniques encourage the listener to become physically and
emotionally involved in recorded performance.

129. **Dines, Michael, and Laura Way, eds**. 2017. *Postgraduate Voices in Punk Studies:
Your Wisdom, Our Youth*. Newcastle upon Tyne: Cambridge Scholars Publishing. vi, 166 p. Illustrations and Bibliography. ISBN: 9-781-44387-476-2.

Represents an academic collection to draw upon postgraduate research in
exploring the punk scene. Spans both local and global contexts. Covers a range

of interdisciplinary discourse and builds on diversity of existing academic work in punk studies. Topics include post-punk manifestos, anarcho-punk and rock history; Dutch ultra scene; French hardcore scene; Mexico City's punk women; Johnny Rotten; anarcho-punk; and aesthetics in Gee Vaucher's images of Crass (1979–1984).

130.   **Doggett, Peter**. 2007. *There's a Riot Going On: Revolutionaries, Rock Stars and the Rise and Fall of the '60s Counter-Culture*. Edinburgh & New York: Canongate. 598 p. Illustrations, [16 p.] of plates, Portraits, Bibliography, and Index. ISBN: 9-781-84767-180-6.

A study of how between 1965 and 1972 political activists around the world prepared to mount a revolution. Examines how the Black Panthers to the Gay Liberation Front, the yippie movement, the IRA, and some musicians' rock and soul music supplied the revolutionary tide with anthems and iconic imagery. Examines how musicians John Lennon, Mick Jagger, Bob Dylan, and others were influential in the revolutionary movement. Provides an account of the period and conveys a portrait of the era when revolutionaries turned to rock stars and rock stars dressed up as revolutionaries.

131.   **Donnelly, K. J.** 2015. *Magical Musical Tour: Rock and Pop in Film Soundtracks*. New York: Bloomsbury. vii, 207 p. Bibliography and Index. ISBN: 9-781-62892-128-1.

Examines how the popular music industry has become completely interlinked with the film industry such as Simon and Garfunkel's "The Sound of Silence" in *The Graduate* (1967), the Righteous Brothers' "Unchained Melody" in *Ghosts* (1990), and many others. Provides a survey to engage in the intersection of both the aesthetic and industrial levels of popular music and the film industry. Offer discussions of many films and musicians and detailed case studies of films.

132.   **Duffett, Mark, and Beate Peter, eds**. 2020. *Popular Music and Automobiles*. London: Bloomsbury. viii, 203 p. Illustrations, Bibliography, and Index. ISBN: 9-781-50135-230-0.

Contends that since the 1990s cars and popular music have been constantly associated. Furthermore, as complementary good and intertwined technologies, their relationship has become part of a widely shared experience that connects individuals and society, private worlds, and public spheres. Compiled essays explain the ways in which cars and car journeys have shaped society and how attention to an ongoing relationship can reveal insights about the assertion and negotiation of identity.

133.   **Duffett, Mark, and Jon Hackett, eds**. 2021. *Scary Monsters: Monstrosity, Masculinity, and Popular Music*. New York: Bloomsbury. viii, 280 p. Bibliography and Index. ISBN: 9-781-50131-337-0.

A compilation of essays that focus on popular music and masculinity, which is examined through research into monstrosity. Essays consider discourses associated with rock and pop, gender, myth, and meaning, with a focus on cultural theory. Argues that monstrosity provides a unique perspective on the study of masculinity in popular music culture.

134. **Duffett, Mark**. 2014. *Popular Music Fandom: Identities, Roles, and Practices.* Series: *Routledge Studies in Popular Music*. Abingdon, Oxon: Routledge. vi, 233 p. Bibliography and Index. ISBN: 9-781-13893-697-3.

   Explores popular music fandom from a cultural studies perspective that incorporates popular music studies, audience research, and media fandom. Draws together recent work on popular music studies and integrates a dialogue within the wider field of media fan research. Considers how popular music fandom can be understood as a cultural phenomenon. Also considers topics such as how to define, theorize, and empirically research popular fan culture and how music fandom relates to other roles, practices, and forms of social identity.

135. **Dunbar, Julie C**. 2021. *Women, Music, Culture: An Introduction*. New York: Routledge. xvi, 408 p. Music Examples, Bibliography, and Index. ISBN: 9-780-36713-812-7.

   Prepared for an undergraduate textbook on the history and contributions of women in a variety of musical genres and professions. Includes over one hundred listening experiences and the musical work of women throughout history and includes composers, performers, conductors, technicians, music industry, and personnel in both art music and popular music.

136. **Dunkel, Mario, and Sina A. Nitzsche, eds**. 2019. *Popular Music and Public Diplomacy: Transnational and Transdisciplinary Perspectives*. Series: *Studien zur Popularmusik*. Bielefeld: Transcript. 328 p. Bibliography and Index. ISBN: 9-783-83944-358-3.

   Observes that in the early years of the Cold War, Western nations increasingly adopted strategies of public diplomacy involving popular music. Moreover, while the diplomatic use of popular music was initially limited to such genres as jazz, the second half of the twentieth century saw a growing presence of various popular genres in diplomacy including rock, punk, reggae, and hip-hop. Essays highlight the interrelations of popular music and public diplomacy from transnational perspectives and how diplomatic use has impacted the global musical landscape of the twentieth and twenty-first centuries.

137. **Dunn, Kevin C**. 2016. *Global Punk: Resistance and Rebellion in Everyday Life*. New York: Bloomsbury. 262 p. Bibliography and Index. ISBN: 9-781-62892-605-7.

   Examines the global phenomenon of DIY punk and argues that it provides a powerful tool for political resistance and personal self-empowerment. Draws on examples from across the evolution of punk from the streets of 1976 London (England) to contemporary Jakarta (Indonesia) and others. Integrates both historical and global perspectives and examines the ways pun contributes to the process of disalienation and political engagement.

138.   **Dyndahl, Petter, Sidsel Karlsen, and Ruth Wright, eds**. 2021. *Musical Gentrifi-cation: Popular Music, Distinction, and Social Mobility.* Series: *ISME Global Per-spectives in Music Education.* Abingdon, Oxon: Routledge. 196 p. Illustrations, Bibliography, and Index. ISBN: 9-780-36753-559-9.

A collection of essays that concentrate on the role of popular music in the process of sociocultural inclusion and exclusion in a variety of contexts. Essays approach the phenomenon of musical gentrification from a variety of angles of theoretical and methodological perspectives and with reference to several key issues in pop-ular music, from class, gender, and ethnicity to cultural consumption, activism, hegemony, and musical agency.

139.   **Edgar, Robert, Kristy Fairclough-Isaacs, Benjamin Halligan, and Nicola Spelman, eds**. 2015. *The Arena Concert: Music, Media, and Mass Entertainment.* New York: Bloomsbury. xv, 331 p. Illustrations, Bibliography, and Index. ISBN: 9-781-62892-554-8.

Offers interviews with key designers, discussions of the practicalities of mount-ing arena concerts, mixing and performing live to a mass audience, recollections of the giants of late twentieth-century music in performances, and others. Tracks the evolution of the arena concert and considers design and architecture, celeb-rity and fashion, feminism, ethnographic research, and ideas about humor, live-ness, and authenticity in order to explore and frame the arena concert and how the arena become the real-time center of a global digital network.

140.   **Elferen, Isabella, and Jeffrey A. Weinstein**. *Goth Music: From Sound to Sub-culture.* Series: *Routledge Studies in Popular Music.* New York: Routledge. 162 p. Bibliography and Index. ISBN: 9-780-41572-004-5.

Argues that in the variegated musical landscape of goth, several key consistencies exist. Further argues that not only do these goth substyles share several musical and textual characteristics, but more importantly these aspects of the music are constitutive of goth social reality. Draws on personal experiences in the Euro-pean and North American goth scenes to explore the ways in which the sounds of goth inform the scene's listening practices, its fantasies of other worlds, and its re-enchantment of their own world. Asserts that goth music engendered a musical landscape of its own, a musical chronotype that is driven by nostalgic yearnings.

141.   **Elliott, Richard, and Abigail Gardner, eds**. 2024. "Special Issue: Aging, Time, and Popular Music." *IASPM Journal* 14(1): 1–209. ISSN: 2079-3871.

A special issue that seeks to explore what aging might be or mean for popular music studies. Special issues suggest that aging has not been addressed much across popular music studies, although significant contributions have emerged in relation to aging audiences. Compiled essays focus on aging fans and fandoms, representation, performances, and production from popular music studies, musi-cology, sociology, cultural studies, queer theory, and aging studies. Some of the topics covered include Jacques Greene's aging temporalities; exploring how young adults give meaning to their lifelong music fandom; Julio Valverde's temporal agency through musicking; youth and persona in Paul McCartney's self-titled solo albums; aging, nostalgia, and older punk women's fandom; hermeneutics in Alice Cooper's metamodern menagerie of age; aging female vocalities in musical theater; negotiating genre, style, and contemporality in an intergenerational Irish music ensemble; Molchat Doma, the death of the reader and the birth of the Tik Toker; and the acquisition of digital audio knowledge in the studies of Senegalese beatmakers.

142. **Emerson, Gina**. 2023. *Audience Experience and Contemporary Classical Music: Negotiating the Experimental and the Accessible in a High Art*. Series: *Audience Research*. Abingdon, Oxon: Routledge. xv, 224 p. Illustrations, Bibliography, and Index. ISBN: 9-780-36769-681-8.

Responds to recent debates on cultural participation and the relevance of music composed with the first large-scale audience experience study on contemporary classical music. Provides analysis of how existing audience members experience contemporary classical music and seeks to make date-informed contributions to future discussions of audience diversity and accessibility.

143. **Endsley, Crystal L.** 2023. *Quantum Justice: Global Girls Cultivating Disruption Through Word Poetry*. Austin: University of Texas Press. xii, 268 p. Illustrations, Bibliography, and Index. ISBN: 9-781-47732-805-7.

By facilitating works for girls in Ethiopia, South Africa, Tanzania, and the United States, the author highlights how girls use spoken words to narrate their experiences, dreams, and strategies for surviving and thriving. Examines how girls forecast what is possible for their collective lives. Combines poetry, discourse analysis, photo-voices, and others to forge the feminist theory of "quantum justice," which forefronts girls' relationships with their global counterparts. Emphasizes how the imaginative energy in hip-hop culture can mobilize girls to connect and motivate each other through spoken word performance.

144. **Eriksson, Maria, Rasmus Fleischer, Anna Johansson, Pelle Snickars, and Patrick Vonderau, eds**. 2019. *Spotify Teardown: Inside the Black Box of Streaming Music*. Cambridge: MIT Press. ix, 276 p. Bibliography and Index. ISBN: 9-780-26203-890-4.

Considers how the shift from a logic of ownership of a cultural good to that of market experience influences the practice of individuals. Aims in a critical approach to dismantle Spotify, a Swedish streaming platform launched in 2008. Linked with the destabilization experience of Harold Garfinkel, father of ethnomethodology, the volume aims to open various "black boxes" of streaming model of which Spotify is highly representative. Chapters are interspersed with an experimental intervention linked to Spotify from the analysis of a digital campaign (#backaspotify) to the creation of a puppet label titles, and so forth.

145.   **Evans, Mark**. 2006. *Open the Doors: Music in the Modern Church*. Series: *Studies in Popular Music*. London & Oakville: Equinox Publishing. xiv, 209 p. Illustrations, Bibliography, and Index. ISBN: 9-781-84553-492-9.

Links modern church music with influences from popular music. Presents a study of the struggle between secular forces from which new surveys concerning how popular music is used in churches around the world. In the context of the history of Western congregational songs, the volume concludes that music, like other cultural elements of contemporary Christianity, has been widely secularized. It argues that this secularization is a global phenomenon fed by the explosive growth of the contemporary church music industry—worth more than nine hundred million dollars in annual revenue—which has seen the large secular music companies acquiring independent labels in many cases to the distress of the faithful.

146.   **Everett, Walter**. 2023. *Sex and Gender in Pop/Rock Music: The Blues Through the Beatles to Beyoncé*. New York: Bloomsbury. 272 p. Online Appendix, Bibliography, and Index. 9-781-50134-595-1.

Observes that following the 1960s sexual revolution, rock and pop have continued to map the societal understanding of sexuality, feminism, and gender studies. Offers an investigation of how subsequent pop music has maintained that tradition. Discusses the gendered performance and biographical experiences of individual musicians, including Patti Smith, Rufus Wainwright, Etta James, and Frank Ocean, and how their invented personae contribute to musical representations of sexuality. Evaluates lyric structure and symbolic languages of these artists and overall emphasizes how popular music, while a commodity art form, reflects the diversity of human sex and gender.

147.   **Everett, Walter, ed**. 2000. *Expression in Pop-Rock Music: A Collection of Critical and Analytical Essays*. Series: *Studies in Contemporary Music and Culture, v. 2; Garland Reference Library of the Humanities, Volume 2102*. New York & London: Routledge. xii, 372 p. Illustrations Music Examples, Bibliography, and Index. ISBN: 0-81533-160-6.

This collection of essays by scholars in musicology and music theory specializing in popular music presents a wide range of approaches to understanding artistic expression in rock. Essays cover artists such as Frank Zappa, U2, Genesis, The Cure, Tori Amos, and Sarah McLachlan with a focus on analytical approaches to the craft of composition, general stylistic concerns, and the listener's role in the process.

148.   **Ewens, Hannah**. 2020. *Fangirls Scenes From Modern Music Culture*. Previously published, London: Quadrille, 2019. Series: *American Music Series (Austin, Tex.)*. Austin: University of Texas Press. ix, 239 p. Bibliography. ISBN: 9-781-47732-210-9.

Concentrates on hundreds of fans from the United Kingdom, United States, and Japan to discuss the story of music fandom using its own voices over scenes from modern pop and rock music history. Uncovers the importance of fan devotion, how Ariana Grande represents both tragedy and resilience to her followers, and what it means to meet an artist like Lady Gaga in person, members of BeyHive, and others.

149.   **Eyerman, Ron, and Andrew Jameson**. 1998. *Music and Social Movements: Mobilizing Traditions in the Twentieth Century*. Series: *Cambridge Cultural Social Studies*. Cambridge & New York: Cambridge University Press. xi, 191 p. Bibliography. ISBN: 0-52162-045-7.

Examines the mobilization of cultural traditions and formulation of new collective identities through the music of activism. Combines theoretical arguments with historical-empirical studies of nineteenth-century populists and twentieth-century labor and ethnic movements. Focuses on the interrelations between music and social movements in the United States and the transfer of these experiences in Europe. Specific chapters examine folk, country, Black music, music of the 1960s, and music of the Swedish progressive movements to link political sociology of social movements to cultural theory.

150.   **Fairchild, Charles**. 2008. *Pop Idols and Pirates: Mechanisms of Consumption and the Global Circulation of Popular Music*. Series: *Ashgate Popular & Folk Music Series*. Aldershot & Burlington: Ashgate. ix, 82 p. Bibliography and Index. ISBN: 9 780 75166 383-6.

Argues that the music industry has been waging some very significant battles in recent years, reacting to numerous interrelated crises that have been provoked by globalization, digitalization, and extensive commercialization of public culture. Presents two interrelated cases of crisis and opportunity that include the music industry's epic struggle over piracy and the "idol" phenomenon. Examines how both are explicit attempts to control and justify the ways in which the music industry makes money from popular music through specific kinds of relationships with consumers and others. Presents analysis of the battle against piracy and analysis of "idol" and the emerging promotional culture of the music industry, and much more.

151.   **Farrugia, Rebekah**. 2012. *Beyond the Dance Floor: Female DJs, Technology, and Electronic Dance Music Culture*. Chicago & Bristol: University of Chicago Press & Intellect Books. 171 p. Music Examples, Appendix, Bibliography, and Index. ISBN: 9-781-84150-566-4.

A study of women who create electronic dance music. Focuses on the relationship between these women and the conception of gender and technology that continue to inform the male-dominated culture surrounding electronic dance music. Explores several issues such as the politics of identity and representation, the bonds formed by women within the DJ community, and the role female DJs and producers play in dance music culture and in the large public space.

152.   **Fast, Susan, and Craig Jennex, eds**. 2019. *Popular Music and the Politics of Hope: Queer and Feminist Interventions*. New York: Routledge. xii, 338 p. Illustrations, Bibliography, and Index. ISBN: 9-781-35167-781-3.

A compilation of essays that explore the theme that popular music is a vital site where ideas about gender and sexuality are imagined and disseminated. Compiled essays consider the many ways in contemporary popular music performances that gender and sexuality are politically engaged and even radical. Essay topics include Beyoncé's *Lemonade*; Janelle Monaé's Afrofuturism, vision, queer music diaspora; Beyoncé, the Dixie Chicks and the art of outlaw protest; disability, gender, and life-writing in the twenty-first century; racial politics of post-millennial British soul; rewriting the political imaginary in rock music memoir; sounds of the Halluci Nation—decolonizing race, masculinity, and global solidarities with A Tribe Called Red; Afro-South Asian hip-hop and R&B; hip-hop dialogues, sampling, and the Canadian popular mainstream; electro-pop; genders, genres, generations; anthems, genres, and the queer voice; resisting politics of aging—Madonna and the value of female labor in popular music; Vera Lyn 100—retirement, aging, and legacy for national treasure; and singing in administrative segregation at Louisiana correctional institute for women.

153. **Faupel, Alison, and Vaughn Schmutz**. 2010. "Gender and Cultural Contestation in Popular Music." *Social Forces* 89(2): 685–707. ISSN: 1534-7605.

Examines the gendered native of cultural legitimacy and consecration in popular music. Explores which factors affect the likelihood that female performers achieve consecrated status and how those decisions are discursively legitimated.

154. **Feld, Steven**. 1995. "From Schizophonia to Schismogenesis: The Discourses and Practices of World Music and World Beat." In *The Traffic in Culture: Refiguring Art and Anthropology*, George E. Marcus and Fred R. Myers, eds. Berkeley: University of California Press. ix, 380 p. Illustrations, Bibliography, and Index. ISBN: 0-52008-846-8.

Concerns the struggles over musical propriety in the discourses and commodification practices that sound the contemporary global traffic of world music and world beat. Focuses on complex layering of representations emanating from voices that are differentially positioned as academics, journalists, fans, musicians, critics, and consumers. Argues that their perspectives indicate a play of shared and contested assumptions about who speaks authoritatively and what outcomes are at stake for world music production and creativity. Furthermore, these discourse positions are constructed, asserted, circulated, and implicitly understood as signposts of an array of artistic and political investments.

155. **Fernandes, Sujatha**. 2011. *Close to the Edge: In Search of the Global Hip-Hop Generation*. Sydney: New South. xi, 204 p. Illustrations and Bibliography. ISBN: 9-781-74224-568-3.

Inspired by hip-hop as a youth in the 1980s, the author embarks on a journey into street culture around the world. Considers whether hip-hop can change the world. Investigates hip-hop from the south side of Chicago to the barrios of Caracas, Venezuela, and Havana, Cuba, and the urban city of Sydney, Australia. Grapples with the question of global voices and local critiques and the rage that underlies both.

156. **Ferrett, D**. 2020. *Dark Sound: Feminine Voices in Sonic Shadow*. Series: *Ex: Centrics*. New York & London: Bloomsbury. ix, 255 p. Bibliography and Index. ISBN: 9-781-50132-580-9.

Examines the concept of "dark sound," a strand of contemporary music that links the ideas of death, desire, and violence with women's gender studies. Provides a series of case studies that involve Moor Mother, Anna Calvi, Björk, Chelsea Wolfe, and Diamanda Galás. Argues that the extreme limits of transgressions of dark sound do not simply imply the limits of language but also are tied to a cultural and historical association between darkness and the feminine within music and music discourse.

157. **Firth, Simon**. 1978. *The Sociology of Rock*. London: Constable. 255 p. Illustrations, Tables, Bibliography, and Index. ISBN: 9-780-09460-220-5.

Examines the consumption, production, and ideology of rock music. Begins with a critical analysis of youth culture and considers both sociological theories and media images. Argues that in order to understand youth music one must first understand youth leisure, and by analyzing the place of different youth groups in production it is possible to make sense of different uses and meanings of rock music.

158. **Firth, Simon**. 1996. *Performing Rites: On the Value of Popular Music*. Cambridge: Harvard University Press. viii, 352 p. Bibliography and Index. ISBN: 9-780-67466-195-0.

Reflects and expounds on popular music by asking several questions: what we talk about when we talk about music; what's good, what's bad, what's high, what's low; and why such distinctions matter. These questions are employed as forms of engagement to evaluate popular music and musicians. Considers hundreds of songs and writers ranging through and beyond the twentieth century and puts the Pet Shop Boys and Giacomo Puccini, rhythm, lyric, voice, and technology into a dialogue about the undeniable impact of popular aesthetics in everyday life. Argues that listening itself is a performance, both social gesture and bodily response, and popular songs have not only merited aesthetic judgments but also demanded them and shaped our understanding of what all music means.

159. **Fischerman, Diego**. 2004. *Efecto Beethoven: Complejidad y Valor en la Música de tradición Popular (The Beethoven Effect: Complexity and Value in Popular Music Tradition)*. Series: *Paidós Diagonales, No. 7*. Buenos Aries & Barcelona: Paidós. 151 p. Spanish text. Bibliography. ISBN: 9-789-50120-507-7.

Employing a classical/popular music paradigm, the volume deals with topics that concern popular music, popular music and society, and the philosophy and aesthetics of music. Offers a proposition that in 1963 the Beatles created a recording of Chuck Berry whose lyrics ensured that rock 'n' roll music would never stop and that it was possible to rock 'n' roll on Beethoven. Suggests that the mention of Beethoven was not accidental and that there is an idea of art that crystallizes around his figure of the myth that romanticism created with him. Argues that an aesthetic idea in which suffering of the artist and the notion of struggle are essential and whose value in the field of music is defined by the conditions of abstraction, depth of expression of conflicts, complexity, and difficulty of composition, interpretation, and listening.

160. **Fischlin, Daniel, and Eric Porter, eds**. 2021. *Sound Changes: Improvisation and Transcultural Difference*. Ann Arbor: University of Michigan Press. 288 p. Illustrations, Bibliography, and Index. ISBN: 9-780-47213-242-3.

Responds to a need in improvisation studies for more work that addresses the diversity of global improvisatory practices. Argues that by beginning to understand the material experiences of sonic realities that are different from our own, we can address the host of other factors that are imported or sublimated in performance. Compiled essays provide case studies drawn from Africa, Asia, the Americas, and Oceania, offer an introduction to a range of musical expressions across the globe in which improvisation plays a key role, and demonstrate that improvisation is a vital site to produce emergent social relationships.

161. **Fisher, Joseph B., and Brian Flota, eds**. 2011. *The Politics of Post-9/11 Music: Sound Trauma, and the Music Industry in the Time of Terror*. Farnham, Surrey & Burlington: Ashgate. 232 p. Bibliography and Index. ISBN: 9-781-31555-431-0.

A compilation of essays that investigate the politics of a variety of post-9/11 music scenes. Extends discussions beyond the acts associated with September 11 attacks of U2, Toby Keith, The Dixie Chicks, and Bruce Springsteen. Compiled essays offer a new conceptualization of what constitutes "political music." Essays cover several topics that include the rise of the Internet music distribution, Christian punk rock, rap music in the Obama era, and nostalgia for 1960s political activism.

162. **Fitzgerald, Josh**. 2019. "Peace Up, A-town Down: Exploring the Evolution of Popular Music." *American Journal of Qualitative Research* 3(1): 72–92. ISSN: 2576-2141.

A study that thematically examines the lyrical change in popular music across three decades. Argues that examining the lyrical characteristics of popular songs over time may give some insight into how people were feeling at a certain point in time. Illustrates how a particular song is most popular over a specific year and how this song is structured lyrically and contributes to a better understanding of society in general.

163. **Fosbraey, Glenn, ed**. 2022. *Coastal Environments in Popular Music: Lost Horizons*. Series: *Routledge Advances in the History of Bioethics*. Abingdon, Oxon: Routledge. 184 p. Bibliography and Index. ISBN: 9-781-03213-795-7.

Examines how popular music can approach subjects of biopolitics, climate change, solastalgia, and anthropomorphizing alongside its more common diet of songs about love, dancing, and break-ups all while satisfying its primary remit of being entertaining and listenable. Compiled essays examine popular music through a range of topics from romance to climate change.

164. **Franklin, Marianne I**. 2021. *Sampling Politics and the Geocultural.* New York: Oxford University Press. xii, 345 p. Illustrations, Maps, Bibliography, and Index. ISBN: 9-780-19085-551-2.

Explores the geocultural politics of music listening. Considers sampling as a material of music and not simply a digital technique or restricted to one sort of music making. Addresses an unexplored dimension in studies of the relationship between music (any sort) and politics of the day. Incorporates archival research, listening, musical analysis, interviews with artists, and so on.

165. **Friedman, Jonathan, ed**. 2013. *Routledge History of Social Protest in Popular Music.* Series *Routledge Histories.* New York: Routledge. xvii, 412 p. Illustrations, Bibliography, and Index. ISBN: 9-780-20312-488-8.

Comprised of a series of essays that analyze the trends, musical formats, and rhetorical devices used in popular music to illuminate the human condition. Compares and contrasts musical offerings in several countries in different context from the nineteenth century to the present day. Aims to be an introduction to the history of social protest music that is ideal for popular music studies, art history, and sociology of music courses. Essays cover individuals such as Frank Zappa and Bono and topics such as civil rights anthems and soul music; gender and women in rap and hip-hop; and international protests in Latin pop, Guinea-Bissau, South Africa, Palestine, Asia, and much more.

166. **Friedman, Jonathan**. 1994. *Cultural Identity and Global Process.* Series: *Theory, Culture and Society.* London: Sage. 288 p. Bibliography and Index. ISBN: 9-780-80398-638-1.

Explores the interface between global processes, identity formation, and the production of culture. Examines ideas ranging from world systems theory to postmodernism and investigates the relations between the global and the local to demonstrate how cultural fragmentation and modernist homogenization are equally constitutive trends in global reality. Also examines the interdependency of world markets and local cultural transformation and demonstrates the complex interrelations between globally structured social processes and the organization of identity.

167. **G. W. L**. 1995. "A Letter From Pete Seeger: Pop, Rock, and Coca-Colonization." *Canadian Folk Music* 29(4): 4–8. ISSN: 0829-5344.

Emphasizes that the young of other countries must not forget their own music and to listen to music of all the world. Discusses the history of United States' pop and folk music and its influences. Stresses that the music-loving person of the future will learn and be influenced by the richness of global musical culture, such as the music of South Africa and the gamelan orchestras of Indonesia.

168.   **Gamble, Steven**. 2021. *How Music Empowers: Listening to Modern Rap and Metal*. Abingdon, Oxon: Routledge. 188 p. Illustrations, Bibliography, and Index. ISBN: 9-780-36733-955-5.

Argues that empowerment is the key to unlocking the long-standing mystery of how music moves us. Draws on research in embodied cognitive social psychology and cultural studies. Provides a new way of understanding how music affects listeners. Develops the latest conceptions of what it is to be human and investigates the experience of listening to popular music in everyday life.

169.   **Garcia, Thomas, ed**. 2017. *Global Popular Music*. San Diego: Cognella. xvi, 276 p. Illustrations and Maps. ISBN: 9-781-51652-586-7.

Examines popular music in a global context. Features readings that examine the commonalities and differences among different popular music traditions in the Americas, Africa, Asia, and Europe. Explores the ways in which each tradition developed, evolved, eventually disseminated and how they gained global reach. Explores various music traditions that include blues, samba-reggae, mariachi, Afro-pop, bhangra, rap, K-pop, and others.

170.   **Gardner, Abigail, ed**. 2019. *Ageing and Contemporary Female Musicians*. 154 p. Illustrations, Bibliography, and Index. ISBN: 9-781-03209-153-2.

Focuses on aging within contemporary popular music. Argues that context, genres, memoirs, racial politics, and place all contribute to how women are "aged" in popular music. Frames contemporary musicians as canonical grandmothers, Rude Girls, neo-Afrofuturists, and memoirists, introducing dynamism into the concept of aging.

171.   **Garofalo, Reebee, ed**. 1992. *Rockin' the Boat: Mass Music and Mass Movements*. Boston: South End Press. viii, 333 p. Illustrations and Bibliography. ISBN: 9-780-89608-428-5.

Concerns the relation between mass-mediated popular musics and political struggles around the world. Topics and geographical areas covered are varied and include understanding mega-events; rock rebellions and mass media hegemony; Nelson Mandela, concerts, and mass culture; Rock Against Racism; rock music and political change in East Germany; rock musical subculture in socialist Hungary in the 1960s; pop music, cultural identity, and political opposition in China; popular music in Hong Kong in response to the Chinese student movement; Australian aboriginal music; social protest and popular music in Hawaii; anti-hegemonic aspects of African popular music; *rock nacional* and dictatorship in Argentina; music beyond apartheid; popular music and the civil rights movement, women's music; nationalist thoughts in Black music and culture; and Chicano rock.

172.   **Garofalo, Reebee, Erin T. Allen, and Andrew Snyder, eds**. 2020. *Honk!: A Street Band Renaissance of Music and Activism*. New York: Routledge. xii, 279 p. Illustrations, Bibliography, and Index. 9-780-36703-070-4.

A compilation of essays that focus on the recent transnational revival of street bands. Essays provide a view into the diverse manifestation of cultural activity that mobilizes communities to reimagine the public space, protest injustice, and celebrate community. Topics include circulation of repertoire, innovative musical pedagogies, musical engagement with protest, and various theories of activism including social dynamics of gender, race, and class.

173.   **Garofalo, Reebee**. 1993. "Whose World, What Beat: The Transnational Music Industry, Identity, and Cultural Imperialism." *The World of Music* 35(2): 16–32. ISSN: 0043-8774.

Argues that there have always been occasional hints even in the United States pop market that the international flow of popular music is more complicated than we like to think. Presents and discusses reviews of the research and theories that have permeated discussions about popular music and world popular music genres. Suggests that the transnational flow of music is often envisioned as a vertical flow from more powerful nations to less powerful ones or as center-periphery models with music moving from developed countries, especially the United States, to the rest of the world with accompanying images of overpowering, displacing, or destroying local cultures.

174.   **Gault, Erika, and Travis Harris, eds**. 2020. *Beyond Christian Hip-Hop: A Move Toward Christians and Hip-Hop*. Series: *Studies in Hip-Hop and Religion*. Abingdon, Oxon & New York: Routledge. ix, 311 p. Bibliography and Index. 9-780-36718-511-4.

A compilation that explores the inception of Christians and hip-hop and the multiple outcomes of this section and lays out the ways in which Christians and hip-hop overlap and diverge. Brings together African diasporic cultures, lives, memories, and worldviews. The essays explore three major themes: identifying hip-hop, irreconcilable Christianity, and boundaries. Essays bring together these various considerations and show through these three themes that the complexities of the intersection of Christians and hip-hop encompass more than rap music; it is an African diasporic phenomenon.

175.   **Gebesmair, Andreas, and Alfred Smudits, eds**. 2016. *Global Repertoires: Popular Music Within and Beyond the Transnational Music Industry*. Abingdon, Oxon, & New York: Routledge. Originally published by Aldershot & Burlington: Ashgate, 2001. xi, 176 p., Illustrations, Music Examples, Bibliography, and Index. ISBN: 9-780-75460-526-3.

A collection of papers that were presented at a conference on music and globalization organized by the International Research Institute for Media Communication and Cultural Development (known as MEDIACULT) and held in November 1999 in Vienna, Austria. The papers focus on popular music in the twentieth and twenty-first centuries and embrace the world's popular music from jazz to many other popular genres. The papers also focus on the changing conditions of music production and distribution in a globalized world.

176.   **Geffen, Sasha**. 2020. *Glitter Up the Dark: How Pop Broke the Binary*. Austin: University of Texas Press. viii, 254 p. Bibliography and Index. ISBN: 9-781-47732-083-9.

Ponders the theme of whether our love of popular music is innately queer. Begins with the Beatles and moves to the present day to identify artists of all stripes who performed outside the limitations of their assigned genders. Includes discussions of trans artists like Wendy Carlos and openly gender-bending artists like David Bowie, Prince, and other artists whose work and performance complicate the binary. Covers the origins of house and disco in gay clubs and the utopia of the dance floor, the genderless technology of hip-hop, and artists like Missy Elliott who embody masculine virtues.

177.   **Gibson, Chris, and Andrew Warren**. 2021. *The Guitar: Tracing the Grain Back to the Tree*. Chicago: University of Chicago Press. 284 p. Illustrations, Maps, Bibliography, and Index. ISBN: 9-780-22676-382-8.

Focuses on musical instrument making and the timbers and trees from which guitars are made. Chronicles the authors' explorations around the world to guitar festivals, factories, remote sawmills, Indigenous lands, and distant rainforests to search behind the scenes of how guitars are made, where guitar timbers ultimately come from, and the people and skills involved along the way. Also provides insight on the human exploitation of nature, colonialism, industrial capitalism, and cultural change.

178.   **Giddens, Anthony**. 2000. *Runaway World: How Globalization Is Reshaping Our Lives*. Originally published, London: Profile Books, 1999. New York. Routledge. 124 p. Bibliography and Index. ISBN: 0-41592-719-6.

Demonstrates how globalization impacts every human on earth. Examines the global marketplace and extends inquiry beyond a conventional economic approach to look at more universal issues. Describes how changing currents in international finance are destabilizing countries, and much more.

179.   **Gilbert, Jeremy, and Ewan Pearson**. 1999. *Discographies: Dance Music, Culture, and the Politics of Sound*. London & New York: Routledge. xii, 195 p. Bibliography and Index. ISBN: 9-780-20301-206-2.

Presents research based on experiences of disco, hip-hop, techno, drum 'n' bass, and garage. Examines the transatlantic dance scene of the last twenty-five years. Discusses the problems posed by contemporary dance culture of both academic and cultural study. Also discusses issues of technology, club space, drugs, the musical body, gender, sexuality, and pleasure. Suggests why politicians and agencies as diverse as the independent music press and public broadcasting should be so hostile to this cultural phenomenon.

180.   **Gill, Jon I., ed**. 2021. *Underground Rap as Religion: A Theopoetic Examination of a Process Aesthetic Religion*. Series: *Routledge Studies of Hip-Hop and Religion*. Abingdon, Oxon & New York: Routledge. ix, 189 p. Bibliography and Index. ISBN: 9-781-31514-255-5.

Employs a secular religion methodology to put forward an aesthetic philosophy for the rap portion of underground hip-hop. Draws from Alfred North Whitehead's notion/process thought, a theopoetic argument. Argues that it is not simply the case that God is the "poet of the world," but rather rap can in fact be the poet (creator) of its own from of quasi-religion. Offers a unique look at the religious workings and implications of underground rap and hip-hop.

181. **Glitsos, Laura**. 2019. *Somatechnics and Popular Music in Digital Contexts.* Series: *Pop Music, Culture, and Identity.* Cham: Palgrave MacMillan. xi, 158 p. Bibliography and Index. ISBN: 9-783-03018-121-5.

Offers a synthesis of the emerging practice and field of somatechnics with popular music studies. Focuses on popular music consumption and listening practices through body-emotion perspectives. Investigates the complex interrelationships between technologies and how these impact the listening experiences as mediated by the body-emotion.

182. **Goldman, Vivian**. 2019. *Revenge of the She-Punks: A Feminist Music History From Poly Styrene to Pussy Riot.* Austin: University of Texas Press. 210 p. Index. ISBN: 9-781-47731-654-2.

Probes four themes that include identity, money, love, and protest to explore what makes punk such a liberating art form for women with her visceral style. Integrates interviews, history, and experience with topics that include Patti Smith's song "Free Money," Tamar-Kali whose name pays homage to a Hindu goddess and her Gullah ancestors in her music, Poly Styrene's daughter discusses the punk anthem "Identity," and so forth.

183. **Gomez, Jeff**. 2024. *Math Rock.* Series: *Genre A 33 1/3 Series.* New York: Bloomsbury. 152 p. ISBN: 9-798-76510-337-1.

Examines how math rock, a trance-like progressive metal music with indie rock and jazz influences, has been captivating and challenging listeners for decades. Examines how math rock has been associated with bands such as King Crimson, Black Flag, Don Caballero, Slint, American Football, Toe, Elephant Gym, Covet, and many others. Examines math rock as a global phenomenon and offers interviews with prominent musicians, producers, and critics spanning the globe.

184. **Gracyk, Theodore**. 2001. *I Wanna Be Me: Rock Music and the Politics of Identity.* Series: *Sound Matters.* x, 292 p. Bibliography and Index. ISBN: 1-56639-902-5.

Considers how rock music shapes, limits, and expands our notions of who we can be in the world. Envisions rock as a mass art, open-ended and open to diverse (but not limited) interpretations. Discusses how rock music constitutes part of the cultural apparatus from which individuals mold personal and political identities and so forth.

185. **Gracyk, Theodore**. 2013. *On Music.* Series: *Thinking in Action.* New York: Routledge. xiii, 156 p. Bibliography and Index. ISBN: 9-780-41580-777-7.

Considers what music is for and whether it is the same in a Haydn symphony, the jazz fusion of Jaco Pastorius, a raga by Ravi Shankar, or an improvised song of grief in Papua New Guinea. Offers an opinionated survey of examples with some fundamental and long-standing debates about the nature of music. Places an emphasis on instrumental music, but examples are also drawn from many cultures including Western classical music, jazz, folk, and popular music.

186.   **Grant, Peter**. 2017. *National Myth and the First World War in Modern Popular Music*. Series: *Palgrave Studies in the History of Subcultures and Popular Music*. London: Palgrave Macmillan. xi, 303 p. Illustrations, Bibliography, and Index. ISBN: 9-781-13760-139-1.

Examines the role of popular music in constructing the myth of the First World War. Observes that since the late 1950s, over fifteen hundred popular songs from more than forty countries have been recorded that draw inspiration from the war. Incorporates an interdisciplinary approach that locates popular music within the framework of "memory studies" and presents an analysis of how songwriters are influenced by their country's "national myths." Investigates popular music and memory, songwriting and memory, and transnational perspectives. Discusses a wide range of musical examples that include the great chansonniers Jacques Brel and Georges Brassens, folk masters including Al Stewart and Eric Bogle, rock icons Iron Maiden and Bolt Thrower, and female icons Diamanda Galás and PJ Harvey.

187.   **Greenwald, Andy**. 2003. *Nothing Feels Good: Punk Rock, Teenagers, and Emo*. New York: St. Martin's Griffin. xii, 321 p. Index. ISBN: 9-781-46683-492-7.

Examines popular music in terms of bands like Dashboard Confessional, Jimmy Eat Wood, and Thursday and the relationship between young people and music that sets them on a road of self-discovery and self-definition known as emo. Provides a case study of emo as more than a genre but an essential rite of teen-agehood. Examines from the 1980s and 1990s the story of emo from inside out and explores the way this movement is taking shape.

188.   **Gregory, Georgina**. 2002. "Masculinity, Sexuality, and the Visual Culture of Glam Rock." *Journal of Culture & Communication* 5: 37–60. ISSN: 2247-4404.

Defines glam rock as a musical style accompanied by a flamboyant dress code that emerged during the early 1970s. Examines the representation of masculinity that occurred during the late 1960s and 1970s that led eventually to the glam rock phenomenon. Discusses the impact of social change, including the legisla-tion of homosexuality and the growth of the women's liberation movement and their effect on male representation. Also discusses glam rock and other musical subcultures, fashion, and the retailing to men of a "unisex" style to demonstrate how men's wear became increasingly feminized, culminating in the adoption of full transvestism by male performing artists like David Bowie.

189.   **Gregory, Georgina**. 2012. *Send in the Clones: A Cultural Study of the Tribute Band*. Series: *Studies in Popular Music*. Sheffield & Bristol: Equinox Publishing. 184 p. Illustrations, Bibliography, and Index. ISBN: 9-781-78179-015-1.

Seeks to understand the phenomenon of the tribute band by linking it to other types of intimate entertainment such as "ghost" cover and parody bands. Demonstrates the impact of changing cultural Zeitgeist on the evolution of popular music tributes, showing how tributes can be related to other examples of retrospection. Explores the working life of musicians involved in the bargain basement end of the live music industry using interviews and firsthand observations to show the trials and tribulations of paying homage and audiences at tribute events, fandom, and so forth.

190.   **Gregory, Georgina**. 2019. *Boy Bands and the Performance of Pop Masculinity*. Abingdon, Oxon & New York: Routledge. ix, 167 p. Illustrations, Bibliography, and Index. ISBN: 9-781-13864-731-2.

Provides a historical study of the boy band from the Beatles to One Direction, placing the modern male pop group within the wider context of the twentieth and twenty-first centuries' popular music and culture. Examines pop masculinity as exhibited by boy bands that links the evolving expression of gender and sexuality in the boy band to wider economic and social change that has resulted in new ways of representing what it is to be a man. Explores the challenges of defining the boy band phenomenon, its origin and history from the 1940s to the present, the role of management and marketing, the performance of gender and sexuality, and the nature of fandom and fan agency.

191.   **Grenier, Line, and Jocelyne Guilbault**. 1990. "Authority Revisited: The Other in Anthropology and Popular Music." *Ethnomusicology* 34(3): 381–397. ISSN: 0014-1836.

Concentrates on some of the issues raised by the latest findings in anthropology, the alternatives being developed, and their relevance for scholars working on different objects of study. Offers a critical examination of the anthropological diagnosis of one of the central issues and focuses on that of the "Other," and continues with a focus on popular music studies to examine the ways in which the study is being addressed, and so forth.

192.   **Grimes, Matt, and Michael Dines, eds**. 2020. *Punk Now! Contemporary Perspectives of Punk*. Series: *Global Punk Series*. Bristol: Intellect. xiii, 223 p. Illustrations, Bibliography, and Index. ISBN: 9-781-78938-174-0.

A compilation of essays that explore contemporary and non-Anglophone punk as well as its most anti-establishment tendencies. Collected essays stem from the second Punk Scholars Network International Conference and Postgraduate Symposium. Essays are intended to inform about punk in today's culture and punk at the margins.

193.   **Grimes, Matt, Russ Bestley, Michael Dines, and Paula Guerra, eds**. 2019. *Punk Identities, Punk Utopias*. Series: *Global Punk Series*. Bristol: Intellect. 260 p. Illustrations, Bibliography, and Index. ISBN: 9-781-78938-412-3.

Extends a critical inquiry that reflects broader social, political, technological concerns impacting punk scenes around the world, from digital technology and new media to gender, ethnicity, identity, and representation. Compiled essays draw from interdisciplinary areas of cultural studies, musicology, and the social sciences to present a compilation based on the notions of identities, ideologies, and cultural discourse surrounding contemporary global punk scenes.

194.   **Grupe, Gerde, ed**. 2013. *Ethnomusicology and Popular Music Studies*. Series: *Grazer Beiträge zur Ethnomusikologie, Bd. 25*. Aachen: Shaker Verlag. vii, 293 p. Illustrations, CD-ROM, and Bibliography. ISBN: 9-783-8402-389-3.

A compilation of papers that were presented at the international Symposium on Ethnomusicology and Popular Music (Symposium Ethnomusikologie und Popularusikschung) at the University of Music and Performing Arts, Graz, Austria. Topics include popular music as a challenge to ethnomusicology; string bands in Vanuatu; the mbira/chimurenga case study from Zimbabwe; xylophonic music on electric guitars; popular actor networks; ethnification of commercialized cultures; contribution of ethnomusicology to popular music studies; transcultural rhythm and blues and the dawn of metal; adapting bandari in Iranian popular music; and ethnomusicology, ethnography, and popular music audiences.

195.   **Guesde, Catherine**. 2021. "Approaches du sauvage: la formation du goût pour le metal extrême (Approaching Wild Sounds: The Formation of a Taste for Extreme Metal)." *Volume! La revue des musiques populaires—The French Journal of Popular Music Studies* 18(1) [Special Issue: *Back to Work!*]: 137–149. French and English texts. ISSN: 1950-568X.

Makes inquiries into how extreme metal fans come to develop an appreciation for a music whose sounds are usually deemed harsh. Draws upon the tools of the sociology of taste. Integrates a study of the love for extreme metal from an aesthetic perspective. Identifies the steps and listening strategies involved in its function and seeks to label its evolution and whether it can be described as an initiation.

196.   **Guilbault, Jocelyne**. 1993. "On Redefining the 'Local' Through World Music." *The World of Music* 35(2) [Special Issue: *The Politics and Aesthetics of "World Music"*]: 33–47. ISSN: 0043-8774.

Argues that since the early 1980s much literature in the social sciences has sought to explain the processes involved in restructuring and transforming the political and economic world order. Further argues that within this framework, many critics have emphasized the globalization of culture and the cultural industries and new technologies involved in the process of change. Highlights concerns with how the status of the "local" has been transformed within contemporary societies but also why and from whom it has been vitally important to redefine it today. Employs a discussion on these notions and the phenomenon of "World Music" as a case study and point to access and in theorizing politics of popular music culture.

197.   **Haddon, Mimi**. 2020. "What Is Post-Punk?" In *Genre and Identity in Avant-Garde Popular Music, 1977–82*. Ann Arbor: University of Michigan Press. viii, 226 p. Bibliography and Index. ISBN: 9-780-47213-182-2.

Examines how a new wave of music strongly influenced the politics and sounds of post-punk but more commercial success followed close on punk in the late 1970s with groups as Think Joy Division, The Raincoats, Human League, Public Image Ltd, The Slits, and others. Focuses on post-punk's push beyond the tropes of rock and how punk was challenged beyond the music's cultural value and commercial success. Demonstrates how post-punk's emphasis on artifice, politics, and eclecticism paved the way for broader gender representation, spanning from glam and new wave to indie rock.

198.　**Häger, Andreas**. 2018. *Religion and Popular Music: Artists, Fans, and Cultures.* Series: *Bloomsbury Studies in Religion and Popular Music.* Bloomsbury. vi, 263 p. Bibliography and Index. ISBN: 9-781-35000-147-3.

Explores encounters between music, fans, and religion. Examines several popular music artists including Bob Dylan, Prince, and Katy Perry and considers the way religion comes into play in their work and personas. Genres explored include folk, rock, metal, and electronic dance music. Case studies originate form a variety of geographic and cultural contexts with a focus on nationalism and hard rock in Russia, fan culture in Argentina, and punk and Islam in Indonesia.

199.　**Hamm, Charles**. 1995. *Putting Popular Music in Its Place.* Cambridge & New York: Cambridge University Press. xii, 390 p. Bibliography and Index. ISBN: 0-5214-719-8.

Contains a compilation of previously published essays between 1970 and 1993 that focus on the context of popular music and its interrelationship with other styles and genres. Topics covered include the anti-slavery sentiment, rock 'n' roll, soul music, Irving Berlin, cultural control of music in South Africa and China, and the impact of modernism.

200.　**Hanly, Francis, and Tim May**. 1989. *Rhythms of the World.* London: BBC Books. 128 p. Illustrations, Map, Music Examples, and Portraits. ISBN: 9-780-56320-790-0.

Supplements a television BBC series titled "Rhythms of the World," offering insight and a map of world music that covers approximately thirty-three different centers ranging over Eastern Europe, the Caribbean, Africa, Latin America, United States, and Pakistan. Provide profiles, traditions, and issues behind the explosion of world music.

201.　**Hansen, Kai A., Eirik Askerøi, and Freya Jarman, eds**. 2020. *Popular Musicology and Identity: Essays in Honor of Stan Hawkins.* Abingdon, Oxon & New York: Routledge. xviii, 224 p. Illustrations, Bibliography, and Index. ISBN: 9-781-13832-288-2.

A compilation of essays in honor of Stan Hawkins, whose work has been a major influence on the musicological study of gender and identity since the early 1990s. Compiled essays reach into a range of musical contexts, eras, and idioms to critically investigate the discursive structures that govern the processes through which music is mobilized as a focal point for negotiating and assessing identity. Essays provide accounts for the state of musicology at the onset of the 2020s while also offering a platform further advancing the critical study of popular music and identity. Provides an up-to-date resource for scholars across fields as popular music studies, musicology, gender studies, and media studies.

202.   **Harker, Dave**. 1980. *One for the Money: Politics and Popular Song*. London: Hutchinson. 301 p. Bibliography and Index. ISBN: 9-780-09140-730-8.

Focuses on popular music and emphasizes the conditions of production instead of consumption. Examines the relation between popular music and mass communication industries. Demonstrates the complexity of several theoretical perspectives by Adorno and others that relate to the study of popular music, culture industry, and so forth.

203.   **Harkins, Paul, and Nick Prior**. 2021. "(Dis)Locating Democratization: Music Technologies in Practice." *Popular Music and Society* 45(1) [Special Issue: *Music, Digitalization, and Democracy*]: 84–103. ISSN: 0300-7766.

Examines the concept of democratization and explains why it has been applied in unhelpful ways to the study of music. Focuses on three examples to illustrate the real-world complexities involved in the adoption of new technologies that are often seen as democratic by dint of their widespread use. Argues that for socially located actors with music-making devices, it prompts detailed questions about who is participating, how, and under what socioeconomic conditions. Suggests a move beyond the term democratization to an application that is specific to the field of popular music.

204.   **Harkins, Paul**. 2020. *Digital Sampling: The Design and Use of Music Technologies*. New York & London: Routledge. xi, 195 p. Illustrations, Bibliography, and Index. ISBN: 9-780-81538-164-8.

Focuses on the design and use of sampling technologies that have shaped the sound of popular music since the 1980s. Explores the Fairlight CMI and how artists such as Kate Bush and Peter Gabriel used it to sample the sounds of everyday life. Also explores E-mu Systems and the use of its keyboards and drum machines in hip-hop, used across a range of musical worlds including United States/United Kingdom garage folk music, electronic music, and others.

205.   **Harris, Travis**. 2019. "Can It Be Bigger Than Hip-Hop: From Global Hip-Hop Studies to Hip-Hop." *Journal of Hip-Hop Studies* 6(2) [Special Issue: *If I Ruled the World: Putting Hip-Hop on the Atlas*]: 17–70. ISSN: 2331-5563.

Presents that global hip-hop studies has grown with scholars from several disciplines that have published numerous journal articles, books, dissertations, theses, presentation at academic conferences, and courses taught on global hip-hop. Traces the history and examines key authors and intellectual interventions, methods, and theories in the field. Employs an interdisciplinary methodology with participant observations of local hip-hop. Also examines numerous scholarly texts assembled into a global hip-hop studies bibliography.

206. **Harrison, Ann, and Tony Rigg, eds. 2021.***The Present and Future of Music and Law*. London: Bloomsbury. xx, 283 p. Illustrations, Bibliography, and Index. ISBN: 9-731-50136-777-9.

A compilation of essays that focuses on how the music business is a multifaceted, transnational industry that operates within complex and rapidly changing political, economic, cultural, and technological contexts. Compiled essays present case studies written by experts in their fields that examine a range of key topics at the points where music law and the post-digital music industry intersect and much more.

207. **Hatch, David, and Stephen Millward**. 1987. *From Blues to Rock: An Analytical History of Popular Music*. Series: *Music and Society*. Manchester: University of Manchester. ix, 217 p. Illustrations, Music Examples, Discography, Bibliography, and Index. ISBN: 0-71901-489-1.

Sets out to be an analytical historical study of popular music that combines with more compatible and useful techniques from sociology, social psychology, and linguistics. Suggests that popular music owes its coherence as a tradition to the musical elements and structure, which provide its musical parameters that distinguish it from other traditions. Focuses more on popular music history than on musical analysis and emphasizes that the core of popular music lies in the blues, with less emphasis and discussion of rock, soul, heavy metal, punk, and others.

208. **Hawkins, Stan**. 2016. *Queerness in Popular Music: Aesthetics, Gender Norms, and Temporality*. Series: *Routledge Studies in Popular Music*. New York & London: Routledge. ix, 243 p. Illustrations, Music Examples, Bibliography, and Index. ISBN: 9-781-13882-087-6.

Investigates the phenomenon of queering in popular music and video, interpreting the music of numerous pop artists, styles, and idioms. Focuses on artists such as Lady Gaga, Madonna, Boy George, Diana Ross, Rufus Wainwright, David Bowie, Azealia Banks, Zebra Katz, Freddie Mercury, the Pet Shop Boys, George Michael, and others. Builds on the concept of queerness upon existing theories of opacity and temporality, which involves a creative interdisciplinary approach to musical interpretation. Advocates a model of analysis that involve both temporal-specific listening and biographic-oriented viewing.

209. **Hawkins, Stan**. 2017. *Settling the Pop Score: Pop Texts and Identity Politics*. Previously published, Aldershot & Burlington: Ashgate, 2002. Series: *Ashgate Popular and Folk Music Series*. London: Routledge. xiv, 220 p. Illustrations, Discography, Bibliography, and Index. ISBN: 0-75460-351-2.

Argues that the analysis of popular music forces us to rethink the assumptions that underpin our approaches to the study of Western music. Moreover, it brings to the forefront an idea that many musicologists still find uncomfortable that commercial production and consumption can be aligned with artistic authenticity. Explores the relationships that exist between music, spectatorship, and aesthetics through a series of case studies of pop artists from the 1980s and 1990s, including Madonna, Morrissey, Annie Lennox, the Pet Shop Boys, and Prince, who represent the diversity of cultures, identities, and sexualities that characterized the start of the MTV boom.

210. **Haworth, Catherine, and Lisa Colton**. 2015. *Gender, Age, and Musical Creativity*. Series: *Ashgate Popular and Folk Music Series*. New York: Routledge. 238 p. Bibliography and Index. ISBN: 9-780-36759-907-2.

Incorporates an interdisciplinary approach to issues of identity and its representation by examining intersections of age and gender in relation to music and musicians across a wide range of periods, places, and genders, including female patronage in Renaissance Italy; the working-class brass band in northern England; twentieth-century jazz and popular music cultures; and the contemporary new music scenes.

211. **Haynes, Jo**. 2013. *Music, Difference, and the Residue of Race*. New York: Routledge. 179 p. Appendix, Bibliography, and Index. ISBN: 9-780-41587-921-7.

Argues that race and music seem to be fatally entwined in a way that involves both creative and ethnic hybridity and ongoing problems of racism. Presents a sociological analysis of the relationships between race and music. Examines ideas of race critical to the understanding of music genres and preference. Also examines "love of difference" via music contributions to contemporary perspectives of racism.

212. **Hayward, Philip, ed**. 2004. *Off the Planet: Music, Sound, and Science Fiction Cinema*. Bloomington: Indiana University Press. vii, 214 p. Illustrations, Music Examples, Bibliography, and Index. ISBN: 9-780-86196-644-8.

A diverse collection of essays that focus on aspects of music, sound, and science fiction cinema. Includes a detailed historical introduction to the development of sound and music in the genre. Individual chapters analyze key films, film series, composers, and directors in the postwar era.

213. **Hebdige, Dick**. 2002. *Subculture: The Meaning of Style*. Originally published, London: Routledge, 1979. London & New York: Routledge. viii, 195 p. Bibliography and Index. ISBN: 9-780-20332-540-7.

Focuses on Britain's postwar youth subculture styles as symbolic forms of resistance. Draws from Marxist theorists, literary critics, French structuralists, and American sociologists. Presents a model for analyzing youth subcultures and argues that each subculture undergoes the same trajectory. Outlines the individual style differences of specific subcultures such as Teddy boys, mods, rockers, skinheads, and punks. Concerned with Britain's postwar music-centered White working-class subcultures. Emphasizes historical, class, race, and socioeconomic conditions that surrounded the formation of each subcultural group.

214. **Heiser, Marshall**. 2022. *Popular Music, Power, and Play: Reframing Creative Practice*. New York: Bloomsbury. 190 p. Bibliography and Index. ISBN: 9-781-50136-274-3.

Argues that the art of record production is today within the reach of all and the rise of the ubiquitous DIY project studio and Internet streaming have made it so. Reassesses the myriad processes and wider sociocultural context through the lens of creativity studies, play theory, and cultural psychology. Provides firsthand interviews with Jerry Harrison (Talking Heads), Bill Bruford (King Crimson, Yes), and others whose work has influenced the way records are made today.

215. **Henseler, Christine, ed**. 2012. *Generation X Goes Global: Mapping Youth Culture in Motion*. New York: Routledge. 372 p. Bibliography and Index. ISBN: 9-780-20310-021-9.

A series of essays that can have topical and research relevance in the study of youth culture and popular music research. Essays engage critics' understanding of Generation X as a global phenomenon and trace the global and local flows that determine the identity of each country's youth from the 1970s to contemporary times. Essays explore the converging properties of Generation X through fields of literature, media studies, youth culture, popular culture, philosophy, feminism, and political science.

216. **Herbst, Jan-Peter, and Mark Mynett**. 2021. "Nail the Mix: Standardization in Mixing Metal Music?" *Popular Music and Society* 44(5): 6228–6249. ISSN: 0300-7766.

Explores how the proliferation of affordable digital tools and the availability of specialist knowledge have affected the mixing stage of metal music productions. Asks whether a standard methodology is apparent in producers' use of templates and presets, processing of audio, and choice of tools. Presents an analysis of metal mixes on the platform Nail the Mix. Findings suggest that although producers follow a vaguely defined methodology for technical reasons, they have leeway for individuality and creativity.

217. **Hermes, Kristen**. 2022. *Performing Electronic Music Live*. Series: *Audio Engineering Society Presents*. New York: Routledge, a Focal Press Book. 304 p. Illustrations, Bibliography, and Index. ISBN: 9-780-36734-073-5.

Offers approaches, tools, and techniques for electronic music performance from DJing, DAWS, MIDI controllers, traditional instruments, live sound design, hardware setups, custom software, and hardware to live visuals, venue acoustics, and live show promotion. Incorporates case studies and contrasting tutorials by successful artists. Explores the different ways that memorable experiences are created on stage. Also features interviews with accomplished musicians and practitioners.

218.   **Hesmondhalgh, David, and Keith Negus, eds**. 2002. *Popular Music Studies.* London: Arnold & New York: Oxford University Press. ix, 272 p. Illustrations, Bibliography, and Index. ISBN: 0-34076-247-0.

A collection of essays that are interdisciplinary in scope and coverage. Topics in popular music studies include, among many others, listening practices; conceptions of mainstream to a variety of transnational appropriations; meaning, power, and value; gender and popular song in South Africa; popular music and masculinity; popular music and audience perception; categories and crossovers; and discussions of popular music genres such as salsa, calypso, electronic dance music.

219.   **Hesmondhalgh, David, and Leslie M. Meier**. 2018. "What the Digitalization of Music Tells Us About Capitalism, Culture, and the Power of the Information Technology Sector." *Information, Communication and Society* 21(11): 1555–1570. ISSN: 1369-118X.

Examines striking but underanalyzed features of culture under capitalism, using the example of music, that the main ways in which people gain access to cultural experience are subject to frequent, radical, and disorienting shifts. Aims to provide a macro-historical multicausal explanation of changes in technologies of musical consumption, emphasizing the mutual imbrication of the economic interests with sociocultural transformation, and so forth. Argues that disruptions caused by the recent digitalization of music are consistent with longer processes whereby music has been something of testing ground for the introduction of new cultural technologies.

220.   **Hesselink, Nathan**. 2021. "Western Popular Music, Ethnomusicology, and Curricular Reform: A History and a Critique." *Popular Music and Society* 44(5): 558–578. ISSN: 0300-7766.

Examines the intersections between popular music studies, ethnomusicology, and curricular reform in college and universities in the United States and the United Kingdom. Includes arguments and analysis that are scrutinized through the rubric of the positioning of Western popular music in ethnomusicology. Argues that ethnomusicology itself must undergo reforms before being held up as a model to emulate for educational transformation.

221.   **Hibbert, Ryan, ed**. 2023. *Lit-Rock: Literary Capital in Popular Music.* New York: Bloomsbury. viii, 264 p. Bibliography and Index. ISBN: 9-781-50135-472-4.

A compilation of essays that discuss the relationship between popular music and literature in conjunction with the connection between high and low art. Topics include authorship, authenticity, David Bowie, Joni Mitchell, and literature of confession; the amateur poetry of Taylor Swift; punk, post-punk, and poetry; and others.

222.   **Hijleh, Mark**. 2019. *Towards a Global Music History: Intercultural Convergence, Fusion, and Transformation in the Human Musical Story.* Abingdon,

Oxon: Routledge. vii, 241 p. Music Examples, Bibliography, and Index. ISBN: 9-780-36766-336-0.

Concentrates on how to explain the globalized world in the early twenty-first century and its beginnings. Outlines an understanding of the human musical story as an intercultural and ultimately a transcultural one with travel and trade as the primary conditions and catalyst across the Afro-Eurasian Old-World Web, the Silk Road, the rise of al-Andalus and its influences through the Iberia Peninsula, and the fusion of European, African, and Indigenous music to the exchanges of technology.

223.   **Hilder, Thomas R., Henry Stobart, and Shzr Ee Tan, eds**. 2017. *Music, Indigeneity, Digital Media*. Series: *Eastman/Rochester Studies in Ethnomusicology, v. 6*. Rochester: University of Rochester Press. viii, 224 p. Bibliography and Index. ISBN: 9-781-78204-921-0.

A compilation of essays that offer diverse perspectives on the encounter between Indigenous music and digital technologies. Compiled essays explore how digital media, whether CD, VCD, the Internet, mobile technology, or the studio, have transformed and become part of the fabric of Indigenous cultural expression across the globe. Essays address issues such as transnationalism and sovereignty; production and consumption; subjectivity and ownership, archives, and transmission; and the virtual and the posthuman.

224.   **Hill, Rosemary, and Karl Spracklen, eds**. 2020. *Heavy Fundamentalism: Music, Metal, and Politics*. Previously published, Oxford: Inter-Disciplinary Press, 2010. Leiden & Boston: Brill. 156 p. Bibliography and Index. ISBN: 9-781-84888-017-7.

A compilation of essays that focus on different aspects of heavy metal music. Topics covered include metal community and aesthetics of identity; the self-destructive lifestyle of heavy metal; power relations in heavy metal and Christian fundamentalist performance; the power of Northern Europe in extreme metal; White power, black metal, and reflection on composing; heavy metal's portrayal of war; gender, sex, and power in the death metal scene; the representation of women letter writers in *Kerrang!* magazine; power, gender, and the communicative discourse of the black metal scene; Estonian metal subculture; power, volume, and the brain; the flattened supertonic within and outside heavy metal music; and mixing the extreme modern metal genre.

225.   **Hill, Rosemary**. 2016. *Gender, Metal, and the Media: Women Fans and the Gendered Experience of Music*. Series: *Pop Music, Culture, and Identity*. London: Palgrave Macmillan. ix, 184 p. Illustrations, Charts, Bibliography, and Index. ISBN: 9-781-13755-441-3.

Deals with women rock music fans, sexism, and groupies. Challenges the idea that heavy metal is masculine music and that all women fans are groupies. Explores the musical pleasure offered by metal to women fans. Offers new thinking about hard rock and metal music and concerning what it is like to be a woman fan in a sexist environment.

226.   **Hill, Sarah, ed**. 2022. *One-Hit Wonders: An Oblique History of Popular Music*. London: Bloomsbury. 260 p. Bibliography and Index. ISBN: 9-781-50136-840-0.

Provides a series of essays that focus on one-hit wonders from the 1950s to the present day with a view toward understanding both the mechanics and success and the sociomusical contexts within which such songs became hits. Includes discussions of some artists who might have aspired to success but only managed one hit, while others enjoyed lengthy careers after their initial chart success. Provides not only a history of popular music taste but also rumination on the changing nature of the music industry and the mechanics of fame.

227.   **Hjelm, Titus, Keith Kahn-Harris, and Mark LaVine, eds**. 2013. *Heavy Metal: Controversies and Counterculture*. Series: *Studies in Popular Music*. Sheffield: Equinox Publishing. viii, 250 p. Illustrations, Bibliography, and Index. ISBN: 9-781-84553-940-5.

An anthology that examines heavy metal, now over forty years old, which has developed into a diverse and multifaceted genre. Provides a thorough investigation of how and why metal becomes controversial, and how metal "scenes" are formed. Also examines how the relationship between metal and society, including fans, musicians, and the media, shapes the culture of heavy metal.

228.   **Hoad, Catherine, ed**. 2019. *Heavy Metal Music, Texts, and Nationhood: (Re)sounding Whiteness*. Series: *Emerald Studies in Metal Music and Culture*. Bingley: Emerald. Cham: Springer. vii, 260 p. Illustrations, Bibliography, and Index. ISBN: 9-783-03067-619-3.

Addresses how Whiteness is represented in heavy metal scenes and practices both as a site of academic inquiry and force of cultural significance. Argues that Whiteness and more specifically White masculinity has been given normative value that obscures the contradictions of women and people of color and affirms the exclusory understanding of belonging that have featured in the metal scenes of Norway, South Africa, and Australia.

229.   **Hoad, Catherine, Geoff Stahl, and Oli Wilson, eds**. 2022. *Mixing Pop and Politics: Political Dimensions of Popular Music in the 21st Century*. New York: Routledge. 234 p. Illustrations, Bibliography, and Index. ISBN: 9-780-36724-809-3.

Provides an explanation of the complex politics of popular music in its contemporary formations. Compiled essays cover a range of international artists and genres, from South African hip-hop to Polish punk, and address topics such as climate change and environmentalism, feminism, diasporic identity, political parties, music making as labor, the far right, conservatism and nostalgia, and civic engagement.

230.   **Hogarty, Jean**. 2017. *Popular Music and Retro Culture in the Digital Era*. Series: *Routledge Advances in Sociology*. New York: Routledge. 138 p. Bibliography and Index. ISBN: 9-781-13867-670-1.

Explores the trend of retro and nostalgia within contemporary popular music culture. Employs empirical evidence obtained from a case study of fans' engagement with older music. Presents the argument that retro culture is the result of an inseparable mix of cultural and technological changes, especially the rise of a new generation and cultural mood along with the encouragement of new technologies. Appeals to advanced popular music studies, critical studies, media studies, and sociology and music.

231. **Holmes, Thom**. 2016. *Electronic and Experimental Music: Technology, Music, and Culture, 5th ed.* Abingdon, Oxon & New York: Routledge. xxi, 565 p. Illustrations, Bibliography, and Index. ISBN: 9-781-13879-272-2.

An extensive and revised resource geared to the need of students and instructors. Provides a comprehensive history of electronic music and covers key composers, genres, and techniques used in both analog and digital synthesis.

232. **Holt, Fabian**. 2007. *Genre in Popular Music*. Chicago: University of Chicago Press. xiv, 224 p. Illustrations, Music Examples, Tables, Bibliography, and Index. ISBN: 9-780-22635-040-0.

Provides new insight into why we debate music categories and why those terms are unstable and always shifting. Through a collection of case studies, it examines not only the different reactions to the *O Brother, Where Art Thou?* motion picture soundtrack, but also the impact of rock and roll's explosion in the 1950s and 1960s on country music and jazz, and how jazz and indie music scenes in Chicago have intermingled to expand borders of their respective genres. Concludes that genres are an integral part of musical culture and fundamental both to musical practice and experiences and to social organization of musical life.

233. **Holt, Macon**. 2019. *Pop Music and Hip Ennui: A Sonic Fiction of Capitalist Realism*. New York: Bloomsbury. 208 p. Illustrations, Discography, Filmography, Bibliography, and Index. ISBN: 9-781-50134-666-8.

Provides imaginative and analytical resources to explore contemporary popular music to investigate the ambivalences of contemporary culture and the potentials in it for change. Examines the multiplicities contained in contemporary pop from sensation to abstraction and from the personal to the political. Unravels the assumption embedded in the cultural and critical analysis of popular music. Suggests new ways to understand the experience of living in the sonic atmosphere it produces.

234. **Homan, Shane, ed**. 2006. *Access All Eras: Tribute Bands and Global Pop Culture*. Maidenhead, Berkshire: Open University Press. xi, 255 p. Illustrations, Bibliography, and Index. ISBN: 9-780-33521-691-8.

Examines the tribute and cover band phenomenon and its place within the global popular music industry. Also examines music industry attitudes towards imitation. Focuses on other issues such as copyright and the use of multimedia performance techniques to deliver the "authentic" tribute experience.

235.   **Homan, Shane, Martin Cloonan, and Jennifer Cattermole, eds**. 2020. *Popular Music Industries and the State: Policy Notes*. Series: *Routledge Studies in Popular Music*. London & New York: Routledge. viii, 249 p. Bibliography and Index. ISBN: 9-780-36759-797-9.

Presents a study of the relationships between government and the popular music industries and compares three Anglophone nations: Scotland, New Zealand, and Australia. Emphasizes that at a time when issues of globalization and locality are seldom out of the news, musicians, fans, government, and industries are forced to reconsider older certainties about popular music activity and their roles in production and consumption circuits. Compiled essays are based on several themes: the changing role of states and industries in popular music activity; assessment of the central challenges of smaller nations versus larger global music media markets; comparative analysis of music policies and debates between nations; and analysis of where and why the state intervenes in popular music activities, and more.

236.   **Hood, Marguerite**. 1931. "Practical Listening Lessons: Are They Possible?" *Music Supervisors Journal* 17(5): 21–22. ISSN: 2329-0803.

An opinion commentary by an early president of the National Association of Music Education (NAfME), who emphasized that music education must be connected in some way with a personal knowledge, feeling, or idea on the part of the average listener. Encourages a greater emphasis the study of popular music in music education.

237.   **Horner, Bruce, and Thomas Swiss, eds**. 1999. *Key Terms in Popular Music and Culture*. Malden: Blackwell. x, 260 p. Illustrations, Bibliography, and Index. ISBN: 0-63121-263-9.

Integrates a series of essays that collectively address the question of what we are talking about when we talk about popular music. Draws upon work in feminist, postcolonial, cultural studies and the disciplines of musicology and literary criticism. Maps the competing perspectives on one of the key terms in ongoing debates on the meaning of popular music and culture. Also discusses the history of continuities and conflicts in its meaning and how each essayist has come to adopt such a position.

238.   **Howard, Jay R., and John M. Streck**. 1999. *Apostles of Rock: The Splintered Word of Contemporary Christian Music*. Lexington: University of Kentucky Press. 308 p. Discography, Bibliography, and Index. ISBN: 9-780-81314-805-2.

Examines the contemporary Christian music (CCM) phenomenon, as some see CCM performers as ministers or musical missionaries while others define them as entertainers or artists. Examines how the movement evokes a variety of responses concerning the relationship between Christians and culture. Discusses such Christian musicians as Amy Grant, Michael W. Smith, DC Talk, Sixpence None the Richer, and others.

239. **Howell, Amanda**. 2015. *Popular Film Music and Masculinity in Action: A Different Tune*. Series: *Routledge Advances in Film Studies*. New York: Routledge. 188 p. Bibliography and Index. ISBN: 9-780-36786-656-3.

Offers a perspective on the contemporary pop scene as how masculinities not seen or heard before become part of post–World War II American cinema. Addresses an eclectic mix of films from Elvis Presley to John Travolta, star vehicles of Jerry Bruckheimer–produced blockbuster action films, and work of musically innovative directors Melvin Van Peebles, Martin Scorsese, Gregg Araki, and Quentin Tarantino. Draws scholarship from popular music studies and the pop score as well as feminist films and media studies.

240. **Huq, Rupa**. 2006. *Subculture, Pop, Youth, and Identity in a Postcolonial World*. London & New York: Routledge. viii, 217 p. Bibliography and Index. ISBN: 9-780-20349-139-3.

Employs case studies and interviews with consumers and producers, including Noel Gallagher and Talvin Singh. Investigates a series of musically centered global youth cultures and re-examines the link between music and subcultures. Topics include rethinking subculture for the twenty-first century; age and youth, diversifying discourses beyond subculture; theorizing youth popular music meanings; bhangra, post-bhangra, and rai music; deconstructing difference in dance music; subculture and club culture at the turn of the century; rap and the use of hip-hop culture; identity and nation in grunge, Britpop, and beyond; and rethinking youth and pop beyond subculture.

241. **Hyden, Colleen, and N. Jane McCandless**. 1983. "Men and Women as Portrayed in the Lyrics of Contemporary Music." *Popular Music and Society* 9(2): 19–26. ISSN: 000-7766.

Examines how the media and contemporary music have been frequently considered agents of socialization and as purveyors of sex role stereotypes. Discusses research that suggests that because of the pervasiveness of popular music among young people, popular music serves as a socializing agent in the lives of its audience. Argues that popular music teaches people ways of understanding themselves and their social relation and may also encourage them to view popular music figures of the mass media as authority figures whose expressed opinions become legitimate.

242. **Inda, Jonathan, and Renato Rosaldo, eds**. 2002. *The Anthropology of Globalization: A Reader*. Series: *Blackwell Readers in Anthropology*. Maiden: Blackwell. xii, 498 p. Bibliography and Index. ISBN: 9-781-40513-612-9.

A compilation of essays that focus on the increasing interconnection of people around the world and the culturally specific ways in which these connections are mediated. Compiled essays ground the study of globalization ethnographically by locating global processes in everyday practice. Addresses the global flow of capital, people, commodities, and ideologies. The essays also offer extensive geographic coverage from Africa, Asia, the Caribbean, Europe, and North America.

243.   **Inglis, Ian, ed**. 2006. *Performance and Popular Music: History, Place, and Time*. Series: *Ashgate Popular and Folk Music Series*. Aldershot, Hants & Burlington: Ashgate. xvii, 205 p. Bibliography and Index. ISBN: 9-780-75468-157-1.

Observes that since the emergence of rock 'n' roll in the early 1950s, there have been several live musical performances that were not only memorable in themselves but became influential in the way they shaped the subsequent trajectory and development of popular music. Moreover, each in its own way introduced new styles and provided templates for others to follows. The essays in this collection explore the processes by examining some of these specific occasions when such transformations occurred. They reveal that it is often through the disruptive dynamics of performance and interaction between performance and audience that pattern of change and innovation can best be recognized. They discuss performances from the Beatles, Bob Dylan, Queen, Michael Jackson, Madonna, Woodstock, Live Aid, and others.

244.   **Inglis, Ian, ed**. 2003. *Popular Music and Film*. London & New York: Wallflower Press. 205 p. Bibliography and Index. ISBN: 9-781-90336-472-7.

A compilation of essays that focus on the growing presence of popular music in film and offers contemporary research in film studies. Compiled essays are written by an international group of academics and researchers. Essays explore issues such as the changing roles and functions that music performs.

245.   **Ingraham, Mary, Joseph So, and Roy Moodley, eds**. 2016. *Opera in a Multicultural World: Coloniality, Culture, Performance*. Series: *Routledge Research in Music*. New York: Routledge. 278 p. Music Examples, Bibliography, and Index. ISBN: 9-780-36759-879-2.

Critically explores the relevance and expressions of multicultural representation of and in Western European operatic genres in the modern world. Reveals their approaches to reflecting identity, transmitting meaning, and inspiring creation as well as the ambiguities and the contradictions that occur across the time-place(s) of their performance. Considers a broad repertoire that includes Canadian operas and Chinese and African American performances, as well as works by Franz Joseph Haydn, Richard Strauss, Giacomo Puccini, and Richard Wagner and the performances spanning three continents and over two centuries.

246.   **International Advisory Editors**. 2005. "Can We Get Rid of the 'Popular' in Popular Music? A Virtual Symposium With Contributions From the International Advisory Editors of *Popular Music*." *Popular Music* 24(1): 133–145. ISSN: 0261-1430.

Reports on a virtual symposium participated by the Editorial Group of *Popular Music* journal regarding how the group has been discussing the term "popular" and considering its epithetic role next to "music." Considers how some of the editors have questioned what the term now means, partly because it has been used less in media studies and cultural sociology over the last few years, Also, considers how other editors have pointed out the fact that it remains a vital concept, even a rallying point, in certain fields such as musicology and politics.

247. **Istvandity, Lauren, Sarah Baker, and Zelmaire Cantillon, eds**. 2019. *Remembering Popular Music's Past: Memory-Heritage-History*. London & New York: Anthem Press. vi, 244 p. Bibliography and Index. ISBN: 9-781-78308-969-7.

Seeks to capitalize on the growing interest globally in the preservation of popular music's material past and on scholarly explorations of the ways in which popular music as heritage is produced, legitimized, and conferred cultural and historical significance. Considers the spaces, practices, and representations that constitute popular music heritage to elucidate how popular music's past is lived in the present. Focuses on the transformation of popular music heritage and the role of history and memory in the process.

248. **James, Robin**. 2015. *Resilience and Melancholy: Pop Music, Feminism, Neoliberalism*. Arlesford, Winchester, & Washington: Zero Books. ix, 223 p. Bibliography. ISBN: 9-781-78279-598-8.

Remixes a connection between music, society, and power. Considers works of critical theorists Theodor Adorno and Max Horkheimer who diagnosed the relationship between popular music and the broader social world. Argues that contemporary music relies on noise and dissonance and resources for productivity as raw materials for the reproduction of social life. Also argues that noise making as the means of musical, cultural, and social production is emblematic of neoliberalism's demand for resilience in the face of trauma and loss. Resilience discourse is what ties together contemporary popular music aesthetics, neoliberal capitalism, and racism/sexism.

249. **James, Robin**. 2017. "Post-Feminism's Sexual Contact and Electronic Dance Music's Queered Femme Voices." *Dancecult—Journal of Electronic Dance Music Culture* 9(1) [Special Issue: *Women and Electronic Dance Music Culture*]: 28–49. ISSN: 1947-5403.

Argues that post-feminism's new sexual contact grants other privileged White women the things traditionally denied women as a class, namely economic success and self-ownership of their bodies. Considers three ways White women and femme musicians across electronic dance music use vocal authorized voices to reimagine post-feminist practices. Examines Brooklyn band bottoms, Berlin techno collective Decon/Recon, and Australian American pop star Sia, who all use "voice" to craft femininities that deviate from post-feminist gender norms.

250. **James, Robin**. 2022. "Feminist Aesthetics, Popular Music, and the Politics of the 'Mainstream.'" In *Feminist Aesthetics and Philosophy of Art: Critical Visions, Creative Engagements*, L. Ryan Musgrave, ed. Netherlands: Springer. 290 p. Bibliography and Index. ISBN: 9-781-40206-836-2.

Argues that while feminist aestheticians have long interrogated gendered, raced, and classed hierarchies in the arts, feminist philosophers still do not talk much about popular music. Even though Angela Davis and bell hooks have seriously engaged popular music, they are often situated on the margins of philosophy. With this argument, the volume offers a study of popular music and the case of popular music that points out feminist aesthetics to some of its own limitations and unasked questions. Addresses the paucity of work in feminist philosophy and popular music by applying insights from other areas of feminist aesthetics to questions of popular music using feminists', specifically Julia Kristeva's, notion of female genius and the female genius spectator.

251. **Jameson, Fredric, and Masao Myoshi, eds**. 1998. *The Cultures of Globalization*. Series: *Post-Contemporary Interventions*. Durham: Duke University Press. xvii, 393 p. Illustrations, Maps, Bibliography, and Index. ISBN: 0-82232-157-2.

Presents an international collection of essays that consider the process of globalization as it concerns the transformation of the economic into the cultural and vice versa; the rise of consumer cultures around the world; the production and cancellation of forms of subjectivity; and the challenges it presents to national identity, local culture, and transnational forms of everyday life. Discusses overlapping themes of transnational experiences and describes how the global character of technology, communication networks, consumer culture, intellectual discourse, the arts, and mass entertainment have all been affected by recent worldwide trends.

252. **Jarman-Ivens, Freya, ed**. 2007. *Oh Boy! Masculinities and Popular Music*. London: Routledge. vii, 279 p. Illustrations, Maps, Music Examples, Bibliography, and Index. ISBN: 9-780-41597-820-0.

A compilation of essays that examine how forms of masculinities are negotiated, constructed, represented, and addressed across a range of popular music texts and practices. Compiled essays study the concept of masculinity in performance and appearance and how both male and female artists have engaged with notions of masculinity in popular music. Topics include constructions of masculinity in Freddie Mercury and Justin Hawkins; negotiating masculinity in an Indonesian popular song; queer voices and musical genders; and others.

253. **Johannsen, Igor**. 2019. "Configurations of Space and Identity in Hip-Hop: Performing 'Global South.'" *Journal of Hip-Hop Studies* 6(2) [Special Issue: *If I Ruled the World: Putting Hip-Hop on the Atlas*]: 183–205. ISSN: 2331-5563.

Examines the spatiality of culture, specifically hip-hop and the reverberations between space and identity. Deconstructs and contextualizes the Global South by discussing the practices of respective hip-hop communities to diagram the oversimplifications inherent in those seemingly natural spatial terms. Argues that researching hip-hop in the Global South necessitates the realization that hip-hop is not only a local but also an international phenomenon in which practitioners and fans as well as audiences and critics are able to contribute to a common transregional discourse.

254. **Johannson, Ola, and Thomas L. Bell, eds**. 2016. *Sound, Society, and the Geography of Popular Music*. Previously published, Burlington: Ashgate, 2009. London & New York: Routledge. xiv, 305 p. Illustration, Maps, Bibliography, and Index. ISBN: 9-781-31560-993-5.

An edited volume that features case studies from the United States, Canada, the Caribbean, Australia, and Great Britain. Compiled essays present contemporary innovative spatial perspectives on music and further an understanding of broader social relations and trends, including identity, attachment to place, cultural economies, social activism, and politics.

255. **Johnson, Bruce, and Martin Cloonan**. 2009. *Dark Side of the Tune: Popular Music and Violence*. Series: *Ashgate Popular and Folk Music Series*. Farnham & Burlington: Ashgate. xiv, 238 p. Filmography, Bibliography, and Index. ISBN: 9-780-75469-960-6.

Focuses on what is described as the "dark side" of popular music. Examines the ways in which popular music has been deployed in association with violence. Addresses the physiological and cognitive foundations of sounding/hearing and provides a historical survey of examples of the nexus between music and violence from pre-biblical times to the late nineteenth century. Also concentrates on the emergence of technologies by which music can be electronically augmented, generated, and disseminated.

256. **Johnson, Imani K**. 2022. *Dark Matter in Breaking Cyphers: The Life of Africanist Aesthetics in Global Hip-Hop*. New York: Oxford University Press. 256 p. Bibliography and Index. ISBN: 9-780-19085-670-0.

An in-depth study of hip-hop focusing on the dance circle (called the cypher) as a common signifier of breaking culture known more for its spectacular moves than as a ritual practice with foundations in Africanist aesthetics. Expresses that those foundations evident in expressive qualities like call and response, the aural kinesthetic, the imperative to be the original, and others are essential to cyphering's enduring presence on the global stage. Centers on the voices of practitioners in a study of breaking events in cities across the United States, Canada, and Europe.

257. **Johnson, Jake, Masi Asare, Amy Coddington, Daniel Goldmark, Raymond Knapp, Oliver Wang, and Elizabeth Wollman**. 2019. "Divided by a Common Language: Musical Theater and Popular Music." *Journal of Popular Music Studies* 31(4): 32–50. ISSN: 1533-1598.

A compilation of essays that stem from a symposium to consider one of scholarship's persistent examples of separation by a common language—that of popular music and musical theater. Compiled essays are grounded on the notion that popular music studies embrace a large and dynamic variety of musical styles and over the years have produced journals and conferences, as well as academic degree programs both within and outside of music departments. Compiled essays also support the notion that studies in musical theater, like studies in popular music, are likewise on the rise.

258.   **Jones, Carys W**. 2008. *The Rock Canon: Canonical Values in the Reception of Rock Albums*. Series: *Ashgate Popular and Folk Music Series*. Aldershot & Burlington: Ashgate. 169 p. Bibliography and Index. ISBN: 9-781-13824-789-5.

Explores the emerging reflections of values, terms, and mechanisms from the canon of Western literature and classical music in the reception of rock music. Examines the concept of canon as theorized by scholars in the fields of literary criticism and musicology. Investigates for canonical facets in the reception of rock music as represented by the following albums: Bob Dylan's *Highway 61 Revisited*; the Beach Boys' *Pet Sounds*; the Beatles' *Revolver*; the Velvet Underground's *The Velvet Underground & Nico*; Van Morrison's *Austral Weeks*; Marvin Gaye's *What's Going On*; the Rolling Stones' *Exile on Main St.*; Patti Smith's *Horses*; the Sex Pistols' *Never Mind the Bollocks: Here's the Sex Pistols*; and Nirvana's *Nevermind*.

259.   **Jones, Ellis**. 2021. *DIY Music and the Politics of Social Media*. Series: *Alternate Takes: Critical Responses to Popular Music*. New York: Bloomsbury. 236 p. Bibliography and Index. ISBN: 9-781-50135-964-4.

Explores the significant challenges faced by artists navigating the DIY/cultural landscape. Examines how anti-commercial musicians operate in the competitive attention-seeking world of social media, how they deal with a new abundance of data and metrics, and how they present their activity as cultural resistance. Demonstrates that a platform-enabled DIY approach is now the norm for a wide array of cultural practitioners.

260.   **Jones, Simon**. 1995. "Rocking the House: Sound System Cultures and the Politics of Space." *Journal of Popular Music Studies* 7: 1–24. ISSN: 1533-1598.

Investigates cultural and musical practices that revolve around the reproduction and reception of recorded music as a form of public entertainment. Focuses on the technological and institutional configuration of the "sound system" in various genres of Black music, disco, and dance cultures. Shows how sound systems have become the focus of various musical, technological, and sound practices that have articulated cultural space. Seeks to answer the inquiry of what occurs when these practices separate outside the boundaries of authored, legitimate, leisure space, and how they become subject to forms of social control and legal regulations.

261.   **Jones, Stacy H**. 2007. *Torch Singing: Performing Resistance and Desire From Billie Holiday to Edith Piaf*. Series: *Ethnographic Alternatives*. Previously published, Aldershot, Hants & Burlington: Ashgate, 2003. Lanham: AltraMira Press/Rowman & Littlefield. xii, 282 p. Bibliography and Index. ISBN: 9-780-75910-659-8.

Presents torch singing as a more complicated phenomenon than the familiar trope of a woman lamenting her victimhood. Observes the blues singer as if they are possibly performing critiques of the lyrics they sing. Reveals points of contact in the opposition between spectators and performers, emotion and intellect, and love and power.

262. **Jori, Anita**. 2017. *The Discourse Community of Electronic Dance Music*. Bielefeld: Transcript Verlag. 240 p. Bibliography and Index. ISBN: 9-783-83945-758-0.

Offers perspective on examining electronic dance music communities. Provides an overview on the language use and discourse characteristics of the EDM community. Integrates methodology of linguistic discourse analysis and cultural studies.

263. **Kahn-Harris, Keith**. 2007. *Extreme Metal: Music and Culture on the Edge*. Oxford & New York: Berg. x, 194 p. Illustrations, Discography, Bibliography, and Index. ISBN: 9-780-85785-081-2.

Explores the global extreme metal scene. Include interviews with band members and fans from countries ranging from the United Kingdom and the United States to Israel and Sweden. Demonstrates the power, subtlety, and often surprising nature of a frequently misunderstood music form.

264. **Kajanová, Yvetta**. 2013. "The Rock, Pop and Jazz in Contemporary Music Studies." *International Review of the Aesthetics and Sociology of Music* 44(2): 343–359. ISSN: 0351-5796.

Notes that research on jazz, rock, and pop music has a relatively brief history when compared with the one-hundred-fifty-year tradition of classical musicology. Also notes that the first research on jazz was conducted in the 1950s. Topics are divided into several sections: rock, pop, and jazz education in Central Europe; research and rock, pop, and jazz within musicology and non-musicological disciplines; research methods—comparative analysis, historiography; and others.

265. **Kaplan, E. Anne**. 1987. *Rocking Around the Clock: Music Television, Postmodernism, and Consumer Culture*. Series: *Routledge Library Editions*. New York & London: Routledge. ix, 196 p. Illustrations, Videography, Bibliography, and Index. ISBN: 0-41633-370-2.

Examines the cultural context of MTV and its relationship to the history of rock music. Focuses on MTV as a commercial institution, the context of production and exhibition of videos, advertisements, and others. Also focuses on rock videos, gender issues in videos by both male and female stars, and the wider implications of MTV.

266. **Kärjä, Antti-Ville**. 2022. *The Popular and the Sacred in Music*. Abingdon, Oxon & New York: Routledge. 210 p. Illustrations, Bibliography, and Index. ISBN: 9-781-03202-503-2.

Argues that music as form of art whose name derives from ancient myths is often thought of as a pure symbolic expression and associated with transcendence.

Further argues that music is also a universal phenomenon and a profound marker of humanity and these features make music a sphere of activity where sacred and popular qualities intersect and amalgamate. Stresses the extended and multiple dimensions of the sacred and the popular and challenges conventions taken for granted and the rigid conceptualization of both popular and sacred music. Focuses on the cultural politics of labeling music either as popular or sacred and the disciplinary and theoretical implications of such labeling.

267.   **Kasinitz, Philip, and Marco Martinello, eds.** 2020. *Music, Immigration, and the City: A Transatlantic Dialogue.* Series: *Ethnic and Racial Studies.* Abingdon, Oxon: Routledge. viii, 160 p. Bibliography and Index. ISBN: 9-780-36733-570-0.

A compilation of essays from the research of social scientists and music scholars that examine the role of migrant and migrant-descended communities in the production and consumption of popular music. Essay topics include hiphop in Liège and Montreal; politics of Mexican folk music in Los Angeles; ethnic boundaries in Naples; tango in the Argentine diaspora; Alevi music among Turks in Germany; history of soca in Brooklyn; and the recreation of "American" culture by children of immigrants on the Broadway stage.

268.   **Katz, Mark**. 2020. *Build: The Power of Hip-Hop Diplomacy in a Divided World.* New York: Oxford University Press. xvii, 232 p. Illustrations, Bibliography, and Index. ISBN: 9-780-19005-611-7.

Reveals the power of art to bridge cultural divides, facilitate understanding, and express and heal trauma. Draws from approximately one hundred fifty interviews with hip-hop artists, diplomats, and others in more than thirty countries and explores the tensions and ambiguities in the relationship between art and the state. Suggests that hip-hop at its best can promote positive, productive international relations between people and nations and has the power to build global community when it is so desperately needed.

269.   **Kaye, Lenny**. 2022. *Lightning Striking: Ten Transformative Moments in Rock and Roll.* New York: Ecco Press. xv, 496 p. Bibliography and Index. ISBN: 9-780-06244-920-7.

Explores ten crossroads of time and place that define rock and roll, characters, and visionaries, how each generation came to be, and how it was discovered by the world. Time and places explored include Cleveland 1952; Memphis 1954; New Orleans 1957; Philadelphia 1959, Liverpool 1962; San Francisco 1967; Detroit 1969; New York City 1975; London 1977; Los Angeles 1984/Norway 1993; and Seattle 1991.

270.   **Keil, Charles, and Steven Feld**. 2005. *Music Grooves: Essays and Debates, 2nd ed.* Tucson: Fenestra. Previously published, Chicago: University of Chicago Press, 1994. viii, 402 p. [4 p.] of plates, Illustrations, Bibliography, and Index. ISBN: 9-781-58736-412-9.

Explores the dual themes of musical participation and musical mediation. Expresses a desire for a more reflexive, experimental discourse in music and society. Discussions and topics range from jazz, blues, polka, soul, rock, world beat, rap, karaoke, and other genres to major scholarly debates in music theory and pop culture studies. Covers vital issues in media studies, ethnomusicology, pop cultural studies, anthropology, and society and discusses music from America, Greece, Cuba, Africa, and Papua New Guinea and from diverse artists such as James Brown, Aretha Franklin, Li'l Wally Jagiello, Bo Didley, Walt Solek, Madonna, Paul Simon, Miles Davis, Thelonious Monk, and Billie Holiday.

271. **Kennedy, Victor**. 2013. *Strange Brew: Metaphors of Magic and Science in Rock Music*. Newcastle upon Tyne: Cambridge Scholars. 145 p. Bibliography and Index. ISBN: 9-781-44384-846-6.

Employs the title "Strange Brew" from the title of a hit song from Cream's album *Disraeli Gears*, which featured the most psychedelic cover art. The song is what most postmodern scholars influenced by Frederic Jameson would refer to as pastiche, combining lyrics about love and witchcraft with a note-for-note homage to Albert King's song, "Oh Pretty Woman." Traces the evolution of psychedelic music from its roots in rock 'n' roll and the blues to its influence on popular music in contemporary times. Demonstrates how metaphor is used to create the effects of songs and their lyrics and how words and music came together as both cause and effect of the cultural revolution of the 1960s.

272. **Klein, Bethany, ed**. 2020. *Selling Out: Culture, Commerce, and Popular Music*. New York: Bloomsbury. vi, 193 p. Bibliography and Index. 9-781-50133-934-9.

Examines the relationship between popular music and consumer brands, product placement, music videos, promotions, and so forth. Traces the evolution of selling out debates in popular music cultures and considers what might be lost when the boundary between culture and commerce is dismissed as a relic.

273. **Klein, Bethany, Leslie M. Meier, and Devon Powers**. 2017. "Selling Out: Musicians, Autonomy, and Compromise in the Digital Age." *Popular Music and Society* 40(2): 222–238. ISSN: 0300-7766.

Explores how popular music making and perspectives on selling out have been shaped by digitalization, promotionalism, and globalization. Argues that charges of "selling out" and debates about the boundaries of cultural autonomy have played a pivotal role in the development of popular music as a legitimate and serious art form. Further argues that with promotional strategies and commercial business practices now practically inseparable from the core activities previously associated with music making, the relevance of such concepts and the values that underpin them are questioned by industry experts, musicians, and fans.

274. **Klump, Brad**. 1999. "Origins and Distinctions of the 'World Music' and 'World Beat' Designations." *Canadian Perspectives in Ethnomusicology/Perspectives Canadiennes en Ethnomusicologie* 19(2): 50–15. French and English texts. ISSN: 0710-0353.

Traces the origins and uses of the musical classifications of "world music" and "world beat." Claims that the term world beat was first used by the musician and

DJ Dan Del Santo in 1983 for his syncretic hybrids of American R&B, Afrobeat, and Latin popular music styles. In contrast, the term world music was coined independently by at least three different groups: European jazz critics (ca. 1963), American ethnomusicologists (1965), and British record companies (1987). Further claims that applications range from the musical fusions between jazz and non-Western musics to a marketing category used to sell almost any music outside the Western mainstream.

275.   **Kotarba, Joseph A., ed**. 2018. *Understanding Society Through Popular Music, 3rd ed*. New York: Routledge. xvi, 256 p. Illustrations, Bibliography, and Index. ISBN: 9-781-13880-652-8.

An edited volume of essays that were written for Introductory Sociology and Sociology of Popular Culture classes. Uses popular music to illustrate fundamental social institutions, theories, sociological concepts, and processes. Uses music as a social phenomenon of great interest to draw students to their study and social life. Topics include music and social media, hip-hop culture, religion, politics, and music, class and gender, youth culture, and so forth.

276.   **Kramer, Lucia**. 2010. "From Flam Rock to Cock Rock: Revis(it)ing Rock Masculinities in Recent Feature Films." In *Performing Masculinities*, Rainer Emig and Anthony Rowland, eds. Houndmills, Basingstoke & New York: Palgrave Macmillan. xiii, 240 p. Illustrations, Bibliography, and Index. ISBN: 9-780-23057-798-5.

Provides an outline of the depiction of rock in film and investigates the constructions of rock masculinities in the feature films *Rock Star, Almost Famous, Still Crazy*, and *Velvet Goldmine*. Interprets the first three films as representative of the dominant strategies of representing male rock stardom in streamlined independent cinema supporting a construction of rock as a male cosmos streaked by homophobia, misogyny, and a gendered conception of fandom. Whereas *Velvet Goldmine*, in contrast, is marked by a narrative structure and a discussion of ideas that deliberately uphold ambivalences and uncertainties on the topics of art, theatricality, love, and sexuality.

277.   **Kronenburg, Robert**. 2017. *This Must Be the Place: An Architectural History of Popular Music Performance Venues*. New York: Bloomsbury. xviii, 286 p. [16 p.] of plates, Bibliography, and Index. ISBN: 9-781-50131-927-3.

Examines the design and form of popular music architecture and charts how it has been developed in ad hoc ways by nonprofessionals such as building owners, promoters, and the musicians themselves as well as professionally by architects, designers, and construction specialists. Focuses on Europe and North America with coverage on Australia, Asia, and South America and explores audience experiences and how venues such as bar rooms, stadiums, and so forth have influenced the development of different music scenes.

278.   **Kuhlke, Olaf, ed**. *Global Moments: Dance, Place, and Hybridity*. Lanham: Lexington Books. xii, 191 p. Bibliography and Index. ISBN: 9-780-73917-182-0.

A compilation of essays that focus on the relationship between global mobility and dance. Compiled essays are interdisciplinary research in scope and examine how diffusion of global cultures has impacted dance and even gives new meaning to the everyday spaces where dance occurs. Essay topics include Irishness and step dancing in Newfoundland and Labrador; dancing in Berlin, Germany, 1989–2006; tango; salsa cosmopolitanism; and others.

279.   **Laing, Dave**. 2008. "World Music and the Global Music Industry: Flows, Corporations, and Networks." *Popular Music History* 3(3): 213–231. ISSN: 1740-7133.

Provides a sketch of the main features of the global macro economy of music followed by comments on world music and its relation to the macro economy. Contains key financial data of the worldwide music industry in global regions, and the corporate structures of the major international music companies are analyzed. Also discusses the main characteristics of vocal music as a "genre market" and a subset on the global music industry.

280.   **Lashua, Brett, and Joseph Minadeo**. 2014. "*One Day on Earth*: Music Documentary Film-Making and Global Soundscapes." In *Sounds of the City: Popular Music, Place, and Globalization, Volume 1*. Series: *Leisure Studies in a Global Era*, Brett Lashua, Karl Spracklen, and Stephen Wagg, eds. Houndmills, Basingstoke, Hampshire & New York: Palgrave Macmillan. xii, 323 p. Illustrations, Bibliography, and Index. ISBN: 9-781-13728-311-5.

Considers Bruce Chatwin's (in his book *Songlines*) notions of musical phrase as a map of reference. Posits that music is a memory bank for finding one's way around the world. The volume is concerned less with the sounds of a particular city than with ways of using music as means of finding one's way around the world. Addresses the question of intersections of music and filmmaking and explores the documentary *One Day on Earth* (2012) as a case study through which to explore relations of music and place from the immensity of the global to the intimately tiny.

281.   **Lashua, Brett, Karl Spracklen, and Stephen Wagg, eds**. 2014. *Sounds of the City: Popular Music, Place, and Globalization, Volume 1*. Series: *Leisure Studies in a Global Era*. Houndmills, Basingstoke, Hampshire & New York: Palgrave Macmillan. xii, 323 p. Illustrations, Bibliography, and Index. ISBN: 9-781-13728-311-5.

A compilation of essays that explore the ways in which Western-derived music connects with globalization, hybridity, consumerism, and the flow of culture. Essays are geared for both local terrain and as global crossroads with topics of selected cities in the United States, Canada, Europe, Indonesia, and Australia, which remain fascinating spaces of cultural contestation and meaning-making via the composing, playing, recording, and consumption of popular music.

282.   **Lashua, Brett, Karl Spracklen, Stephen Wagg, and M. Selim Yavuz, eds**. 2019. *Sounds of the City: Popular Music, Place, and Globalization Volume 2*. Series:

Leisure Studies in a Global Era. Cham: Palgrave Macmillan. xviii, 443 p. Illustrations, Bibliography, and Index. ISBN: 9-783-31994-080-9.

A compilation of essays that draw on expansive scholarship regarding the relations between music and cities and the global flows between music and urban experiences. Essays comment on the global city as a nexus of moving people, changing places, and shifting social relations, asking what popular music can indicate about cities and vice versa.

283. **Lee, Marshall**. 2011. "The Sociology of Popular Music, Interdisciplinarity, and Aesthetic Autonomy." *British Journal of Sociology* 62(11): 154–174. ISSN: 1468-4446.

Considers the impact of interdisciplinarity on sociological research by focusing on the academic study of popular music. Argues that popular music studies is an area of research characterized by interdisciplinarity, and in keeping with broader intellectual trends this approach is assumed to offer significant advantages. Further argues that popular music studies is broadly typical of contemporary intellectual and governmental attitudes regarding the best way to research specific topics. Suggests that considering musical specificity is a necessary component of a sociology of popular music, and some possibilities for developing a materialist sociology of music is outlined.

284. **Leggiewie, Claus, and Erik Meyer, eds**. 2017. *Global Pop das Buch zur Weltmusik (Global Pop the Book on World Music)*. Stuttgart: J. B. Metzler Verlag. 392 p. German text. Bibliography and Index. ISBN: 9-783-47602-636-1.

Integrates a series of essays that describe the phenomenon of world music in different contexts. The essays introduce central terms and offer a vivid description of characteristics of musical genres. The term "world music" is discussed from different perspectives, including current developments in "World Music 2.0," which is characterized by digitization and online communication. Topics include world music and politics, fusion, folk music, ethnomusicology, religion, inter- and transculturality, pop music cultures, sampling, archives, klezmer, tourism, migration, discourses in global pop, festivals Africa, Peter Gabriel, Ry Cooder, Alan Bern, Manu Chao, and much more.

285. **Leonard, Marion**. 2007. *Gender in the Music Industry: Rock, Discourse and Girl Power*. Series: *Ashgate Popular and Folk Music Series*. Aldershot & Burlington: Ashgate. 252 p. Bibliography and Index. ISBN: 9-781-35121-826-9.

Explores different representations of masculinity offered by and through rock music. Examines how female rock performers negotiate this gendering of rock music. Also focuses on how notions of gender affect the everyday experiences of all rock musicians within the context of the music industry.

286. **Levande, Meredith**. 2007. "Women, Pop Music, and Pornography." *Meridians: Feminism, Race, Transnationalism* 8(1): 293–321. ISSN: 1536-6936.

Demonstrates how a connection between media ownership deregulation and the mega-media companies that profit from adult entertainment have pushed pornographic imagery into the mainstream. Argues that nowhere is this situation more evident than with women in popular music whose images have become increasingly hypersexualized.

287. **Lieb, Kristin**. 2013. *Gender, Branding, and the Modern Music Industry: The Social Construction of Female Popular Music Stars*. New York: Routledge. xxiii, 194 p. Bibliography and Index. ISBN: 9-781-13806-416-4.

Combines interview data with music industry professionals with theoretical frameworks from sociology, mass communication, and marketing to explain and explore the gender differences of female artists' experiences. Provides insight into the rigid process that transforms female artists of various genres into female pop stars. Discusses several topics that include sexual attractiveness over talent, competitiveness for record deals, female pop star image, short-term brands, and so forth. Also explores the sociological forces that drive women into different representations and the ramifications for the greater social world.

288. **Liebersohn, Harry**. 2019. *Music and the New Global Culture: From the Great Exhibition to the Jazz Age*. Series: *Big Issues in Music*. Chicago: University of Chicago Press. 338 p. Illustrations, Tables, Bibliography, and Index. ISBN: 9-780-22622-126-5.

Traces the origins of global music to a handful of critical transformations that took place between the mid-nineteenth and early twentieth centuries. Demonstrates musical responses to globalization in diverse areas that include metropolises of India and China and remote settlements in South America and the Arctic. Offers discussion about global movement and feelings about music in the world. Topics covered include music's global archive, a global empire of sound, and others.

289. **Ling, Jan**. 2003. "Is 'World Music' the 'Classical Music' of Our Time?" *Popular Music* 22(2): 235–240. ISSN: 0261-1430.

Contends that "world music" as a common definition cannot be based on musical material or on musical functions. Moreover, it refers to a form of music that is enjoyed by a very sophisticated young middle-class public who combine their music interest and new sounds from different parts of the world with a progressive interest in what is going on in the peace and environmental movements, among others. Suggests that all music called "world music" was from the beginning promoted by academic expertise, which was very much involved in marketing.

290. **Lipsitz, George**. 1994. *Dangerous Crossroads: Popular Music, Postmodernism, and the Poetics of Place*. London & New York: Verso. viii, 192 p. Illustrations, Bibliography, and Index. ISBN: 1-85984-435-0.

Surveys world music's intercultural fusions. Focuses on and provides theoretical notions concerning world music production in Havana, Port-au-Prince, Kingston, Budapest, Paris, London, New York, Los Angeles, and Tokyo. Explores the fusion of immigrant and mainstream cultures displayed in world music, including rap, jazz, reggae, zouk, bhangra, juju, swamp pop, and Puerto Rican and Chicago punk. Also explores the ways in which ethnic differences in popular music enable musicians in aggrieved populations to enjoy the rewards of mainstream culture while boldly stating their divergence from it and how it offers a utopian model of intercultural cooperation while at the same time making a spectacle out of ethnicity and reinforcing ethnic divisions.

291.   **Lipsitz, George**. 2007. *Footsteps in the Dark: The Hidden Histories of Popular Music*. Minneapolis: University of Minnesota Press. xxv, 343 p. [16 p.] of plates, Illustrations, Bibliography, and Index. ISBN: 9-780-81665-019-4.

Posits that most popular songs are short-lived because they appear suddenly and, if they catch on, seem to be everywhere at once before disappearing into obscurity. However, some songs resonate deeply and often in ways that reflect broader historical and cultural changes. This study illuminates these secret meanings by offering imaginative interpretations of a wide range of popular music genres from jazz and salsa to rock. Using several examples, it discusses such topics as the emergence of an African American techno music subculture in Detroit as a contradictory case of digital capitalism and the prominence of banda, merengue, and salsa music in the 1990s as an expression of changing Mexican, Dominican, and Puerto Rican nationalism. Also examines race and popular music in jazz and others.

292.   **Lohlker, Rüdiger**. 2014. "Hip-Hop and Islam: An Exploration into Music, Technology, Religion, and Marginality." *Wiener Zeitschrift für die Kunde des Morgenlandes* 104: 115–135. ISSN: 0084-0076.

Considers the global landscape of hip-hop and offers theoretical notions that hip-hop is a unique expression that has crossed social, cultural, and national boundaries. Moreover, hip-hop is not only a phenomenon in the United States popular culture but also has been appropriated and transformed by local artists in different parts of the world such as in Europe, South America, Africa, Middle East, Asia, Australia, and so forth. Points out that local artists in many parts of the world who are searching for emancipation and empowering avenues use hip-hop to express such sentiments in various ways. Concentrates on how hip-hop is performed with explicit references to Islam. Suggests that hip-hop in its Islamic role and other contexts is one of the most pertinent examples for the cultural role of technology.

293.   **Longhurst, Brian, and Danijela Bogdanovic**. 2014. *Popular Music and Society, 3rd ed.* Previously published, 1995. Cambridge: Polity Press. xvi, 277 p. Illustrations, Bibliography, and Index. ISBN: 9-780-74565-365-5.

A revised and updated edition that explores the study of popular music in the context of wider debates in sociology and media and cultural studies. Begins by examining the ways in which popular music is produced and then explores its structure as text and the ways in which audiences understand its music. Includes overview and critical theoretical approaches to existing studies that have shaped the discipline. Topics covered include the popular music industry; the social production of music; history, politics, and sexuality; Black music; genres and social constructions; texts and meaning; performance, dance, distinction, and the body; effects; American and subcultures; fans, production, and consumption; and beyond subcultures and fans.

294. **Loos, Helmut**. 2018. "World Music or Regionality? A Fundamental Question for Music Historiography." *Music in Society* 2018: 13–22. ISSN: 2303-5722.

Elaborates on and considers theoretical notions surrounding the term "world music." Argues that the term can be seen in a larger context as a phenomenon of postmodernism in that the challenge to the strict laws and boundaries of modernism form a connection between regionally and global meaning to be established. Discusses several categories of music that began to dissolve with modernism. Suggests that historical-critical musicology must adapt to a transformed state of consciousness in world music categories. Doing so will allow for several promising perspectives to unfold.

295. **Lopez Cano, Rueben**. 2005. "Más allá la Intertextualidad: Tópicas Musicaes, Esquemas Narrativos, Ironíca y Cisismo en la Habridación Musical de la Era Global (More From the Intertextuality: Musical Topics, Narrative Themes, Irony and Cynicism in the Musical Hybridization of the Global Era)." *Nassarre: Revista Aragonésa de Musicología; Zaragoza* 2005: 59–76. Spanish text with English summary. ISSN: 0213-7305.

Explores the compositional elements of twentieth- and twenty-first-century popular music by examining how structures and techniques are not new but mimic pre-existing genres, songs, and other compositions. Focuses on intertextuality between popular music genres. Presents examples that include harmonic structure found in bolero that was used in romantic rock ballads by the Beatles and Elvis Presley. Also focuses on four trends in popular music: references to fragments of specific pieces in new works; a pre-existing melody theme or unifying item that serves as the basis for a new work; a fragment of an existing piece that is included in a new composition; and allusions to pre-existing styles.

296. **Lovesey, Oliver**. 2022. *Popular Music Autobiography: The Revolution in Life-Writing by 1960s' Musicians and Their Descendants*. Series: *Popular Music (New York, N.Y.)*. New York: Bloomsbury. 256 p. Bibliography and Index. ISBN: 9-781-50135-583-7.

Argues that the 1960s saw the nexus of the revolution in popular music by a postwar generation amid demographic upheavals and shifts in technology. Moreover, the musicians associated with this period have produced a large amount of important autobiographical writing. Offers an examination of these works in the forms of formal autobiographies and memoirs, auto-fiction, songs, and self-fashioned museum exhibitions within the context of the recent expansion of interest in autobiography, disability, and celebrity status. Suggests that these writings express an anxiety over musical originality and authenticity. Includes discussions of Cosey Fanni Tutti, Brett Anderson, Moby, Patti Smith, Bob Dylan, and others.

297.   **Lull, James**. 1992. *Popular Music and Communication, 2nd ed.* Series: *Sage Focus Editions, v. 89.* Newbury: Sage Publications. viii, 247 p. Illustrations, Bibliography, and Index. ISBN: 0-80393-916-7.

A collection of essays that demonstrate how young people all over the world know how powerfully music communicates. Topics covered include the communicative potential of modern music recording technologies; popular music and social dance; the visual pleasures of music video; how musicians themselves articulate their communicative intentions; disruption caused by popular music in the political upheavals of Eastern Europe; the cultural roles of popular music among Vietnamese immigrants in the United States; and others.

298.   **Lynch, Gordon**. 2006. "The Role of Popular Music in the Construction of Alternative Spiritual Identities and Ideologies." *Journal for the Scientific Study of Religion* 45(4): 481–488. ISSN: 0021-8294.

Sets forth a discussion in the wider context of the decline of institutional religion among young adults, the rise of alternative spiritualities, and the mediatization of religion. Explores the significance of popular music in the development of alternative spiritual identities and ideologies. Provides a summary of research in the field by Christopher Partridge and Graham St. John. Argues that they demonstrate the encoding of alternative spiritual symbols and ideologies into certain forms of popular music. Concludes that researchers in the field of religions and popular music need to draw more on theories and methods developed in ethnomusicology and sociology of music.

299.   **Mainsbridge, Mary**. 2021. *Body as Instrument: Performing With Gestural Systems in Live Electronic Music.* New York: Bloomsbury. 192 p. Bibliography and Index. ISBN: 9-781-50136-854-7.

Explores how musicians interact with movement-controlled performance systems, producing sounds imbued with their physical signature. Explores how using motion-tracking technology, performers can translate physical actions into sonic processes creating or adapting novel gestural systems that transcend the structure and constraints of conventional music instruments. Provides interviews with influential artists in the field that includes Laetitia Sonami, Atu Tanaka, Pamela Z, Julie Wilson-Bokowiec, Sarah Hayes, Mark Coniglio, Garth Paine, and the Bent Leather Band.

300.   **Malone, Christopher, and George Martinez Jr., eds**. 2015. *The Organic Globalizer: Hip-Hop, Political Development and Movement Culture.* London & New York: Bloomsbury. xiii, 276 p. Bibliography and Index. ISBN: 9-781-50130-229-9.

A collection of critical essays that take the position that hip-hop holds political significance through an understanding of its ability to at once raise cultural awareness and expand civil society's focus on social and economic justice through institution building and engagement in political activism and participation. Compiled essays assert hip-hop's importance as an "organic globalizer" and that it holds promise through cultural awareness and identification/recognition of social creation and the institutionalization of independent alternative institutions, political activism, and others.

301.   **Manuel, Peter**. 1988. *Popular Musics in the Non-Western World*. New York: Oxford University Press. x, 287 p. Illustrations, Music Examples, Bibliography, and Index. ISBN: 0-19505-342-7.

Examines all major non-Western urban styles from genres such as reggae and salsa to lesser-known regional styles of Latin America, the Caribbean, Africa, the Middle East, non-Western Europe (Greece, Yugoslavia, Portugal), Asia, and the Near East. Establishes parameters that distinguish popular music from both folk and classical music. Defines popular music as music centered with the mass media in mind and reproduced on a large-scale basis as salable commodity of the dialectics of nationalism and acculturation, tradition and modernity, urban and rural aesthetics, and grassroots spontaneity and corporate or bureaucratic manipulation.

302.   **Manuel, Peter**. 1995. "Music as Symbol, Music as Simulacrum: Postmodern, Pre-Modern, and Modern Aesthetics in Subcultural Popular Musics." *Popular Music* 14(2): 227–239. ISSN: 0261-1430.

Argues that postmodern aesthetics has come to be recognized as a salient feature of much popular culture including music. Moreover, the syncretic popular musics created by subcultures may reflect multiple cultural orientations by combining postmodern and more traditional characteristics. Suggests that punk rock and rap music can be seen to combine postmodern techniques of pastiche, bricolage, and black irony with modernist sociopolitical protest.

303.   **Marshall, Lee, and Dave Laing, eds**. 2014. *Popular Music Matters: Essays in Honour of Simon Firth*. New York: Routledge. 252 p. Bibliography and Index. ISBN: 9-780-36766-920-1.

A series of essays by leading scholars such as Robert Christgau, Antoine Hennion, Peter J. Martin, Philip Tagg, and others in honor of the works of Simon Firth. Essays focus on sociology and industry, as well as aesthetics and values that reflect themes in Firth's research and writings that can also be found as topics in popular music studies. Essays are constructed to provide an essential resource for those working in popular music studies, musicology, sociology, and critical and media studies.

304.   **Martin, Bill, and Robert Fripp**. 2015. *Avant Rock: Experimental Music From the Beatles to Björk*. New York: Open Court. Series: *Feedback (Chicago, Ill.), v. 3*. xvi, 269 p. Bibliography and Index. ISBN: 9-780-81269-500-7.

Explores avant rock music that emerged from the social and political upheaval of the sixties. Covers the music from its early stages and reveals its influence on avant rock musicians such as John Cage and Cecil Taylor to those more closely related to rock like James Brown and Parliament/Funkadelic. Follows the development of avant rock through the sixties with bands such as the Beatles, the Who, Jimi Hendrix, the Velvet Underground, King Crimson, Brian Eno, Stereolab, Mouse on Mars, Sonic Youth, and Jim O'Rourke. Critiques the work of all important avant rock bands and individual artists from the well known to the most obscure and provides an annotated discography.

305.   **Mazierska, Ewa, and Georgina Gregory, eds**. 2015. *Relocating Popular Music*. Series: *Pop Music, Culture, and Identity*. Houndmills, Basingstoke, Hampshire & New York: Palgrave Macmillan. xi, 253 p. Bibliography and Index. ISBN: 9-781-13746-337-1.

Deals with popular music history and criticism, and music and globalization. Integrates a focus of colonialism and tourism to analyze types of music movements, such as transporting music from one place to another or historical period to another, hybridizing it with a different style and furnishing it with new meaning. Also discusses music in relation to music videos, graphic arts, fashion, and architecture. Essay topics include spaces of protest in Turkish popular music; the sense of place in baile funk music; Serbia popular music 1999; popular music in Tallinn, Estonia; Mancunian music (Manchester, United Kingdom); Abby Road and Beatles heritage, and others.

306.   **Mazierska, Ewa, Les Gillon, and Tony Rigg, eds**. 2020. *Popular Music in the Post-Digital Age: Politics, Economy, Culture, and Technology*. New York: Bloomsbury. xi, 292 p. Illustrations, Bibliography, and Index. ISBN: 9-781-50133-837-8.

A collection of essays and case studies that explore the relationship between various macro environmental factors such as politics, culture, and technology captured by terms such as "post-digital" and "post-Internet." Discusses the creation, monetization, and consumption of music and what changes in the music industry can indicate about wider shifts in economy and culture. Covers issues such as curation algorithms, block chain, careers of mainstream and independent musicians, festivals, and clubs to inform greater understanding and better navigation of the popular music landscape within a global context.

307.   **McCarthy, Cameron, ed**. 1999. *Sound Identities: Popular Music and the Cultural Politics of Education*. Series: *Counterpoints (New York, N.Y.)*. New York: Peter Lang. xiii, 490 p. Bibliography and Index. ISBN: 0-820-44139-2.

Integrates a sustained reflection on the sociocultural implications of youth consumption of popular music such as rap, heavy metal, calypso, and salsa. Argues that young people construct their identities through the social formation of boundaries and it is important to discuss how social, cultural, and political boundaries are created through popular music. Compiled essays provide a range of theoretical and empirical research of popular music and youth consumption.

308. **McClain, Jordan M., and Myles E. Lascity**. 2020. "Toward the Study of Framing Found in Music Journalism." *Popular Music and Society* 43(1): 20–33. ISSN: 0300-7766.

Explores the boundaries of framing and its promise for studying the alternative domain of music journalism. Examines the characteristics of music journalism and of framing within it and discusses the reasons and potential in connecting concepts of research, political communication, music journalism's core customs, and critical uses such as race, gender, sexuality, and celebrity woven into the popular culture content of such media coverage.

309. **McFadyen, Scot and Sam Dunn, directors**. 2008. *Global Metal*. Montreal: Films Seville. DVD. 95 Minutes. Dialogue in English and French. OCLC Number: 7-6245-787-1.

A documentary that follows metal fan and anthropologist Sam Dunn on a journey through Asia, South America, and the Middle East. Explores the world's emerging music scenes from Indonesian death metal to Chinese black metal to Iranian thrash.

310. **McKay, George**. 2015. *The Pop Festival: History, Music, Media, Culture*. New York Bloomsbury. xx, 234 p. Bibliography and Index. ISBN: 9-781-62356-820-7.

Considers how popular music festivals are one of the strikingly successful and enduring features of seasonal popular cultural consumption by young people and older generations of enthusiasts. Discusses a range of topics from pop and rock to folk, jazz, and techno, under the stars and canvas, dancing in the streets, and much more. Provides scholarship in cultural studies, media studies, musicology, sociology, and history to explore the music festival as a key event in the cultural landscape and one of the major interests of young people as festival goers themselves and as students.

311. **McLeese, Don**. 2010. "Straddling the Cultural Chasm: The Great Divide Between Music Criticism and Popular Consumption." *Popular Music and Society* 33(4) [Special Issue: *Popular Music and Journalism*]: 433–447. ISSN: 0300-7766.

Argues that although there has long been a divide in popular music between critical response and marketplace reception, there is a greater extending wall beyond musical taste to modes of consumption. Further argues that technology has transformed both journalism and popular music in profound and interrelated ways; journalism in general and music journalism face wide challenges; and radical change has created a disconnect that is as much a generational as a technological divide that music journalists must bridge to stay relevant.

312. **McLeod, Ken**. 2016. *We Are the Champions: Politics of Sports and Popular Music*. Series: *Ashgate Popular and Folk Music Series*. London: Routledge. x, 257 p. Bibliography and Index. ISBN: 9-781-31554-759-6.

Concentrates on the paradoxical and often conflicting relationship-associated modes of leisure and entertainment. Incorporates how music is used as an active part of sporting events, such as anthems, chants/cheers, and intermission entertainment. Ties together several threads of sports and popular culture.

313. **McLeod, Ken**. 2018. Vaporwave: Politics, Protest, and Identity." *Journal of Popular Music Studies* 30(4): 123–142. ISSN: 1533-1598.

Investigates various aspects of the popular online music genres known as vaporwave to understand how it functions as a form of socioeconomic critique while problematizing aspects of identity. Discusses some of the prominent features and objectives of vaporwave and analysis of the most well-known examples of vaporwave, Macintosh Plus album, *Floral Shoppe* (2011). Also, explores the relationship of vaporwave to techno-Orientalism and the genre's recent pernicious co-option by the conservative alt-right movement in the form of fashwave and Trumpwave.

314. **McLeod, Ken**. 2020. *Driving Identities: At the Intersection of Popular Music and Automotive Culture*. Series: *Ashgate Popular and Folk Music Series*. Abingdon, Oxon, & New York: Routledge. 275 p. Illustrations, Bibliography, and Index. 9-781-03223-616-2.

A study that examines the long-standing connections between popular music and the automotive industry and how this relationship has helped to construct and reflect various sociocultural identities. Challenges common assumptions regarding the divergences between industry and art and reveals how music and sound are used to suture the divide between human and non-human. Also explores the relationship between popular music automobiles and the mutual aesthetic and stylist influences that have historically left their mark on both industries.

315. **McMillin, Divya C., Joost de Bruin, and Jo Smith, eds**. 2018. *Place, Power, Media: Mediated Responses to Globalization*. New York: Peter Lang. vi, 232 p. Illustrations and Bibliography. ISBN: 9-781-43315-472-0.

An interdisciplinary compilation that can inform research in global popular music studies. Compiled essays explore how media practices and communication rituals are connected to larger economic, social, and political processes in a globalizing world. Compiled essays explore how daily, mundane, and interpersonal processes shape our place in the world.

316. **Mednicov, Melissa L**. 2018. *Pop Art and Popular Music: Jukebox Modernism*. New York: Routledge. 150 p. Bibliography and Index. ISBN: 9-781-35118-739-8.

Offers an interdisciplinary approach to pop art through a recuperation of popular music into historical understandings of the movement. Examines jukebox modernism as a procedure by which pop artists used popular music within their works to disrupt decorous modernism during the 1960s. Examines how artists such as Peter Blake, Pauline Boty, James Rosenquist, and Andy Warhol respond to pop music for reasons of emotional connectivity, issues of fandom, and identity.

317. **Meier, Leslie**. 2017. *Popular Music as Promotion: Music and Branding in the Digital Age*. Cambridge & Malden: Polity Press. vii, 200 p. Bibliography and Index. ISBN: 9-780-74569-221-0.

Argues that business-as-usual has been transformed across the music industries in the post-CD age. Provides a critique of the ways major music labels have successfully adapted to digital challenges and what is at stake for music makers and cultures. Examines how recording artists are positioned as artist-brands and popular music as a product to be licensed by consumer and media brands. Also examines key consequences of shifting business models, marketing strategies, and the new common sense in the music industries: the gatekeepers and colonization of popular music brands.

318. **Melillo, James**. 2020. *The Poetics of Noise From Dada to Punk*. New York: Bloomsbury. vii, 198 p. Bibliography and Index. ISBN: 9-781-50135-991-0.

Constructs a literary history of noise through poetic sound and performance and traces how poets figure noise in the disfiguration of poetic voice. Presents a series of case studies that range from verse by ear witnesses to World War I, dadaist provocations, jazz modernist, song and poetry, New York City punk rock, contemporary sound poetry, noise music, and others.

319. **Meyers, John P**. 2015. "Still Like Old Time Rock and Roll: Tribute Bands and Historical Consciousness in Popular Music." *Ethnomusicology* 59(1): 61–81. ISSN: 0014-1836.

Integrates ethnographic description of several tribute band performers and a critical reading of popular music discourse to explain historical consciousness and examines the role that tribute bands are playing in its development. Argues that tribute bands construct and partake in this new attitude that treats the events of popular music with historical respect and legitimacy. Focuses on rock music as a case study and provides an example of how events from the past can be remade and reconfigured into "history."

320. **Middleton, Richard**. 1990. *Studying Popular Music*. Milton Keynes & Philadelphia: Open University Press. vii, 328 p. Illustrations, Music Examples, Bibliography, and Index. ISBN: 9-780-33515-276-6.

Draws on a dialectical conception of musical development, genre, and meaning. Outlines a historical map of popular music studies that offer a way for a constructive critique of existing musical histories, Theodor Adorno's pessimistic picture of music in twentieth-century "mass culture," and the various theories of musical production and reproduction in contemporary capitalist societies. Also focuses on an analysis of popular music to examine approaches drawn from musicology, folklore, anthropology, cultural studies, and so forth.

321. **Middleton, Richard**. 1993. "Popular Music Analysis and Musicology." *Popular Music* 12(2): 177–190. ISSN: 0261-1430.

Argues that since their beginnings, popular music studies have conducted an implicit and sometimes explicit dialogue with musicology. Moreover, the musicological side of this conversation has often been marked by insult, incomprehension, or silence. Further argues that popular music scholars for their part have tended to concentrate on musicology's deficiencies. Contends that musicology is changing at the same time and that recent work in popular music studies suggest a confidence, manifesting itself in part in a willingness to engage with and adapt mainstream methods.

322.   **Mills, Peter**. 2012. *Media and Popular Music*. Edinburgh: Edinburgh University Press. vii, 168 p. Bibliography. ISBN: 9-780-74862-749-3.

Analyzes the relationship between temporary media and popular music, via both the mediation of music and music as mediator. An analysis provides a series of original interviews with key practitioners and major and independent label bosses. Among those interviewed include Mark Ellen, editor of *Smash Hits*, Q, *Mojo*, and *The Word* magazines, Mark Cooper, producer of *Later... With Jools Holland*, and others. Considers the experiences of the interviewees and observations in order to explore the ways popular music is produced, marketed, and distributed.

323.   **Mitchell, Tony, ed**. 2001. *Global Noise: Rap and Hip-Hop Outside the USA*. Series: *Music/Culture*. Middletown: Wesleyan University Press. 336 p. Illustrations, Discography, Videography, Bibliography, and Index. ISBN: 9780-81956-501-3.

An edited volume of essays comprised of international scholars that explore hip-hop in Europe, Canada, Japan, South Korea, Australia, and New Zealand. The essays explore hip-hop in these geographical regions within their social, cultural, and ethnic contexts. Topics covered include postcolonial hip-hop in France and rap and hip-hop culture in the 1980s and 1990s; Islamophobia; hip-hop in the United Kingdom; rap in Germany; Negu Gorriak and the Basque Country (Spain) political imagery; hip-hop in Italy; hip-hop in Japan; street dance and the club scene; rap and hip-hop and dance in South Korea; Sydney-style hip-hop; Māori and Pacific Islander hip-hop in Aotearoa/New Zealand; and rap in Canada.

324.   **Mitchell, Tony, Peter Doyle, and Bruce Johnson, eds**. 2000. *Changing Sounds: New Directions and Configurations in Popular Music*. Sydney: Faculty of Humanities and Social Sciences, University of Technology. 438 p. Illustrations and Bibliography. ISBN: 9-78-186365-364-0.

A compilation of papers presented at the tenth annual International Association for the Study of Popular Music, held in July 1999 at the University of Technology in Sydney Australia. Compiled papers consider new trends and directions in popular music and popular music studies for the new millennium.

325.   **Mitsui, Tōru, and Shuhei Hosokawa, eds**. 2001. *Karaoke Around the World: Global Technology, Local Singing*. Series: *Routledge Research in Cultural and*

Media Studies. London: Routledge. xi, 206 p. Illustrations, Music Examples, Bibliography, and Index. ISBN: 0-41516-371-4.

Situates karaoke as technology, place, and musical behavior in its social and cultural constructs. Explores the karaoke phenomenon in Japan and other cultures. Compiled essays explore the influence of karaoke in such areas as the United Kingdom, North America, Italy, Sweden, South Korea, and Brazil. Essays are also divided into three parts based on geography and explore various facets of these issues that involve people, co-singers, and listeners.

326. **Moberg, Marcus**. 2015. *Christian Metal: History, Ideology, Scene*. Series: *Bloomsbury Studies in Religion and Popular Music*. London: Bloomsbury. xii, 188 p. Illustrations, Bibliography, and Index. ISBN: 9-781-47257-983-6.

Argues that Christian metal has always defined itself in contrast to its non-Christian secular counterpart, but it stands out from nearly all other forms of contemporary Christian music through its unreserved use of metal's main visual and aesthetic traits. Further argues that Christian metal is a rare example of a direct combination and highly controversial form of popular music and its culture. Explores the phenomenon of Christian metal, its history, main characteristics, development, diversification, and key ideological traits from its formative years in the early 1980s to the present day.

327. **Moore, Allan F**. 2003. *Analyzing Popular Music*. Cambridge & New York: Cambridge University Press. ix, 270 p. Illustrations, Discography, Filmography, and Index. ISBN: 9-780-51148-201-4.

A compilation of essays that focus in some way on the question, how do we know music that impacts everyday life experience? The topics covered are varied and include popular music analysis, analyzing the words in popular songs, exoticism in film music, house music as rhetoric, the role of performance and meaning, Marxist music analysis, modernism and mass culture, new wave rock of the 1970s, listening in popular music, and popular music and ethnomusicology.

328. **Moorefield, Virgil**. 2005. *The Producer as Composer: Shaping the Sounds of Popular Music*. Cambridge: MIT Press. xix, 143 p. Discography, Bibliography, and Index. ISBN: 9-780-26213-457-6.

Traces the evolution with detailed discussions of works by producers and producer-musicians including Phil Spector, George Martin, Brian Eno, Bill Laswell, Trent Reznor, Quincy Jones, and the Chemical Brothers. Examines technological developments in terms of new techniques, tape editing, overdubbing, compression, and so forth that allowed artists to become their own producers. Describes the importance of disco, hip-hop, remixing, and other forms of electronic music production in shaping the sound of contemporary popular music.

329. **Morrison, Sarah**. 2008. "Music Makers: Popular Culture in Music Education—Can Pop Be Relevant? Using Popular Music to Address Issues of Racism." *Canadian Music Educator* 49(3): 52–54. ISSN: 0008-4546.

Presents a commentary that discusses the unique opportunity to address or challenge racism or prejudiced thoughts through the study of popular music. Suggests that there are both negative and positive examples of prejudices that can be drawn from popular music history. Further suggests that popular music concerts such as Live Earth have been used as ways of bringing people together for a common cause or goal.

330.　**Moy, Roy**. 2015. *Authorship Roles in Popular Music: Issues and Debates*. Series: Routledge *Studies in Popular Music*. Abingdon, Oxon & New York: Routledge. xxxi, 153 p. Bibliography and Index. ISBN: 9-781-13878-067-5.

Applies the critical concept of authorship theory to popular music by employing different aspects of production and creativity. Contextualizes key concepts of authorship relating to gender, race, technology, originality, and genius and raises important issues about the critical construction of authenticity, value, class, nationality, and genre. Employs a range of case studies as examples and investigates areas such as studio production, composition, DJing, collaboration, performance, and audience.

331.　**Moylan, William, Lori Burns, and Mike Alleyne, eds**. 2023. *Analyzing Recorded Music Collected Perspectives on Popular Music Tracks*. Abingdon, Oxon: Routledge. xxviii, 415 p. Illustrations, Music Examples, Bibliography, and Index. ISBN: 9-780-36754-631-1.

A collection of essays that focus on the study of recorded popular music and explore how the record shapes the song from a variety of perspectives. Essays examine a collection of diverse songs from a range of genres and points in history spanning the years 1936–2020.

332.　**Mueller, Charles A**. 2008. *The Music of the Gothic Subculture: Postmodernism and Aesthetics*. Ph.D., dissertation. Tallahassee: Florida State University. vii, 238 p. Music Examples and Bibliography. OCLC Number: 7-85833-557-3.

A musicological study that uses the methodology of Dick Hebdige's theory of subcultures to demonstrate how bands used gothic significance and aesthetics as way to sharpen and continue the social commentary of the punk movement. Examines how the artists recognized the masculine logic of power and control as the root cause of many social problems and embraced seduction and female signifiers as subversive devices. Also examines how goth bands purged their music and image as characteristics associated with masculinity and composed songs dealing with gyno-centered trauma, domestic abuse, and everyday cruelty. Their songs typically treated sex as a source of danger rather than pleasure. Musical artists featured in the study include Bauhaus, The Cure, Christian Death, Siouxsie and the Banshees, The Sisters of Mercy, and others.

333.　**Mullen, John**. 2019. *Popular Song in the First World War: An International Perspective*. Series: *Ashgate Popular and Folk Music Series*. Abingdon, Oxon: Routledge. x, 259 p. Bibliography and Index. ISBN: 9-780-36758-539-6.

Examines what popular music meant to people across the world during the First World War. Examines song repertoires and musical industries from around the world on both sides of the Great War as well as from neutral countries. Topics include lyricists, theater chains owners, cross-dressing singers, fado composer, and stage Scotsman or rhyming soldier, whether they came from Serbia, Britain, the United States, Germany, France, Portugal, or elsewhere.

334. **Nasir, Kamaludeen M**. 2020. *Representing Islam: Hip-Hop of the September 11 Generation*. Series: *Framing the Global Book Series*. Bloomington: Indiana University Press. xii, 206 p. Bibliography and Index. ISBN: 9-780-25305-303-9.

Explores the tensions between Islam and the global popularity of hip-hop, including attempts by the hip-hop *ummah*, or community, to draw from the struggle of African Americans to articulate the human rights abuses Muslims face. Explores state management of hip-hop culture and how Muslim hip-hoppers are attempting to "Islamize" the genre's performers and jargon to bring the music more in line with religious requirements, which may be even more fraught for female artists who struggle with who has the right to speak for Muslim women. Also investigates the vibrant underground hip-hop culture that exists online.

335. **Negus, Keith, and Pete Astor**. 2015. "Songwriters and Song Lyrics: Architecture, Ambiguity, and Repetition." *Popular Music* 34(2): 226–244. ISSN: 0261-1430.

Argues for an architectural approach to the popular song, a perspective that treats songwriters as architects rather than romantically inspired expressive artists. Offers implications that listeners are indeed dancing and thinking about architecture when responding to popular songs, and it is an awareness of this that informs the practices of songwriters. The use of the term "architecture" is intended to mean those recognizable characteristics of songs that exist as enduring qualities regardless of a particular performance, recording, or version.

336. **Negus, Keith**. 2019. "Nation-States, Transnational Corporations, and Cosmopolitans in the Global Popular Music Economy." *Global Media and China* [Special Issue: *Asian Popular Music: Transnationality and Globalization*] 4(4): 403–418. ISSN: 2059-4364.

Addresses changing debates about globalization in the growth of digital media. Emphasizes how popular music is shaped by enduring tensions between nation-state attempts to control territorial borders, the power of transnational corporations aiming to operate across these borders, and emergent cosmopolitan practices that offer a cultural challenge to these borders. Outlines how popular music is influenced by physical place. Also highlights the cultural and political importance of the nation-state for understanding the context within which musical creativity occurs.

337. **Neumeir, Beate, ed**. 2009. *Dichotonies: Gender and Music*. Series: *American Studies (Munich, Germany); v. 181*. Heidelberg: Universitätsverlag Winter. 372 p. Illustrations and Music Examples. ISBN: 9-783-82537-326-9.

A compilation of essays that stem from papers presented at the Klang Körper conference held in Cologne, Germany, in June 2008. Contains essays by international scholars from the fields of gender studies, cultural theory, and music studies. Compiled essays cover a wide range of music genres and theoretical perspectives regarding the concept of gender and sexuality pervading in musical production and performance as well as consumption. Music genres covered include classical, popular music gangsta rap, and liederspiel.

338. **Novak, David**. 2011. "The Sublime Frequencies of New Old Media." *Public Culture* 23(3): 603–634. ISSN: 0899-2363.

Describes a recent intervention into the circulation of "world music," which has been associated since the 1950s with the academic field of ethnomusicology and since the 1980s with the music industry categories of "world music" and "world beat." Argues that both contexts have been substantially transformed in recent years by an underground distribution of sound recordings in North America. Further argues that as world music becomes part of online culture, its new leadership has realigned against hegemonic frameworks of intellectual property. This new world music, sometimes called "World Music 2.0," disengages from earlier collaborations (e.g., Paul Simon, Peter Gabriel, and David Byrne) and hybrid genres of world music in the late 1980s and 1990s that provoked a broad scholarly critique of its production and marketing as a thinly vested form of musical imperialism.

339. **O'Brien, Lucy**. 2020. *She Bop: The Definitive History of Women in Popular Music, revised edition*. London: Jawbone Press. 420 p. Illustrations, Discography, Bibliography, and Index. ISBN: 9-781-91103-667-8.

Draws on numerous original interviews with female artists and women working behind the scenes in A&R, marketing, music publishing, and production. Presents a history of women in popular music from the 1920s to contemporary times. Interviews stem from artists such as Eartha Kitt and Nina Simone to Debbie Harry and Beyoncé. Charts out how women have negotiated "old boy" power networks to be seen to get their music heard. Also incorporates information on more contemporary artists such as Lizzo, Billie Eilish, and many others.

340. **Osumare, Halifu**. 2001. "Beat Streets in the Global Hood: Connective Marginalities of the Hip-Hop Globe." *Journal of American & Comparative Cultures* 24(1/2): 171–181. ISSN: 1537-4726.

Provides a historical and critical study of what can be described as "global hip-hop." Observes that rap music has spread around the world since the 1970s and has created a global hip-hop youth culture. Explores a variety of issues relating to marginalization. Topics addressed include rap music, hip-hop culture, dance parties, popular culture, and internationalization.

341. **Pabón-Colón, Jessica N**. 2018. *Graffiti Grrlz: Performing Feminism in the Hip-Hop Diaspora*. New York: New York University Press. xii, 263 p. Illustrations, Portraits, Bibliography, and Index. ISBN: 9-781-47989-593-9.

Introduces and focuses on the world of women graffiti artists. Draws on the lives of numerous women in twenty-three countries. Argues that graffiti art is an unrecognized but crucial space for the performance of feminism. Demonstrates how it builds communities of artists, reconceptualizes the hip-hop masculinity of these spaces, and rejects notions of girl power.

342.   **Palmer, Landon**. 2020. *Rock Star/Movie Star: Power and Performance in Cinematic Rock Stardom*. Series: *Oxford Music/Media*. New York: Oxford University Press. 290 p. Illustrations, Bibliography, and Index. ISBN: 9-780-19088-840-2.

Examines the casting of rock stars from Elvis Presley to Madonna. Offers a perspective on the role of stardom within the convergence of media industries. Provides archival resources to demonstrate how rock stars have often proven themselves to be prominent film workers, exploring this terrain of platform old and new.

343.   **Palmer, Roy**. 2008. *The Sound of History: Songs and Social Comment*. Previously published, Oxford & New York: Oxford University Press, 1988. Oxford & New York: Farber & Farber. xx, 361 p. Illustrations, Music Examples, Discography, Bibliography, and Index.

Presents a survey, anthology, and social history of popular song. Provides discussions of popular song that tell us of life's pleasures and pains from the cradle to the grave, work and play, sports, sex, loving and leaving, and so forth.

344.   **Partridge, Christopher H**. 2015. *Mortality and Music: Popular Music and the Awareness of Death*. Series: *Bloomsbury Studies in Religion and Popular Music*. London: Bloomsbury. vii, 222 p. Bibliography and Index. ISBN: 9-781-47253-451-4.

Draws on a range of bands and genres and examines the ways in which popular music has responded to our awareness of inevitability of death and the anxiety it can evoke. Explores bereavement, depression, suicide, violence, gore, and fans' responses to the deaths of musicians. Argues for the social and cultural significance of popular music's treatment of mortality and existence.

345.   **Pauwke, Berkers, and Julien Schaap**. 2018. *Gender Inequality in Metal Music Production*. Series: *Emerald Studies in Metal Music and Culture*. Bingley: Emerald. xx, 149 p. Illustrations, Maps, Bibliography, and Index. ISBN: 9-781-78714-674-7.

Examines how for over four decades scholars have been investigating male dominance both symbolically and numerically within popular music. Offers a systematic and larger scale overview of gender inequality in metal music production and how many women compared to men are participating in metal bands and what the causes are for differences in participation.

346.   **Peddie, Ian, ed**. 2017. *The Resisting Muse: Popular Music and Social Protest*. Series: *Ashgate Popular and Folk Music Series*. Previously published, Aldershot &

Burlington: Ashgate, 2006. London: Taylor and Francis. xxiv, 228 p. Illustrations, Bibliography, and Index. ISBN: 0-75465-113-4.

A compilation of essays that examine the various ways in which popular music has been deployed as anti-establishment and how such opposition both influences and responds to the music produced. Examines the forms of music and aims of social protest music, which are contingent upon the audience's ability to invest the music with the appropriate political meaning. Artists, genres, theses, and organizations covered include Aboriginal rights and music; Bauhaus, Black Sabbath; Billy Bragg; Bono; cassette culture; The Capitol Steps; class; The Cure; DJ Spooky; drum and bass; Eminem, Farm Aid; Foxy Brown; folk; Goldie; gothicism; Woody Guthrie; heavy metal; hip-hop; independent/home publishing; Iron Maiden; Live Aid; Marilyn Manson; Bob Marley; MC Eiht; Minor Thread; Motown; Queen Latifah; race; rap; Rastafarianism; reggae; The Roots; Diana Ross; Rush; Salt-n-Pepa; 7 Seconds; Roxanne Shanté; Siouxsie and the Banshees; The Sisters of Mercy; Michelle Shocked; Bessie Smith; straight edge, Sunrize Band; Bunny Wailer; Wilco; Bart Willoughby; Wirrinyga Band; and zines.

347. **Peddie, Ian**. 2011. *Popular Music and Human Rights: Two-Volume Set*. Series: *Ashgate Popular and Folk Music Series; Popular Music and Human Rights*. Farnham: Ashgate. Two Volumes (220 p. & 220 p.). Discography, Bibliography, and Index. 9-781-40943-758-1.

Argues that popular music has long understood that if human rights are at all attainable, they involve a struggle without end. Moreover, the rights to imagine individual will, the right to some form of self-determination, and the right to self-legislation have long been at the forefront of popular music's approach to human rights. The two-volume set includes Volume I. British and American Music and Volume II. World Music. Topics covered are varied and include punk music; globalization; blues; women's and human rights; Bruce Springsteen; and others.

348. **Perchard, Tom, ed**. 2009. *From Soul to Hip-Hop*. London: Routledge. 568 p. Bibliography and Index. ISBN: 9-781-31509-381-9.

A compilation of essays that address some of the most visible, durable, and influential of African American musical styles as they developed from the mid-1960s into the twenty-first century. The volume explores soul, funk, pop, rhythm and blues, and hip-hop both singly and in their many convergences and in writings that have often become regarded as landmarks in Black scholarship. Compiled essays employ a wide range of methodologies and document important and emergent trends in the study of these styles as they have spread around the world.

349. **Peterson, James B**. 2017. *Hip-Hop Headphones: A Scholar's Critical Playlist*. New York: Bloomsbury. x, 286 p. Illustrations, Bibliography, and Index. ISBN: 9-781-50130-825-3.

Features definitions, lectures, academic essays, and other scholarly discussions and resources to document the scholarship of Dr. James B. Peterson, founder of Hip-Hop Scholars, an organization devoted to developing the educational potential of hip-hop. Defines hip-hop from multidisciplinary approaches that embrace the elemental forms of hip-hop culture.

350.   **Peterson, Marina**. 2016. "Emergent Sound: Labor, Materiality, and Nonrepresentational Music." *Popular Music and Society* 39(3) [Special Issue: *The Worlds of Popular Music*]: 317–331. ISSN: 0300-7766.

Considers what it would mean to rethink music as emergent, to think of ephemerality in relation to potentiality. Focuses on the multidimensional relationship between sounds and labor and takes up sound of work, the circulation of sound across mediums of liveliness and mediation during the 1940s recording bans, and the noisy and contradictory silences of these bans, especially those working with folk musicians who were often in solidarity with labor and continue to record.

351.   **Phillipov, Michelle**. 2012. *Death Metal and Music Criticism: Analysis at the Limits*. Lanham: Rowman & Littlefield. 178 p. Bibliography and Index. ISBN: 9-780-73916-459-4.

Contextualizes the discussion of death metal via substantial overview of popular music studies as a field. Highlights how the premium placed on political engagements in popular music studies not only circumscribes an understanding of the complexity and specification of death metal but other musical styles as well. Offers an analysis of death metal's sonic and lyrical extremity and shows how violence and aggression can be figured as sites of pleasure and play in death metal.

352.   **Pirker, Eva U., and Judith Rahn, eds**. 2023. *Afrofuturism's Transnational Trajectories: Resistant Imaginaries Between Margins and Mainstream*. New York: Routledge. 132 p. Illustrations, Bibliography, and Index. ISBN: 9-781-03241-498-0.

A collection of essays that were originally published as a special issue in the journal *Critical Studies in Media Communication*. Essays contextualize Afrofuturism's diverse approaches in the past and present through investigations into overlapping horizons between Afrofuturist agendas and other intellectual or artistic movements that include Pan-Africanism, debates about civil rights, decolonial debates, and transnational modernisms. Essays also explore Afrofuturist approaches in the twenty-first century across media cultures and from a transcultural perspective.

353.   **Plasketes, George**. 2016. *B-Side, Undercurrents and Overtones: Peripheries to Popular Music, 1960 to the Present*. Series: *Ashgate Popular and Folk Music Series*. Previously published, Burlington: Ashgate, 2009. Abingdon, Oxon & New York: Routledge. xii, 209 p. Bibliography and Index. ISBN: 9-781-13825-768-9.

Adapts the iconic "A-Side/B-Side," dichotomy from the 45 rpm records for use as a unique conceptual, critical, historical, and cultural framework for exploring and theorizing together a variety of popular music and media texts. Topics include Terry Melcher surf music of the 1960s; Geffen records, Neil Young; music and movie musicality; Ry Cooder; world music; Paul Simon's *Graceland*; pop rock sitcom cameo; and others.

354.   **Plastino, Goffredo, ed**. 2003. *Mediterranean Mosaic: Popular Music and Global Sounds*. New York: Routledge. viii, 336 p. Illustrations, Discography, Bibliography, and Index. ISBN: 9-780-41593-655-2.

An edited volume that demonstrates the Mediterranean region's rich history of cross-cultural interactions. The essays compile scholarly research that offer innovative approaches to the multicultural music traditions of the region. The topics covered include klapa singing, Spanish folk and pop music, Moroccan world beat, pop-rai local and globalization, Tunisian reinterpretation of ma'luf, Spanish tinge in Egyptian music, Israeli pop music, Akdeniz scene, Greek and Croatian pop music traditions, musica Mediterranea in Italy, and so forth.

355.   **Poulakis, Nick, ed**. 2022. "Music, Documentaries, and Globalization From World Music to World Cinema." *Popular Music Research Today-Revista Online de Divulgación Musicologica* 4(2): 7–21. ISSN: 2659-6482.

Deals with the relationship between sound and image as expressed in the cinematic genre of music documentary. Explores the way in which musical cultures are expressed audiovisually through filmic representation of music performances, artists, and groups. Applies a critical approach and examines how the films *Buena Vista Social Club* (1999) and *Café de los Maestros* (2008) became vehicles to investigate images and sounds of music in everyday life with an emphasis on their creation and interpretation procedures.

356.   **Powers, Devon**. 2016. "Popular Music Studies." In *International Encyclopedia of Communication Theory and Philosophy*, Klaus B. Jensen, and Robert T. Craig, eds. Series: *Wiley-Blackwell-ICA International Encyclopedia of Communication*. Maiden: John Wiley & Sons. Four Volumes. Bibliography and Index. ISBN: 9-781-11876-680-4.

Argues that to trace the connections between popular music studies and communication research is to recognize the nebulous, interdisciplinary, and often uncertain character of both fields of study. Further argues that tracing their linkage requires thinking about the place of music in several adjacent fields—sociology, psychology, journalism, and American studies, as well as how communication has conceived of popular media such as television, film, and radio. Provides some revelations that arise from considering popular music studies and communication research, what popular music studies has offered, and so forth.

357.   **Prato, Greg**. 2018. *The Yacht Book: The Oral History of the Soft, Smooth Sounds of the 70s and 80s*. London: Jawbone Press. 278 p. Illustrations and [16 p] of plates. ISBN: 9-781-91103-629-6.

Defines yacht rock as popular music played while carousing aboard a yacht in the 1970s and 1980s. Provides a historical and critical study of rock music in the 1970s and 1980s and discusses the music of artists whose songs and albums fall under the category of yacht rock. Artists discussed and interviewed include Fleetwood Mac, the Eagles, the Doobie Brothers, Toto, and others.

358. **Prendergast, Mark J.** 2003. *The Ambient Century: From Mahler to Moby: The Evolution of Sound in the Electronic Age.* London: Bloomsbury. xii, 498 p. Illustrations, [16 p.] of plates, Discographies, Bibliography, and Index. ISBN: 0-74754-213-9.

Expands the classical musical horizons of Gustav Mahler, Eric Satire, and Claude Debussy to the revolutions in electronic music initiated by Karl Stockhausen and John Cage, the Indian-influenced minimalism of Philip Glass, and Terry Riley and Brian Eno. Also covers the epoch-defining rock music of the Beatles and Jimi Hendrix and the electronic creations of Kraftwerk, Goldie, and Trance. Discusses how drift technology, minimalism, the rock era, and techno is earthed by the development of ambient sounds. Explores electronics, new ideas, and mass consumption aided in the development of ambient as the "classical music" of the future.

359. **Prior, Nick.** 2012. "Digital Formations of Popular Music." *Réseaux* 2(172): 66–90. ISSN: 0751-7971.

Presents a broad attempt to take stock of some of the challenges, dilemmas, and issues sparked by a focus on digital formation in music where *formations* are loosely configured amalgamations of discursive, technical, and material. Discusses the totalizing styles of rock, folk, and jazz as "meta-genres" that retain a certain solidarity on the map of popular music.

360. **Prior, Nick.** 2013. "Bourdieu and the Sociology of Music Consumption: A Critical Assessment of Recent Developments." *Sociology Compass* 7(3): 181–193. ISSN: 1751-9020.

Considers the impact of Pierre Bourdieu's ideas on the sociology of music, the debate sparked in its wake, and the attempt at "post-Bourdieusian" sociology. Also considers to what extent Bourdieu's claims about social stratification and music consumption are still relevant and whether they are sophisticated enough to deal with the specific ways that we interact with musical form.

361. **Przybylski, Liz.** 2023. *Sonic Sovereignty: Hip-Hop, Indigeneity, and Shifting Popular Music Mainstreams.* Series: *Postmillennial Pop.* New York: New York University Press. 336 p. Illustrations, Bibliography, and Index. ISBN: 9-781-47981-691-0.

Offers a frame to listen for the effects of expressive culture in the world. Experiments with possibilities of listening in relation to time and perspectives. Reflects across time and vantage point so that readers can listen backwards and forwards into possible futures.

362. **Purcell, Natalie J.** 2003. *Death Metal Music: The Passion and Politics of a Subculture.* Jefferson: McFarland. 242 p. Photographs, Appendices, Bibliography, and Index. ISBN: 9-780-78641-585-4.

Investigates the demographic trends, attitudes, philosophical beliefs, ethical systems, and behavioral patterns within the death metal scene. Situates death metal in the subculture and lends insight into the psychological and social functions of many forbidden and illicit entertainment forms. Includes analysis and interviews of rock stars, radio hosts, and fans.

363.   **Purdy, Stephen**. 2021. *Flop Musical of the Twenty-First Century: Part I: Creatives.* Abingdon, Oxon: Routledge. xii, 293 p. Illustrations, Bibliography, and Index. ISBN: 9-780-36776-112-7.

Offers a historical narrative of a group of musicals that cost millions and had spectacular potential but bombed. Examines the production and focuses on several infallible theater creatives. Grounds the discussions by examining what the legendary creators of *Les Misérables*, pop superstar Elton John, Julie Taymour, and others have in common besides being inspired storytellers of iconic Broadway musicals.

364.   **Qirko, Hector**. 2014. "Consumer Authentication of Popular Music in the Global Postmodern." *Popular Music and Society* 37(3): 219–312. ISSN: 0300-7766.

Explores the role that consumers play in determining if music and the artists who produce it belong in a particular popular music genre that is accomplished socially and musically. Explores the effects of globalization and postmodernity on popular music authentication through analysis of print and web consumer responses to two late 1990s recordings of Marc Ribot y Cubanos Postizos and Bueno Vista Social Club. Suggests that even in global postmodern popular music, authentication is likely to remain important to consumers in the formation and maintenance of group identity.

365.   **Quirk, Tim, and Jason Toynbee**. 2005. "Going Through the Motion: Popular Music Performance in Journalism and in Academic Discourse." *Popular Music* 24(3) [Special Issue: *These Magic Moments*]: 399–413. ISSN: 0261-1430.

Argues that popular music performance raises important questions about music making as process, and these questions are addressed through dealing with a further issue relating to the difference between music journalism and academic discourse on music. Examines the film of The Who playing at the Isle of Wight in 1970 and demonstrates how Pete Townsend's performance moves through a cycle of incompetence to the extraordinary paradoxically formulaic performance that prompts sincerity on the part of Townsend.

366.   **Radano, Ronaldo, and Tejumola Olaniyan, eds**. 2016. *Audible Empire: Music, Global Politics, Critique*. Series: *Refiguring American Music*. Durham: Duke University Press. xi, 418 p. Illustrations, Bibliography, and Index. ISBN: 9-780-82235-986-9.

An edited volume of essays that reconsiders the processes and mechanisms of empire. Shows how musical practice has been crucial to its spread around the world. The essays cover a large number of genres, times, politics, and geographies.

Topics include the effective relationships between jazz and cigarettes in China, the sonic language of the United States–Mexico border, the critiques of post-9/11 United States empires by desi rappers, and the role of tonality in the colonization of Africa. In addition, whether focusing on Argentine tango, theorizing anti-colonist sound, or reexamining the music industry of post-apartheid, the essays show how Audible has been a central component in the creation of imperialist notions of reason, modernity, and culture.

367. **Rae, Casey.** 2019. *William S. Burroughs and the Cult of Rock 'n' Roll.* Austin: University of Texas Press. 304 p. Bibliography and Index. ISBN: 9-781-47731-866-9.

Offers insight into how William S. Burroughs—fictionist, essayist, and author of *Naked Lunch*—influenced music's counterculture. Reveals the transformations in music history that can be traced to Burroughs. Discusses Burroughs' rise to fame among many musicians of the 1960s, 1970s, and 1980s when it became a rite of passage to hang out with Burroughs or to experiment with his cut-up techniques for producing lyrics as the Beatles and Radiohead did. Also discusses Burroughs' relationship with other musicians such as David Bowie, Patti Smith, and Lou Reed.

368. **Rambarran, Shara.** 2021. *Virtual Music: Sound, Music, and Image in the Digital Era.* London: Bloomsbury. x, 238 p. Illustrations, Bibliography, and Index. ISBN. 9-781-50133-360-6.

Explores the interactive relationship of sound, music, and image and its users. Offers a survey of areas involving the historical, technological, and creative practices of virtual music, including its connection with creators, musicians, performers, audiences, and consumers. Examines the innovation surrounding music and illustrates key artists such as Grace Jones and The Weeknd; creators such as King Tubby, Kraftwerk, Mad Villain, and Danger Mouse; audiovisuals in video games and performers such as Cuphead and Gorillaz; and audiences and consumers that contribute to making the musical experience a phenomenon.

369. **Redhead, Steve, Derek Wynne, and Justin O'Connor.** 1997. *The Club Cultures Reader: Readings in Popular Culture.* Oxford: Blackwell. ix, 251 p. Illustrations, [16 p.] of plates, Bibliography, and Index. ISBN: 0-63119-786-9.

Combines description and theory in a pedagogical framework of popular cultural studies. Incorporates a collection of readings on contemporary youth cultures and youth music. Covers rave, disco, and house to northern soul and much more and distinguishes popular cultural studies from some aspects of the theoretical work of contemporary cultural studies. Includes ethnographic research associated with contemporary cultural traditions of youth and popular culture that is consolidated, extended, and applied to contemporary culture in the 1990s.

370. **Regev, Motti.** 2019. "Pop-Rock, Cultural Cosmopolitanism and the Global Cultural Market of Youth Identities." *Youth and Globalization* 1(1): 88–106. ISSN: 2589-5737.

Offers a sociological framework for understanding the function of pop-rock music and its many genres, styles, and related phenomena through the years of influencing cosmopolitan youth identities and cultural cosmopolitanism in general. Develops the notion of a cultural market for youth identities created by the structural emergence of "youth" as an age-based social category. Defines mainstream pop as an emerging potpourri of genres ranging from pop, rock, electronica, rhythm and blues, and hip-hop to big band and jazz.

371.   **Reitsamer, Rosa, and Wolfgang Fichna, eds**. 2011. *They Say I Am Different . . . Popularusik, Szenen und ihre Akteure-innen (They Say I Am Different . . . Popular Music, Scenes, and Their Actors)*. Vienna: Löcker-Verlag. German text. 323 p. Illustrations, Bibliography, and Index. ISBN: 9-783-85409-570-5.

An edited volume of essays that consider how the debate about music scenes, which was initially limited to the Anglophone world, has become significantly international. The volume covers a broad spectrum both geographically and thematically intended to promote discussions about popular music and youth culture. Combines theoretical analysis and empirical studies on local, transnational, and virtual music scenes from the fields of sociology, critical studies, history, and media studies. Expands the established perspectives of popular music research by discussing the changed framework conditions for the formation and existence of music scenes.

372.   **Reynolds, Simon, and Joy Press**. 1996. *The Sex Revolts: Gender, Rebellion, and Rock 'n' Roll*. Cambridge: Harvard University Press. xvii, 410 p. Bibliography and Index. ISBN: 9-780-67480-273-5.

Deals with feminism and music. Considers rock rebellion using gender. Captures the paradox of rock music that is often most thrilling when it is most misogynist and macho. Discusses groups and individuals such as the Rolling Stones, Sex Pistols, the Clash, Public Enemy, and U2, as well as Led Zeppelin, Jim Morrison, Nick Cave, Pink Floyd, Jimi Hendrix, Brian Eno, My Bloody Valentine, Kate Bush, Grace Jones, Joni Mitchell, the Slits, Riot Grrrls, PJ Harvey, Janis Joplin, Courtney Love, Miles Davis, and many others.

373.   **Rice, Timothy, and Dave Wilson**. 2022. "Creating a Global Music History." *Asian-European Music Research Journal* 10: 1–6. ISSN: 2701-2689.

Considers concepts and discourses for global music history. Argues that all global music histories will of necessity be written from some position on the globe, not from "outer space." Outlines pedagogical goals for introducing music students to the full range of human music making in present times.

374.   **Richardson, John, ed**. 2017. *An Eye for Music: Popular Music and the Audiovisual Surreal*. Series. *Oxford Music/Media Series*. Oxford & New York: Oxford University Press. xi, 323 p. Illustrations, Music Examples, Bibliography, and Index. ISBN: 9-780-19536-736-2.

Discusses the tendencies in popular and audiovisual expression since the 1990s that resemble those found in historical surrealism. Applies several theoretical notions to emerging audiovisual practices including independent cinema, live performances of popular music, cinematic opera, and Internet practices such as syncing and audiovisual mashup. Musicians discussed include Gorillaz, Philip Glass, KT Tunstall, and Sigur Ros. Directors and films discussed include Richard Lanklastes's *Walking Line*; Michael Gondry's *Be Kind Rewind*; Sally Potter's *Yes*; and Tsai Ming-Liang's *The Wayward Cloud*.

375.   **Rietveld, Hilegonda C**. 1998. *This Is Our House: House Music, Cultural Spaces, and Technology*. Series: *Popular Cultural Studies, 13*. Aldershot & Brookfield: Ashgate. ix, 276 p. Discography, Videography, Bibliography, and Index. ISBN: 1-85742-242-2.

Examines how house music has shaped the sound of popular music in the late 1980s and early 1990s. Covers topics from underground dance events to Top of the Pops. Traces the aesthetic and formalistic style and attitude of house music.

376.   **Robertson, Roland**. 1992. *Globalization: Social Theory and Global Culture*. Series: *Theory, Culture, & Society*. London: SAGE. x, 211 p. Bibliography and Index. ISBN: 0-80398-187-2.

Argues that the real nature of globalization is observed while peripheral concerns such as minute economic analysis are overstated. Presents an alternative view that incorporates the economic and cultural aspects of the global scene and in the process connects general social structures to historical developments in the modern world. Offers a distinct cultural flow on the social theory of the contemporary world.

377.   **Robinson, Deanna C., Elizabeth Buck, Marlene Cuthbent, Hanna Adoni, and the International Communication & Youth Consortium**. 1991. *Music at the Margins: Popular Music and Cultural Diversity*. Series: *Communication and Human Values*. Newbury Park: Sage Publications. xiv, 312 p. Bibliography and Index. ISBN: 0-80393-192-1.

A critical study that offers a determination as to whether there is a growing homogenization of the world's popular music or whether there is a combining and/or ever-increasing diversity of song styles and forms. Employing theoretical approaches, the volume focuses on how the process of popular music production is perceived by local musicians. Also considers the debate surrounding popular music's spread, testing a more conventional "cultural imperialism" hypothesis as based on empirical findings from study by the International Communication & Youth Consortium.

378.   **Rodriguez, Carlos A**. 2004. *Bridging the Gap: Popular Music and Music Education*. Lanham: Lexington Books. ix, 247 p. Illustrations, Music Examples, and Bibliography. ISBN: 9-781-56545-158-2.

A collection of essays that address important issues dealing with popular music and music education. They include discussions of many possible definitions of popular music, information on how popular musicians learn, and specific examples of educational programs that incorporate popular, as well as offering suggestions on how to choose high-quality repertoire.

379.   **Rogers, Jim**. 2013. *The Death and Life of the Music Industry in the Digital Age*. New York: Bloomsbury. 236 p. Bibliography and Index. ISBN: 9-781-78093-160-9.

Challenges the conventional wisdom that the Internet is killing the music industry. Demonstrates how technological innovations and transnational music companies have formulated response strategies to negate the harmful effects of the Internet. Documents how the radical transformative potential of the Internet is being suppressed by legal organizational innovations, and more.

380.   **Rollefson, J. Griffith, Warrick Moses, Jason Ng, Patrick Marks, Steve Gamble, and Ophelia McCabe**. 2023. "Networking Global Hip-Hop Knowledges: The CIPHER Method." *Ethnomusicology* 67(3): 430–464. ISSN: 0014-1836.

Comprised of a global hip-hop knowledge mapping project using ethnographic, digital, and arts research methods to comprehend the emergences and flows of the culture's deeply local but immanently global intertextualities. Offers a network and develops ideas from six of CIPHER's global hip-hop researchers, elaborating the project in method as well as in theory. Models a community of engaged CIPHER methods of tracking thematic, conceptual, and archetypal relationships and presents preliminary findings of four interrelated case studies.

381.   **Rovira, James, ed**. 2023. *Women in Rock, Women in Romanticism: The Emancipation of the Female Will*. Series: *Routledge Interdisciplinary Perspectives on Literature*. New York: Routledge. 234 p. Illustrations, Bibliography, and Index. ISBN: 9-781-03206-984-5.

A collection of essays that explore the interrelationships between contemporary female musicians and eighteenth- and nineteenth-century art, music, and literature. Essays explore the music and videos of contemporary musicians, including Erykah Badu, Beyoncé, the Carters, Hélène Cioux, Missy Elliot, the Indigo Girls, Janet Jackson, Janis Joplin, Natalie Merchant, Joni Mitchell, Janelle Monaé, Alanis Morissette, Siouxie Sioux, Patti Smith, St. Vincent (Annie Clark), and Alice Walker, through the lenses of pastoral themes, Afrofuturism, gothic influences, female gothic perspectives, and literary connections.

382.   **Rovner, Lisa, director**. 2021. *Sisters With Transistors*. London: Media Films. DVD. 85 Minutes. OCLC Number: 1-31408-426-7.

An important documentary that informs research in popular music, contemporary music, women and gender, electronic/digital, film, and sound studies. Narrated by Laurie Anderson, the film conveys the story of electronic music female pioneers, composers who embraced machines in their liberating technologies to transform how we produce and listen to music in contemporary times. Provides and maps out a new history of electronic music through women, including Clara Rockmore, Daphne Oram, Bebe Baron, Pauline Oliveros, Delia

Derbyshire, Maryanne Amacher, Eliane Radique, Suzannr Ciani, Wendy Carlos, and Laurie Spiegel, whose radical experimentation with machines redefined the boundaries of music.

383. **Rowe, David**. 1995. *Popular Cultures: Rock Music, Sports, and the Politics of Pleasure*. Series: *Media, Culture and Society Series*. London: SAGE. 184 p. Bibliography and Index. ISBN: 0-80397-700-X.

Focuses on two major forms of popular culture: rock music and sports. Outlines key issues involved in the understanding of the diverse aspects of popular culture. Examines how rock music and sports encapsulate the contradictory elements of popular culture, the tensions between the commercial manufacture and marketing of popular products, and their potential for articulating a resistive independence. Demonstrates that popular culture cannot be adequately understood without a clear grasp of the ways in which economic, ideology, and culture interrelate.

384. **Rowe, Paula**. 2018. *Heavy Metal Youth Identities: Researching the Musical Empowerment of Youth Transitions and Psychosocial Wellbeing*. Series: *Emerald Studies in Metal Music and Culture*. Bingley: Emerald. 183 p. Bibliography and Index. ISBN: 9-781-78756-849-5.

Draws on interviews with metal youth and examines why they were first attracted to metal during high school. Also examines how metal youth used metal music and identities as coping strategies and the ways their metal affiliations took on further significance for helping them make important decisions about what to do with their lives post-school.

385. **Roy, Elodie, and Eva M. Rodriguez, eds**. 2022. *Phonographic Encounters: Mapping Transnational Cultures of Sound, 1890–1945*. Series: *Cultural Study of Popular Music*. New York & London: Routledge. xiv, 268 p. Illustrations, Portraits, Bibliography, and Index. ISBN: 9-780-36743-921-7.

A cross-disciplinary collection of essays that illuminate the history of early phonography from a transnational perspective. Provides case studies from China, Australia, United States, Latin America, Sweden, Germany, Spain, Portugal, France, and Italy. Explores moments of interaction and encounter as well as tensions between local and global understandings of recording technologies. Draws on archival sources often previously unavailable in English and moves beyond Western-centric narratives of early phonography and beyond the strict confines of the recording industry.

386. **Rudden, Patricia S**. 2007. *Singing for Themselves: Essays on Women in Popular Music*. Newcastle: Cambridge Scholars. ix, 280 p. Bibliography. ISBN: 9-781-84718-345-3.

A compilation of essays that examine various artists and movements that have come to new conclusions about the ways in which female artists have contributed to the past decades of pop, rock, blues, and punk. The essays examine such major artists as Etta James, Laura Nyro, Patti Smith, Ferron, Björk, and Melissa

Etheridge and suggest new ways to view music that is already part of our culture. Other essays focus on groups as Indigo Girls, Dixie Chicks, and Destiny's
Child to stress that the girl groups' tradition is still alive and well but with additional new dimensions. Also included is a three-essay section on Joan Jett and
the Riot Grrrls phenomenon that sheds new light on their implications for artistic expression. Also includes an annotated bibliography of academic writing on
women in rock.

387.   **Russell, Dave**. 1993. "The Social History of Popular Music: A Label Without a
        Cause." *Popular Music* 12(2): 139–154. ISSN: 0261-1430.

        A review of some of the recent developments within the social history of popular
        music and as a stimulus for further work and argument. Focuses on and suggests
        that the study of popular music may be relevant to the study both in and of
        other countries and of other historical periods. Suggests that "popular" music is
        broadly defined in the study to accommodate both aesthetic and social usages
        of the term, driven by interests and possibly influenced by the methodological
        imperatives of social history.

388.   **Rutten, P. 1991**. "Popular Music on the National and International Markets."
        Cultural Studies 5(3): 294–305. ISSN: 0950-2386.

        An early study that focuses on how one of the most notable developments in the
        world's popular music in the postwar era has been the growing internationaliza-
        tion of its sound. Examines how those musical genres that have left the strongest
        mark on popular music in the world have originated in the United States and
        to a lesser extent the United Kingdom. Presents a historical conversation and
        analysis of the developments of genres such as rock 'n' roll, funk, disco, rap, hip-
        hop, and house in the United States and "beat" and punk music in the United
        Kingdom, which have had a substantial influence on the continental Western
        European music scene. Traces the prominent position of the United States as a
        global cultural trendsetter, and so forth.

389.   **Sadler, D**. 1997. "The Global Music Business as an Information Industry: Rein-
        terpreting Economies of Culture." *Environment and Planning A: Economy and
        Space* 29(1): 919–936. ISSN: 0308-518X.

        Argues that the music business should be regarded as an activity trading in
        information. Offers a review of key themes in the conceptualization of the music
        industry within economic tradition and tensions between creativity and com-
        merce between global and local processes, and the characterization of the indus-
        try in terms of the flexible specialization and reflexive accumulations.

390.   **Samson, Guillaume**. 2013. "Musical Transculturations and Identitarian Dynam-
        ics." *L'Homme* 3: 215–235. ISSN: 0439-4216.

        Investigates whether the concept of creolization applies to music. Creolization is
        presented as potentially useful to study interdependence between music creation
        processes specific to situations of cultural change resulting from internal forces,

factors, and mechanisms defining Creole identity that accompany or justify such processes. Discussion topics include popular styles such as jazz, salsa, soul, funk, and others.

391. Sanneh, Kelefa. 2021. *Major Labels: A History of Popular Music in Seven Genres*. New York: Penguin. xx, 476 p. Bibliography and Index. ISBN: 9-780-52555-959-7.

Presents the entire history of popular music over the fifty years, traced through the big genres that have defined and dominated it, including rock, country, punk, rhythm and blues, dance, and hip-hop. Weaves music's evolution from Black Sabbath to Black Friday to Beyoncé and beyond as a popular form, a huge and economic force, and an essential component to our identities.

392. Sardinha, João, and Richardo Campos, eds. 2016. *Transglobal Sounds: Music, Youth, and Migration*. London: Bloomsbury. x, 237 p. Bibliography and Index. ISBN: 9-781-50131-196-3.

A compilation of essays and case studies that seek to articulate between musical nationalism and a sense of place. The essays present a transnational, comparative, and multi-level approach to the relationship between youth, migration, and music, as well as the aesthetic intersection between the local and the global and between agency and identity. They concentrate on migrant youth and the impact of music in diaspora settings and on the lives of individuals and collectives engaging with broader questions of how new modes of identification are born out of the social, cultural, historical, and political interfaces between youth, migration, and music.

393. Scanlan, John. 2022. *Rock 'n' Roll Plays Itself: A Screen History*. London: Reaktion Book, distributor, Chicago: University of Chicago Press. 256 p. Illustrations, Music Examples, Bibliography, and Index. ISBN: 9-781-78914-572-4.

Explores rock's relationship with the moving image over seven decades in cinema, television, music video, advertising, and YouTube. Shows how rock music was exploited, how it inspired film pioneers, and the film transformations it caused over more than half a century. Examines rock from Elvis Presley to David Bowie, from Scorpio Rising to the films of Scorsese and DIY documentarists as Don Letts, conveying the story of rock from birth to old age through its on-screen life.

394. Schleifer, Ronald. 2013. *Modernism and Popular Music*. Cambridge & New York: Cambridge University Press. xx, 233 p. Illustrations, Bibliography, and Index. ISBN: 9-781-10700-505-1.

Argues that traditionally ideas about twentieth-century "modernism," whether focused on literature, music, or the visual arts, have made a distinction between "high art" and the "popular" arts of best-selling fiction, jazz, and other forms of popular music and commercial art. Demonstrates how George Gershwin, Cole Porter, Thomas "Fats" Waller, and Billie Holiday can be considered as artistic expression equal to those of the traditional high art practices in music and literature. Combines details to the language and aesthetics of popular music with an examination of its early twentieth-century performance dissemination through the new technology of radio and phonograph. Explores the "popularity" of pop music in order to reconsider received and seemingly self-evident truths about the differences between high art and popular art and about twentieth-century modernism altogether.

395.   **Schloss, Joseph G., and Jeff Chang**. 2014. *Making Beats: The Art of Sample-Based Hip-Hop, 2nd ed.* Series: *Music/Culture.* Middletown: Wesleyan University Press. 273 p. Bibliography and Index. ISBN: 9-780-81957-481-7.

A study and research conducted among hip-hop producers that explore goals, methods, and values in the art of sample-based hip-hop creation. Focuses on a variety of topics from hip-hop artists' pedagogical methods to the African diasporic rock of the sampling process to the social significance of digging for rare records. Examines the ways hip-hop artists have managed to create a form of expression that reflects their creative aspirations, moral beliefs, political values, and cultural affinities.

396.   **Seago, Alex**. 2000. "'Where Hamburgers Sizzle on an Open Grill Night and Day?': Global Pop Music and . . ." *American Studies* 41(2/3): 119–137. ISSN: 0026-3079.

Explores the condition of global pop music in the context of globalization theory. Topics include the association of American pop music and cultural imperialism. Other topics discussed include the cultural trends in popular music styles and aesthetics, consideration of the hegemony of Western music, and the influence of multinational media in many parts of the world.

397.   **Sellheim, Nikolas**. 2016. "Black and Viking Metal: How Two Extreme Music Genres Depict, Construct, and Transfigure the (sub-)Arctic." *Polar Record* 52(2): 509–517. ISSN: 0032-2474.

Explores how two heavy metal subgenres black and Viking metal approach and utilize narratives associated with the "North." Employs the use of lyrics of black and Viking metal bands different forms of utilizations come to fore ranging from narratives of death to the raging Northman. Also explores musical expression as a source for generating extreme conceptual settings.

398.   **Seroussi, Edwin**. 2022 "Diasporas and Global Musical Network: Jewish Perspectives." *Asian-European Music Research Journal* 9: 1–8. ISSN: 2701-2689.

Suggests that the COVID-19 pandemic not only dictated daily routines but also scholarly concerns and that global networks should also be a more pertinent concern for musicologists in the present time than ever before. Further suggests that human connectivity is an essential ingredient of a global vision of history and of music history and that music studies are relative latecomers to the idea of global history as a conceptual framework for research but not in practice.

399. **Shahriari, Andrew C**. 2018. *Popular World Music, 2nd ed*. New York: Routledge. xxv, 220 p. Illustrations, Maps, Music Examples, Bibliography, and Index. ISBN: 9-781-13868-446-1.

An appropriate educational source and/or textbook for introducing popular music genres and artists from around the world. Discusses international musical styles such as reggae, salsa, K-pop, and many others with a comprehensive listening-oriented introduction to mainstream culture. Focuses on specific music styles and artists such as Bob Marley, Carmen Miranda, ABBA, Ladysmith Black Mambazo, and others.

400. **Shank, Barry**. "Abstraction and Embodiment: Yoko Ono and the Weaving of Global Musical Networks." *Journal of Popular Music Studies* 18(3): 282–300. ISSN: 1524-2226.

Discusses the role of Yoko Ono as a leader in the avant-garde movement in the 1960s in the development of conceptual and performance art. Examines how Yoko Ono's inclination to perform a variety of rock-and-dance-based popular music styles has attained an insoluble intertwining of mind and body, which is a basic characteristic of Japanese activism.

401. **Sheinbaum, John J**. 2019. *Good Music: What It Is and Who Gets to Decide*. Chicago: University of Chicago Press. xiii, 289 p. Illustrations, Bibliography, and Index. ISBN: 9-780-22659-338-8.

Explores traditional models for valuing music. Provide examples such as Handel's oratorios, Beethoven's and Mahler's symphonies, jazz improvisations, and Bruce Springsteen. Argues that metaphors of perfection do justice to neither the perceived strengths nor the assumed weaknesses of the music question.

402. **Shelchy, Russell P., and Jeremy Taylor, eds**. 2022. *Sonic Histories of Occupation: Experiencing Sound and Empire in a Global Context*. London & New York: Bloomsbury. 256 p. Illustrations, Bibliography, and Index. ISBN: 9-781-35022-808-5.

An edited volume of essays that examines how auditory environments in different contexts have contributed to understanding foreign occupation and colonialism and how they have given rise to historical music cultures. Examines how sound and music are implicated in the control and discipline of people under occupation. Essays incorporate case studies that focus on relationships between occupation and the bodily senses, voice and occupation, memory, sound, and so forth. Highlights case studies in Asia, North America, North Africa, and Europe.

403. **Shuker, Roy**. 2016. *Understanding Popular Music Culture, 5th ed*. London & New York: Routledge. vi, 298 p. Bibliography and Index. ISBN: 9-781-13890-785-0.

A revised and expanded fifth edition that provides an accessible and comprehensive introduction to the production, distribution, consumption, and meaning of popular music and the debates that surround popular culture and popular music. Reflects the continued proliferation of popular music studies, the new music industry in the digital age, and the emergence of new stars. Updates include two new chapters titled "The Real Thing: Authenticity, Covers and the Canon," and "Time Will Pass You By: Histories and Popular Memory," providing new case studies on artists that include the Rolling Stones, Lorde, One Direction, and Taylor Swift. Includes further examples of musical tastes, genres, and performers through additional coverage of electronic dance music, and much more.

404.   **Siddiqi, Asif, ed**. 2023. *One-Track Mind: Capitalism, Technology, and the Art of the Pop Song*. Series: *Ashgate Popular and Folk Music Series*. Abingdon, Oxon: Routledge. xii, 393 p. Illustrations, Bibliography, and Index. ISBN: 9-780-36755-372-2.

A compilation of essays that focus on sixteen iconic tracks from the history of popular music. The volume is arranged chronically in order of release date of the tracks and spanning approximately five decades. Compiled essays zigzag across the cultural landscape to present the history of popular music through psychedelic rock, Afro-pop, Latin pop, glam rock, heavy metal, punk, post-punk, adult contemporary rock, techno, hip-hop, and electro-pop.

405.   **Sisco, David, and Laura Joseph**. 2022. *Performing in Contemporary Musicals*. Abingdon, Oxon: Routledge. xvi, 235 p. Illustrations, Bibliography, and Index. ISBN: 9-781-03207-985-1.

Focuses on the skills performers must possess when tackling shows that are newly written, in development, or somewhere in between. Examines myths about contemporary musical theater. Analyzes the development timelines of musicals from around the world and how performers can become invaluable to a creative team by developing the skills needed to move a new musical forward.

406.   **Sloan, Nate, and Charlie Harding**. 2020. *Switched on Pop: How Popular Music Works & Why It Matters*. New York: Oxford University Press. 201 p. Illustrations, Music Examples, Bibliography, and Index. ISBN: 9-780-19005-665-0.

Based on the eponymous podcast and analysis of Top 40 hits. Incorporates sixteen case studies that shift pop music from the background to the forefront and illuminates the essential musical concepts behind two decades of chart-topping songs. Incorporates discussions of popular repertoire from Britney Spears, Beyoncé, Outkast, Kendrick Lamar, Ariana Grande, Kelly Clarkson, Jay Z, Kanye West, Paul McCartney, Justin Timberlake, Rihanna, Carley Rae Jepsen, and so forth.

407.   **Slobin, Mark**. 2008. *Global Soundtracks: Worlds of Film Music*. Series: *Music/ Culture*. Middletown: Wesleyan University Press. xxiii, 387 p. Illustrations, Bibliography, and Index. ISBN: 9-780-81956-881-6.

A collection of essays that provide a historical and critical study of the worlds of film music. Compiled essays provide analysis of films from China, India, Indonesia, Egypt, Nigeria, Latin America, the Caribbean, and the United States. Compiled essays also provide a variety of key films, periods, and studio practices.

408.   **Smith, Angela**. 2014. *Women Drummers: A History From Rock and Jazz to Blues and Country*. Lanham: Rowman & Littlefield. xviii, 271 p. Discography, Bibliography, and Index. ISBN: 9-780-81088-835-7.

Combines archival research with personal interviews of over fifty female drummers representing more than eight decades in music history. Offers a vivid picture of their struggles to overcome discrimination not only as professional musicians but also in other parts of their lives. Outlines the evolution of woman drummers from pre-biblical times, when women held important leadership roles, to their silencing during the Middle Ages, to their changing roles in contemporary times.

409.   **Smolko, Tim, and Joanna Smolko**. 2021. *Atomic Tunes: The Cold War in American and British Popular Music*. Bloomington: Indiana University Press. viii, 355 p. Illustrations, Bibliography, and Index. ISBN: 9-780-25305-616-0.

Presents a musical history of the Cold War. Examines how during the Cold War over five hundred songs were written about nuclear weapons, fear of the Soviet Union, civil defense, bomb shelters, and others. Demonstrates the widespread concern among musicians coping with the effect of communism on American society and the threat of a nuclear conflict of global proportions.

410.   **Smudits, Alfred, and Andreas Gebesmair, eds**. 2001. *Global Repertoires: Popular Music Within and Beyond the Transnational Music Industry*. Series: *Ashgate Popular and Folk Music Series*. Aldershot, Hants & Burlington: Ashgate. xi, 176 p. Illustrations, Music Examples, Bibliography, and Index. ISBN: 0-754-60526-4.

An edited volume of essays that stem from a conference on music and globalization organized by the International Research Institute for Media, Communication and Cultural Development (Mediacult), held November 4–8, 1999, in Vienna, Austria. The essays approach the functions and operations of popular music in contemporary societies. Discusses issues of globalization and accesses the role the music industry plays in the process to analyze its strategies and the reactions they provide. Concerns mainly with the commercial face of popular music. As a compilation, the essays can be gathered into three headings: music industry, globalization, and case studies that provide insight into one, the other, or both.

411.   **Soni, Manish**. 2001. *Mystic Chords: Mysticism and Psychology in Popular Music*. New York: Algora Pub. 244 p. Bibliography. ISBN: 9-781-89294-147-3.

Focuses on popular music artists such as Bob Dylan, Bob Marley, the Beatles, and other rock artists and examines how these artists have drawn on the same primal source from which mythology, dreams, and poetic insight arise. Employs references to passages from the Bhagavad Gita, the Bible, Carl Jung, Sigmund Freud, Joseph Campbell, and the Tao Te Ching. Offers highlights of some of the parallels between psychology, mysticism, religion, and contemporary arts as they contribute to a human quest for greater meaning.

412.   **Spicer, Mark**. 2011. *Rock Music*. Series: *Library of Essays on Popular Music*. Farn-
        ham & Burlington: Ashgate. xxix, 474 p. Illustrations, Music Examples, Bibliog-
        raphy, and Index. ISBN: 9-781-31508-863-1.

        Compiles twenty essays from among the leading scholars writing on rock music
        published in academic journals over two decades. Diverse essays reflect the wide
        approaches that scholars in various disciplines have applied to the study of rock
        music. Essays range from those that address historical, sociological, cultural, and
        technological factors that gave rise to rock music to those that focus primarily on
        analysis of the music itself.

413.   **Spracklen, Karl**. 2020. *Metal Music and the Re-Imagining of Masculinity,
        Place, Race, and Nation*. Series: *Emerald Studies in Metal Music and Culture*.
        Bingley: Emerald. vii, 272 p. Discography, Bibliography, and Index. ISBN:
        9-781-83867-445-8.

        Focuses on metal music and popular music and popular music as a form of lei-
        sure. Argues that in the modern age, popular music has become part of popular
        culture and a heavily contested collection of practices and industries that con-
        struct place, belonging, and power.

414.   **St. John, Graham**. 2009. *Technomad: Global Raving Counter Cultures*. Series:
        Studies in Popular Music. London & Oakville: Equinox. xii, 312 p. Illustrations,
        Bibliography, and Index. ISBN: 9-781-84545-546-0.

        Explores the pleasurable and activist trajectories of post-rave. Examines
        sound system culture, sonic societies, international parties, counter-colonial
        interventions, and other movements. Also investigates how dance party has
        been harnessed for transgressive and progressive ends for manifold freedoms.
        Draws on ethnographic, netographic, and documentary research. Provides
        commentary about post-rave trajectory through various local sites and global
        scenes. Focuses on the unique developments in the techno-culture such as
        Spiral Tribe, teknivals, psytrance, Burning Man, Reclaim in the Streets, and
        Earthdream.

415.   **St. John, Graham**. 2010. *Local Scenes and Global Culture of Psytrance*. Series:
        Routledge Studies in Ethnomusicology. London & New York: Routledge. x, 259 p.
        Illustrations, Bibliography, and Index. ISBN: 9-780-41589-816-4.

        An edited volume that stems from a textual symposium of formative research
        on the culture of global psytrance (psychedelic trance). Addresses the diverse
        transnationalism of this contemporary electronic dance music phenomenon
        with a host of interdisciplinary research on psytrance as a product of intersect-
        ing local and global trajectories. Contributes to theories of globalization, post-
        modernism, music scenes and technology, dance ritual, counterculture, youth
        subculture, neotribes, the carnivalesque, and spirituality. Introduces psytrance
        in Goa (India), the United Kingdom, Israel, Japan, the United States, Italy, Czech
        Republic, Portugal, and Australia.

416. **Stahl, Geoff, and Giacomo Bottà, eds**. 2019. *Nocturnes: Popular Music and the Night.* Series: *Pop Music, Culture, and Identity.* Cham: Springer International & Palgrave MacMillan. xvii, 280 p. Illustrations, Bibliography, and Index. ISBN: 9-783-31999-786-5.

An edited volume of essays that examine the relationship between night and popular music. Essays in this volume are geographical and interdisciplinary in scope and explore how the problems, promises, and paradoxes of the night and music play off one another to produce spaces of silence and sanctuary as well as underpinning strategies designed to police, surveil, and control movements and bodies.

417. **Steinbrecher, Bernhard**. 2021. "Mainstream Popular Music Research: A Musical Update." *Popular Music* 40(3–4): 406–427. ISSN: 0261-1430.

Reviews studies that examine internationally circulating music that has reached the upper echelon of all-genre single charts in the twenty-first century. Provides examples for the analysis of sonic aesthetics that are embedded in a particular frame of cultural debate, which in the study is conceptualized as mainstream popular music. Provides discussions regarding prevailing objectives, methods, and findings as well as elaboration on how future research might advance understanding of the aesthetics within discourses of mainstream popular music and contemporary culture at large.

418. **Steingrass, Gerhard, ed**. 2002. *Songs of the Minotaur: Hybridity and Popular Music in the Era of Globalization: A Comparative Analysis of Rebetika, Tango, Rai, Flamenco, Sardana, and English Urban Folk.* Series: *Research in Popular Music and Jazz; No. 9.* Münster & London. Lit. x, 325 p. Bibliography and Index. ISBN: 3-82586-363-8.

An edited volume that focuses on popular music, dance, and folk music in a global perspective. Topics include the global economy of music—how the major labels define the Latin music market; hybridization and the rebetika; politics of the hybridization in rai music; hybridization in tango; hybridization and its meaning in the Catalan music tradition; flamenco as the basis of heretical identities; flamenco fusion and new flamenco as postmodern phenomena; hybrid phenomena in popular culture and English urban folk; and topology of hybrid forms in popular music.

419. **Stephan, Michael, and Trevor Pateman**. 2016. *A Transformation Theory of Aesthetics.* Originally published in 1990. Series: *Routledge Library Editions, Aesthetics.* London & New York: Routledge. xii, 242 p. Illustrations, Bibliography, and Index.

Expounds on how we perceive and respond to the visual image that has been a traditional concern of psychology, philosophers, and art historians. Breaks new ground by linking findings that relate to visual image and everyday life and consequences, representations of pictures, and aesthetic experiences. Draws on new theory of picture perception and aesthetic response. Argues that images can generate in us a complex pattern of mental change or transformation.

420.   **Stewart, Francis**. 2017. *Punk Rock Is My Religion: Straight Edge Punk and Religious Identity*. New York: Routledge. xiii, 175 p. Illustrations, Bibliography, and Index. ISBN: 9-780-36788-443-7.

Employs a focus and detailed study of straight edge punk, a subset in which adherents abstain from drugs, alcohol, and casual sex. Argues that traditional modes of religious behaviors and affiliations are being rejected in favor of ideals within a variety of spaces and experiences including popular culture. Engages with questions of identity construction through concepts such as authenticity, community, symbolism, and music and furthers the debate on what is meant by the concepts of "religion" and "secular."

421.   **Stockton, Will, and D. G. Gibson**. 2020. *The 33 1/3 B-Sides*. New York: Bloomsbury. 231 p. Bibliography and Index. ISBN: 9-781-50134-294-3.

An anthology that features compact essays from past 33 1/3 authors on albums that consume them but about which they do not write. Essays explore often overlooked and underrated albums and focus on artists such and Leonard Cohen, Bob Dylan, the New York Dolls, the Rolling Stones, the Durutti Columns, R.E.M., Rites of Spring, Jane's Addiction, Del Amitri, Sinead O'Connor, Billy Idol, and many others.

422.   **Stokes, Martin**. 1994. *Ethnicity, Identity, and Music: The Musical Construction of Place*. Series: *Berg Ethnic Identities Series*. Berg & Oxford: Oxford University Press. x, 212 p. Bibliography and Index. ISBN: 9-780-85496-877-0.

Examines the significance of music in the construction of identities and ethnicities and suggest ways to understand music as a social practice. Focuses on the role of music in the construction of national and regional identities, the media and postmodern identity, concepts of authenticity, aesthetics, meaning, performance, world music, and the use of music as a focus for discursive evocation of place.

423.   **Stokes, Martin**. 2004. "Music and the Global Order." *Annual Review of Anthropology* 33: 47–72. ISBN: 9-780-82431-933-5.

Offers theoretical notions of music and globalization that may be of benefit to research in global pop studies. Makes assertions that music is used as a metaphor of global social cultural processes and constitutes an enduring process by and through which people interact within and across cultures. Argues for an approach to musical globalization and contextualization of genres, styles, and practices that circulate across cultural borders in specific institutional sites and histories.

424.   **Stratton, Jon**. 2009. *Jews, Race, and Popular Music*. Series: *Ashgate Popular and Folk Music Series*. x, 227 p. New York: Routledge. Bibliography and Index. ISBN: 9-780-75466-804-6.

Focuses on Jews as a radicalized group in popular music of America, Britain, and Australia during the late twentieth and twenty-first centuries. Provides case studies that examine the American, British, and Australian music industries. Discusses how the racialized positioning of Jews, which is sometimes similar but often different in each of the societies, affected the kinds of music with which Jews have been involved.

425. **Straw, Will, ed**. 1995. *Popular Music: Style and Identity*. Montreal: Centre for Research on Canadian Cultural Industries and Institutions. iv, 323 p. Illustrations and Bibliography. ISBN: 0-77170-459-3.

A compilation of papers that were presented at the seventh International Association for the Study of Popular Music in 1993 in Stockton, California. Compiled papers are varied and include those based on historical and critical analysis of popular music and identity.

426. **Straw, Will**. 1988. "Music Video in Its Contexts: Popular Music and Post-Modernism in the 1980s." *Popular Music* 7(3) [Special Issue: *Music Video and Film*]: 247–266. ISSN: 0261-1430.

Argues that writing on music and video has had two distinctive moments in its brief history. Furthermore, this includes the wave of treatments that have tended to come from the culture surrounding rock music and from those who were primarily interested in music video as something that produced effects on that music. Also argues that the two claims were expressed in the terms and contexts of rock journalism.

427. **Strohm, Reinhard**. 2018. *Studies in Global History of Music: A Balzan Musicology Project*. Series: *SOAS Musicology Series*. Abingdon, Oxon & New York: Routledge. 502 p. Bibliography and Index. ISBN: 9-781-31516-397-0.

Promotes a post-European thinking that is based on the idea that a global history of music cannot be one single hegemonic history. Compiled essays explore the paradigms and terminologies that might describe a history of many different voices. The essays address historical practices and interpretations of music in different parts of the world from Japan to Argentina and from Mexico to India. Essays consider sociopolitical and historical circumstances that have affected music in the various regions and address aspects that Western musical historiography has tended to neglect even when looking at its own culture of performance, dance, nostalgia, topicality, enlightenment, and the relationships between traditional, classical, and popular music concerning European, Asian, and Latin American interpretations of each other's musical traditions.

428. **Strong, Catherine**. 2016. *Grunge: Music and Memory*. Series: *Ashgate Popular and Folk Music Series*. Abingdon, Oxon: Routledge. 192 p. Bibliography and Index. ISBN: 9-781-13826-857-9.

Argues that grunge has been perceived as the music that defined Generation X and decades after the height of the movement, there is still considerable interest in its rise and fall and its main figures such as Kurt Cobain and Courtney Love. Explores how grunge has been remembered by the fans that grew up with it and asks how memory is both formed by and forms popular culture. Explores the relationship between media, memory, and music fans and demonstrates how different groups can use and shape memory as part of an ongoing struggle for power in society. Shows that although grunge challenged many social structures, the way it and youth itself are remembered often work to reinforce the status quo.

429. **Strong, Catherine, and Barbara Lebrun**. 2015. *Death and the Rock Star*. Series: *Ashgate Popular and Folk Music Series*. Farnham, Surrey: Ashgate. xii, 224 p. Bibliography and Index. ISBN: 9-780-36759-806-8.

Explores the reception od dead rock stars, "rock" being taken in the widest sense as the artists discussed belong to the genre of rock 'n' roll (Elvis Presley), disco (Donna Summer), pop and pop-rock (Michael Jackson, Whitney Houston, Amy Winehouse), punk, post-punk (GG Allin, Ian Curtis), rap (Tupac Shakur), folk (the Dutchman André Hazes), and world music (Fela Kuti). Examines the contrasting ways in which male and female dead singers are portrayed in the media.

430. **Studwell, William E., and David Lonergan**. 1999. *The Classic Rock and Roll Reader: Rock Music From Its Beginning to the 1970s*. Series: *Haworth Popular Culture*. New York: Routledge & Taylor & Francis. xii, 278 p. Indexes. ISBN: 9-781-31772-068-3.

A collection of essays that inform about an era that shaped culture and future musical trends. Discusses hundreds of rock 'n' roll and non-rock compositions included in rock history. Also examines the music that preceded early rock, the music that followed early rock, and the numerous non-rock songs that flourished during the classic rock period.

431. **Szabo, Victor**. 2023. *Turn On, Turn In, Drift Off: Ambient Music's Psychedelic Past*. New York: Oxford University Press. xi, 376 p. Illustrations, Bibliography, and Index. ISBN: 9-780-19069-930-7.

Offers a rethinking of the history and socio-aesthetics of ambient music as a popular music genre with roots in the psychedelic countercultures of the late twentieth century. Narrates how anglophone audio producers and DJs between the mid-1990s and the century's end commodified drone-and-loop-based records as ambient audio—slow, spare, spacious audio sold as artful personal media for creating an atmosphere for fostering contemplation, transformation awareness, and stilling the body.

432. **Tagg, Philip, and Robert Clarinda, eds**. 2003. *Ten Little Title Tunes: Towards Musicology of the Mass Media*. New York: The Mass Media Music Scholarship Press. xvi, 898 p. Illustrations, Music Examples, Bibliography, and Index. ISBN: 0-97016-842-X.

Documents the paramusical association with hundreds of listeners to ten extracts of music played without visual accompaniment but potentially usable in television or film contexts. Deals with the links between listener connotations and musical structures in the global, Anglo-United States American mass media culture of the late twentieth century. Offers analysis of musicogenic categories of thought with serious ideological potential.

433. **Taylor, Jodie**. 2012. *Playing It Queer: Popular Music, Identity and Queer World-Making*. Bern: Peter Lang. xii, 254 p. Illustrations, Bibliography, and Index. ISBN: 9-783-034305-532.

Provides a study of the relationship between popular music and queer self-fashioning and (sub)cultural world-making. Offers a survey and critical evaluation of relevant literatures on queer identity and political debates, as well as of popular music, identity, and the (sub)cultural. Contextualizes within a detailed history of queer sensibilities and creative practices, drag, queercore, feminist music, camp, and club cultures within translocal scenes that capture the meaning and value of popular music.

434. **Taylor, Timothy D**. 2001. *Strange Sounds: Music, Technology, and Culture*. New York: Routledge. x 279 p. Illustrations, Bibliography, and Index. ISBN: 0-41593-684-5.

Argues that the advent of digital technology may mark the most fundamental change in the history of Western music since the invention of notation and that technology is a fundamentally social notion and its uses are informed by people's experiences and memories. Further argues that technological changes are spurred by social demands and bear upon social practices. Digital technologies must meet the expectations of producers, musicians, and listeners who have in turn transformed the ways in which music is made and consumed. Thus, to study the reciprocal effects of technological changes and musical transformation amounts to looking at the world with new glasses that could enable one to see important phenomenon in a new light of cultural interaction, globalization, and others.

435. **Taylor, Timothy D**. 1997. *Global Pop: World Music, World Markets*. New York: Routledge. xxiii, 271 p. Illustrations, Discography, Filmography, Bibliography, and Index. ISBN: 0-41591-871-5.

Examines the rise of "world musics" and "world beat" and some of the musicians associated with these new genres such as Peter Gabriel, Ladysmith Black Mambazo, and Johnny Clegg. Draws on a wide range of sources including academic writings, popular culture, cyber content, interviews, and the music itself. Examines the range of discourses employed around the world. Demonstrates how the central concepts of authority are wielded by musicians, fans, and other listeners and looks at some of these musics in detail, examining ways they are caught up in forms of domination and resistance. Explores how some cross-collaborations may fashion new musics and identities through innovative combinations of sound and style.

436. **Terkourafi, Marina, ed**. 2010. *The Languages of Global Hip-Hop*. London: Continuum. xii, 351 p. Bibliography and Index. 9-781-44111-639-0.

A selection of essays that take the view that hip-hop should not be viewed with a dichotomous dynamic in mind and that the dynamic does not arise solely outside the continental United States. Provides close analysis of the facts and reveals a complex situation where market pressures, local (musical) traditions, linguistic and semiotic factors, intelligibility, and each country's particular historico-political past conspire to yield new hybrid expressive genres. Topics include German migrant hip-hop; Arabic, English, and Verlan in French rap; Egyptian hip-hop; Hungarian hip-hop; German gangsta rap lyrics; and South Korean hip-hop.

437.   **The Subcultures Network, eds**. 2014. *Subcultures, Popular Music, and Social Change*. Newcastle upon Tyne: Cambridge Scholars Press. xvii, 304 p. Illustrations, Bibliography, and Index. ISBN: 9-781-44385-945-5.

Offers empirical studies regarding how style-based subcultures, scenes, and tribes have pulsated through the history of social, economic, and political change. Topics include 1940s zoot suiters and hepcats; 1950s rock 'n' rollers, beatniks, and Teddy boys 1960s surfers, rudeboys, mods, hippies, and bikers; 1970s skinheads, soul boys, rastas, glam rockers, funksters, and punks; heavy metal, hip-hop, casual, goth, rave, hipster, and clubber styles of the 1980s; 1990 noughties, and more.

438.   **Thorley, Mark, and Gerhard Roux**. 2017. "Global Patchbay: Developing Popular Music Expertise Through International Collaboration." In *Popular Music Today-Proceedings of the International Association for the Study of Popular Music*, Julia Merrill, ed. Series: *Systematische Musikwissenschaft*. Wiesbaden: Springer VS. 298 p. Bibliographies. ISBN: 9-783-65817-739-3.

Shares the practice of Global Patchbay, an initiative aimed to bring together universities and practitioners around the world to exploit the potential of collaborative learning in music. Project stems from partners in the United Kingdom and the United States and continues with others from South Africa, Australia, and New Zealand. Discusses how such collaborations have included recording projects, mixing projects, acoustic design projects, and other production technologies.

439.   **Tofalvy, Tomas, and Emilia Barna, eds**. 2020. *Popular Music, Technology, and the Changing Media Ecosystem: From Cassettes to Stream*. Series: *Popular Music, Culture, and Identity*. Cham: Palgrave Macmillan. xix, 258 p. Illustrations, Bibliography, and Index. ISBN: 9-783-030446-659-8.

A compilation of essays that utilize a cross-disciplinary approach that integrates concepts and perspectives of popular music studies, media studies, science and technology, and sociology. Avoids technological determination and focuses on the social and economic embeddedness of technology and the critical construction of technology. Topics include community and change in relationship to popular music; culture and technology; music scenes as infrastructures; media, technology, and the reproduction of underground cultural capacity; digitalization and the symbolic power of the music industries; streaming in the music industry; race and ethnicity; authenticity and digital popular music bands; music in 1990s China; cassette format in twenty-first-century Japan; online music scenes; the fan-artist relationship; Galician underground scene; and the political comedy mashup.

440.   **Torell, Kurt**. 2022. *Rock and Roll, Social Protest, and Authenticity: Historical, Philosophical, and Cultural Explorations*. Lanham: Lexington Books. 190 p. Illustrations, Bibliography, and Index. ISBN: 9-781-79365-563-9.

Explores the relationships between rock and roll, social protest, and authenticity to consider how rock and roll could function as a social protest music. Discusses the nature and origins of rock and roll and the nature of social protest and social protest music within the wider contexts of the evolution of the commercial music industry and the social and technological infrastructure developed for the mass dissemination of popular music. Examines causes of public disapproval originally expressed toward rock and roll, social protest, subversive qualities, commercialization, and so forth.

441.   **Toynbee, Jason, and Byron Dueck, eds**. 2011. *Migrating Music*. Series: *Culture, Economy, and the Social*. Abingdon, Oxon & New York: Routledge. xiv, 256 p. Illustrations, Map, Bibliography, and Index. ISBN: 9-780-20384-175-4.

A compilation of essays that focus on how migrants bring music from their homelands to the metropolis. Also focuses on how music migrates via the media, world music, hip-hop, bossa nova, and others. Compiled essays provide case studies around the world and demonstrate how migrating music is key to the construction of a still emerging global cosmopolitan imagination. Some of the music and geographic areas discussed include the Mediterranean, Morocco, Paris (France), Tehran (Iran), Fiji, United Kingdom, Afghanistan, New York, Bombay (India), Netherlands, Finland, and others.

442.   **Turner, Kathleen, ed**. 2015. *This Is the Sound of Irony: Music, Politics, and Popular Culture*. Series: *Ashgate Popular and Folk Music Series*. Farnham, Surrey: Ashgate. xii, 257 p. Illustrations, Music Examples, Bibliography, and Index. ISBN: 9-780-36759-928-7.

A compilation of essays that explore the linkages between irony and the comic, the tragic, the remembered, the forgotten, the co-opted, and the resistant. Essays cover the nineteenth to twentieth centuries in America, Europe, and Asia via a range of ironies through issues such as race, religion, class, the political Left and Right, country, punk, hip-hop, folk, easy listening, and the technologies that make possible the popular music experience. Essays are intended to create new methodologies and apply existing theories of irony to musical works.

443.   **Turner-Graham, Emily**. 2012. "Resistance Never Looked So Good: Women in White Power Music." In *White Power Music: Scenes of the Extreme-Right Cultural Resistance*, Anton Shekhovtsov and Paul Jackson, eds. Northampton: RWM Publications. 129 p. Illustrations, Bibliography, and Index. ISBN: 9-780-95220-389-6.

Included in a series of essays that focus on the role in the shifting phenomenon of White power music more often associated with masculinity. Focuses on the role of women in White power music and how they help to preserve an ultra-nationalist and racial narrative and other issues such as censorship, extreme-right music scenes.

444.   **Unger, Matthew**. 2016. *Sound, Symbol, Sociality: The Aesthetic Experience of Extreme Music*. Series: *Palgrave Pivot*. London: Palgrave Macmillan. xiii, 137 p. Illustrations, Bibliography, and Index. ISBN: 9-781-13747-834-4.

A study based on ethnographic research within the extreme music community on how symbols of authenticity and defilement fashion social experience. Interprets aesthetic resonances to understand contemporary identity, politics, and social relation. Develops an argument that internal composition of the community's music and sound symbols that shapes, reflects, and constrain patterns of identity, difference, and transgression.

445.   **Valijärvi, Ritta-Liisa, Charlotte Doesburg, and Amanda DiGioia, eds**. 2021. *Multilingual Metal Music: Sociocultural, Linguistic, and Literary Perspectives on Heavy Metal Lyrics*. Series: *Emerald Studies in Metal Music and Culture*. Bingley: Emerald Publishing. xiii, 291 p. Illustrations, Bibliography, and Index. ISBN: 9-781-83909-949-6.

A compilation of essays that explore the textual analysis of heavy metal lyrics written in other languages than English, including Japanese, Yiddish, Latin, Russian, Hungarian, Austrian, German, and Norwegian. Essay topics include national and minority identity, politics, wordplay, parody, local/global, intertextuality, and adaptation.

446.   **Van der Merwe, Peter**. 1989. *Origins of the Popular Styles: The Antecedents of Twentieth-Century Popular Music*. Oxford: Clarendon Press & New York: Oxford University Press. xiii, 352 p. Music Examples, Bibliography, and Index. ISBN: 9-780-19316-121-4.

Analyzes popular music from a musicological as opposed to a sociological, biographical, or political point of view. Presents a survey of Western popular music in all its forms—blues, ragtime, music hall, waltzes, marches, parlor ballads, and folk music. Uncovers the common language that unites the styles. Examines the split between "classical" and "popular" Western music in the nineteenth and twentieth centuries and sheds light on the "serious" music of the time. Chapter contents include historical background—Europe and the Near East, Africa, and North America; theoretical foundation; the blues (African origins, British blues origins, blues harmony, twelve bar blues); parlor music and ragtime; and final reflections.

447.   **Varas-Diáz, Nelson, Jeremy Wallach, Esther Clinton, and Daniel N. Araujo, eds**. 2023. *Defiant Sounds: Heavy Metal in the Global South*. Lanham: Rowman & Littlefield. 418 p. Bibliography and Index. ISBN: 9-781-79365-185-3.

A compilation of essays related to the Global South to reflect on the roles of heavy metal music throughout their respective regions. Essays position metal music at the epicenter of region-specific experiences of oppression marked by colonialism, ethnic extermination, political prosecution, and war. They stress how metal music is used throughout the Global South to face these oppressive experiences, foster hope, and promote an agenda that seeks to build a better world. Areas and topics covered include Aotearoa Indigenous metal; Navajo Nation metal scene; metal in the Middle East and North Africa; Argentine metal; Asian American metal; East Africa metal; metal music in Egypt, Iran, and Syria; Caribbean metal; Indonesian metal; and Moroccan metal.

448. **Verbood, Marc, and Amanda Brandellero**. 2016. "The Globalization of Popular Music 1960–2010: A Multilevel Analysis of Music Flows." *Communication Research* 45(4): 603–627. ISSN: 0093-6502.

Offers a cross-national multilayered analysis of music flows between 1960 and 2010. Advances previous studies of cultural globalization and focuses on global and country levels while adding to the individual level of music flows. Analyzes the international composition of pop charts in nine countries by mapping trends, comparing countries, and conducting multivariate analyses.

449. **Verbood, Marc, and Sharon Noord**. 2016. "The Online Place of Popular Music: Exploring the Impact of Geography and Social Media on Pop Artists' Mainstream Media Attention." *Popular Communication: The International Journal of Media and Culture* 14(2): 59–72. ISSN: 1540-5702.

A study that can be useful in global pop studies and social media research. Examines the extent to which social media can reduce inequalities in mainstream media attention between artists from central cities (e.g., New York, London) in popular music production versus more peripheral cities. This study distinguishes between media attention by institutionally embedded music critics and lay users on the Internet.

450. **Von Appen, Ralf, and Mario Dunkel, eds**. 2019. *(Dis-)Orienting Sounds-Machtkritische Perspektiven auf populäre Musik ((Dis-)Orienting Sounds: Power-Critical Perspectives on Popular Music)*. Series: *Beiträge zur Popularmusikforschung*. Bielefeld: Transcript Verlag. German text with English summary. 310 p. Bibliography and Index. ISBN: 9-783-83765-058-7.

Contends that popular music offers listeners a sociocultural orientation and positioning. Associated with this are power structures, such as the relationship between the sexes, generations, ethnic groups, and social milieus, that popular music can produce but also break up so that disorientation or new orientation can arise. Compiled essays analyze such processes critically and on several levels including neo-sexism in indie rock, feminist counter strategies, sexualized images in Africa and Eastern Europe, and others.

451. **Wagner, Christoph**. 1999. "Early (World)-Music: Über das Comeback ethnischer Musik aus der Shellack-Ära (Early (World)-Music: On the Comeback of

Ethnic Music From the Shellac Era)." *Neue Zeitschrift für Musik* 160(1): 48–50. ISSN: 0945-6995. German text with English summary.

Takes historical and critical approaches to investigating the commercial recording industry and the various geographic areas and styles that have influenced the industry. Describes early commercial recording activities in Asia, Africa, and Latin America with a focus on the companies Odeon (in Germany) and Gramophone (in England). Also traces the successive waves of Hawaiian music, jazz, and Caribbean music.

452. **Waksman, Steve**. 2001. *Instrument of Desire: The Electric Guitar and the Shaping of Musical Experience*. Cambridge: Harvard University Press. xi, 373 p. Illustrations, Discography, Bibliography, and Index. ISBN: 9-780-67400-065-0.

Explores the historical and cultural significance of the electric guitar and how and why the instrument has had a broad musical and cultural impact. Topics covered include Charlie Christian, the electric guitar, and the Swing Era; Les Paul's new sound; Chet Atkins and the Nashville Sound; racial distortions—Muddy Waters, Chuck Berry, and the electric guitar in Black popular music; Jimi Hendrix and the meaning of Blackness; the MC5 and the politics of noise; and heavy metal–cock rock, colonialism, and Led Zeppelin.

453. **Walden, Joshua S., ed**. 2013. *Representation in Western Music*. Cambridge: Cambridge University Press. xvi, 316 p. Bibliography and Index. ISBN: 9-781-10702-157-0.

Offers a comprehensive study of the roles of representation in the composition, performance, and reception of Western music. Essays present new research about musical representation with particular focus on Western art and popular music from the nineteenth century to the present day. Essay topics cover instrumental music, opera, popular song, dance, cinema, and music videos.

454. **Wall, John, ed**. 2007. *Music, Metamorphosis and Capitalism: Self, Poetics, and Politics*. Newcastle upon Tyne: Cambridge Scholars. xxiv, 129 p. Illustrations, Music Examples, Bibliography, and Index. ISBN: 9-781-44380-799-9.

An edited volume of essays that examine various kinds of music from several perspectives including the sociopolitical, aesthetic, and psychological. Compiled essays focus on diverse categories of rock-pop, new music, rap, metal, and music video. The essays are historically based and engage self-consciously in the deconstruction of music genres.

455. **Wall, Tim**. 2013. *Studying Popular Music Culture, 2nd ed*. Los Angeles: SAGE. 332 p. Bibliography and Index. ISBN: 9-781-44620-771-0.

A study that seeks to incorporate the strands of the musical text, the industry that produces it, and the audiences that give it meaning. Covers several areas that include histories of popular music, their traditions, and cultural, social, economic, and technical factors; industries and institutions, production, new technology, and new entertainment media; musical forms; meaning and representation; and audiences and consumption. Learning methodology is provided through a set of case studies engaging activities and suggestions for further reading.

456. **Wallach, Jeremy, Harris M. Berger, and Paul D. Greene, eds**. 2011. *Metal Rules the World: Heavy Metal Music Around the World*. Durham: Duke University Press. 381 p. Illustrations, Bibliography, and Index. ISBN: 9-780-82234-716-3.

A compilation of essays that explore the dynamics of masculinity, class, race, and ethnicity in metal scenes; the place of metal in the music industry; and the ways that disfranchised youth use metal to negotiate modernity and social change. Essays cover metal scenes in Brazil, Canada, China, Easter Island, Indonesia, Israel, Japan, Malaysia, Malta, Nepal, Norway, Singapore, Slovenia, and the United States.

457. **Walser, Robert**. 2014. *Running With the Devil: Power, Gender, and Madness in Heavy Metal Music, 2nd ed*. Series: *Music/Culture*. Middletown: Wesleyan University Press. Originally published in 1993, Hanover: University Press of New Hampshire. xxvii, 230 p. Illustrations, [12 p.] of plates, Discography, Bibliography, and Index. ISBN: 0819552526 & 9-780-81957-515-9.

A comprehensive musical, social, and cultural analysis of heavy metal music. Explores how and why heavy metal music works both musically and socially. Employs an in-depth study to investigate contemporary formation of identity, community, and gender and power.

458. **Warner, Simon**. 2014. *Text and Drugs and Rock 'n' Roll: The Beats and Culture From Kerouac to Kurt Cobain*. New York: Bloomsbury. xix, 521 p. Bibliography and Index. ISBN: 9-780-82641-664-3.

Explores the interaction between two of the most powerful sociocultural movements in the postwar years—the lifelong forces of the Beat Generation and the musical energies of rock and its attendant culture. Examines the interweaving strands of influence by Jack Kerouac, Allen Ginsberg, William Burroughs, and others in the 1940s and 1950s cultivated by major rock figures who emerged after 1960—Bob Dylan, the Beatles, David Bowie, the Clash, Kurt Cobain, and others.

459. **Watson, Harry L., and Jocelyn Neal**. 2013. *Southern Cultures: Global Southern Music, Issues, Enhanced E-Book*. Series: *University of Carolina at Chapel Hill Center for the Study of the American South* 19(1): 1–120. ISBN: 9-781-46960-904-1.

A special issue of *Southern Cultures*. Topics covered include the south meets Senegal as hip-hop goes transatlantic; Hawaiian steel guitar and the Southern musical landscapes; poet Allen Ginsburg and bluesman James "Son" Thomas; Aussie Elvis impersonators; a United Kingdom scholar offering a new perspective on the study of the blues; and music pirates and bootlegging in the South.

460.   **Weisbard, Eric**. 2004. *This Is Pop: In Search of the Elusive at Experience Music Project*. Cambridge: Harvard University Press. vii, 389 p. Illustrations, Bibliography, and Index. ISBN: 9-786-67401-321-6.

A publication that stems from Seattle's Music Project that captures the academic, critical, musical, and literary in an impromptu dialogue that suggests the breadth and vitality of pop inquiry in contemporary times. Topics covered include popular music and popular prose; European thoughts on American music; jazz; Sister Rosetta Tharpe and women in rock and blues; Chitlin Circuit; movie music from Max Steiner to Marvin Gaye; post-soul, Ray Davies, and the Kinks; authenticity, gendering, and personal voice; marketing authenticity and manufacturing authorship; translating the Wailers into rock; rock 'n' roll in contemporary times; compression pop; the rise and fall of a hip-hop tradition; massiveness, materiality, and the Top 40; and unoriginality in pop.

461.   **Werner, Ann, Tami Gadir, and Sam De Boise**. 2020. "Broadening Research in Gender and Music Practice." *Popular Music* 39(3–4): 636–651. ISSN: 0261-1430.

Builds on research concerning gender and music practice in terms of skewed musical canons, ratios and quotas of gender representation, unfair treatment and power dynamics, and the exclusionary enmeshment with music technologies. Offers a critical reading of what "gender" is understood to be, how it has been studied, and how gendered power has been challenged in order to suggest new areas for research of gender and music practice.

462.   **Wetzel, Richard D**. 2012. *The Globalization of Music in History*. Series: *Routledge Studies on History and Globalization*. New York: Routledge. ix, 197 p. Bibliography and Index. ISBN: 9-780-41587-475-5.

Offers a contextualization of a globalized process that has since ancient times involved the creation, use, and worldwide movement of songs, instrumental music, musical drama, music with dance, concert, and secular popular and religious music. Contributes to the growing awareness of the power of music to provide insight into those things that all cultures and civilizations hold in common and that promote noble virtues. Also contributes to theoretical perspectives in ethnomusicology, musicology, music therapy, and global music.

463.   **Wheaton, R. J**. 2023. *Trip-Hop*. Series: *33 1/3 Series*. New York: Bloomsbury. 164 p. ISBN: 9-781-50137-360-2.

Focuses on trip-hop, a label cast upon music that in the early 1990s sounded from boundaries of dub, hip-hop, electronic, jazz, soul, and psychedelia. Examines albums as Massive Attack's *Blue Lines and Protection*; Portishead's *Dummy*, Tricky's *Maxinquay*, and DJ Shadow's *Endtroducing*, and other records on labels like Mo' Wax and Ninja Tune that seemed to speak to a sense of collective alienation and disenchantment with the end of the twentieth century. Seeks to dislocate trip-hop and instead understand the music within wider and more interesting aesthetic traditions.

464.   **Whelan, Andrew, and Rachael Nowak**. 2018. "Vaporwave Is (Not) a Critique of Capitalism: Genre Work in an Online Music Scene." *Open Cultural Studies* 2: 451–462. ISSN: 2451-3474.

Contends that vaporwave first emerged in the early 2010s as a genre of music characterized by extensive sampling of earlier "elevator music," such as smooth jazz, easy listening, and muzak. Explores how the narrative of vaporwave as an aesthetic critique of late capitalism has been developed, articulated, and disputed through this genre work. Focuses on the limits around these narrative functions as a pedagogical or sensitizing device, instructing readers and listeners in how to understand and discuss musical affect, the nature and function of descriptions of music, and the nature of critique and of capitalism as something meriting such critique.

465.   **White, Bob, ed**. 2011. *Music and Globalization: Critical Encounters*. Bloomington: Indiana University Press. 248 p. Bibliography and Index. ISBN: 9-780-25322-365-4.

An edited volume that explores the dynamics that enable or hinder cross-cultural communication through music. Compiled essays demonstrate how the careful historical and ethnographic analysis of global music can show how globalization operates and what if anything consumers can do with it.

466.   **Whiteley, Shelia, Andy Bennett, and Stan Hawkins, eds**. 2017. *Music, Space, and Place:Popular Music and Cultural Identity*. Series: *Ashgate Popular and Folk Music Series*. Aldershot, Hants, & Burlington: Ashgate; London: Routledge. x, 224 p. Illustrations, Bibliography, and Index. ISBN: 9-780-75465-574-9.

A compilation of essays that examine the urban and rural spaces in which music is experienced, produced, and consumed. Essays focus on the musical processes of music, place, and identity where these processes are shaped by specific musical practices and by the pressures and dynamics of political and economic circumstances. Essays offer discourses in several different parts of the world including Cuba, France, Italy, New Zealand, and South Africa,

467.   **Whiteley, Shelia, and Jennifer Rycenga, eds**. 2006. *Queering the Perfect Pitch*. New York: Routledge. xix, 308 p. Illustrations, Bibliography, and Index. ISBN: 9-780-41597-805-7.

A compilation of essays that situate queering within the discourse of sex and sexuality in relation to popular music. Compiled essays address the changing debates with gay, lesbian, and queer discourse in relation to the dissemination of musical texts, performers, cultural production, and sexual meaning. Essays situate music within the broader patterns of culture that both mirrors and actively reproduces. The essays are divided into four sections:

Queering Borders; Queer Spaces; Hidden Histories; and Queer Thoughts, Mixed Media.

468.   **Whiteley, Shelia, and Jedediah Sklower, eds**. 2014. *Counterculture and Popular Music*. Series: *Ashgate Popular and Folk Music Series*. Burlington: Ashgate. xx, 295 p. Illustrations, Bibliography, and Index. ISBN: 9-781-47242-107-4.

An edited volume that focuses on "Counterculture," a term that emerged in the late 1960s and has been redeployed in more recent decades in relation to other forms of cultural and sociopolitical phenomena. This volume provides new academic scrutiny of the concept of counterculture and a critical examination of the period and its heritage. Compiled essays examine how music played a significant part in the way that the counterculture authored space in relation to articulations of community by providing a shared sense of collective identity.

469.   **Whiteley, Shelia, ed**. 1997. *Sexing the Groove: Popular Music and Gender*. London & New York: Routledge. xxxvi, 353 p. Music Examples, Discography, Bibliography, and Index. ISBN: 9-780-41514-671-5.

A compilation of essays that offer debates about how popular music performers, subcultures, fans, and texts construct and deconstruct masculine and feminine identities. Essays provide a wide range of case studies from Mick Jagger to Riot Grrrls and demonstrate that there is nothing natural, permanent, or immovable about the regime of sexual difference that governs society and culture.

470.   **Whiteley, Shelia**. 2000. *Women and Popular Music: Sexuality, Identity and Subjectivity*. London & New York: Routledge. x, 246 p. Illustrations, Discography, Bibliography, and Index. ISBN: 9-781-13512-173-0.

Explores the changing roles of women musicians and the ways in which their songs resonate in popular culture. Examines the counterculture's reactionary attitudes to women through the lyrics of the Beatles and the Rolling Stones. Explores the ways in which artists like Janis Joplin and Joni Mitchell confronted issues of sexuality and freedom, redefining women's participation in the industry, and assesses the personal cost of their achievements. Also considers how personalities such as Annie Lennox, Madonna, and k.d. Lang have confronted issues of gender stereotypes and sexuality through pop videos and so forth.

471.   **Wiatrowski, Myc, and Cory Barker, eds**. 2013. *Popular Culture in the Twenty First Century*. Newcastle upon Tyne: Cambridge Scholars Publishing. xx, 178 p. Bibliography and Index. ISBN: 9-781-44386-444-2.

A collection of papers that were presented at the first annual Ray Browne Conference held at Bowling Green State University. Papers address the ways that popular culture surrounds us through products, movies, popular music, literature, and technology. Papers engage with these issues and suggest a diverse selection of contemporary scholarship from a wide variety of perspectives.

472. **Wicke, Peter**. 1990 "Rock Music: Dimensions of a Mass-Medium Meaning Through Popular Music." *Canadian University Music Review/Revue des Musiques des Universites Canadiennes* 10(2): 137–156. French and English texts. ISSN: 0710-0353.

Offers debates on the rock song as art. Ponders the question of what meaning, significance, and value can reside in the musical, gestural, and visual materials of a rock song. Expresses that this question leads into uncharted areas and produces another question: does the high degree of stereotyping to be found in the music allow any kind of differential meaning? Suggests that it is always possible to cite examples from the wide variety of this kind of music, which apparently testifies to the existence of differentiated musical structures of an aesthetic resulting from other forms of commercial music.

473. **Wicke, Peter, and Rachael Fogg, translator**. 2011. *Rock Music: Culture, Aesthetics, and Sociology*. Cambridge: University Press. xii, 228 p. Discography and Bibliography. ISBN: 9-780-52139-914-2.

Translation of *Rockmusik*, originally published in 1990, deals with philosophy and aesthetics, social aspects, and popular culture of rock music. Examines how rock music has changed the face of modern music and examines what the fascination is, its significance in contemporary society, and what cultural values it reflects. Addresses these issues and offers a study of rock music, tracing its development through Elvis Presley and the Beatles.

474. **Wilcox, Felicity, ed**. 2022. *Women's Music for the Screen: Diverse Narrative in Sound*. Series: *Routledge Music and Screen Media Studies*. New York: Routledge. 240 p. Illustrations, Bibliography, and Index. ISBN: 9-780-36721-026-7.

Compiled essays concentrate on the works and lives of female-identifying screen composers. Integrates composer profiles, exclusive interview excerpts, and industry case studies to showcase the achievements of women that reflect on the systemic gender biases women have faced in an industry that has long excluded them. Women composers covered include Bebe Baron, Delia Derbyshire, Wendy Carlos, Annie Dudley, Rachel Portman, Hildur Guðnadottir, Mica Levy, Winifred Phillips, and others.

475. **Williams, Justin A**. 2010. "The Construction of Jazz Rap as High Art in Hip-Hop Music." *Journal of Musicology* 27(4): 435–459. ISSN: 0277-9269.

Argues that multiple factors contributed to the elevation of jazz as high art in mainstream media reception by the 1980s and that the stage was set for hip-hop groups such as Gang Starr, A Tribe Called Quest, and Digable Planets to engage in a relationship with jazz as art and heritage. Suggests that jazz codes in the music helped create a rap music subgenre commonly branded as "jazz-rap." Discusses the creation of hierarchies, value judgments, and the phenomenon of elite status within music genres.

476.   **Wodtke, Larissa**. 2021. *Dance-Punk*. Series: *33 1/3 Series*. New York: Blooms-
        bury. 162 p. Bibliography and Index. ISBN: 9-781-50138-186-7.

        Suggests that beginning in the late 1970s, as an offshoot of disco and punk,
        dance-punk is difficult to define and is referred to as disco-punk and funk-punk,
        which skirts, overlaps, and blurs into other genres including post-punk, post-
        disco, new wave, mutant disco, and synthpop. Explores the historical and cul-
        tural conditions of the genre as it appeared in the late 1970s and 1980s and again
        in the early 2000s. Examines bands such as Gang of Four, ESG, Public Image
        Ltd., LCD Soundsystem, the Rapture, and Le Tigre in terms of tension between
        blurring of the rhetoric and emotion in dance music and the cynical and ironic
        and associated with post-punk.

477.   **Wojcik, Pamela R., and Arthur Knight, eds**. 2001. *Soundtrack Available: Essays
        on Film and Popular Music*. Durham: Duke University Press. x, 491 p. Illustra-
        tions, Bibliography, and Index. ISBN: 0-82232-080-3.

        A compilation of essays that attempt to fill the gap of minimal serious writing
        on film soundtracks that feature popular music. Essays include detailed analy-
        sis of individual films as well as historical overview of genres, styles of music,
        and approaches to film scoring with a cross-cultural emphasis. Essayists focus
        on movies that use popular songs from a variety of genres including country,
        bubble-gum pop, disco, classical, jazz, French cabaret, and showtunes. Films
        discussed range from silent to musicals and from dramatic and avant-garde
        film to documentaries in India, France, England, Australia, and the United
        States.

478.   **Wolfe, Paula M**. 2019. *Women in the Studio: Creativity, Control, and Gender in
        Popular Music Sound Production*. Series: *Ashgate Popular and Folk Music Series*.
        Abingdon, Oxon & New York: Routledge. 224 p. Bibliography and Index. ISBN:
        9-781-31554-671-1.

        Discusses gendered notions of creativity and examines the significant under-
        representations of women in studio production. Offers research-based inter-
        views and firsthand observation that demonstrate that patriarchal frameworks
        continue to form the backbone of the music industry establishment, but that
        women's work in the creation of sound presents a potent challenge to gender
        stereotyping, marginalization, and others.

479.   **Wrazen, Louise, and Fiona Magowan eds**. 2015. *Performing Gender, Place, and
        Emotion in Music: Global Perspectives*. Series: *Eastman/Rochester Studies in Eth-
        nomusicology*. Rochester: University of Rochester Press. 216 p. Illustrations, Bib-
        liography, and Index. ISBN: 9-781-58046-543-4.

        Presents a range of ethnographic case studies from around the globe that offers
        new ways of thinking about the interconnectivity of gender, place, and emotion
        in musical performance. Interweaves these three concepts from a cross-cultural

perspective. Compiled case studies demonstrate how a one-dimensional theoretical focus implicates the others across different regions around the globe.

480.   **Wrobel, David M**. 2010. "Western Themes in Contemporary Rock Music, 1970–
        2000: A Lyric Analysis." *American Music Research Center Journal* 10: 83–100.
        ISSN: 1058-3572.

        Provides an overview of the pervasiveness of Western themes in recent rock
        marked by a special emphasis on lyrical, narrative context rather than musical,
        formal construction and by carefully qualified attempts at linking lyrical content
        to cultural trends. Suggests that rock songs can be viewed as social and cultural
        history documents but that care needs to be taken in linking lyricists' influences
        and intentions to specific cultural trends. Moreover, linkages can be difficult
        to establish and influences may be subconsciously processed by the individual
        artist.

481.   **Young, Richard A., ed**. 2002. *Music, Popular Culture, Identities*. Series: *Critical
        Studies (Amsterdam, Netherlands)*. Amsterdam: Rodopi. 360 p. Bibliography and
        Index. ISBN: 9-789-00433-412-0.

        A collection of essays that focus on music as an expression of local, ethnic, social,
        and other identities. Essays focus on popular traditions and contemporary forms
        from several regions that include Italian popular music; flamenco in Spain; chal-
        lenges of traditional music in Bulgaria; boerenrock and rap in Holland; Israeli
        extreme heavy metal; jazz and pop in South Africa; musical hybridity and pol-
        itics in Côte d'Ivoire; the Mexican corrido; popular music and dance in Cuba;
        bossa nova in Brazil; and Somali immigrants and refugee youths and Iranians in
        exile in the United States.

482.   **Yu, Peter**. 2014. "How Copyright Law May Affect Popular Music Without Our
        Knowing It." *UMKC Law Review* 83(2): 363–401. ISSN: 0047-7575.

        Explores several questions about popular music that can be illuminated by
        greater insight into copyright law and the music business. Examines why some
        pop songs last fewer than five minutes; why professional songwriters are dissat-
        isfied with Pandora and Spotify; the European compact disc in the United States;
        YouTube and ASCAP/BMI licenses; digital downloads, sales, and licenses; and
        royalty rates for sheet music.

483.   **Zak, Albin**. 2007. *The Poetics of Rock: Cutting Tracks, Making Records*. Berke-
        ley: University of California Press. xvii, 259 p. Bibliography and Index. ISBN:
        9-780-52092-815-2.

        Presents an exploration of recording consciousness and compositional process
        from the perspective of those who make records. Examines the crucial roles
        played by recording technologies in the construction of rock music. Demon-
        strates how songwriters, musicians, engineers, and producers contribute in the
        creative process.

484.   **Zhang, Qian, and Keith Negus**. 2021. "Stages, Platforms, Streams: The Economies and Industries of Live Music After Digitalization." *Popular Music and Society* 44(5): 539–557. ISSN: 0300-7766.

Argues that digital corporations and social media platforms are shaping the
changing value and experience of live music by introducing new platforms of
commodities into a live experience economy and integrating live music into a
digital attention economy. Illustrates how platforms are exerting greater influence within the music industries as streaming extends live music from an activity associated with a real place to an extended experience in real time.

2

Theory, Methodology, and Musicianship Studies

485. **Abbey, Eric J., and Colin Helb, eds**. 2016. *Hardcore Punk and Other Junk*. Lanham: Rowman & Littlefield. 228 p. Bibliography and Index. ISBN: 9-780-73917-605-4.

A collection of essays that offer theoretical perspectives of punk music, which is considered aggressive through the world. Essays cover local underground bands in Detroit, Michigan, to Puerto Rico and across Europe and demonstrate the importance of aggressive music in society. Essays offer discussions about the politics and values of extreme hardcore and so forth.

486. **Aguilar, Ananay, Ross Cole, Matthew Pritchard, and Eric Clarke, eds**. 2020. *Remixing Music Studies: Essays in Honour of Nicholas Cook*. New York: Routledge. 234 p. Illustrations, Bibliography, and Index. ISBN: 9-780-36750-133-4.

A collection of essays by the students of Nicholas Cook that question the place of academic study in contemporary time, future paths, how music relates to society and constructs meaning through it, and how it transcends the social, remixing the discipline and attempting to address all musics on an equal basis. Essays also raise questions from Cook's work in critical musicology from notation, historiography, and performance to place music's role in multimedia such as virtual reality and video games.

487. **Alev, Simeon**. 2020. *Jazz and Psychotherapy: Perspectives on the Complexity of Improvisation*. Series: *SEMPRE Studies in the Psychology of Music*. London: Routledge. 288 p. Bibliography and Index. ISBN: 9-781-03208-173-1.

Blends the insights of musicians and psychologists from D. W. Winnicott to Gregory Bateson to Ornette Coleman and explores improvisation to reveal its potential to transform experiences. Argues that what we share with the professional

DOI: 10.4324/9781003507345-2

improvisers known as psychotherapists and jazz musicians is the reality of not knowing what those around us or even ourselves are going to do next. Provides revolutionary approaches to human development and creative expression embodied in these two seemingly disparate twenty-first-century traditions.

488. **Anderton, Chris, and Sergio Pisfil**. 2022. *Researching Live Music: Gigs, Tours, Concerts, and Festivals*. Series: *SEMPRE Studies in the Psychology of Music*. London: Routledge. xiv, 255 p. Illustrations, Music Examples, Bibliography, and Index. ISBN: 9-780-36740-500-7.

Draws on a range of methodological and theoretical approaches to provide a critical resource on live music processes. Demonstrates how live music events have become central to raising and discussing broader social and cultural issues. Incorporates case studies from Argentina, Australia, France, Jamaica, Japan, New Zealand, Switzerland, and Poland.

489. **Antokoletz, Elliott**. 2013. *A History of Twentieth Century Music in a Theoretical-Analytical Context*. New York: Routledge. xvi, 506 p. Illustrations, Bibliography, and Index. ISBN: 9-780-41588-187-6.

Provides an account of genres and concepts of twentieth-century art music organized topically by aesthetic, stylistic, technical, and geographical categories. Integrates within the larger context of social economic and cultural frameworks. Also integrates musical issues with political, cultural, and social conditions that have a significant impact on the course of twentieth-century musical tendencies and styles.

490. **Antović, Mihalio**. 2022. *Multilevel Grounding: A Theory of Musical Meaning*. Series: *SEMPRE Studies in the Psychology of Music*. London: Routledge. vii, 158 p. Illustrations, Music Examples, Bibliography, and Index. ISBN: 9-780-36746-738-8.

Develops a new approach to musical meaning of multilevel grounded semantics and addresses the paradox that music seems full of meaning yet there is little consensus among listeners on what exactly this meaning communicates. Combines insights from the fields of philosophy of the mind, cognitive science, semiotics, linguistics, and music cognition, employing a broad range of examples from traditional, classical, and popular music into a theoretical system.

491. **Archibald, Paul**. 2014. "Searching for the First Bass Drum Pedal: Rock Harmonicas to Viennese Pianos." *Popular Music History* 9(3): 285–305. ISSN: 1740-173.

Contends that the drum kit is an instrument of great importance to most forms of popular music since its conception in the late nineteenth century. Presents a history of the bass drum pedal that predates the drum kit earlier than previously considered.

492. **Attali, Jacques, Brian Massumi, translator, Frederic Jameson, foreword, and Susan McClary, afterword**. 1985. *Noise: The Political Economy of Music*. Series: *Theory and History of Literature, Volume 16*. Minneapolis: University of Minnesota Press. xiv, 179 p. Bibliography and Index. ISBN: 0-81661-286-2.

Argues that music does not reflect society but foreshadows new social formations. Moreover, music is not simply a reflection of culture but a harbinger of change and an anticipatory abstraction of the shape of things to come. Employs the metaphor of "noise" as a model of cultural historiography. Refers specifically to the reception of musics that sonically rival normative social order, drawing on historical vanguardism for radical soundscapes of the Western continuum that express structurally the course of social development.

493. **Attas, Robin**. 2019. "Music Theory as Social Justice: Pedagogical Applications of Kendrick Lamar's *To Pimp a Butterfly.*" *Music Theory Online* 25(1): 1–13. ISSN: 1067-3040.

Employs the use of Kendrick Lamar's *To Pimp a Butterfly* (*Butterfly*) as a case study to demonstrate possible ways that music theorists can integrate their discipline with the world at large. Suggests that the album draws attention to the genre of hip-hop and its political history, incorporates Lamar's rich and unique musical language, and discusses issues of race and racism in the United States in a compelling way. Demonstrates how *Butterfly* offers three methods for bringing social justice into the music theory classroom, but many hip-hop albums could be used to teach standard core theory topics with the social justice agenda left implicit.

494. **Bates, Elliot**. 2013. "Popular Music Studies and the Problems of Sound, Society, and Method." *IASPM Journal* 3(2) [Special Issue: *Popular Music Studies in the Twenty-First Century*]: 15–32. ISSN: 2079-3871.

Investigates four inquiries in relation to three dominant Anglophone popular music studies journals—*Popular Music and Society*; *Popular Music*; and *Journal of Popular Music Studies*. Inquires include what interdisciplinary and multidisciplinary means within popular music studies; the extent to which popular music studies has developed canonic scholarship; the motivations for two scholarly groups—Dancecult and ASARP—to break away from popular music studies and the forms of music analysis; and the kind of musical material commonly employed within popular music studies. Suggests that the field would greatly benefit from a true engagement with anthropological theories and methods and that the "chaotic" conceptualization of musical structuration and the critical discourse would likewise benefit from attention to recorded sound production aesthetics.

495. **Bennett, Andy**. 2002. "Researching Youth Culture and Popular Music: A Methodological Critique." *British Journal of Sociology* 53(3): 451–466. ISSN: 1468-4446.

Argues for the need for critical evaluation on the qualitative research methodology in sociological studies of the relationship between youth culture and popular music. Illustrates that there is currently an absence of critical debate concerning methodology in the field of sociological research. Examines this absence by analyzing how early research on youth and music rejected the need for empirical research and relying instead on theories and concepts drawn from cultural

Marxism. Also illustrates how the legacy of this early body of work in youth and music research manifests in current research.

496. **Bhabha, Homi K**. 2004. *The Localization of Culture, 2nd ed.* Previously published in 1994. Series: *Routledge Classics*. New York & London: Routledge. 404 p. Bibliography and Index. ISBN: 9-780-41533-639-0.

A theoretical work that may inform some theoretical perspectives in global popular music studies research. Reconsiders notions of identity, cultural agency, and national affiliation. Provides a theory of cultural hybridity and employs concepts such as mimicry, interstice, and liminality to argue that cultural production is always most productive where it is most ambivalent.

497. **Biamonte, Nicole**. 2010. "Triadic Model and Pentatonic Patterns in Rock Music." *Music Theory Spectrum* 32(2): 95–110. ISSN: 0195-6167.

Contends that pitch syntax of mainstream rock music comprises a variety of tonal, modal, blues-based, and chromatic elements. Further contends that traditional constructs of scale-degree theory and harmonic functionality, while originally attributed to art music, can be usefully modified to address elements of rock music that do not conform to tonal norms. Offers an examination of the context and function of some harmonic structures unique to rock music that cannot be interpreted in conventional tonal terms: double-plagal and Aeolian progressions and triad-double scale systems.

498. **Bjerstedt, Sven**. 2021. *Storytelling in Jazz and Musicality in Theatre Through the Mirror.* London: Routledge. 144 p. Bibliography and Index. ISBN: 9-780-36777-578-0.

Focuses on two examples of conceptual mirror reflectivity: narrativity in jazz music and musicality in spoken theater. Suggests that these metaphors are shown to be significant to the practice and reflection of performing artists through their ability to mediate holistic views of what is of crucial importance in artistic practices, analysis, and education.

499. **Blacking, John**. 1981. "Making Artistic Popular Music: The Goal of True Folk Music." *Popular Music* 1 [Special Issue: *Folk or Popular? Distinctions, Influences & Continuities*]: 72–82. ISSN: 0261-1430.

Offers theoretical perspectives that focus on distinctions of styles within a society's music, social, and functional differentiation, and mutual communication. Examines the distinctions between sacred and secular music between music for the young and old or men and women.

500. **Bolden, Tony**. 2020. *Groove Theory: The Blues Foundation of Funk.* Series: *American Made Music Series; Mississippi Scholarship Online.* Jackson: University of Mississippi Press. 280 p. Illustrations, Bibliography, and Index. ISBN: 9-781-49683-052-4.

Presents an innovative history of funk music focused on the performers regarded as intellectuals who fashioned a new aesthetic. Utilizes musicology, literary studies, performance studies, and African American intellectual history to explore what it means for music or any cultural artifact to be funky. Undertakes a theoretical examination of the development of funk and the historical conditions in which Black artists reimagined their music. Also provides historical and biographical studies of key funk artists who transfigured elements of blues tradition into new styles and visions.

501. **Borgo, David**. 2022. *Sync or Swarm: Improvising Music in a Complex Age, revised edition*. New York: Bloomsbury. xvii, 236 p. Illustrations, Music Examples, Compact Disc, Bibliography, and Index. ISBN: 9-781-50136-887-5.

Provides a study of musical improvisation using theories from cultural and cognitive studies and the emerging sciences of chaos and complexity. Explores with a systematic approach and expands outward in scope from the perspective of a solo improviser to that of a group interacting in performance and over time to the network dynamics that bind together performers, listeners, educators, and promoters into a musical community. Features new sections that highlight electro-acoustic improvisation, transcultural improvisation, and concomitant issues of human-machine interaction and postcolonial cultural studies.

502. **Borthwick, Stuart, and Ron Moy**. 2005. *Popular Music Genres: An Introduction*. New York: Routledge. 256 p. Bibliography and Index. ISBN: 9-780-41597-369-4.

Offers a schematic approach to a range of popular music genres and examines them in terms of their antecedents, histories, visual aesthetics, and sociopolitical contexts. Offers insights into the relationship between popular music, cultural history, economies, politics, iconography, production techniques, marketing, and music structures.

503. **Bowman, Peter**. 1997. "So You Want to Be a Rock 'n' Roll Scholar—Well You Need to Get an MBA." *Canadian University Music Review/Revue des Musiques des Universites Canadiennes* 18(1) [Special Issue: *Crossing Borders: Interdisciplinary Studies by Canadian Scholars*]: 52–65. French and English Texts. ISSN: 0710-0353.

Employs a study of Stax Records, a record label based in Memphis, Tennessee, from the late 1950s through December 1975 when it was forced into involuntary bankruptcy to problematize what has often been a tendency within popular music scholarship to attempt to understand the political economy of the recording industry primarily via the mechanical application of Marxist theory on a micro level. Examines the relationship between CBS Records and Stax Records from 1972 through 1975, concluding that to fully understand the nature of the distribution agreement between the two companies, one needs to consider on a micro level the different modi operandi of independent and major labels, differences in the retail world of Black and White America, and individual agency.

504. **Braae, Nick, and Kai A. Hansen, eds**. 2019. *On Popular Music and Its Unruly Entanglements*. Cham: Palgrave MacMillan. xiii, 269 p. Illustrations, Bibliography, and Index. ISBN: 9-783-03018-099-7.

A compilation of essays that explores the many ways in which popular music is entwined within social, cultural, musical, historical, and media networks. Essays discuss diverse genres as mainstream pop, hip-hop, classic rock, instrumental synthwave, video game music, amateur ukulele groups, and others. They also present a wide range of methodology and theoretical positions.

505. **Brackett, David**. 1995. *Interpreting Popular Music*. Cambridge & New York: Cambridge University Press. xiv, 260 p. Bibliography and Index. ISBN: 9-780-52022-541-1.

Focuses on how we analyze the effects of popular music and its meaning. Draws from the disciplines of cultural studies and music theory to demonstrate how listeners form opinions about popular songs and how they come to attribute a rich variety of meanings to them. Explores several genres of popular music through recordings of Hank Williams, James Brown, Billie Holiday, Bing Crosby, and Elvis Costello. Develops a set of tools for looking at both the formal and the cultural dimensions of popular music of all kinds.

506. **Braquinski, Nikita**. 2022. *Mathematical Music: From Antiquity to Music AI*. Abingdon, Oxon: Routledge. vi, 136 p. Illustrations, Bibliography, and Index. ISBN: 9-781-03206-219-8.

Integrates a concise history of how mathematics was used to create music. Topics include ratios in antiquity to random combinations in the seventeenth century, twentieth-century statistics and contemporary artificial intelligence, and others. Topics are grounded in research findings from musicology and history of technology.

507. **Byun, Chong H. C.** 2016. *The Economics of the Popular Music Industry: Modelling from Microeconomic Theory and Industrial Organization*. New York: Palgrave MacMillan. viii, 128 p. Illustrations, Bibliography, and Index. ISBN: 9-781-13746-705-8.

Employs modeling from microeconomic theory and industrial organization to demonstrate how consumers and producers have responded to major changes in the music industry. Examines the important role of technology in changing its structure as new methods of creating and accessing music prove to be a double-edged sword for creators and producers. Considers how the business of music affects creativity and how artists continue to produce creative output in the face of business pressures, the erosion of copyright enforcement, and rampant online piracy.

508. **Capitain, Wouter**. 2017. "Edward Said on Popular Music." *Popular Music and Society* 40(1): 49–60. ISSN: 0300-7766.

Provides a comprehensive overview and a critical analysis of Edward Said's public statements on popular music. Argues that Said, strongly creates dissonance with his interventions in postcolonial and political theories. Also argues that in these reflections of popular music, Said voices problematic elitist, orientalist, and universalist claims.

509. **Chagas, Paulo C., and Jaiyue C. Wu, eds**. 2021. *Sounds From Within: Phenomenology and Practice*. Series: *Numanities—Arts & Humanities in Progress (NAHP, Volume 18)*. Cham: Springer. x, 252 p. Bibliography and Index. ISBN: 9-783-03072-507-5.

   A compilation of essays that transform phenomenology, music, technology, and cultural arts from within. Compiled essays explore concepts such as embodiment, art and technology mindfulness, mediation, time and space, self and emptiness, and cultural historical preservation. The volume offers close studies on music, phenomenology theory involving experimental music teaching, and more.

510. **Clancy, Martin, ed**. 2023. *Artificial Intelligence and Music Ecosystems*. Abingdon, Oxon: Routledge. x, 184 p. Illustrations, Bibliography, and Index. ISBN: 9-780-36740-577-9.

   A compilation of essays that highlight the opportunities and rewards associated with the application of artificial intelligence (AI) in the creative arts. Essays feature a range of voices, including interviews with Jacques Attali, Holly Herndon, and Scott Cohen, and offer interdisciplinary approaches to ethical and technical questions with AI. Essays also consider the perspectives of developers, students, and artists as well as the wider themes of law, ethics, and philosophy, serving as valuable resources for those studying and working in the creative arts field.

511. **Clement, Brett**. 2023. *Rock Tonality Amplified: A Theory of Modality, Harmonic Foundations, and Tonal Hierarchy*. Series: *Routledge Studies in Music Theory*. New York: Routledge. xii, 184 p. Illustrations, Bibliography, and Index. ISBN: 9-781-03229-144-4.

   Presents an in-depth study of rock tonality. Develops a comprehensive music theory designed to make sense of several essential components of tonality. Learning methodology is based on how to locate chords as they appear through various methods to understand and predict harmonic resolution tendencies and to identify the function of chords as they appear in musical contexts. Offers a conceptual framework to describe tonal relations that are played out through entire songs.

512. **Collins, Karen**. 2011. *From Pac-Man to Pop Music: Interactive Audio in Games and New Media*. Series: *Ashgate Popular and Folk Music Series*. Farnham, Surrey & Burlington: Ashgate. 224 p. Bibliography and Index. ISBN: 9-781-40942-903-6.

   Considers digital interactive audio as the future of audio in media, especially for video games, web pages, theme parks, museums, art installations, and theatrical events. Provides a framework for understanding the history, issues, and theories surrounding interactive audio. Presents the work of academics, composers, and sound programmers.

513. **Covach, John, and Graeme M. Boone, eds**. 1997. *Understanding Rock: Essays in Musical Analysis*. New York: Oxford University Press. xiii, 219 p. Music Examples, Bibliography, and Index. ISBN: 9-781-60256-076-5.

A compilation of essays on rock music that covers diverse aspects of the music itself to close and sophisticated analytical scrutiny. The essays are contributed by scholars in musicology and music theory. Their topics include progressive rock, the Beach Boys, experimental music, blues transformation in the music of Cream, k.d. lang's feminist revision, Paul Simon's crisis of chromaticism, a study of music cognition, and tonal expressive ambiguity in "Dark Star."

514. **Curry, Ben**. 2015. "Blues Music Theory and the Songs of Robert Johnson: Ladder, Level, and Chromatic Cycle." *Popular Music* 34(2): 245–273. ISSN: 0261-1430.

Explores the notion of ladder, level, and chromatic cycle as an insightful set of theoretical tools in analyzing the music of Robert Johnson. Employs the analytical approach of Gerhard Kubik and the spatially oriented analytical methods of neo-Riemannian theory. Notions of ladder, level, and chromatic cycle are explored with close reference to Johnson's "Kindred Woman," through a more general consideration of the scale-degree content of his vocal parts.

515. **Dannenberg, Roger B., Nicolas E. Golo, Dawen Liang, and Guangyu Xia, eds**. 2014. "Methods and Prospects for Human-Computer Performance of Popular Music." *Computer Music Journal* 38(2): 36–50. ISSN: 1531-5169.

A study that examines how computers are often used in performance of popular music but most often in very restricted ways such as in keyboard synthesizers, where musicians are in complete control of pre-recorded sequence music where musicians follow the computer's drums or click track. Argues that a little-explored possibility is the computer as highly autonomous performer of popular music capable of joining a mixed ensemble of computers and humans.

516. **Davis, James A., and Christopher Lynch, eds**. 2022. *Listening Across Borders: Musicology in the Global Classroom*. Series: *Modern Musicology and the College Classroom*. New York: Routledge. vi, 171 p. Illustrations, Bibliography, and Index. ISBN: 9-780-36713-567-6.

Provides tools and techniques for integrating a global approach to music history within the framework of the roots, challenges, and benefits of internationalization into the modern music curriculum. Compiled essays provide discussions of internationalized methods in a global age. Essays are divided into three parts: Creating Global Citizens; Teaching With Case Studies of Intercultural Encounters; and Challenges and Opportunities.

517. **Dawe, Kevin**. 2010. *The New Guitarscape in Critical Theory, Cultural Practice, and Musical Performance*. Series: *Ashgate Popular and Folk Music Series*. Farnham, Surrey: Ashgate. xx, 227 p. Illustrations, Bibliography, and Index. ISBN: 9-780-75466-775-9.

Argues for a reassessment of guitar studies in light of more recent musical, social, cultural, and technological developments that have taken place around the instrument. Draws from studies in science and technology, design theory, material culture, cognition, sensual culture, gender and sexuality, power and agency, ethnography (real and virtual), and globalization.

518. **Diederichsen, Diedrich**. 2023. *Aesthetics of Pop Music*. Series: *Theory Redux*. Cambridge & New York: Polity Press. 176 p. Bibliography and Index. ISBN: 9-781-50955-202-3.

Develops a theory and draws on interdisciplinary discourse from sociology, cultural studies, media studies, and ethnography. Argues that pop music is not so much a form of music as a constellation of different social media channels, social spaces, and behavioral systems of which music is only a part. Further argues that the appeal of pop music is primarily shaped by sound technologies, studio discipline, staging, and performance, rather than compositions and subjective expressions.

519. **Drabløs, Per Elias**. 2016. *The Quest for the Melodic Electronic Bass: From Jameson to Spenner*. Series: *Ashgate Popular and Folk Music Series*. New York: Routledge. 252 p. Bibliography and Index. ISBN: 9-780-36787-963-1.

Examines how the double bass, the preferred bass instrument in popular music during the 1960s, was challenged and subsequently superseded by the advent of a new electronic bass instrument. Incorporates interviews with players from this era, numerous transcriptions, and elaborations of twenty bass-related features. Also offers a critical study of four key players who provided the case studies for examining the performance practice of the melodic electronic bass.

520. **Duniker, Ben, and Denis Martin**. "In Search of the Golden Age of Hip-Hop Sound (1986–1996)." *Empirical Musicology Review* 12(1/2): 80–100. ISSN: 1559-5749.

Presents a methodology for developing, transcribing, and analyzing a body of one hundred hip-hop tracks released during the Golden Age. Analyzes eight categories of aurally salient musical and production parameters: tempo, orchestration and texture, harmony, form, vocal and lyric profiles, global and local production effects, vocal doubling and backing, and loudness and compression. Organizes the analysis of data into three trend categories: trends of change, trends of prevalence, and trends of similarity. Argues that these trends form a generalized model of the Golden Age hip-hop sound that considers both global and local contexts.

521. **Echard, William**. 2017. *Popular Music: A History Through Musical Topic Theory*. Series: *Musical Meaning and Interpretation*. Bloomington: Indiana University. 291 p. Bibliography and Index. ISBN: 9-780-25302-659-0.

Explores the historical development of psychedelic music and its various stylistic incarnations as a genre unique for its fusion of rock, soul, funk, folk, and electronic music. Incorporates the theory of musical topics and traces the stylistic evolution of psychedelic from its reception in the early 1960s with the Beatles' *Rubber Soul* and *Revolver*, the Kinks, and Pink Floyd to the German experimental bands and psychedelic funk of the 1970s with a special emphasis on Parliament/Funkadelic. Concludes with a look at the 1980s and early 1990s and the free festival scene, rave culture, and neo-jam bands.

522.   **Eusterbrock, Linus**. 2023. "Mobile Safe Spaces and Preset Emotions: Making Music With Apps as a Digital Technology of the Self." *Popular Music and Society* 46(1): 50–69. ISSN: 0300-7766.

Demonstrates that music apps used in technology of the self shape musicians' self-constitution and allow a complex interplay between music, place, and the self. Argues that music production with apps can promote practices of self-government but also serve as a tool of self-empowerment and critique.

523.   **Ewell, Philip**. 2023. *On Music Theory and Making Music More Welcoming for Everyone*. Series: *Music and Social Justice*. Ann Arbor: University of Michigan Press. 332 p. Bibliography and Index. ISBN: 9-780-47205-502-9.

Offers a Black perspective on the state of music theory and to confront the field's White supremacist roots. Undertakes an analysis to unpack the mythologies of Whiteness and Westernness with respect to music theory. Speaks directly about the anti-Blackness of music theory and the anti-Semitism of classical music writ large. Suggests a creative space in which those who have been marginalized in music theory can thrive.

524.   **Fagge, Roger, and Nicolas Pillar, eds**. 2017. *New Jazz Conceptions: History, Theory, Practice*. Series: *Warwick Series in the Humanities*. Abingdon, Oxon: Routledge. 220 p. Bibliography and Index. ISBN: 9-780-36788-676-9.

A collection of essays that capture the cutting edge of the developing methodologies and growing interdisciplinary nature of the field. Essays are intended to break down barriers previously maintained between jazz histories, theorists, and practitioners, with emphasis on interrogating binaries of national/local and professional/amateur.

525.   **Farber, Barry A**. 2007. *Rock 'n' Roll Wisdom: What Psychologically Astute Lyrics Teach Us About Life and Love*. Series: *Sex, Love & Psychology*. Westport: Praeger. xxxiii, 190 p. Bibliography and Index. ISBN: 9-780-31308-280-1.

Considers theoretical perspectives concerning rock and lyrics and their influences from an unusual vantage point of a psychologist who considers the interplay between lyrics and society. Employs rock lyrics to understand the human psyche. Draws connections between Freud and rock star perspectives.

526.   **Farrell, Isabel, and Kenton Mann**. 1995. *Music Unlimited: The Performer's Guide to New Audiences*. Series: *Performing Arts Series*. Abingdon, Oxon: Routledge. x, 68 p. Index. ISBN: 9-783-71865-526-7.

Designed to be music performers' companion that informs performers make decisions as they prepare performances. Describe some of the situations in which performers will find themselves and the techniques that work for performers while performing in community venues.

527. **Fink, Robert, Melinda Latour, and Zachary Wallmark, eds**. 2018. *The Relentless Pursuit of Tone: Timbre in Popular Music*. New York: Oxford University Press. xvii, 386 p. Illustrations, Bibliography, and Index. ISBN: 9-780-19998-522-7.

A compilation of essays that engage the entire history of popular music as recorded sound from the 1930s to the present under four large categories. "Genre" describes how sonic signatures define music identities and publics; "Voice" considers the most naturalized musical instrument, the human voice, as a racial and gendered signifier; "Instrument" tell stories of some iconic popular music machines—guitars, strings, synthesizers, and their distinctive sounds; and "Production" puts it all together, asking structural questions.

528. **Firth, Simon**. 2019. "Remembrance of Things Past: Marxism and the Study of Popular Music." *Popular Music* 16(1) [Special Issue: *Music and Socialism*]: 141–155. ISSN: 0261-1430.

Considers the role of Marxism in the history of popular music studies. Combines the sociology of knowledge with a personal memoir and its argument that in becoming a field of scholarly interest, popular music studies drew both from Marxist theoretical arguments about cultural ideology in the 1950s and 1960s and from rock writers' arguments about the role of music shaping socialist bohemianism in the 1960s and 1970s. Argues that popular music taken seriously academically meant taking it seriously politically. Furthermore, once established as an academic subject, popular music studies were absorbed into both established music departments and vocational and commercial music courses.

529. **Fitzgerald, Jon**. 2003. *Popular Music Theory and Musicianship*. East Lismore: Hazelmount. vii, 249 p. Illustrations, Bibliography, and Index. ISBN: 9-780-97505-680-6.

Examines basic music theory from a popular music perspective. Provides a workbook that includes written tasks with answers, music reading practice, and aural exercises and practical activities to help students assimilate theoretical concepts.

530. **Folse, Stuart**. 2004. "Popular Music as a Pedagogical Resource for Musicianship: Contextual Listening, Prolongations, Mediant Relationships, and Musical Form." *Journal of Music Theory Pedagogy* 18: 65–79. ISSN: 2013-2017.

Considers how popular music can be advantageously applied toward one pedagogical problem—the aural recognition of basic tonal prolongations. Demonstrates how in recent trends in music scholarship have emphasized the importance of popular music through in-depth analysis and historical studies. Argues that popular music can provide teachers of undergraduate musicianship courses with an unlimited supply of pedagogically relevant examples that make lasting impressions on students.

531.   **Gallardo, Cristobal**. 2000. "Schenkerian Analysis and Popular Music." *Trans-Revista Transcultural de Música* 5: 1–11. ISSN: 1697-0101.

Integrates Schenkerian analysis as the most disseminated approach to analyze Western tonal music, at least in the European-speaking world. Examines how in the last decades there have been many attempts to apply Schenkerian analysis to other musical transitions than the one it was created for in terms of Western art tonal music. Examines how these attempts include Western art Medieval and Renaissance music, Western folk music, non-Western music, and Western popular music. Discusses some significant Schenkerian analysis of popular music in order to obtain conclusions about the applicability of this kind to this type of music in general other than repertoires of Western art music.

532.   **Gauvin, Hubert L**. 2018. "Drawing Listener Attention in Popular Music: Testing Five Musical Features Arising From the Theory of Attention Economy." *Musicae Scientiae* 22(3): 291–304. ISSN: 1029-8649.

Argues that changes in the last thirty years have influenced the way people consume music, not only granting immediate access to a much larger collection of songs but also allowing listeners to instantly skip songs. Examines whether popular music compositional practices have changed in the last thirty years in a way that is consistent with economic principles.

533.   **Glitsos, Laura**. 2019. *Somatechnics and Popular Music in Digital Contexts*. Cham: Palgrave MacMillan. xi, 158 p. Bibliography and Index. ISBN: 9-783-03018-122-2.

Synthesizes the emerging practice and field of somatechnics with popular music studies. Presents an approach to popular music consumption and listening practices through the body-emotion perspective. Also investigates the complex interrelationships between technologies and music and how these impact the listening experience as mediated by the body system.

534.   **Graham, Stephen**. 2010. "(Un)Popular Avant-Garde: Underground Popular Music and the Avant-Garde." *Perspectives of New Music* 48(2): 5–20. ISSN: 0031-6016.

Discusses underground popular music, particularly in its role as an index of what can be described as popular avant-garde. Introduces the field of underground music, summarizing its history, aesthetics, and practitioners. Also concentrates on the proposed yoking together of the concept of the avant-garde with underground music and investigates a meaningful way to consider underground music to articulate, rehabilitate, and repurpose the notion of avant-garde.

535.   **Green, Lucy**. 2002. *How Popular Musicians Learn: A Way Ahead for Music Education*. Series: *Ashgate Popular and Folk Music Series*. New York: Routledge. 250 p. Bibliography and Index. ISBN: 9-780-75463-226-9.

Explores the nature of popular musicians' informal learning practices, attitudes, and values, the extent to which these changed over the last forty years, and the experience of the musicians in formal music education. Offers insights into how we might reinvigorate the musical involvement of the population through a comparison of the characteristics of informal popular music learning with those of more formal music education.

536.   **Guilbault, Jocelyne**. 1997. "Interpreting World Music: A Challenge in Theory and Practice." *Popular Music* 16(1): 31–44. ISSN: 0261-11430.

Focuses on theoretical approaches to the issue of meanings in "world music" practices. Addresses how such musical cultures take meanings, and what meanings are constructed by such cultures. Include discussions and examples of world musics that embody a hybrid character that embrace attentiveness to musical, social, or political change occurring elsewhere, and so forth.

537.   **Hadley, Susan, and George Young, eds**. 2012. *Therapeutic Uses of Hip-Hop*. New York: Routledge. xlii, 385 p. Illustrations, Music Examples, Bibliography, and Index. ISBN: 9-780-41588-473-0.

A series of essays generated from experienced therapists who examine the multiple ways that rap and hip-hop can be used in therapy by listening and discussing, performing, creating, or improvising. Compiled essays can be divided into three sections: the historical and theoretical perspectives of rap and hip-hop; descriptions of firsthand experiences of using the music with at-risk youth; and discussions of the ways in which each therapist has used rap and hip-hop with clients with specific diagnoses.

538.   **Hemmings, Jan**. 2016. *Methoden der Erforschung Populärer Musik (Methods for Researching Popular Music)*. Series: *Systematische Musikwissenschaft; Research (Wiesbaden, Germany)*. Wiesbaden: Springer. German and English texts. 534 p. Illustrations, Music Examples, Bibliography, and Index. ISBN: 9-783-65811-496-1.

Focuses on methods and introduces the field of systematic musicology/scientific study of popular music. Written from the perspective of a musicologist, the volume aims to appeal equally to students, scholars, and scientists from disciplinary and interdisciplinary contexts. Chapter topics covered include musicology and popular musicology: a theoretical framework model; technology and production; textual analysis; semiotic analysis; gender studies and performativity; empirical research; contextual analysis; economic analysis; music industry and copyright; globalization; history and historiography; and the definition of popular music.

539.   **Herbst, Jan-Peter, and Jonas Menze**. 2021. *Gear Acquisition Syndrome: Consumption of Instruments and Technology in Popular Music*. Huddersfield: University of Huddersfield Press. 282 p. Illustrations, Bibliography, and Index. ISBN: 9-781-86218-184-7.

Defines gear acquisition syndrome, also known as GAS, which is commonly understood as a musician's unrelenting urge to buy and own instruments and equipment as an anticipated catalyst of creative energy and bringer of happiness. Provides research from popular music studies, music technology, cultural and leisure studies, consumption research, sociology, psychology, and psychiatry. Offers a theoretical framework and empirical studies of online communities and offline music stores that allow for the consideration of musical, social, and personal motives that influence the way musicians think about and deal with equipment.

540.   **Hoag, Melissa, ed**. 2023. *Expanding the Canon's Black Composers in the Music Theory Classroom*. New York: Routledge. 286 p. Illustrations, Bibliography, and Index. ISBN: 9-781-03206-827-5.

A collection of essays that demonstrate why diversification is badly needed and help faculty expand their teaching with practical classroom-oriented lesson plans focusing on teaching music theory with music by Black composers. Essays are arranged to resemble a typical music theory curriculum, with topics progressing from basic to advanced and moving from fundamentals, diatonic harmony, and chromatic harmony to popular music and music of the twentieth and twenty-first centuries.

541.   **Holt, Fabian**. 2021. *Everybody Loves Live Music: A Theory of Performance Institutions*. Series: *Big Issues in Music*. Chicago: University of Chicago Press. 344 p. Illustrations, Tables, Music Examples, Bibliography, and Index. ISBN: 9-780-22673-840-6.

Demonstrates how festivals and other institutions of musical performance have evolved in recent decades from once meaningful sources of community and culture to those increasingly consumed by corporate giants. Examines a diverse range of case studies such as Lollapalooza, Coachella, Glastonbury, and others. Offers a theory of performance institutions.

542.   **Istvandity, Lauren**. 2019. *The Lifetime Soundtrack: Music and Autobiographical Memory*. Series: *Transcultural Music Studies*. Sheffield & Bristol: Equinox. 156 p. Bibliography and Index. ISBN: 9-781-78179-628-3.

Integrates the theoretical position that when music becomes integrated into personal memories, an invitation to remember is provided through both purposeful listening activities and incidental engagement within the everyday, and the result is a metaphorical canon in music that accompanies these experiences. Investigates musically motivated autobiographical memories as they relate to the lifetime soundtracks in order to provide further understanding of their occurrence, nuance, emotionality, and function for individuals.

543.   **Ito, John P**. 2021. *Focal Impulse Theory: Musical Expression, Meter, and the Body*. Series: *Musical Meaning and Interpretation*. Bloomington: Indiana University Press. xx, 376 p. Illustrations, Music Examples, Tables, Bibliography, and Index. ISBN: 9-780-25304-993-3.

Argues that music is surrounded by movement and that these actions are not just a visual display but reveal what it really means for musicians to move to the beat, organize the flow of notes from beat to beat, and shape the sound produced. Further argues that through the development of "focal impulse theory," it demonstrates how performers' choices in movement with the meter can transform the music's expressive contours.

544.   **Johnson, Julian**. 2002. *Who Needs Classical Music? Cultural Choice and Musical Value*. Oxford: Oxford University Press. 140 p. Bibliography and Index. ISBN: 9-780-19514-681-3.

Maintains that music is more than just a matter of taste. While some music provides entertainment or serves as background noise, other music functions as art. Considers the value of classical music in contemporary society. Argues that classical music remains distinctive because it works in quite different ways than most of the other music that surrounds us. Aims to restore classical music's intrinsic aesthetic value and rescue it from a designation as mere signifier of elitism or refinement.

545.   **Julien, Olivier, and Christophe Levaux, eds**. 2018. *Over and Over: Exploring Repetition in Popular Music*. New York: Bloomsbury. xvii, 189 p. Illustrations, Bibliography, and Index. ISBN: 9-781-50132-488-8.

A compilation of essays that address from perspectives of musicology, psychology, sociology, science, and technology the complexity connected to notions of popular music in a variety of musical genres. Essay topics including Tin Pan Alley 32-bar form, modal jazz, electronic dance music, structure, use of repetition from large repetitive structures to micro repetitions, and drones are explored in relation to both specific and large-scale issues and contexts.

546.   **Kahr, Michael, ed**. 2022. *Artistic Research in Jazz: Positions, Theories, Methods*. New York: Routledge. xxii, 201 p. Illustrations, Music Examples, Bibliography, and Index. ISBN: 9-780-36722-595-7.

A collection of essays that present an in-depth discourse on shared and specific approaches to artistic research in jazz. Essays aim at an understanding of the specificity of current practices, both improvisational and composed. Topics addressed throughout consider the cultural, institutional, epistemological, philosophical, ethical, and practical aspects of jazz as well as the influence of race, gender, and politics.

547.   **Kamp, Michiel, Tim Summers, and Mark Sweeney, eds**. 2016. *Ludomusicology: Approaches to Video Game Music*. Sheffield: Equinox. 240 p. Illustrations, Bibliography, and Index. ISBN: 9-781-78179-197-4.

A compilation of essays that suggest a variety of new approaches to the study of game music and develop new ways of conceptualizing and analyzing game music. They consider other critical issues, including the distinction between game play and music play, how notions of diegesis are complicated by video game interactivity, the importance of cinema aesthetics in game music, the technicalities of game music production, and the relationships between game music and music traditions.

548. **Kastner, Julie, and Saleel Menon**. 2019. "Popular Music in Choir: Helping Students 'Find Their Voices.'" *Music Educators Journal* 106(1): 48–54. ISSN: 0027-4321.

Describes the possibilities for using popular music to support singing with good technique, developing music literacy, and exposing students to new repertoire. Explores how music teachers can incorporate popular music into their classes using student-led creative projects, as well as how they can develop parameters to help facilitate students' learning in these activities.

549. **Kladder, Jonathan R., ed.** *Commercial and Popular Music in Higher Education: Expanding Notions of Musicianship and Pedagogy in Contemporary Education.* Series: *CMS Pedagogies and Innovations in Music.* New York: Routledge. xiv, 122 p. Illustrations, Bibliography, and Index. ISBN: 9-781-03210-719-6.

A collection of essays with examples of pedagogy in emerging areas of popular and commercial music. Essays offer practical insight and provide a theoretical framework for today's music educators. They also demonstrate how a constructivist approach to music pedagogy enables student-led, real-world leading in higher education and consider how diversity, equity, and inclusion intersect with teaching popular music performance.

550. **Kramer, Lawrence**. 2007. *Why Classical Music Still Matters.* Berkeley: University of California Press. viii, 241 p. Bibliography and Index. ISBN: 9-780-52093-364-4.

Explores the sources of classical music's power in a variety of settings from concert performance to film and television and others to the historical trauma of September 11. Addressed to a wide audience. Affirms the continued value of classical music, defined as a body of nontheatrical music produced since the eighteenth century with a single aim of being listened to, by revealing what its values are and specific beliefs, attitudes, and meanings. Admits that classical music needs a broader, more up-to-date rationale.

551. **Langlois, Tony, ed.** 2017. *Non-Western Popular Music.* Series: *Library of Essays on Popular Music.* Farnham: Ashgate; New York: Routledge. xxvii, 608 p. Illustrations, Bibliography, and Index. ISBN: 9-780-75462-984-9.

A compilation of essays that provide a diverse and contemporary overview of theoretical research in the field. Draws on scholarly writing from a range of disciplines and approaches through case studies from a wide range of non-Western popular music contexts. Essay topics include issues of popular music in Turkey, Cambodia, Bulgaria, Singapore, Kurdish popular song, Israeli-Egyptian popular music, South Africa, Hong Kong, Arab-Jewish music, Cuba, India, Zimbabwe, Nigeria, North India, Japan, Afghanistan, Indonesia, so forth. Other topics include interpreting world music, rap music, global discourse, theory and practice, and others.

552. **Lee, Gavin S. K**. 2018. *Rethinking Differences in Gender, Sexuality and Popular Music Theory and Politics of Ambiguity.* Series: *Routledge Studies in Popular*

Music. Abingdon, Oxon & New York: Routledge. x, 197 p. Illustrations, Bibliography, and Index.

Argues that in studies of popular music, the concept of difference is often a crucial analysis for detecting social agency. However, the alternative analytic of ambiguity has never been systematically examined. Offers critically oriented case studies that examine the theory of politics of ambiguity. Considers ambiguity to mean that there are both positive and negative implications in any gender and sexuality practice. Covers popular music from around the globe.

553. **Lief, Jason**. 2017. *Christianity and Heavy Metal as Impure Sacred With the Secular West*. Lanham: Rowman & Littlefield. 142 p. Bibliography and Index. ISBN: 9-781-49850-632-8.

Explores heavy metal music in the context of the secular West from Christianity. Even if the purpose is to critique religion, its usage creates a positive connection with an interpretation of Christianity as a form of cultural critique. Explores how Christianity and heavy metal function within the context of secularity as a form of ideological critique. Employs theories of Emile Durkheim, Max Weber, and Charles Taylor to explore the religious nature of secularism in the West interpreted in the immanent processes of politics and economics.

554. **Lochhead, Judy**. 2016. *Reconceiving Structure in Contemporary Music: New Tools in Music Theory and Analysis*. Series: *Routledge Studies in Music Theory*. New York: Routledge. xiv, 179 p. Illustrations, Music Examples, Bibliography, and Index. ISBN: 9-780-36759-880-8.

Studies music in the Western classical tradition and offers a critique of current analytical and theoretical approaches. Addresses the present fringe status of recent music sometimes described as crossover, postmodern, post-classical, post-minimalist, and others.

555. **Malawey, Victoria**. 2020. *A Blaze of Light in Every Word: Analyzing the Popular Singing Voice*. Series: *Oxford Studies in Music Theory*. New York: Oxford University Press. ix, 99 p. Illustrations, Bibliography, and Index. ISBN: 9-780-19005-224-9.

Presents a conceptual model for analyzing vocal delivery in popular song recordings focused on three overlapping areas of inquiry: pitch, prosody, and quality. Focuses on the sonic and material aspects and other electronic effects that impact voice in recorded music, indie rock to hip-hop, death metal, and so forth.

556. **Marc, Isabelle**. 2015. "Travelling Songs: On Popular Music Transfer and Translation." *IASPM Journal* 5(2) [Special Issue: *Transnational Issue*]: 3–21. ISSN: 2079-3871.

Draws on translation and cultural theories and contends that even through a song is created in a specific national or communitarian context that determines to various degrees its production on reception processes, once it is recorded, reproduced, and disseminated, especially through the global market, it travels and wanders through time and place becoming a transcultural product that can be described as a "travelling song" and by extension "travelling music." Argues that travelling songs are dramatically transformed by their new contexts of reception.

557. **McClain, Jordan M**. 2016. "A Framework for Using Popular Music Videos to Teach Media Literacy." Dialogue: *The Interdisciplinary Journal of Popular Culture and Pedagogy* 3(1) [Special Issue: *Popular Culture Pedagogy: Theory and Application in Academia*]: [Electronic Resource at www.journaldialogue]. OCLC Number: 8-9205-006-3.

Discusses the use of popular music as a tool for teaching media literacy. Address the importance of music videos as popular culture, what other music video research has examined, and what features make music videos a good fit for in-class work investigating media and popular culture. Provides details of a single-class activity for introducing and teaching media literacy using music videos.

558. **McClary, Susan**. 1994. "Paradigm Dissonances: Music Theory, Cultural Studies, Feminist Criticism." *Perspectives of New Music* 32(1): 68–85. ISSN: 0031-6016.

Focuses on a solution to the strife between theory and feminism by introducing a mediating factor, namely cultural studies that offers a loose amalgam of methods, questions, and issues. Suggests that if the gap between a self-sufficient music theory and criticism dealing with issues of gender and sexuality seems impossible to bridge, it is in large part because theorists have so long resisted treating music as a cultural phenomenon. However, under a cultural studies umbrella, it should be possible to both investigate the syntactical conventions that grant coherence to repertoires and to examine the way music participates in the social construction of subjectivity, gender, desire, ethnicity, the body, and so forth.

559. **McClary, Susan**. 2002. *Feminine Endings: Music, Gender, and Sexuality*. Minneapolis: University Minnesota Press. xx, 220 p. Bibliography and Index. ISBN: 9-780-81669-505-8.

Originally published in 1991, the volume intermingles cultural criticism and musical studies in an approach that came to be called "the New Musicology." Offers case studies of works ranging from the canonical operas by Claudio Monteverdi and Georges Bizet to the contemporary, including the performance art of Diamanda Galás and popular songs by Madonna. Focuses on the ways music produces images of gender, desire, pleasure, and the body. Explores the gender-based metaphors that circulate in discourse about music.

560. **McDonald, Chris**. 2000. "Exploring Modal Subversions in Alternative Music." *Popular Music* 19(3): 355–363. ISSN: 0261-1430.

A study that is concerned with a particular set of harmonic practices that rock musicians, particularly those who participate in the domain of guitar-oriented "alternative" rock, have been using with noticeable frequency. Discusses the concept of the *powerchord*, as a device in rock that has facilitated the set of harmonic practices. Discusses the observations from the author's previous research inquiry into the devices that alternative musicians use to differentiate their music from other styles of mainstream rock and from a response to Allan Moore's admonition that there is a very little concern for theorizing analytical method in rock music.

561.   **McIntyre, Phillip**. 2008. "Creativity and Cultural Production: A Study of Contemporary Western Popular Music Songwriting." *Creativity Research Journal* 1: 40–42. ISSN: 1040-0419.

Incorporates the use of ethnographic research methodology to investigate the systems of creativity as it applies to contemporary Western popular music songwriting. Posits that the systems model of creativity partially coupled with the similarity complex approach to cultural production presented by Pierre Bourdieu provides the most useful working platform to investigate the idea of creativity. Concludes that a contemporary Western songwriter's ability to make choices and be creative is both circumscribed and facilitated by knowledge of the domain of contemporary Western popular music and access to knowledge of the field that holds this knowledge allows the conclusion of a more philosophical level, independence of agency, and structure within the workings of the creative system.

562.   **McKay, George**. 2013. *Shakin' All Over: Popular Music and Disability*. Ann Arbor: University of Michigan Press. x, 230 p. Illustrations, Bibliography, and Index. ISBN: 9-780-47207-209-5.

A significant study covering the important intersection of popular music and disability. Offers a cross-disciplinary examination of the ways in which popular music performers have addressed disability in their songs, their live performances, and various media presentations. Examines closely the work of artists such as Johnny Rotten, Neil Young, Johnny Ray, Ian Dury, Teddy Pendergrass, Curtis Mayfield, and Joni Mitchell to investigate such questions as how popular music works to obscure and accommodate the presence of people with disabilities in its cultural practice. Also investigates how popular musicians have articulated the experiences of disability or have used their cultural arena for disability advocacy purposes.

563.   **McKerrell, Simon, and Lyndon C.S. Way, eds**. 2017. *Music as Multimodal Discourse: Semiotics, Power, and Protest*. London: Bloomsbury. xxi, 229 p. Bibliography and Index. ISBN: 9-781-47426-444-0.

Considers musical sound as multimodal communication. Examines the interaction with text, image, and other modes and their relationships to rhythm, instrumentation, pitch, tonality, and melody. Compiled essays draw upon critical discourse analysis, social semiotics and music, and music studies to expose both the function and the semiotic potential of the various modes used in songs and other musical texts.

564.   **Middleton, Richard**. 2000. *Reading Pop: Approaches to Textual Analysis in Popular Music*. Oxford & New York: Oxford University Press. xi, 388 p. Illustrations, Music Examples, Bibliography, and Index. ISBN: 0-19816-612-5.

A compilation of scholarly essays that focus on different approaches to music and theoretical analysis of popular music. Popular musicians covered in the essays include Randy Newman, Prince, James Brown, Chuck Berry, Jimi Hendrix, Irving Berlin, Hank Williams, John Mellencamp, David Bowie, and John Zorn. Analytical topics include popular music approaches, harmonic analysis, theory and methodology, representation progressive and psychedelic rock, postcolonialism, structural relationship of music and images in music videos, and others.

565.   **Middleton, Richard**. 2006. *Voicing the Popular: On the Subjects of Popular Music*. New York: Routledge. viii, 339 p. Bibliography and Index. ISBN: 9-780-41597-590-2.

Draws on approaches from musical interpretation, cultural history, social theory, and psychoanalysis to explore key topics in popular music including race, gender, authenticity, and repetition. Provides examples from across the past hundred years of popular music development but also relating them to the eighteenth and nineteenth centuries. Constructs an argument that relates "the popular" to the unfolding of modernity itself.

566.   **Miklitsch, Robert**. 2006. *Roll Over Adorno: Critical Theory, Popular Culture, Audiovisual Media*. Albany: State University of New York Press. xxi, 262 p. Illustrations, Bibliography, and Index. ISBN: 9-781-42378-038-0.

Investigates the postmodern nexus between elite popular culture as it occurs in the audiovisual fields of music, film, and television ranging from Gershwin to gangsta rap, Tarantino to Tongues United, and Buffy the Vampire Slayer. Argues that the aim of critical theory in the new millennium is to describe and explain these commodities in greater phenomenological detail without losing touch with those evaluative criteria that have historically sustained both kulturkrtik and classical aesthetic.

567.   **Moore, Alan, and Remi Martin**. 2019. *Rock: The Primary Text: Developing a Musicology of Rock, 3rd ed.* Series: *Ashgate Popular and Folk Music Series*. Abingdon, Oxon & New York: Routledge. xxiv, 321 p. Illustrations, Discography, Bibliography, and Index. ISBN: 9-781-13859-210-0.

Features sections on melody, Britpop, authenticity, and intertextuality, and an extended discussion of texture. Argues for the development of musicology particular to rock within the context of the background to the genres, the beat and rhythm, and blues style of early 1960s "progressive" rock and subsequent styles. Explores the fundamental issue of rock as a medium for self-expression and the relationship of this to changing musical styles.

568.   **Moore, Allan**. 2007. *Critical Essays in Popular Musicology*. Aldershot & Burlington: Ashgate. xxii, 608 p. Illustrations and Index. ISBN: 9-780-75462-647-3.

A compilation of essays that reproduces in facsimile form of many of the most important and innovative journal articles and papers in the field of popular musicology. Topics include the context for addressing text and theory of Black music, African American music, and European music, musical competence, rock aesthetics, analyzing popular music, British dance band music of the 1920s and 1930s, theory of popular music harmony, and much more.

569. **Morrison, Matthew D**. 2019. "Race, Blacksound, and the (Re)Making of Musicological Discourse." *Journal of the American Musicological Society* 72(3): 781–832. ISSN: 0003-0139.

Highlights practices of exclusion embedded in musicology, especially in relation to race, racialized people, and race relations to rupture its construed borders and decentralize the normative systems that have come to shape the discipline, its members, and its discourses. Defines the concept of Blacksound—the sonic and embodied legacy of blackface performance as the origin of all popular music, entertainment, and culture in the United States.

570. **Negus, Keith**. 1996. *Popular Music Theory: An Introduction*. Cambridge: Polity Press. 243 p. Bibliography and Index. ISBN: 0-74561-317-9.

Provides a critical introduction to the key theoretical issues and concepts that arise in the study of contemporary popular music. Organized in a way that shows how popular music is created across a series of relationships that link together industry and audiences, producers, and consumers. Examines the equally significant social processes that intervene between and across the production–consumption divide. Also examines how popular music is mediated by technology, cultural, historical, geographical, and political factors.

571. **Nicholls, David**. 2007. "Narrative Theory as an Analytical Tool in the Study of Popular Music." *Music & Letters* 88(2): 297–315. ISSN: 0027-4224.

Explores the ways in which music, lyrics, prose, art works, and other elements can be used to create and describe both single and multiple narratives. Argues that narrative structures truly come into their own at the point where albums begin to function as significant units of music organization. Provide examples of the Beatles' *Norwegian Wood* (1968); Kate Bush's *Wuthering Heights* (1978); The Buggles' *Video Killed the Radio Star* (1979); Genesis's *The Lamb Lies Down on Broadway* (1974); and The Who's *Quadrophenia* (1973).

572. **Niknafs, Nasim**. 2019. "Engaging With Popular Music From a Critical Standpoint: A Concept-Oriented Framework." *Music Educators Journal* 106(1): 25–30. ISSN: 0027-4321.

Examines the concept-oriented framework through which, instead of exploring popular music geographically, one can engage with the wider concept of popular music across cultures. Offers a theoretical framework of a central concept selected by music teachers and students and is centralized by various areas of exploration. Argues that popular music can play an influential transformative and socially just role in improving numerous situations.

573. **Nobile, Drew**. 2020. *Form as Harmony in Rock Music*. New York: Oxford University Press. xxii, 268 p. Illustrations, Music Examples, Bibliography, and Index. ISBN: 9-781-50133-045-2.

Argues that rock songs unfold through a unified musical structure. Considers and incorporates discussions about the process-based approach of classical theorists to popular music scholarship. Offers a comprehensive theory for 1960s, 1970s, and 1980s classical rock repertoire by showing how songs in this genre are not simply a series of discrete elements but rather exhibit cohesive format-harmonic structures across their entire timespan. Also observes and examines how many elements contribute to the cohesion of a song and how rock music of these decades is built around a fundamentally harmonic backdrop and has given rise to distinct types of verses, choruses, and bridges. Discussions of theoretical analysis are presented to demonstrate how artists from Bob Dylan and Stevie Wonder to Madonna consistently turn to the same compositional structures throughout rock's various genres and decades, unifying them under a single musical style.

574. **O'Grady, Pat**. 2023. "Everyday Fidelity: Analyzing Sound Quality in Ubiquitous Listening Practices." *Popular Music and Society* 46(1): 21–34. ISSN: 0300-7766.

Examines wireless headphones and speakers to consider how "ubiquitous listening" practices spare our desires for portability and fidelity. Proposes the term "everyday fidelity" to describe how listeners might seek out distinct levels of fidelity based on their activities at one point in time.

575. **Onsman, Andrys, and Robert Burke**. 2019. *Experimentation in Improvised Jazz: Chasing Ideas*. New York: Routledge. xi, 192 p. Bibliography and Index. ISBN: 9-780-36758-467-2.

Challenges the notion that in the twenty-first century jazz can be restrained by a singularly static definition. Suggests that the worldwide trend for jazz to be marginalized by the mainstream music industry as well as conservatories and schools of music runs the risk of stifling the innovative and challenging aspects of its creativity. Argues that to remain relevant jazz needs to be dynamic, be proactively experimental, and consciously facilitate new ideas to be made accessible to an audience wider than just the innovators themselves.

576. **Osborn, Brad**. 2013. "Subverting the Verse-Chorus Paradigm: Terminally Climatic Forms in Recent Rock Music." *Music Theory Spectrum* 35(1): 23–47. ISSN: 1533-8339.

Defines and demonstrates a formal type of "terminally climatic forms." Examines how these forms that appear frequently in rock after 1990 are characterized by their balance between the expected memorable highpoint of the chorus and the thematically independent terminal climax of the song's actual high point, which appears only once at the end of the song.

577. **Polt, Christopher B**. 2018. "'I Found Someone' . . . Or Did I? Teaching Persona Theory Through Popular Music." *Classical World* 112: 627–647. ISSN: 0009-8418.

Defines persona theory that presents essential for the modern critical study of Latin poetry. Presents an in-class activity designed to introduce students to the concept of the literary persona or persona theory through modern popular music. Outlines how the project fits into a course on Latin love poetry structured around the hypothesis that Roman poetry has more in common with traditions of popular music than with the view of poetry that modern students often bring to college.

578. **Prey, Robert, Marc Esteve Del Valle, and Leslie Zwerwer**. 2022. "Platform Pop: Disentangling Spotify's Intermediary Role in the Music Industry." *Information, Communication & Society* 25(1): 74–92. ISSN: 1369-118X.

Examines whether Spotify is leveling the playing field or entrenching hierarchies between major labels and independent labels. Provides a longitudinal analysis of content owners (major labels and indies) and formats (albums, tracks, or playlists) promoted by Spotify through its Twitter account @Spotify. Offers an empirical study of how Spotify is shaping the consumption of music, and in turn the structure of the recording industry.

579. **Ravn, Susanne, Simon Høffding, and James McGuirk, eds**. 2021. *Philosophy of Improvisation: Interdisciplinary Perspectives on Theory and Practices*. Series: *Routledge Research in Aesthetics*. New York: Routledge. 226 p. Illustrations, Bibliography, and Index. ISBN: 9-780-36754-021-0.

A series of essays that covers philosophical and interdisciplinary perspectives on improvisation. Essays connect the theoretical dimensions of improvisation with different viewpoints on its practice in the arts and the classroom. They also attend to lived experiences of improvisation both within and outside the arts in order to explain the phenomenon and extend the scope of improvisational practices to include the role of improvisation in habit and planned action on both individual and collective levels.

580. **Reid, Anna, Neal Da Costa, and Jeanell Carrigan, eds**. 2021. *Creative Research in Music: Informed Practice, Innovation, and Transcendence*. Series: *ISME Global Perspectives in Music Education Series*. New York: Routledge. x, 237 p. Illustrations, Maps, Bibliography, and Index. ISBN: 9-780-36723-135-4.

A collection of essays that explores what it means to be an artistic researcher in music in the twenty-first century. Essays delineate the varieties of processes that underpin successful artistic research in music and provide examples ranging from Western classic art music to local Indigenous traditions, and from small- to large-scale multi-music and cross-cultural formats.

581. **Robertson, Roland**. 2004. "Globalization or Glocalization?" *Journal of International Communication* 1(1) [Special Issue: *Gulf & Beyond: Broadcasting International Crises*]: 33–52. ISSN: 1321-6597.

A study that may be useful in formulating theoretical perspectives in global popular music research. Deals with the idea of glocalization as a refinement of the concept of globalization. Argues that glocalization has some definite conceptual advantages in the general theorization of globalization and facilitates the thorough discussion of various problems that attend a simple distinction between the global and local. Examines the ways in which localities are produced on a global-wide basis.

582.   **Robinson, Dylan**. 2020. *Hunger Listening: Resonant Theory for Indigenous Sound Studies*. Series: *Indigenous Americas*. Minneapolis: University of Minnesota Press. 328 p. Illustrations, Photographs, Bibliography, and Index. ISBN: 9-781-51790-768-6.

Evaluates how decolonial practices of listening emerge from increasing awareness of our listening positionality. Provides case studies on Indigenous participation in classical, musical, and popular music and examines structures of inclusion that reinforce Western musical values. Also offer examples of "doing sovereignty" in Indigenous performance art, museum exhibition, and gatherings.

583.   **Robinson, Thomas**. 2017. *Popular Music Theory and Analysis*. Series: *Routledge Music Bibliographies*. London & New York: Routledge. ix, 335 p. Bibliography and Index. ISBN: 9-781-13820-632-8.

An annotated bibliography that incorporates a wealth of scholarly works dealing with the theory and analysis of popular music. Features a catalog of music-theoretical and musicological works that is searchable by subject, genre, and song title. Supports emerging scholarship and inquiry for future research in popular music. Includes annotations for articles, books, collections, and dissertations and a song index, subject index, author/editor index, and year index.

584.   **Shadrack, Jasmine H**. 2021. *Black Metal, Trauma, Subjectivity and Sound: Screaming the Abyss*. Series: *Emerald Studies in Metal Music and Culture*. Bingley: Emerald. xxiv, 227 p. Illustrations, Music Examples, Bibliography, and Index. ISBN: 9-781-78756-927-0.

Weaves together trauma, black metal theory, and disability into a story of both pain and freedom. Draws on the many years of black metal guitarist Jasmine Hazel Shadrack and uses autoethnography to explore her own experiences of gender-based violence, misogyny, and the healing power of performance.

585.   **Shenoy, Arun, and Ye Wang**. 2005. "Key, Chord, and Rhythm Tracking of Popular Music Recordings." *Computer Music Journal* 29(3): 75–86. ISSN: 0148-9267.

Proposes a framework to analyze a musical audio signal sampled from popular music recordings to determine its key, provide usable chord transcriptions, and obtain the hierarchical rhythm structure representation containing the quarter note, half note, and whole note. Discusses automatic transcription structural audio and emotion detention in music.

586.   **Shepherd, John**. 1982. "A Theoretical Model for the Sociomusicological Analysis of Music." *Popular Music* 2 [Special Issue: *Theory and Method*]: 145–177. ISSN: 0261-1430.

Offers theoretical motion concerning a model for music. Argues that despite the radical shift in musical and social aesthetics that have been maintained since the turn of the century through successive works of so-called popular music, very little attention has been paid to popular music as a cultural form. Suggests, in consensus with the notions of Jenny Taylor and Dave Laing, that the study of popular music continues to be undervalued in cultural theory.

587. **Shonk, Kenneth L., and Daniel R. McClure**. 2017. *Historical Theory and Methods Through Popular Music, 1970–2000: 'Those Are the New Saints'*. Series: *Pop Music, Culture, and Identity*. London: Palgrave MacMillan. xii, 311 p. Bibliography and Index. ISBN: 9-781-13757-071-0.

Examines the post-1960s era of popular music in the Anglo-Black Atlantic through the prism of historical theory and methods. Employs a series of case studies that mobilizes historical theory and methods underlying different expressions of alternative music functioning within a mainstream music industry. Weaves historical theory and methods through a genre of music expressing a notion of alternativity and explicit positioning of one's expression and counter to the mainstream.

588. **Simonett, Helena**. 2011. "Giving Voice to the 'Dignified Man': Reflections on Global Popular Music." *Popular Music* 30(2) [Special Issue: *Crossing Borders: Music of Latin America*]: 227–244. ISSN: 0261-1430.

Observes that music increasingly links the global and local and vice versa and creates fusions of diverse musical genres and styles. Moreover, the globalization theory has spurred explanations for musical hybridity and cross-fertilization among scholars from different academic fields focusing on music. Presents an argument for the necessity of understanding global cultural interactions and musical appropriations or exchanges in the context of the ambivalences of the globalized mass diffusion and the power asymmetries involved.

589. **Sinnamon, Sarah**. 2021. *Achieving Peak Performance in Music: Psychological Strategies for Optimal Flow*. Abingdon, Oxon: Routledge. xiii, 200 p. Illustrations, Bibliography, and Index. ISBN: 9-780-36748-062-2.

Provides a comprehensive exploration of flow in musical performance. Describes the optimal performance experiences of great musicians and outlines ten psychological steps that can be implemented to facilitate and enhance optimal experiences. Reveals strategies used by experts to prepare themselves emotionally, cognitively, and physically for performances.

590. **Smith, Hazel**. 2016. *The Contemporary Literature-Music Relationship: Intermedia, Voice, Technology, Cross-Cultural Exchange*. Series: *Routledge Interdisciplinary Perspectives on Literature*. New York: Routledge. xii, 202 p. Illustrations, Bibliography, and Index. ISBN: 9-780-36787-241-0.

Explores the relationship between words and music in contemporary texts, examining the way the new technologies are changing the literature-music relationship. Integrates a range of interdisciplinary theories to the area of musico-literary studies, drawing from fields of semiotics, disability studies, musicology, globalization, and others. Argues that conjunctions between words and music create emergent structures and meanings that can facilitate culturally transgressive and boundary interrogating effects.

591.	**Smith, Kenneth M., and Stephen Overy**. 2023. *Listening to the Unconscious: Adventures in Popular Music and Psychoanalysis*. New York: Bloomsbury. 280 p. Bibliography and Index. ISBN: 9-781-50136-849-3.

Presents the history of the unconscious and its related concepts working systematically and contextualizes theories as vital to follow the psychoanalysts' complexity of popular music demonstrated through close readings of individual songs, albums, artists, genres, and popular music practices. Draws from several artists such as Prince, Sufjan Stevens, Robyn, Xiu Xiu, Joanna Newsom, Arcade Five, PJ Harvey, LCD Sound System, and others.

592.	**Solomos, Mak S.** 2020. *From Music to Sound: The Emergence of Sound in 20th- and 21st-Century Music*. Series: *Routledge Research in Music*. Abingdon, Oxon: Routledge. xi, 282 p. Illustrations, Bibliography, and Index. ISBN: 9-781-03208-716-0.

Provides a communication of six musical histories: timbre; noise; listening; immersion; composing with sound; and spaces from Claude Debussy to contemporary music in the early twenty-first century from rock to electronica, musique concréte to current electroacoustic music, and others.

593.	**Solstad, Stein**. 2020. *Expertise in Jazz Guitar Improvisation: A Cognitive Approach*. Series: *SEMPRE Studies in the Psychology of Music*. Abingdon, Oxon: Routledge. xviii, 224 p. Illustrations, Bibliography, and Index. ISBN: 9-781-03207-224-1.

A study of musical interplay and the ways implicit (subconscious) and explicit (conscious) knowledge appears during improvisation. Includes practice-based research, interviews, and interplay with five world-class jazz guitarists: Lage Lund, Jack Wilkins, Ben Monder, Rez Abbasi, and Adam Rogers. Offers a modal matrix for analyzing structure, time, and form in jazz guitar improvisation and musical analysis based on cognitive theory.

594.	**Song, Yading, Simon Dixon, Marcus T. Pearce, and Andrea R. Halpern**. 2016. "Perceived and Induced Emotion Responses to Popular Music." *Music Perception: An Interdisciplinary Journal* 33(4): 472–492. ISSN: 1533-8312.

Examines the difference between perceived and induced emotion for Western popular music using both categorical and dimensional models of emotion. Examines the influence of individual listener differences on their emotional judgment. The study involved several musical experts who were randomly selected from an established dataset of numerous popular songs tagged with one of the four words—happy, sad, angry, and relaxed.

595.	**Source, Richard**. 1995. *Music Theory for the Professional: A Comparison of Common-Practice and Popular Genres*. New York: Ardsley House. xxv, 549 p. Illustrations, Music Examples, Bibliography, and Index. ISBN: 9-781-88015-720-6.

A music theory text that not only addresses the importance of music's syntax in the classical sense but also relates the syntax to current practices and styles. Intended for musicians focusing on aspects of the music business and of popular culture.

596.   **Spilker, Hendrick S**. 2017. *Digital Music Distribution: The Sociology of Online Music Streams*. Series: *Routledge Advances in Sociology*. Abingdon, Oxon: Routledge. x, 207 p. Bibliography and Index. ISBN: 9-780-36787-752-1.

Offers a broad perspective for understanding the paradoxes inherent in new forms of distribution. Covers both production and consumption perspectives and analyzes the change and regulatory issues through original case studies, examining how digital music distribution has both changed and been changed by the critical practices and politicking of youth, parents, music countercultures, artists, brands, record companies, and others.

597.   **Steinbrecher, Bernhard**. 2021. "Mainstream Popular Music Research: A Musical Update." *Popular Music* 40(3–4): 406–427. ISSN: 0261-1430.

A study that reviews studies that examine internationally circulating music that has reached the upper echelon of all-genre single charts in the twenty-first century. Employs examinations as examples for the analysis of sonic aesthetics that are embedded in a particular frame of cultural debate, which in the study is conceptualized as mainstream popular music. Provides discussions of prevailing objectives, methods, and findings, including further discussions on how future research might advance an understanding of the aesthetics within the discourse of mainstream popular music and of contemporary culture at large.

598.   **Sterne, Jonathan.** *The Sound Studies Reader*. New York: Routledge. x, 566 p. Bibliography and Index. ISBN: 9-780-41577-130-6.

A compilation of essays that blend work that self-consciously describes itself as "sound studies" with earlier and lesser-known scholarship of sound. Includes an introduction that acquaints readers with key themes and concepts in sound studies. Also offers further background on the essays with an extensive up-to-date bibliography for further reading in sound studies.

599.   **Stone, Alison**. 2016. *The Value of Popular Music: An Approach From Post-Kantian Aesthetics*. Cham: Palgrave Macmillan. xxxvi, 294 p. Illustrations, Bibliography, and Index. ISBN: 9-783-31946-544-9.

Argues that popular music such as rock 'n' roll is a unified form of music that has positive value and affirms the importance of materiality and body, challenging the long-standing Western evaluation of the intellect above all things corporeal. Further argues that popular music's stress on materiality gives it aesthetic value. Draws on ideas from the post-Kantian tradition in aesthetics by Georg Hegel, Theodor Adorno, and others to demonstrate that popular music gives importance to materiality in its typical structures in how music of this type handles the relations between matter and form, the relations between sound and words, and how it deals with rhythm, meaning, and emotional expression.

600. **Sweers, Britta, and Sarah M. Ross, eds**. 2020. *Cultural Mapping and Musical Diversity*. Series: *Transcultural Music Studies*. Sheffield, South Yorkshire & Bristol: Equinox. xii, 321 p. Illustrations, Bibliography, and Index. ISBN: 9-781-78179-758-7.

A collection of essays that approach the topic of cultural mapping from several thematic perspectives. Topics include the method of cultural mapping; cultural landscapes and music; the politics of intangible cultural heritage; intangible cultural heritage (case studies); musical hybridization; policy making; and others.

601. **Swiss, Thom, John M. Sloop, and Andrew Herman, eds**. 1998. *Mapping the Beat: Popular Music and Contemporary Theory*. Malden: Blackwell. xi, 322 p. Bibliography and Index. ISBN: 1-57718-077-1.

An interdisciplinary compilation of essays that analyzes popular music to understand the world through the social dynamics, cultural production, and consumption of popular music. Attempts to map out contemporary popular music in relation to the best and newest cultural and social theory. Essay topics include spaces of noise and places of music; race, repetition, and difference in hip-hop and dance music; music production, public policy, and the market; rock and gender on the Internet; queers, punks, and alternative acts; scholarship, technology, and music making; history of rock's past through rock covers; patriarchy and feminism in rock music; synergy and corporate culture; Selena's Tejano music and the Borderlands; music-making television for Latin America; materialist ethnography; scenes, spatiality, and migrancy; and politics of noise.

602. **Tagg, Philip**. 1982. "Analyzing Popular Music: Theory, Method, and Practice." *Popular Music* 2 [Special Issue: *Theory and Method*]: 37–67. ISSN: 0261-1430.

Argues that the initial problems of any new field of study is the attitude of incredulity it meets. Moreover, the study of popular music is no exception to the rule and is often confronted with an attitude of bemused suspicion, implying that there is something weird about taking "fun" seriously or finding "fun" in serious things. Suggests that such attitudes are of considerable interest when discussing the aims and method of popular music analysis.

603. **Titlebaum, Mike**. 2021. *Jazz Improvement Using Simple Melodic Embellishment*. New York: Routledge. 322 p. Illustrations, Bibliography, and Index. ISBN: 9-780-36742-742-9.

Teaches fundamental concepts of jazz improvisation by highlighting the development of performance skills through embellishment techniques. Offers a practical and comprehensive source that is ideal for the aspiring improviser focused not on scales and chords but melodic embellishments. Assumes some basic theoretical knowledge and level of musicianship for producing multiple techniques.

604. **Tobias, Evan**. 2019. "Another Perspective: Inquiry, Context, and Popular Music." *Music Educators Journal* 106(1): 64–66. ISSN: 0027-4321.

Reflects on context in relation to popular music, music programs, and curriculum structures. Makes inquiries into how to address popular music, how to address popular music from a technical perspective, how to enact practices that account for sociocultural issues such as equity or cultural appropriations, and so forth.

605. **VanWeelden, Kimberly**. 2018. "Classical Music as Popular Music: Adolescents' Recognition of Western Art Music." *Update: Applications of Research in Music Education* 13(1): 14–24. ISSN: 8755-1233.

A study to determine which "popular" classical repertoire is familiar and predictable to adolescents. Goals of the study, in which students were given thirty classical music excerpts to listen to, include examining if students had heard the music before. Results indicate the various contexts in which students had previously heard the repertoire, including several contemporary media, school music classrooms, and/or live performances.

606. **Varas-Diaz, Nelson, and Niall Scott, eds**. 2016. *Heavy Metal Music and the Communal Experience*. Lanham: Lexington Books. xiii, 216 p. Bibliography and Index. ISBN: 9-781-49850-638-0.

A compilation of essays that critically examines the issue of community formation in metal music with theoretical reflections and empirical research. The essays focus on how metal communities are conceptualized, created, shaped, maintained, interact with their context, and address internal tensions. They provide the field of metal music studies with a state-of-the-art reflection on how metal communities are constructed while also addressing their limits and future challenges.

607. **Verbuč, David**. 2021. "Ethnography in Western Popular Music Research Revisited." *Journal of World Popular Music* 8(2): 207–235. ISSN: 2052-4900.

Focuses on ethnomusicological and popular music studies, examining Western popular music cultures to provide a critique of some of their methods. Suggests a re-emphasis of some of the fundamental ethnographic approaches in studying Western popular music cultures. Examines personal ethnographic research of American DIY venues and scenes as an example of participatory research of living and touring with DIY participants and studying their everyday lives.

608. **Vilotijevic, Marija D., and Ivana Medic, eds**. 2019. *Contemporary Popular Music Studies Proceedings of the International Association for the Study of Popular Music*. Series: *Systematische Musikwissenschaft*. Wiesbaden: Springer. 298 p. Illustrations and Bibliography. ISBN: 9-783-65825-252-6.

A compilation of papers that were presented at the International Association of Popular Music in 2017 in Kassel, Germany. Topics of papers include methodologies; the structure and interpretation of popular music scenes, genres, and repertoires; approaches to education in popular music studies outside the

Anglophone world; and an examination of discursive and technological aspects of numerous popular music phenomena.

609.   **Waite, Si**. 2014. "Sensation and Control: Indeterminate Approaches in Popular Music." *Leonardo Music Journal* 3: 78–79. ISSN: 0961-1215.

Argues that indeterminate techniques borrowed from experimental music can be applied to the composition and performance of popular, song-based material. Makes that case for teaching computer-based systems as collaborations in creating works that are both sensuous and cerebral.

610.   **Washburne, Christopher, and Maiken Derno, eds**. 2004. *Bad Music: The Music We Love to Hate*. New York: Routledge. x, 379 p. Illustrations, Bibliography, and Index. ISBN: 9-780-41594-365-9.

A compilation of essays that consider why some popular musical forms and performers are universally reviled by critics and ignored by scholars despite enjoying larger-scale popularity and how the notion of what makes "good" or "bad" music has changed over the years. The essays examine how popular musical forms as jazz, country, and pop music were all once rejected as "bad" by the academy that now has courses on these and many other popular forms of music.

611.   **Weinstein, Deena**. 1991. *Heavy Metal: A Cultural Sociology*. Series: *Lexington Book Series on Social Issues*. New York: Lexington Books. 331 p. Bibliography and Index. ISBN: 9-780-66921-837-4.

Describes through scholarly discourse the heavy metal culture and explains why it has prompted demands for censorship. Argues that fears of heavy metal stem from a deep misunderstanding of the energetic rebellious culture of metal. Offers an analysis of and discusses many issues associated with the heavy metal phenomenon and attempts to interpret all aspects of the metal world.

612.   **Werner, Ann**. 2023. *Feminism and Gender Politics in Mediated Popular Music*. London: Bloomsbury. 146 p. Bibliography and Index. ISBN: 9-781-50136-850-9.

Engages with feminist theory and previous research about gender and music. Investigates the meaning of current trends relating to gender, feminism, and woman-identified artists in mediated popular music. Examples discussed include artists such as Beyoncé, Lady Gaga, and Taylor Swift. Discusses the media specificity of the different examples, introduces and explains feminist theories and concepts, and analyzes the position of women, gender, equality, and feminism in mainstream popular music in contemporary time.

613.   **Whitt, David, ed**. 2020. *Popular Music in the Classroom: Essays for Instructors*. Jefferson: McFarland. 257 p. Bibliography and Index. ISBN: 9-781-47667-157-4.

A compilation of essays that draws upon the knowledge and expertise of instructors from a variety of disciplines who have taught classes on popular music. Topics covered include the analysis of music genres such as American folk, Latin American protest music, and Black music; exploring the musical catalog and sociocultural relevance of specific artists; and discussing how popular music can be used to teach history, identity, race, gender, and politics.

614. **Williams, James, and Samuel Horlor, eds**. 2022. *Musical Spaces: Place, Performance, and Power.* Singapore: Jenny Stanford Publishing and New York: Routledge. xxx, 460 p. Illustrations, Bibliography, and Index. ISBN: 9-789-81487-785-5.

Explores intersections between multiple scales and kinds of musical spaces. Investigates the broader power structures and place-based identities with a focus on the moments of music making and music environments. Overcomes a Eurocentric focus on a typically narrow range of musics, especially European and North American classical and popular forms, with case studies on a diverse set of genres and global contexts.

615. **Williams, Justin A**. 2022. "'This Year's Model': Toward a Sloanist Theory of Popular Music Production." *The Musical Quarterly* 105(3–4): 320–356. ISSN: 0027-4631.

Defines Sloanism as the production of an updated or upgraded consumer good, sold even before the older product's life cycle has ended. Seeks to answer the questions that relate to what Sloanism looks like (or sounds like) in mainstream popular music production in late-capitalist production as adapted as a strategy for creating mainstream pop hits, using distinct case studies from 1980s popular dance music cycle (Kyle Minogue's "Locomotion" and Janet Jackson's "Rhythm Nation") and 1990s rap conversions (Puff Daddy's "Come With Me" and the Fugees "Killing Me Softly") as examples.

616. **Williams, Matthew**. 2016. "Preference for Popular World Music: A Review of Literature." *Update: Applications of Research in Music Education* 35(3): 31–37. ISSN: 8755-1233.

Contends that calls to widen the types of music used in curricula seem to underscore the importance of research exploring preferences using music other than and in addition to Western art music. Presents a review of the literature that explores nonmusical factors, including external characteristics and listener characteristics as well as musical factors contributing to decisions of musical preference related to popular and world music to aid educators in planning effective and meaningful music activities.

617. **Zak, Vladimar**. 1982. "Asaf'ev's Theory of Intonation and the Analysis of Popular Song." *Popular Music* 2 [Special Issue: *Theory and Method*]: 91–111. ISSN: 0261-1430.

Examines the theoretical writings of Boris Asaf'ev (1884–1949), the founder of Soviet musicology who has contributed to the study of music. Argues that although Asaf'ev did not look particularly at popular music genres, the theory of intonation that underlies his most important research (*Musical Form as Process,* 1963) is universal and can be applied to the study of popular music.

3

Special Issues Published in Scholarly Journals

I. GENERAL TOPICS

618. **Adlington, Robert, and Igor C. Zubillaga, eds**. 2013. "Special Issue: Music and Democratic Transition." *Twentieth-Century Music* 20(1): 2–134. ISSN: 1478-5722.

A special issue that examines how musical practices in different national contexts formed ways of imagining democracy and how these practices participated in the wider social struggle to define freedom and equality in the twentieth century. Essays explore case studies from Greece, Spain, the German Democratic Republic, South Korea, South Africa, and Chile. Topics include sonic narratives of resistance and collective memory; experimenting musically with democracy in late Franconist and post-Franconist Spain; imagining democracy through song in South Korea; music manifestos for anti-capitalist futures in post–World War II East Berlin; rethinking post-authoritarian Chile through popular music; and Fidelio on Robben Island; and South Africa's early democratic project.

619. **Ahlers Michael, and Jan-Peter Herbst, eds**. 2021. "Special Issue: Crisis at Work: Potentials for Change?" *IASPM Journal* 11(1): 2–110. ISSN: 2079-3871.

A special issue inspired by but not limited to the current processes and effects of the COVID-19 pandemic and the global civil rights movements related to "Black Lives Matter," which highlights systematic racism as an epidemic in many societies around the world. Compiled essays reflect a broad range of scholarly and artistic perspectives on crisis in popular music composition and production,

DOI: 10.4324/9781003507345-3

labor, business, education, societies, and culture. Topics include COVID-19, spatiality, and the United Kingdom's live music industry; performing artists in Vienna (Austria); the live music scene in the age of COVID-19; the impact of the COVID-19 crisis on the mental health of EDM DJs; why #BlackLivesMatter(s) to K-Pop's BTS-ARMY; music work and solidarity politics in the age of COVID-19; some thoughts from Greece; cultural policy in Germany; pragmatic White allyship for higher education popular music academics; and hip-hop's musical horizon of hope in dark times.

620.   **Amico, Marta, and Emmanuel Parent, eds**. 2022. "Special Issue: Terrains Communs: Ethnomusicologie et Popular Music Studies [Common Ground: Ethnomusicology and Popular Music Studies]." *Volume! La revue des musiques populaires—The French Journal of Popular Music Studies* 19(2): 7–208. French and English texts. ISSN: 1634-5495.

Explores the crossroads, contracts, and contrasts between two fields of musical knowledge—ethnomusicology and popular music studies. Essay topics include when ethnomusicology tackles music that is produced in recording studios in both the North the and South; queer performance venture into Asturian folklore; bureaucracies producing world music; raggadub and punk music from Marseille; and Manding music (in Burkina Faso) as a mainstream media trend that transforms local African scenes.

621.   **Andean, James, ed**. 2022. "Special Issue: The Sonic and the Electronic in Improvisation, Part 2." *Organised Sound* 27(2): 103–271. ISSN: 1355-7718.

Part 2 of a special issue focuses on the theme of the sonic and electronic aspects of improvisation, presenting various trends among the essays that encompass analyses of improvisation, different improvisational communities, their geographical and aesthetic displacements or connections, and so forth. Essay topics include group performance paradigms in free improvisation and analytical approaches to electroacoustic music improvisation; electronic media and electronic improvisers in Europe at the turn of the millennium; improvisation through performance-installation; gesture and texture in the electroacoustic improvised music of Jin Sangtae, Hong Chulki, and Jetuzi Akiyama; spaces for people—technology, improvisation, and social interaction in the music of Pauline Oliveros; electroacoustic improvisation and the metaphysical imaginary; improvising module synthesizers; material sources, lack of notation, and the presence of collaborators; crafting the language of robotic agents; neural synthesis as methodology for art—anthropology in contemporary music; experiencing sound installations; and material media sonification.

622.   **Andean, James, ed**. 2021. "Special Issue: The Sonic and the Electronic in Improvisation, Part 1." *Organised Sound* 26(1): 1–162. ISSN: 1355-7718.

A special issue that contributes to the academic study of improvisation by offering a platform for improvisers and musicologists to examine improvisation from a perspective that explicitly foregrounds electroacoustic practice.

The issue also offers a range of philosophical, technical, artistic, and other perspectives. Topics covered include fostering intersubjectivity in electronic music improvisation; resistance, mastering agency—improvisation with the feedback-actuated augmented bass; algorithmic improvisation as acousmatic *poiésis*; co-estrangement in live touch and feedthrough in distributed music performance; improvising an augmented violin; designing musical games for electroacoustic improvisation; a spatial performance tool to play the ephemeral and improvise with space to playback speeds; free improvisation as experience; improvising with failing playback media; improvisational listening; developing performer-specific electronic improvisatory accompaniment for instrumental improvisation; François-Bernard Mâche's "Sacred Music"; and the concept of the palimpsest as a model for listening to works that engage multiple layers of technology, aesthetics, and sound.

623.   **Bannister, Matthew, ed**. 2017. "Special Issue: Pop Life: The Popular Music Biopic." *IASPM Journal* 6(2): 1–197. ISSN: 2079-3871.

A special issue dedicated to examining biopics of popular music artists and offering questions regarding the genealogy of the genre, authenticity, remediation, identity, authorship, and stardom. Topics include practice of verisimilitude in popular music; remediating historical performance in popular music biopic; beyond authenticity, beyond romanticism—films about Maanam; biographical films about Elvis Presley and Jim Morrison; and authorship and authorization in "I'm Not There."

624.   **Barna, Emilia, *et al***. 2022. "Special Issue: Popular Music and Populism." *Popular Music* 41(3): 281–416. ISSN: 0261-1430.

Focuses on different aspects of popular music and populism through politics, music styles and genres, and how musicians and society employ pop as musical markers. Essay topics include overview of popular music and populism; populism in Israel and beyond; populist performance(s) in contemporary Greek rap music; the aesthetics of songs commissioned by Hungarian government between 2010 and 2020; populism and far-right popular government and Nueva Canción; and musical challenges to Trump's America and Erdoğan's Turkey.

625.   **Bataille, Pierre, and Marc Perrenoud, eds**. 2021. "Special Issue: Back to Work!" *Volume! La revue des musiques populaires—The French Journal of Popular Music Studies* 18(1): 1–172. French and English texts. ISSN: 1950-568X.

A special journal issue that is dedicated to music as work. Considers more seriously the professional, material, and economic dimensions of practices that are obviously "artistic" and that also unfold in a contrasted and very unequal labor and employment market. Essays included were written by members of the Working in Music International research network. Essay topics include music performer's script and meaning; professional socialization and musical work; typology of tribute bands; dissemination of neo-managerial practices among musicians; function, musicians, technology, and class relationships; Michael

Jackson's *Off the Wall* album; formation and taste for extreme metal; and the soundtrack of *Baby Driver*.

626.   Batchelder, Daniel, ed. 2021. "Special Issue: Music and Sound in Disney." *American Music* 39(2): 133–264. ISSN: 1945-2349.

Concentrates on the impact of the Walt Disney company on modern American culture and the music that has represented an array of media offerings in feature films, television shows, theme parks, musicals, and video games. Essay topics include Snow White and the seventh art, sound, song, and respectability; Walt Disney films and American popular music, 1940–1955; nostalgia for a past futurism; youth and yearning in animated musicals of the Disney renaissance; the foreign and the other in the music of *Mulan* (1998); animated Broadway: Disney and musical theater in the 1990s and early 2000s; music, memory, Pixar; and voicing the French and Tahitian dubbed versions of Disney's *Moana*.

627.   Baumann, Peter Max, Bernhard Hanneken, *et al*. 2001. "Special Issue: Folk Music in Public Performance." *The World of Music* 42(2/3): 1–312. ISSN: 0043-8774.

A special issue that reflects on regional traditions that interrelate with musical diversity and intercultural music making and improvisation. Compiled essays also reflect on how in an era of tourism, migration, festivals, technically determined globalization, and a world that is growing smaller, the conceptualization of cultures and region is expressed through music in differentiated ways. Essay topics include festivals, musical actors, and mental constructs in the process of globalization; concepts and context of the Tanz and Folk Fest Rudolstadt (Germany); concerts and festivals—public performance of folk music in Sweden; Indigenous Australian performers at the Woodfork Folk Festival; Japanese taiko drumming in international performance; Vietnamese music in exile since 1975 and musical life in Vietnam since Perestroika; the Latvian folk music movement in the 1980s and 1990s; Gypsy (Roma) musicians in former Yugoslavia; intercultural encounters in Austria; folklore festivals and their current typology; musicians and audiences at the International Folk Music Festivals in Norway; music and ethnicity in Barcelona (Spain); and folk legends' work on the great hits of rock and popular music.

628.   Baxter-Moore, Nicholas, and Thomas M. Kitts, eds. 2016. "Special Issue: The Live Concert Experience." *Rock Music Studies* 3(1): 1–129. ISSN: 1940-1159.

Addresses selected dimensions of the importance of live music and its relationship to recorded music. Essays emphasize venues where performers and audiences came together, the concept of "ecology" or "environment," the importance of the materiality of the buildings in which live music happens, and so forth. Topics include live concert performances—an ecological approach; the relationship between auditory and visual dimensions in live performances in contemporary technology-based popular music; authentication and (re)-live(d) concert experiences (in between performance and mediatization); Bob Dylan's rolling thunder period; and Bruce Springsteen fans on the live concert experience.

629. **Beard, Danijela S., and Elaine Kelly, eds**. 2019. "Special Issue: Music and Socialism." *Twentieth-Century Music* 16(1): 3–187. ISSN: 1478-5722.

A special issue about music and socialism and how scholars may map out the complex relationships between the two. Topics covered include music, the realist conception of art and the materialist conception of history; Paul Dessau and the hard work of socialist music in the German Democratic Republic (GDR); music for socialism, London 1977; soft socialism, hard realism; partisan song, parody, and intertextual listening in Yugoslav Black Wave film (1968–1972); performances of race and otherness in the GDR; Marxism and the study of popular music; Russian revolution and music; and 1968—mythology matters.

630. **Becker, Sharon, ed**. 2012. "Special Issue: 'Oh Pretty Boy, Can't You Show Me Nothing But Surrender?': The Presence and Importance of Women in Punk Rock." *Women Studies* 41(2): 117–261. ISSN: 0049-7878.

A special issue influenced by the women in punk rock, such as Patti Smith, Annabella Lwin, the Slits, and the Go-Go's, who have occupied both important and contested spaces. This special issue is not structured to comprehensively address the ways punk women practiced the art of punk but provides a glimpse into that world. Topics include punk women and why they matter; re-evaluating the Slits and gender relations in early British punk and post-punk; Riot Grrrl Press, girl empowerment, and DIY self-publishing; deciphering the narratives of lesbian punk rock; vindicating Nancy Spungen from patriarchal historical revisionism; Riot Grrrl challenges to gender power relations in British indie music subcultures; and afterword from Patti Smith to Paramore.

631. **Bello, Juan P., Robert Rowe, Carlos Guedes, and Godfried Toussaint, eds**. 2015. "Special Issue: Cross-Disciplinary and Multicultural Perspectives on Musical Rhythm." *Journal of New Music Research* 44(1): 1–70. ISSN: 0929-8215.

A special issue that is constructed as a follow-up to a workshop titled "Musical Rhythm: Cross-Disciplinary and Multicultural Perspectives," which was held in Abu Dhabi in March 2013. Participants covered topics such as definitions of rhythm, complexity, and syncopation; rhythm similarity; rhythm and trance; free rhythm, pitch, and time; isomorphisms in music; rhythm of the brain; and cross-cultural and culture-specific approaches to rhythm. Compiled essays are constructed to include many of these issues and include comparing memory capacity for musical rhythm in musicians and non-musicians; expressive timbre and timing in rhythmic performance; analysis of Steve Reich's *Clapping Music*; the relation between surface rhythm and rhythmic modes in Turkish Makam music; genre classification to rhythmic similarity; and invariant representations of music with application to unsupervised source identification.

632. **Benhäim, Sarah, Lambert Dousson, and Camille Noûs, eds**. 2022. "Special Issue: Les flops Musicaux (The Flops in Music)." *Transpositions-Musiques et Sciences Sociales* 10: Electronic Resource at https://doi.org/10.4000/transposition.6715. French and English texts. ISSN: 2110-6134.

A special issue that aims to shed light on all the factors that explain the musical flop. Compiled essays analyze the role of intermediaries and prescribers (programming of concert halls, production of records, press, critics, etc.) in the exhibition of or, on the contrary, the invisibilities of artists and their influence on the categories of judgment. Essay topics covered include collision of the music industry, machinations, genre maintenance, and Black Britishness in 1980s pop; Queen's album *Hot Spaces* (1982) and the sway of disappointment; Turkish-German music interplay; improvisational flops—a problematic concert (1969) and controversial LP (1970) of Grupo di Improvvisozione Nouva Consonanza; deconstructing the death of progressive rock; the distinctive flops of Anton Webern in the United States; and others.

633.   **Bennett, Andy, David Cashman, and Natalie Lewandowski, eds**. 2020. "Special Issue: Regional and Rural Popular Music Scenes." *Popular Music and Society* 43(4): 367–467. ISSN: 0300-7766.

Presents theoretical and geographical issues relating to what the editors and writers describe as regional and rural popular music scenes. Essay topics are representative of these issues and include researching regional and rural popular music scenes; toward a critical understanding of an undertheorized issue; a review of local and regional press coverage of Island Empire's contemporary music scene, B.C. (before Coachella); three rural Scottish music scenes—an ethnographic study; Tartar language rap in post-Soviet Kazan; urban myth and rural legends—an alternative take on the regionalism of hip-hop; challenge through cultural heritage in the North Spanish rural musical underground; Okinawa, palimpsestic geography, and octogenarian island idols; and rock music scenes, regional touring, and music policy in Australia.

634.   **Bennett, Andy, and Susanne Janssen, eds**. 2016. "Special Issue: Popular Music, Cultural Memory, and Heritage." *Popular Music and Society* 39(1): 1–149. ISSN: 0300-7766.

Examines particular and locally specific ways that popular music has become an object of memory and in turn a focus for contemporary renditions of history and cultural heritage. Essay topics include the contemporary music archive; popular music, materiality, memorabilia, and memory; traces; meaning and language in Dutch popular music; transnational DIY popular music heritage in Austria; the aesthetic of Slovene popular music; and DIY preservationism in progressive rock.

635.   **Bennett, Samantha, and Eve Klein, eds**. 2016. "Special Issue: Perspectives on Popular Music and Sound Recording." *IASPM Journal* 6(2): 1–197. ISSN: 2079-3871.

Addresses the multiple relationships between popular music and sound recording in the construction of popular music and its cultures. Essay topics include time-based signal processing and shape in alternative rock recording; virtual instruments, simulation, and performativity; documentary filmmaking—live album recording, 1967–1969; creativity in recording studios; the transmedial storyworld of Coldplay's Mylo Xyloto; breath, voice, and authenticity in three recordings (Guarnei Quartet's *Grosse Fuge*, Colin Stetson's "Hunted," and Miley Cyrus's "Wrecking Ball"); analyzing, mixing, and evaluating audio in the mashup community; and kosmische music and its techno-social context.

636.   **Blackman, Shane, and Rob McPherson, eds**. 2021. "Special Issue: Autoethnographic and Qualitative Research on Popular Music." *Riffs: Experimental Writing in Popular Music* 5(2): 4–92. ISSN: 2513-8537.

Offers a critical and analytical engagement on popular music where researchers apply their research imagination to interpret personal, political, and social context of music within a range of settings and genres. Essay authors are interested in descriptions of music and cultures, how work is written, and what it seeks to argue through qualitative methods and autobiography. Essay topics include an autoethnographic journey within the word of John Cage; Julie Driscoll's voice in the blues—a model for autoethnographic performance research; United Kingdom rap and grime; Soundcloud—a creative space for everyone; musical micro-utopias; the role of spectacle in creating successful live music performance; metal music and the reimagining of masculinity and place—an ethnographic reflection on when Grand Magnus came to Keighley.

637.   **Bradby, Barbara, and Dave Laing, eds**. 2001. "Special Issue: Gender and Sexuality." *Popular Music* 20(3): 295–480. ISSN: 0261-1430.

Addresses many questions of how gender and sexual identities have been performed in popular music, on the pop stage, and on the dance floor of the twentieth and twenty-first centuries. Essay topics include all rock and roll is homosocial—the representation of women in the British rock music press; the gendered carnival of pop; vocoders, digitalized female identity and camp; sampling (hetero) sexuality-diva-ness, discipline in electronic dance music; house music, homosexuality, and masculine signification; the fabulous ambivalence of the Pet Shop Boys; beyond pop theory's "butch" construction of male Elvis fans; the rise of calypso feminism—gender-musical politics in the calypso; and PJ Harvey's *Dry* and the drowned virgin-whore.

638.   **Bradshaw, Alan, and Avi Shankar, eds**. 2008. "Special Issue: The Production and Consumption of Music." *Consumption Markets & Culture* 11(4): 225–343. ISSN: 1025-3866.

Compiled essays relate to interrogating and collapsing distinctions between production and consumption particularly with a focus on music. The essays are offered in the context of theoretical notions of Jacques Attali on how the condition of music emerges as a sort of magical domain that can captivate audiences, provide cathartic and embodied experiences, and ground identities and communities but also introduce rich exchange between people and subvert power structures. Essay topics include Jamaican dancehall; Tibet music media and markets; anti-apartheid protect music in post-apartheid South Africa; music and meaning in movies relating to jazz genres; and critical understanding, emotion, and self-identity.

639. **Brandellero, Amanda, Susanne Janssen, Sara Cohen, and Les Roberts, eds**. 2014. "Special Issue: Popular Music as Cultural Heritage." *International Journal of Cultural Heritage* 20(3): 219–355. ISSN: 1352-7258.

Presents the first results of the European research project entitled "Popular Music Heritage Cultural Memory and Music Industries," focusing on localized popular musical histories and their significance for musical audiences and music industries and integrating how popular music feeds into a sense of place as a musical history of localities. Essay topics include popular music as heritage and field practice; unauthorizing popular music heritage and a critical framework; popular music and the culture of heritage; mapping popular music heritage in Slovenia; Slovene popular music as critical heritage; popular music of the 1990s—dance music and the cultural meanings of decade-based nostalgia; invention of rock heritage in Austria; and popular music heritage and British bhangra music.

640. **Bridge, Simone K., Jonathan Stock, and Abi Dunnett, eds**. 2019. "Special Issue: Reflections on the Past, Present & Future of Popular Music Scholarship." *Journal of World Popular Music* 19(2). 208–242. ISSN. 2052-4900.

Comprises scholarly papers that were presented at a roundtable conference panel titled "Reflections on the Past, Present & Future of Popular Music Scholarship," held at the Annual Conference of the Society of Ethnomusicology (SEM) in 2019. Compiled papers explore the development of popular music from a variety of disciplinary backgrounds—ethnomusicology, folklore, anthropology, American studies, and history. Papers and panelists include Reflections on the Past, Present & Future of Popular Music Scholarship; Currents & Contradiction in the Ethnomusicology of Popular Music; Rainforest to Rave: Ethnomusicological Forays Into Popular Music; Academia Against Popular Culture: Popular Culture Against Academia; Popular Music Studies and Interdisciplinarity; and Popular Music in the K-12 Classroom and the Quest for Education Justice.

641. **Brusila, Johannes, Martin Cloonan, and Kim Ramstedt, eds**. 2022. "Special Issue: Music, Digitalization, and Democracy." *Popular Music and Society* 45(1): 1–111. ISSN: 0300-7766.

Integrates a series of essays that deal with issues related to music, digitalization, and democracy. Provides a brief overview of some key approaches to studying the interplay between music, technological development, and democracy. Essays focus on different perspectives such as analysis of an American hip-hop group's self-released trilogy and digital technology; structural changes in the media contexts of the United Kingdom general elections; new digitalization and algorithmic architecture; feminist perspectives on digitalization on musical career in Hungary; and availability, affordability, and use of new digital equipment for gamechangers.

642. **Buch, Esteban, and Violeta Nigro Guinta, eds**. 2013. "Special Issue: Musique et Sexualité (Music and Sexuality)." *Transpositions-Musiques et Sciences Sociales* 9: Electronic Resource at https://doi.org/10.4000/transposition.5467. French and English text. ISSN: 2110-6134.

A special issue that informs studies on popular music and opens questions of gender and sexuality. Essay topics include the role of the exotic element in Massenet's work; retrospective reflections; music and erotic agency; sonic resources and social sexual action; sonic resources and sexual action (Body and Soul 1997); hyperfeminization of Japanese female singers; multiple and sustained climaxes in Icelandic punk rock; techniques of orgasms in electronic dance music; and others.

643. **Burns, Gary, Thomas M. Kitts, Michaela A. Neller, *et al***. 2021. "Special Issue: The Pandemic." *Rock Music Studies* 8(1): 1–96. ISSN: 1949-1159.

Reflects music, music making, musicians, and audiences coping with the COVID-19 pandemic and how it affected the music industry. Topics include coping with loss as a musician in a pandemic; responses and politics and conversations across borders and disciplines; collective nostalgia and community in Tim's Twitter listening party during COVID-19; getting cross-generational listeners to rock during the pandemic; a new paradigm of engagement for the socially distanced artist; charity benefit concerts and *One World Together at Home Event*; jazz, pandemics, and our stubborn humanity; Manu Dibango (1933–2020) and John Price (1946–2020).

644. **Campbell, Patricia S., ed**. 2022. "Special Issue: Girls and Women in Popular Music Education." *Journal of Popular Music Education* 6: 137–282. ISSN: 2397-6721.

A special issue that focuses on the role of girls and women in popular music both in and for popular music education. Essay topics are varied and include Toronto indie musicians; harmonica players; African migrant DJs in Ireland; Brazilian ensembles; Malian musicians, and others.

645. **Cayan, Christopher, ed**. 2020. "Special Issue: Expanding Online Popular Music Education Research." *Journal of World Popular Music* 4(2): 131–266. ISSN: 2397-6721.

A special issue that examines the advancement and positive aspects of enhancing online popular music education research. Essay topics include impediments to incorporating popular music technologies in schools; intersections of popular musicianship on computer sciences practices; content analysis of seven prominent YouTube ukulele channels; learning, consuming, and recreating music on social media; case study of popular music pedagogy; songwriting with digital audio workstations in online community; children's music studio; sociology for music teachers; and popular music technology and creativity.

646. **Clark, Lynn Schofield, ed**. 2006. "Special Issue: Forum on Religion, Popular Music, and Globalization." *Journal for the Scientific Study of Religion* 45(4): 475–496. ISSN: 0021-8294.

An introductory article that brings together an interdisciplinary set of essays from scholars from mass communication, ethnomusicology, religious studies, and the sociology of religion to explore how practices and understandings of religion might be changing in the context of a global, mediated, capitalist marketplace. Each of the essays foregrounds music as a particular cultural form with a unique role to play in the maintenance and change of religion's character and practices in the global marketplace. Argues that music is only one cultural form that is part of our commercialized and globalized experiences of religion.

647.　**Cloonan, Martin, and John Williamson, eds**. 2017. "Special Issue: Popular Music and Labor." *Popular Music and Society* 40(5): 493–612. ISSN: 0300-7766.

Considers where musicians work and the kinds of employees they interact with. Essays in the special issue stem from papers that were presented at a conference called "Working in Music," which was held in Glasgow, Scotland. The essays that are introduced focus on the themes and notion that musicians can be characterized as a particular sort of worker. Essay topics include attitudes to women working in cinema and music 1910–1930; labor organizations and the question of "artistic value" in the first years of the Portuguese Musicians' Class Association 1909–1913; musical mutualism in Valparaiso during the rise of the labor movement (1893–1931); conceptualizing creativity and strategy in the work of professional songwriters; performers' rights in the United Kingdom; and being a musician in France and Switzerland.

648.　**Cohen, Sara, and Jan Fairley, eds**. 2006. "Special Issue: Dance." *Popular Music* 25(3): 345–492. ISSN: 0261-1430.

Contributes research that examines aspects of dance and dance music in the wider world. This special issue was inspired by the integral connection between dance and dance music and sought to address a dearth of work on popular music and actual dancing practices. Compiled essay topics include dance music, dancing, and the BBC in World War II; dance, gender, and popular music in Malawi—the case of rap and ragga; cultural embodiment in Tijuana's Nortec music and dance; dancing machines—dance revolution, cybernetic dance, and musical taste; regulation, governmentality, and the confessional practices of the raving bodies; the politics of dancing in the northern soul scene; the riddim method—aesthetics, practice, and ownership in Jamaican dancehall; and reggaeton, sexuality, gender, and transnationalism in Cuba.

649.　**Cohen, Sara, and John Street, eds**. "Special Issue: Literature and Music." *Popular Music* 24(2): 163–305. ISSN: 0261-1430.

A special issue that stems from several different disciplinary traditions in which to explore a variety of themes. Compiled essays demonstrate how music can be used within fiction to indicate the feelings and sensibilities of the character and how music becomes part of the routine realities of the world depicted in autobiographies. Essay topics include the commonalities between cyberpunk literature and industrial music; blues, criticism, and the signifying trickster; novel responses to the gramophone in twentieth-century literature; Garcia Márquez, macondismo, and the soundscape of vallenato; Keith Emerson's anxiety of influence, style change, and the road to prog superstardom; rock memory and oblivion in post-Franco fiction; Hamlet-voice, music sound; thirty-one songs and Nick Hornsby's pop ideology; jazz at night and the classics in the morning—musical double consciousness in short fiction by Langston Hughes; Jack Kerouac's *On the Road* and the culture of bebop and rhythm 'n' blues; and rock autobiographies.

650. **Cubin, Jenny A**. 2022. "Special Issue: Otobiographies." *Riffs: Experimental Writing in Popular Music* 6(1): 4–96. ISSN: 2513-8537.

A special compilation of essays that intersect with existing debates on listening and reflect on the role listening plays in their creative endeavors regardless of disciplinary approaches. The special issue focuses on Jacques Derrida's "Otobiographies" lecture and the subsequent roundtable discussions. Essay topics open the theory of "otobiographies" to new contexts. Topics include drag lip-sync performance as otobiography; reading and writing sonic fictions on the Internet; the shape of sound—an exploration of moving, felt, embodied hearing technologies on obscure motion; reflections on the life of a sound; Marclay, Derrida; and the afterlife of dead sounds; two music psychology scholars discuss listening practices (Amanda Krause and Steven Brown); and echo as metaphor of voice-ear-world perspectives.

651. **Curran, Georgia, and Mahesh Radhakrishnan, eds**. 2021. "Special Issue: The Value of Ethnographic Research in Music." *Asia-Pacific Journal of Anthropology* 22(2–3): 101–254. ISSN: 1444-2213.

A special issue that emphasizes how ethnographic research in music provides an important lens through which to understand cultural worlds. Essay topics include document, designs, and song of the present; Portuguese Burgher identity and the performance of káfriinha; Teochew Opera in Western Sydney (Australia); hip-hop workshops and intergenerational cultural prolocation in the Central Australian desert; Warlpiri identity in a globalized world—voices of the rainforest; Institute of Papua New Guinea Studies, and others.

652. **Cutietta, Robert A**. 1991. "Special Issue: Popular Music: An Ongoing Challenge." *Music Educators Journal* 77(8): 1–78. ISSN: 0027-4321.

A second special issue on popular music that focuses on how time has changed in the intervening years between the Tanglewood Conference and 1991. Compiled essays emphasize that popular music has permeated almost every aspect of every country, but educationally popular music has been specifically used to entice students into traditional forms of music education. Essays suggest that inherent qualities of popular music and its spontaneity, creativity, contemporary relevance to students, and authenticity are often buried in educational programs.

653. **D'Aquino, Brian, and Oâna Parran, eds**. 2021. "Special Issue: Sounds in the City: Street Technology and Public Space." *Journal of World Popular Music* 8(1): 5–157. ISSN: 2052-4900.

Amplifies the knowledge and intervention of sound practitioners and research-ers to address questions that have arisen about how people experience, value, and interact with music, race, sound, technology, freedom of expression, and their circulation in a globalized world. Topics covered include race, sound, and the future of community; journal entry featuring d'bi.young anitafrika; Tikur sound system; the roots of digital cumbia in sound system culture; making music from below in a southern Italian metropolis; U.N.I.T.Y. sound system; international dialogue between sound women; discovering and rediscovering *Lost Bodies* through Jamaican sound; noise, in/security, and the politics of citi-zenship; and Feminine Hi-Fi.

654.	**De Jong, Nanette, and Barbara Lebrun, eds**. 2019. "Special Issue: Music and Magic." *Popular Music* 39(1): 1–178. ISSN: 0261-1430.

Focuses on the intersection of popular music and the notion of magic, offering a cross-section of many and various ways in which musicians, audiences, and critics apply the notion of popular songs and music events. Essays focus on com-positional and discursive processes that generate rare and intense connections between humans and what practitioners qualify as "magic." Essay topics include sample magic in contemporary hip-hop production; DIY musical activism after Egypt's 2011 revolution; sound, music, and magic in football stadiums; pagan-ism, musical, and visual aesthetics of the musical groups of Florence Welch and Natasha Kahn; new age and extreme metal music culture; and inter-Asian popu-lar music studies and academic discourses.

655.	**Desai-Stephens, Anaar, and Nicole Reisnour, eds**. 2020. "Special Issue: Musical Feelings and Affective Politics." *Culture, Theory, and Critique* 61(2–3): 99–357. ISSN: 1423-5784.

A special issue of essays that support argues that music as sound and practice has an important role to play in evolving conversations on affect as a crucial dimension of political life. Essay topics include Sindhi Sufi music in Western India; the affect-emotion on gap & the efficacy of devotional song in Bali; Alevi-Semah & the Sivas massacre; musical haunting & embodied political histories in an Algerian community; popular music classes & the transmission of "feel" in contemporary India; women's competitive *tufo* dancing in northern Mozam-bique; Cuban street-vendor songs; Arab Winter; musical feeling in an American jail; irony of affect in Sao Paulo, Brazil; sonic politics; musical ethnography and the challenge of/to affect; and citational practices.

656.	**Doubleday, Veronica, ed**. 2008. "Special Issue: Sound of Power: Musical Instru-ments and Gender." *Ethnomusicology Forum* 17(1): 1–162. ISSN: 1941-1912.

A compilation of essays and case studies that focus on musical instruments and gender. The essays offer various ways in which gender meaning is invested in instruments, male dominance over instrumental musicianship, male exclusiv-ity, certain types of instruments played by women, and so forth. Essays cover geographical areas and topics include player and Kacapi zither in West Java,

Indonesia; musical instruments, gender, and fertility in the Bolivian Andes; women and square frame drums in Portugal and Spain; and women and mbira players in Zimbabwe.

657.   **Dreyfus, Kay, and Joel Crotty, eds**. 2010. "Special Issue: In Search of the Sixties." *Musicology Australia* 32(2): 155–318. ISSN: 0814-5857.

A special issue about the 1960s and music trends, local responses, the use of specific topics as a lens onto wider 1960s themes, and others considering the overall significance of the decade in different countries. Essay topics include existential psychedelia and Jimi Hendrix's "The Burning of the Midnight Lamp"; layers of identity in the 1960s surf rock icon Misirlou; popular music in 1960s Iran; music and politics in 1960s Romania; International Society for Contemporary Music in Melbourne (Australia)—forerunners, foundation, and decline; Dr. Val Stephen—a musical experiment of the 1960s; changes in music, the music industry, and musicians' careers in 1960s Melbourne (Australia); and cha-cha-cha to *ciuff ciuff*—modernity, tradition, and the Italian-Australian popular music scene of the 1960s.

658.   **Duffett, Mark, Claude Chastagner, et al**. 2018. "Special Issue: Rock and Love." *Rock Music Studies* 5(1): 1–104. ISSN: 1940-1159.

Takes on thematic issues surrounding rock music and themes of love in scholarly discourses and analysis. Topics covered include uses and refractions of the love song in Leonard Cohen's work; Frank Zappa and the antithetical love song; recounts of listening to the rock band Wilco and implications of love; the infamous nature of the Violent Femmes' (American folk punk band) thwarted love songs; gender, genre, and "Girlville" in Liz Phair's *Girly Sound* (1991); and love lyrics in the time of the Argentinian dictatorship.

659.   **Duffett, Mark, and Koos Zwaan, eds**. 2016. "Special Issue: New Directions in Music Fan Studies." *IASPM Journal* 6(1): 1–163. ISSN: 2079-3871.

Aims to build a bridge with the study of popular music to inspire further investigation of music fandom. Essay topics include studying the "self" in the migrant fandom of David Bowie; diversity in music fandom in LGBTQ lives; teenagers and the use local networks; autoethnographic account of Boyzone fandom; recording collecting in the digital age; fan/celebrity contact as ordinary behavior; and Benjamin KISS—a perspective on music, spectacle, and aura.

660.   **Duffett, Mark, Keith Harris, et al**. 2000. "Special Issue: Place Issue." *Popular Music* 19(1): 1–124. ISSN: 0261-1430.

Focuses on popular music and "place," in which the acceleration in the place of globalization has changed the dynamics within the multiple relationships between culture, identity, and place and has given people a new impetus to rethink and reflect about place in different ways. Topics covered include national identity, global commerce, and the Great Canadian Party; the relationship between global and local within the extreme metal scene; losing the local—Sydney and the OZ rock tradition; festival participation and performing a sense of place; race, space, and place in rap music; a virtual place of musical community; and from Manchuria to the tradition village—on the construction of place via pelimanni music (Finland).

661. **Duffett, Mark, ed**. 2015. "Special Issue: Fandom." *Popular Music and Society* 38(1): 1–99. ISSN: 0300-7766.

Focuses on fandom and fan practices. Essay topics include autechre and electronic dance music; new economy of fandom; online fan fiction; filming concerts for YouTube and cultural capital; fans networking before the digital revolution; and the changing nature of pop fandom and its deployment as a political tool.

662. **Duffett, Mark, ed**. 2013. "Special Issue: Fandom." *Popular Music and Society* 36(3): 299–410. ISSN: 0300-7766.

Offers new areas of research in popular music studies that deal with fandom research. Essay topics include directions in music fan research; the continuing world of European deadheads; music, distinction, and the interloping fan in the *Twilight* franchise; diva worship and the sonic search for queer utopia; Lady Gaga, fan identification, and social media; employing and contesting religious terminology in Django fandom; and ravings of a rock and roll fanatic.

663. **Echard, William, Carlo Nardi, and Hillegonda C. Rietveld, eds**. 2014. "Special Issue: Popular Music Performance." *IASPM Journal* 4(1): 1–142. ISSN: 2079-3871.

Explores the relationship between performance and place. Essays concentrate on how performance is linked to specific places such as venues, the stage, clubs, and festivals establishing associations with scenes, urban and rural areas, regions, and nations. Topics covered include performing Austria—protesting the musical nation; rock clubs and gentrification in New York City; sound system performances and the reception and authenticity in performance; jam sessions in Madrid's blues scene—musical experience in hybrid performance models; transgressive practices within the Leeds extreme metal scene; and online gender equality in extreme metal.

664. **Erlmann, Veit, ed**. 1993. "Special Issue: The Politics and Aesthetics of 'World Music.'" *The World of Music* 35(2): 3–152. ISSN: 0043-8774.

A collection of essays that were originally presented at the Annual Meeting of the Society for Ethnomusicology in 1992. Essays delve into the emerging phenomenon labeled "world beat" and "world music," and how these labels apply to new trends and transnational discourses in popular music. Topics covered include the politics and aesthetics of transnational musics; the transnational music industry, identity, and cultural imperialism; on redefining the "local" through world music; Spanish Caribbean perspective on world beat; local and international trends in Dominican merengue; Black consciousness, samba reggae, and the re-Africanization of Bahian Carnival in Brazil; and the role of women in taarab in Zanzibar.

665.   **Farrugia, Rebekah, and Magdalena Olszanowski, eds**. 2017. "Special Issue: Women and Electronic Dance Music Culture." *Dancecult: Journal of Electronic Dance Music and Culture* 9(1): 1–102. ISSN: 1947-5403.

Seeks to situate women at the center of the cultural production of electronic dance music culture (EDMC) and to highlight their various contributions while acknowledging the intersectional difficulties they face daily. Suggests that highlighting the contributions in this special issue while interrogating the misogyny in EDMC has been foregrounded in recent times and shows no signs of slowing down. Essay topics include listening for Delia Derbyshire in histories of EDMC; electronic dance music's queer femme voices; meritocracy, talent, and post-feminist politics, and women-identified spaces and DJs.

666.   **Fick, Jason, Margaret Schedel, and Brandon Vaccaro, eds**. 2022. "Special Issue: Commercial Music and the Electronic Music Studio-Influence, Borrowings, and Language." *Organised Sound* 27(1): 1–102. ISSN: 1355-7718.

A special issue that stemmed from scholarly research on an electronica duo on an entire album that involved designing, beats, pads, and all with EMS Synthi 100 unit. Issues considered include limitation and powers of oppression affected among disciplines; approaches to the study of electroacoustic music and commercial media production, education, and training in both areas and diversity; stigma limiting factors for hip-hop artists; and others. Compiled essay topics consider many of the issues and include how people are sharing a visual notation to create and recreate acid house music; freewave and Eurorack; Tom Erbe interview; lo-fi today; field recordings over history; analog aesthetics in digital landscapes; conversations on Blacktronika, music technology, and pedagogy layers; topological space in digital popular music, and others.

667.   **Firth, Simon, and Martin Cloonan, eds**. 2008. "Special Issue: Popular Music Policy." *Popular Music* 27(2): 189–339. ISSN: 0261-1430.

A special issue that stems from a seminar organized at the University of Stirling in 2014 on one of a series on cultural policy that assembled scholars and researchers from several European countries. The Stirling seminar suggested that the special issue should be addressed on a broader scale beyond European countries and that would also reflect popular music policy in other geographical areas as well, including from Australia, North America, and the Caribbean. Essays covered include popular music policy and public behavior process; policy and performances in the Caribbean; promotion in Germany through Radio Goethe's cultural export of German popular music to North America; portrait of a politician as a young rocker in Australia; the state of rock in Finland; New Zealand popular music, government, and cultural identity; the crisis of the international music industry; New Zealand on Air and New Zealand pop renaissance; and Canadian content regulations.

668.   **Firth, Simon, and Jan Fairley, eds**. "Special Issue: Radio Issue." *Popular Music* 9(2): 151–258. ISSN: 0261-1430.

Concentrates on the radio as a vital form of media that has influenced popular music and popular music production. Compiled essay topics include an analysis of the role of radio in the diffusion of Black music among Whites in the South of the USA, 1920 to 1960; radio space and industrial time—music formats, local narratives, and technological mediation; the traditional English breakfast show in 1989; the competition for the greater London FM radio license; radio broadcast in Canada—the case of "transformat music"; record sales in the 1980s; human-centered musical studies—towards a charter of musical human rights; and Berlin '91.

669.   **Flath, Beate, Adam Behr, and Martin Cloonan, eds**. "Special Issue: Music Festivals and (Cultural) Policies." *IASPM Journal* 9(1): 1–88. ISSN: 2079-3871.

A special issue that offers geographical research in popular music studies of social, political, cultural policies, and musical activities in the structure and organization of musical festivals. Topics include Falun folk music festival (Sweden); live music associations and the revitalization of the music festival scene (Finland); keeping it country while dancing with the elite (Norway); understanding world music festivals as site of musical education—an ethnographic approach (conducted at WOMAD in the United Kingdom and African festival in Germany); and transmedia festivals and the accelerated cultural sector (Europe).

670.   **Forman, Murray, and Jan Fairley, eds**. 2012. "Special Issue: As Time Goes By: Music, Dance, and Ageing." *Popular Music* 31(2): 193–329. ISSN: 0261-1430.

A special issue inspired by notions about popular songs and how people love to create and play music repeatedly over different periods of time. Compiled essay topics include the positive creative impact of a refresher course for "baby boomer" rock musicians; new generations, older bodies—*danzón*, age, and cultural rescue in the Port of Veracruz, Mexico; popular music and the aesthetics of aging; popular music by elders and for elders; generational music identity among older people; and musical formations of pensioners in late twentieth-century Sweden.

671.   **Fritsch, Melanie, and Hillegonda C. Rietveld, eds**. 2023. "Special Issue: Synergies Between Game Music and Electronic Dance Music in Cultural Contexts." *Journal of Sound and Music Games* 4(1): 1–90. ISSN: 2578-3432.

A special issue that marks the current articulation of a techno culture that brings together diverse cultural forms, practices, discourses, and space to make sense of the current fast-moving digital world just as Neuro Dungeon attempted with their project. Investigates electronic dance music and the legacies of house and techno music made by and for DJs who work the dance floors of nightclubs, raves, and other dance events such as festivals. Compiled essays take a global view within the technocultural context of electronica, and others. Topics covered include rave racing—electronic dance music and immersion and WipEout; industrial techno and SID sound design in the Commodore 64 Game Slipstream; scoring the original soundtrack for an escape room—electronic dance music influence in Nobody—*Vis et ressens*; and songs of rapture—creating a bioshock musical show: an interview with Brendan Jennings.

672. **Fritz, Natalie, and Anna-Katharina Höpflinger, eds**. 2020. "Special Issue: Religion and Popular Music." *Journal for Religion, Film and Media* 6(2): 7–125. ISSN: 2414-0201.

A special issue that explores diverse music genres from Christian rock to heavy metal and flamenco, all of which in some way interact with religion. Essay topics include analysis of "The Rape of the World" by Tracy Chapman and a biblical passage into an ecofeminist dialogue; exploration of how popular music is used to express Christian worldviews; bricolages of religious motifs in heavy metal; opera as an important genre of popular music; combating gender norms in Lady Gaga's song "Judas"; and so forth.

673. **Galloway, Kate, K. E. Goldschmitt, and Paula Harper, eds**. 2022. "Special Issue: Listening In: Musical Digital Communities in Public and Private." *Twentieth-Century Music* 19(1): 361–552. ISSN: 1478-5722.

Considers strategies for circulating music and sound abundantly, secretly, meaningfully, and profitably negotiated at intersections of platforms, creators and communities, aesthetics, algorithms, protocols, and behaviors. Essays expand on recent publications in music and media studies topically, temporally, and geographically. Essay topics include sensing, sharing, and listening to musicking animals across the sonic environments of social media; circulating through online jazz communities; persuasive listening of music podcasts; (re)formatting the twenty-first-century digital sensorium; musical aesthetics and the rise of YouTube in India; exchanging Cuba for one million YouTube views; digital fatigue and stereotype (Brazilian punk superstar Anitta release of "Girl from Rio"); and musical messaging—the social/anti-social affordance of WhatsApp.

674. **Galloway, Kate, K. E. Goldschmitt, and Paula Harper, eds**. 2020. "Special Issue: Platforms, Labor, and Community in Online Listening." *American Music* 38(2): 125–261. ISSN: 1945-2349.

Integrates a series of essays and authors analyzing a variety of aspects of listening and how corporate and vernacular musical engagement takes place in twenty-first-century digital culture. Compiled essay topics include the long history of the 2017 Spotify "fake music" scandal; counterfeiting attention on the streaming music economy; Chance the rapper, Spotify, and musical categorization in the 2000s; the entailment of participation in digital music platforms; receiving, remixing, recuperating "Rebecca Black-Friday"; and fan culture and circulating the materiality of Taylor Swift musical greeting cards on YouTube.

675. **Gammon, Vic, Katherine K. Preston, Carole Pegg, *et al***. 1984. "Special Issue: Performers and Audiences." *Popular Music* 4: 1–406. ISSN: 0261-1430.

Expands on Volume Three of *Popular Music* journal that made the point of stressing the interconnections between production and consumption, which affect not only the structure and genesis of the musical product through the relations of market to producers. This special issue presents an alternate notion of reception or music use into the entire cycle constituted by the circulation of musical goods. Essay topics include class expression and popular song texts in mid-nineteenth-century Britain; popular music in the "Gilded Age"—musicians' gigs in late nineteenth-century Washington, DC; factors affecting the musical choices of audiences in East Suffolk, England; trends and taste in Japanese popular music—a case study of the 1982 Yamaha World Popular Music Festival; music and meaning behind the Dykes—the new wave of Dutch rock groups and their audiences; listening behavior and musical preference in the age of "transmitted music;" music in the streets—the example of Washington Square Park in New York City; the Walkman effect; pity Peggy Sue; Maybelle—meaning and the listening subject; rock and roll and the empowerment of everyday life; rock music and politics in Italy; and technology, politics, and contemporary music.

676. **Gavanas, Anna, and Bernardo A. Attias, eds**. 2011. "Special Issue: The DJ." *Dancecult: Journal of Electronic Dance Music and Culture* 3(1): 1–132. ISSN: 1947-5403.

Specifically addresses the relations of pleasure and power that intersect in the space between the DJ, the dancefloor, and the rest of the club world. Essay topics include White gay aesthetics at the Saint (New York City), 1980–84; DYI careers of techno and drum 'n' bass in Vienna (Austria); city, place, and uncanny bass; DJ culture, mobility, and science fictions of listening; DJ Goa Gi; turntablism and controllerism in the twenty-first century (Part I): nomads in sound, vol. 2; meditation on the death of vinyl; turntablism of doom; Swedish techno; and reproduction of power and pleasure at the Amphi Festival in Cologne (Germany).

677. **Goldman, Jonathan, Fanny Gribenski, and João Romão, eds**. 2020. "Special Issue: Opening the Doors to the Studio." *Contemporary Music Review* 39(6): 639–794. ISSN: 0749-4467.

A special issue that aims to investigate the notion of electronic music studios as "laboratories of the arts," instead opening their doors to the outside to examine their technological, cultural, political, and economic inscription. Employs the imagery of "door opening" to highlight circulation between studios and between studios and many other institutions, fields of practices, and sociopolitical contexts. Essay topics include a connected history and geography of studios; electronic music and sound engineering at the WDR (Studio for Electronic Music in Cologne, Germany); music studios as spaces of collective creativity in the context of electronic dance music in Angola; Halim El-Dabh (Egyptian-born composer) at the Columbia-Princeton Electronic Center; experimental studio for Polish radio; probing Gordon Mumma's studio heuristic through a digital recreation of *Mesa* (1966); collecting sounds and nationalizing interior soundscapes and Milton Babbitt and the RCA synthesizer.

678. **Green, Lucy, Don Lebler, and Rupert Till, eds**. 2015. "Special Issue: Popular Music and Education." *IASPM Journal* 5(1): 1–211. ISSN: 2079-3871.

Focuses on popular music education as a subject that is often under-explored despite increasing numbers of popular music courses and other education provision. Compiled essays include contributions discovering developments in several countries such as Argentina, Australia, Brazil, Canada, Germany, Singapore, and the United States. Topics covered include a range of approaches that explore technology, hermeneutics, theory, guitars, jazz, songwriting, DIY/DIWO, politics, and music industry perspectives. Compiled essays are structured to present popular music education in a more forceful presence in popular music studies.

679. **Hartwig, Marcel, Ulf Schulenberg,** *et al*. 2017. "Special Issue: American Rock Journalism." *Rock Music Studies* 4(1): 1–88. ISSN: 1940-1159.

Inspired by an inquiry that ponders what happens when one sees the American rock critic not only as a transnational but also as an Americanist. Special issue concepts stem from papers that were presented at an international conference on American rock journalism at the University of Siegen, Germany, in 2014, where American and German scholars and journalists offered discourse on the subject. Topics covered include the creation of rock journalism in the mid-1960s; visions and versions of America—Greil Marcus's rock journalism as cultural criticism; nostalgia and authenticity in representation of 1980s indie rock and hardcore punk; what is "American" in American rock journalism; Ryan Gosling, Roddy Dangerblood, and the rebellious genealogy of *Thrasher* magazine; pastiche, parody, and rock journalism in Bret Easton Ellis's *American Psycho* (1991) and Kanye West's *Yeezus* (2012).

680. **Horn, David, and Dave Laing, eds**. 1991. "Special Issue: The 1890s." *Popular Music* 10(1): 1–114. ISSN: 0261-1430.

Offers studies on trends, technological innovations, and popular music styles in the decades of the 1890s. Essay topics include popular music and the phonograph in the 1890s; blues and jazz in 1890: from quadrille to the stomp—the Creole origins of jazz; indecency and vigilance in late-Victorian music halls; social protest and oppositional ideology in popular Hawaiian music; the ethics of digital audio-sampling—engineers' discourse; and world record sales.

681. **Housewright, Wiley L**. 1969. "Special Issue: Youth Music: A Special Report." *Music Educators Journal* 56(3): 43–76. ISSN: 0027-4321.

A compilation of essays generated at a time when popular music was rarely included in school music programs and was widely believed to be inappropriate for school settings. Essays stem from the fact the many music educators needed curriculum or to be able to include popular music in their programs. Essays provide philosophical rationales for the inclusion of popular music education, some theoretical knowledge of rock music, and descriptions of exemplary programs. Suggests that there is much to be gained from the study of any musical creation such as rock, soul, blues, folk, and jazz that cannot be ignored.

682. **Hustwitt, Mark, *et al*.** 1983. "Special Issue: Producers and Markets." *Popular Music* 3: 1–270. ISSN: 0261-1430.

Focuses on production, markets, and economics in the process of popular music creation. Divided into three sections: In the Past; The Contemporary Music Industry: Organization and Ideology; and Modes of Musical Production. Topics covered within the sections include the production of dance music in Britain; Hoagy Carmichael and the cultural revolution of racism; the recording industry and the growth of a mass media; the role of Welsh phonographic industry in the development of the Welsh language pop/rock/folk scene; aspects of the popular music record industry in Japan; some institutional aspects of pop and rock in Hungary; capitalism and romantic ideology in the record business; anti-musicology of the pop song; rock music as a recording art; notation and identity in contemporary popular music; and productivity of repetition in pop music.

683. **Inglis, Ian, ed.** 2010. "Special Issue: Popular Music and Journalism." *Popular Music and Society.* 33(4): 431–580. ISSN: 0300-7766.

Covers discourse surrounding the working practices and ideologies of journalism, employing historical, cross-cultural, and comparative perspectives. Compiled essays are presented as case studies that consider the changing roles of those who write about music. Essay topics include the great divide between music criticism and popular consumption; *Let It Rock*, 1972–75; the rock critic and the changing real; *Rockrgrl*, rock, and representation; coverage of popular music since 1955 from the United States, France, Germany, and the Netherlands; popular music fanzines, rock criticism public, and intellectuals; and the British press and the Beatles.

684. **Jacke, Christoph, Martin James, and Ed Montano, eds.** 2014. "Special Issue: Music Journalism." *IASPM Journal* 4(2): 1–132. ISSN: 2079-3871.

Focuses on music journalism and engages a continuing analysis of music journalism's "golden age" and an ongoing consideration of music journalism's scholarly research in a global perspective. Essay topics include the trajectory of popular music criticism; Italian teen pop press and genres in the 1950s; United States hip-hop journalism and female artists; alternative journalism in Madrid's blues scene; and dispatches from the dancefloor and Clubland in Print (United Kingdom).

685. **Jacobsen, Marion, ed.** 2008. "Special Issue: Accordion Culture." *The World of Music* 50(3): 1–141. ISSN: 0043-8774.

A special issue dedicated to research focusing on the development, history, and musical influence of the accordion in various genres and styles and in different geographical areas. Essay topics include the accordion and the process of musical globalization; Irish button accordions; female accordionists in Dominican merengue tipico; Italian, accordions, and a pluralistic vision of ethnicity in New York City; transformation of the accordion in twentieth-century China; and the accordion and ethnic Whiteness —toward a new critical organology.

686. **Johnson, Bruce, and Martin Cloonan, eds**. 2011. "Special Issue: Popular Music and Violence." *Popular Music and Society* 34(1): 1–112. ISSN: 0030-7766.

Offers scholarly discourse on the controversy over music and violence, warning stickers on recordings, moral rights, and the higher proposition of popular music studies and lyrical song content. Essay topics include domestic violence and Americanized calypso; Throbbing Gristle and the mediatized roots of noise in/as music; music as punishment in the United States legal system; how musicians from Beirut react to war and violence; iPod and the link between passive listening and violence; and symbolic violence, education, and Kanye West.

687. **Jones, Ellis, and Jeremy Morris, eds**. 2022. "Special Issue: Podcasting and Popular Music." *Radio Journal: International Studies in Broadcast and Audio Media* 20(1): 1–212. ISSN: 1476-4504.

Focuses on podcasting and popular music and argues that framing music and podcasts as competing sounds permits new contributions to several important areas of media study. Topics covered include competing sounds of podcasts and popular music; exploring listener motivations for engagement with music podcasts; inclusive modes of musical analysis in *Switched on Pop*; pop music form, creation, and reception through *Song Explorer* podcast; finding online community in COVID-19 lockdown; the sonic strategies and technologies of listening alone together in *The World According to Sound's In*; and new synergies between the podcast and music industries—Spotify play the rhythm.

688. **Keller, Damián, Marcelo Queiroz, Marcelo S. Pimenta, and Regis Faria, eds**. 2011. "Special Issue: New Paradigms for Computer Music." *Journal of New Music Research* 40(1): 189–276. ISSN: 0929-8215.

A special issue that stems from the Brazilian Symposium on Computer Music in 2009 that focused on how sound and music technology are constantly forcing the reinvention of methods, goals, tools, and standards in computer music, bringing forth new paradigms. Essays in this special issue address many of these issues and include profiling new paradigms in sound and music technologies; principles for music creation by novices in networked music environments; real-time uses of low-level sound descriptors as event detection functions; microtiming patterns and interactions with musical practices in samba music; efficient binaural rendering of moving sound sources using HRTF interpolation; interacting with 3D reactive widgets of musical performance; and convergent trends toward ubiquitous music.

689. **Kirkegaard, Annemette, and Jonas Otterbeck, eds**. 2017. "Special Issue: Music Censorship." *Popular Music and Society* 40(3): 257–362. ISSN: 0300-7766.

Integrates a collection of essays that address issues of music censorship. Compiled essays take their departure from the perception that musical sound in its complexity plays a major role in silencing musicians and artists. Essay topics include pop music, social violence, and self-censorship; discourses of self-censorship and authenticity in two Finnish metal bands; pop music, socialism, and the church in East Germany; rock music censorship in Czechoslovakia between 1969 and 1989; censorship of pop music in school music education; and globalization of United States' corporate music self-censorship.

690. **Klein, Bethany, ed**. 2011. "Special Issue: Popular Music and Marketing." *Popular Music and Society* 34(4): 397–502. ISSN: 0300-7766.

Brings together a range of research perspectives, objectives of study, and methods to develop a fuller picture of the relationship between commercial culture and popular music culture. Essay topics include recording artists, brands, and rendering authority; music, transmedia advertising, and Brasilidade in the 2006 World Cup; British Asian independent record labels and cultural politics of difference; music radio and the recording industry; advertisement and construction of decision-making power in MTV's *Making the Band*; and "Bumble Boogie" and American sound recordings.

691. **Laing, Dave, and Simon Firth, eds**. 1988. "Special Issue: Music Video and Film." *Popular Music* 7(3): 247–371. ISSN: 0261-1430.

A special issue that concentrates on writing on music and video in popular music and writing on popular music styles and genres. Essay topics include music video in its contexts—popular music and postmodernism in the 1980s; a systems approach to the relationship between the phonogram/videogram industry and music television; country music video; music video use and educational achievement—a Swedish study; music television as billboards of postmodern difference; the Harry Hammond Archive; Institute of Popular; and on Simon Firth's "Copyright and the Music Business."

692. **Larkey, Edward, *et al*.** 2000. "Special Issue: Global Popular Music: The Politics and Aesthetics of Language Choice." *Popular Music and Society* 24(3): 1–156. ISSN: 0300-7766.

Focuses on the theme of language and popular music. Essay topics include language choice in German popular music; interactional work of the MC in drum 'n' bass; the use of "resistance vernaculars" in hip-hop in France, Italy, and Aotearoa/ New Zealand; Ricky Martin; the politics of chronology, crossover, and language within the Latin(o) music "Boom"; language choice in Tanzania and Malawi at the crossroads of language; musics and emotions in Kathmandu (Nepal); and popular music and language choice in France.

693. **León, Javier, ed**. 2014. "Special Issue: Music, Music-Making, and Neoliberalism." *Culture, Theory, and Critique* 55(2): 129–271. ISSN: 1473-5784.

Explores the relationship that music and musicians have with social and economic processes associated with neoliberalism. Essay topics include Jacques Attali, Michel Foucault, and biopolitics; fields, genres, and brands; playback singing and public femaleness in South India; music collaboration in postsocialist Tirana, Albania; the neoliberal self in the Andean Peruvian music industry;

music, youth development, and neoliberalism in South Africa; and music, money, and morality at Thailand's Red Shirt protest.

694. **Levaux, Christophe, and Christophe Pirenne, eds**. 2021. "Special Issue: Experts-Non-Experts: Participative Knowledge Construction in Popular Music: Controversies and Historiography." *Volume! La revue des musiques popularies-The French Journal of Popular Music Studies* 18(2): 1–199. French and English texts. ISSN: 1634-5495.

Offers a retrospective and critical refection on the original vocation of popular music studies. Brings to light topics that are seldom studied and even occasionally discredited. Envisions collaborations between experts and non-experts during the knowledge-building process. Essay topics include prehistory of popular music studies and establishing folk music as an object of studies; rethinking object biography in popular music studies; study and teaching popular music; popular music and musicological education and research in France; a citizen study of popular music; from Erik Satie to the Smashing Pumpkins, variations on the term "world music"; accounts of music circulation; and screens, mediation, and authenticity in the popular concert.

695. **Long, Paul, and Nicholas Gebhardt, eds**. 2019. "Special Issue: Listening Again to Popular Music as History, Part 2." *Popular Music History* 12(3): 253–339. ISSN: 1740-7133.

Part 2 of a special issue dedicated to the question of history in popular music studies. Essays take a further step to examine the nature of sources and what they can tell about the kinds of histories that are produced. Essays focus on the many ways in which the production of historical narratives about popular music raises questions of how the past is experienced and what such encounters come to mean for different groups and individuals. Topics covered include music, materiality, and biographical memory; dance as a source of popular music historiography; listening again to popular music history; and *The Old Grey Whistle Test* as a tastemaster for British album-oriented rock audiences in the early 1970s.

696. **Long, Paul, and Nicholas Gebhardt, eds**. 2019. "Special Issue: Listening Again to Popular Music as History, Part 1." *Popular Music History* 12(2): 147–246. ISSN: 1740-7133.

A special issue that explores the meaning of different acts of retrieval among popular history music scholars. Reflects on the nature of thinking and methodology of popular music history scholars, historical narratives, and the potential for popular musicians to act as public historians. Essay topics include the perennial forgetting of girls in music; Chicano rap as historical source; pirate radio broadcasts as historical and musical artifact; and Slim Dusty, country music, and Aboriginal history.

697. **Lovesey, Oliver, ed**. 2020. "Special Issue: Woodstock University." *Popular Music and Society* 43(2): 121–230. ISSN: 0300-7766.

Considers the legacy of the Woodstock Music and Arts Festival that has become an overarching idea as much as a brief historical event representing the ethos of the 1990s counterculture in a type of fetishized shorthand. Essays included fall into two categories: the participant observations of performers and attendees of Woodstock and related festivals and the reflections of cultural historians on the aspects of the festival, its representation, and its legacy. Addresses the educational interface of the festival by including the voices of performers attending Woodstock and other festival attendees who went on to become professors and through the reflections of other cultural historians, some of whom would use Woodstock as a teachable moment within the emerging field of popular music studies.

698. **Lovesey, Oliver, ed**. 2017. "Special Issue: Popular Music and the Postcolonial." *Popular Music and Society* 40(1): 1–110. ISSN: 0300-7766.

Examines the relationship of popular music and the postcolonial. Compiled essays explore popular music in line with the developments in sound technology and exchange in the Black Atlantic that took place in an era of decolonialization. Essay topics include decolonizing the ear; royalism and popular music in postcolonial Uganda; popular songs and resistance in Kenya; popular music and the young postcolonial state of Cameroon; Edward Said on popular music; Occitan music revitalization; and Irish republican music.

699. **Madden, David, ed**. 2019. "Special Issue: Ageing with EDMC." *Dancecult: Journal of Electronic Dance Music and Culture* 11(1): 1–116. ISSN: 1947-5403.

Brings age/aging studies in contact with electronic dance music culture by highlighting the work of EDMC theorists and practitioners. Offers scholarship connected with a growing group of researchers undertaking historical cultural studies of popular music. Essay topics include the queering of the Pet Shop Boys; LCD sound systems in EDM; youth, adulthood, and aging in contemporary British EDMC; social morphologies and neurosis in the genesis of an EDM beat; aging in Belo Horizonte's (Brazil) rap music scene; interview with Genesis Breyer P. Orridge, Travelers, and sound systems protest; death of British drum 'n' bass music; aging and dance music culture; and live performance of spatial EDM.

700. **Manuel, Jeffery, et al**. 2008. "Special Issue: Popular Music as Cultural Heritage." *Popular Music and Society* 31(4): 417–553. ISSN: 0300-7766.

Deals with popular music and its relationship to cultural heritage. Essay topics include creating country music's social origins; Eric Clapton's changing conception of "Blackness"; Aboriginal contemporary music as Australian cultural heritage; the Englishness of punk/Sex Pistols; mashups and the metaphysics of sound recording; and musical archives and authentic performance.

701. **McKay, George, ed**. 2009. "Special Issue: Popular Music and Disability." *Popular Music* 28(3): 293–461. ISSN: 0261-1430.

Explores the common cultural and social territory of popular music and disability, which has been a neglected topic. Compiled essays are situated within interdisciplinary perspectives from disability studies, popular music studies (including musicology), cultural studies, performance studies, gender, and theory. The essays contribute to the critical dialogue of recent years around disability culture as one corrective to popular music studies. Essay topics include Connee Boswell and a jazz discourse of disability in jazz; Johnny Ray in context; popular music and polio with reference to Ian Dury; the (re)marketing of disability in pop—Ian Curtis and Joy Division; songs and their lyrics in the Disability Arts; a popular music project and people with disabilities community in Hamburg, Germany; hearing (dis)abled masculinities; and teaching, accessibility, and creativity in popular music education.

702.   **Mera, Miguel, and Anna Morcom, eds**. 2009. "Special Issue: Screened Music: Global Perspectives." *Ethnomusicology Forum* 18(1): 1–181. ISSN: 1741-1912.

A special issue of *Ethnomusicology Forum* that stems from the "Sound Music and Moving Image" conference held at the Institute of Music Research (University of London) in 2007. Compiled essays explore screened music from a variety of disciplinary, theoretical, and methodological perspectives. Essay topics include screened music, trans-contextualization, and ethnomusicological approaches; Mbaqanga, Bollywood, and film music; documentary production in Andean Peru; Hindi film music; Balinese Kecak in film; Singapore and state-produced music video; Icelandic pop music video and music documentary; and Central Asian film music as a subcultural system.

703.   **Middleton, Richard, ed**. 1994. "Special Issue: Mellers at 80." *Popular Music* 13(2): 127–238. ISSN: 0261-1430.

A special issue dedicated to Wilfrid Mellers, who was a pioneer in the academic field of popular music, particularly within the musicological community. Regards Mellers as making it possible for professors of music to discuss popular music in an academic environment. Offers a range of essays covering aspects of some of the topics on which Mellers himself has written as a tribute to the role in opening them up for further research. Essay topics include music, culture, and interdisciplinarity—reflections and relationships; genre, performance, and ideology in the early songs of Irving Berlin; Caliban reheard—new voices on jazz and American consciousness; contesting meaning in *Porgy and Bess*; "ethnic" music traditions in the USA/Black music; country music, others, all, scrutiny to subcultures: notes on literary critic in popular music; women singers as composer-poets; renewal and revelation—Wilfrid Mellers at York; Wilfrid Mellers—a selective bibliography; and from refrain to rave—the decline of figure and the rise of ground.

704.   **Middleton, Richard, and David Horn, eds**. 1989. "Special Issue: Performances." *Popular Music* 4: 131–214. ISSN: 0261-1430.

Focuses on different aspects of performance in popular music from a global perspective. Topics covered include *musica mizrakhit*—ethnicity and class culture in

Israel; dance bands and dance halls in Greenock (Scotland), 1944–55; hot swing and the dissolute life—youth, style, and popular music in Europe, 1939–49; popular music in Australia, 1955–1963; legitimacy, authenticity, and community in folk's politics; the when, where, and who in pop lyrics—the listener's prerogative; Son House, 1902–88; the big get bigger; and the Center for Popular Music.

705. **Middleton, Richard, ed**. 1985. "Special Issue: Continuity and Change." *Popular Music* 5: 1–392. ISSN: 0261-1430.

Centers on the notion that popular music studies have mostly focused on contemporary forms and has left the historical dimensions relatively untheorized and has contributed to a separation between central preoccupation and other perspectives. Compiled essays are constructed to focus on different historical moments that have also contributed to popular music studies. Essay topics include articulating musical meaning/reconstructing musical history/locating the "popular"; Count Basie and the piano that swings the band; cultural "fusions"—aspects of British West Indian music in the USA and Britain 1918–1951; visions of change and continuity in rock music; Soviet crusade against sentimentality and high pathos—popular music in Fascist Germany; rock 'n' roll in a very strange society; borrowing, syncretism, hybridization—the Paris revue of the 1920s; role conflict and the professional musician in Hawai'i; and major trends of change in Jewish oriental ethnic music in Israel.

706. **Middleton, Richard, ed**. 1982. "Special Issue: Theory and Method." *Popular Music* 2: 1–243. ISSN: 0261-1430.

Focuses on theory and method in popular music studies. Compiled essays integrate a search and discussions of appropriate theories and methodologies of popular music research. Essay topics are varied and include analysis of affect in popular music; theory, method, and practice; Asaf'ev's theory of intonation and analysis of the popular song; urbanization of African music; popular song in nineteenth-century Britain; taste in popular music; research into musical genres; Adorno and popular music; method and binarism in blues and Black culture; and others.

707. **Middleton, Richard, ed**. 1981. "Special Issue: Folk or Popular? Distinctions, Influences & Continuities." *Popular Music* 1: 1–203. ISSN: 0261-1430.

One of the early issues that focuses on issues of determinants and theoretical notions of folk and popular music. Essay topics include making artistic popular music—the goal of true folk; a music of your own; the making of the Tyneside concert hall; Son House, Muddy Waters, Robert Johnson, and the development of traditional blues; gospel boogie—White Southern gospel music in transition, 1945–55; cross-cultural perspectives in the case of Afghanistan; God, modality, and meaning in some recent songs of Bob Dylan; and the ideology of folk and the myth of the rock community.

708. **Mitchell, Tony, and Theo van Leeuwen, eds**. 2009. "Special Issue: Music and the Production of Place." *Transforming Cultures eJournal* 4(1): 1–291. ISBN: 1833-8542.

A special issue that developed from a series of papers given at a symposium held at the University of Technology, Sydney, Australia, in May 2008. Accompanied essays examine and focus on various ways in which music and musicians produce place in terms of "psychogeographies" of living spaces, cityscapes, and landscapes. Essays are grounded on theoretical notions as defined by Guy Debard in 1955 as the study of the precise law and special effects of the geographical environment, consciously organized or not, on the emotions and behavior of individuals or through the transnational evolution of lost homelands, spaces of migration, or syncretic expressions of place. Essays cover a variety of topics from art music to world music as well as rock, dance music, jazz, reggae, and hip-hop and places—Australia, Fiji, Iceland, Antarctica, Tasmania, United States, and so forth—both where they are produced and what they produce.

709.   **Moist, Kevin M., Ozan Baysal, *et al.*** 2018. "Special Issue: Global Psychedelia and Counterculture." *Rock Music Studies* 5(3): 197–323. ISSN: 1940-1159.

A special issue that offers various perspectives on the countercultural and psychedelic imaginary from a global focus. Essays emphasize discoursing about counterculture and psychedelia should be based on plural perspectives rather than on singular notions. Essay topics include reconsidering "Anadolu pop" (Turkey); counterculture within a counterculture—New Zealand psychedelic rock and the moral guardians of the '60s and '70s; the 1960s/1970s psychedelia music movement in Poland; *rak en rol*—the influence of psychedelic culture in Philippine music; psychedelic territories—exile and sonorities in Caetano Veloso and Gilberto Gil (Brazil); and Italian progressive rock as Indigenous psychedelia.

710.   **Negus, Keith, and John Street, eds.** 2016. "Special Issue: Music and Alcohol." *Popular Music* 35(2): 161–295. ISSN: 0261-1430.

Intended as a contribution to understanding the role of alcohol in music as a facet of historical change, human interaction, individual creative practice, economic behaviors, and political process. Essays explore how the meaning and making of popular music and the actions and attitudes of musicians are mediated by alcohol. Topics covered include drink, song, and politics in early England; temperance battle songs; alcohol, creativity, and performance anxiety; songs and messages about alcohol in remote Central Australia; alcohol sponsorship at Glasgow Jazz Festival, 1987–2001; experiences of alcohol-related misbehavior by audiences and its impact on performance; and the saga of the Licensing Act 2003.

711.   **Negus, Keith, and John Street, eds.** 2002. "Special Issue: Music and Television." *Popular Music* 21(3): 245–390. ISSN: 0261-1430.

A special issue that concerns how television has been conspicuously neglected in studies of popular music and music has been notably absent from most accounts on television. Compiled essays seek to address questions about television form and scholars of television to write about music. Topics covered include musicians and opportunity in early television, 1948–55; the uneasy relationship of music and television; children's television and popular music; authentic boy bands on TV—performers and impresarios in The Monkees and making the band; tracking British television—popular music as stock soundtrack to the small screen; the changing sound world of UK television indents; music and documentary; and television's problem with (classical) music.

712. **Neuenfeldt, Karl, ed**. 2007. "Special Issue: Indigenous Peoples, Recording Techniques, and the Recording Industry." *The World of Music* 49(1): 1–231. ISSN: 0043-8774.

A special issue that focuses partly on Indigenous peoples being recorded by researchers and commercial producers, and on Indigenous peoples doing recording themselves. This special issue also provides insights on aspects of "recording culture," the active process and the culture of recording. Topics covered include engaging of Indigenous peoples with recording technology, and techniques, the recording industry, and researchers; Sámi perspectives on Indigenous CD production in Northern Europe; producing Aboriginal music and maleness in a Central Australian recording studio; innovation and connections in Chuukese popular music and contemporary recording; recording and reviving Rotuman music via a collaborative Rotuman/Fijian/Australian CD project; Australian women and contemporary music recording technologies; Easter Island music and the voice of Luis Avaka "Kiko" Pate; studios at home in the Solomon Islands; celebrity, technology, and the creation of an Indigenous music recording industry; and Fiji blues.

713. **Parent, Emmanuel, ed**. 2011. "Special Issue: Peut-on-parler de musique noire? ("What Is It We Call "Black Music"?)." *Volume! La revue des musiques popularies—The French Journal of Popular Music Studies* 8(1): 1–328. French and English texts. ISSN: 1634-5495.

A special issue of selected papers from an April 2010 conference in Bordeaux, France, based on critical discussion of Phillip Tagg's famous letter and questioning ways of apprehending a popular music field that was easily identified (blues, jazz, reggae, rap, etc.) without being able to define it precisely. Compiled essays tackle the subject to deconstruct the use of racial categories in music without abandoning such terms that have been shaping practices for centuries. Essay topics include George Walker in non-existence and reality of the idea of "Black music"; how the tango become Argentinian; sama, a genre of folk music that is not traditional African or Westernized but uniquely Brazilian; authenticity and musicality in maracatu dance in Pernambuco (Brazil); Afro-Uruguayan candombe; examples of Afro-Mexican cumba and chilena in Costa Chica; and South African jazz.

714. **Pietila, Tuulikki, ed**. 2009. "Special Issue: World Music: Roots and Routes." *Collegium* 6: 1–156. ISSN: 1796-2986.

A special issue that examines world music from diverse perspectives and positions. Compiled essays were originally presented as part of a two-day conference titled "World Music and Small Players in the Global Music Industry," held at the Danish Institute for International Studies in Copenhagen in August 2005. Essay topics include world music and the global music industry—flows, corporations, networks; national versus regional, many versus few—the dilemma facing the collection societies; traditional music and the world music marketplace; Ghana and the world music boom; globalization and commercialization of Caribbean music; diasporic music in a time of war; the invisible conduit from the world to the ears of human beings; and improvised performance in world music—finding the violin's unexpected places.

715. **Pitts, Stephanie, ed**. 2010. "Special Issue: Understanding Audience Experience." *Journal of New Music Research* 39(2): 109–181. ISSN: 0929-8215.

A special issue concerned with why audience members are attracted to musical events, what they experience when they are there, and how their enthusiasm can be sustained and spread to increase social engagement in the arts. Essay topics include new audiences for classical music experiences of non-attenders at live orchestral concerts; understanding jazz audiences—listening and learning at the Edinburgh (Scotland) Jazz & Blues Festival; exploring educational and musical values in youth performances; attending musical performances—teachers' and students' expectations and experiences at a youth program in Madrid (Spain); experimenting with fandom, live music, and the Internet—applying insights from music fan culture to new media production; and exhibiting popular music— museum audiences, inclusion, and social history.

716. **Polak, Rainer, Kevin Dawe, Deborah Wong, *et al***. 2000. "Special Issue: Local Musical Traditions in the Globalization Processes." *The World of Music* 42(3): 1–168. ISSN: 0043-8774.

A special issue where contributors were asked to offer essays on themes that included how the clash of culture affects regional musical culture; in what way do the modern forms of polarity influence traditional music groups; and their understanding of themselves, music and musicians, and globalizing marketplace. The reference to "local" is understood as a social construct whose interpretation and broader relationship to global culture depends on the actors involved. Essay topics include jembe laying in Bamako (Mali), West Africa, and beyond; roots music in the Global Village—Cretan (Crete) ways of dealing with the world at large; Taiko and the Asian/American body; musical systems of intergenre relationships in Hong Kong; Shaanxi Qinpai erhu tradition; and local and global traditional musical instruments and modernization.

717. **Powell, Bryan, Gareth D. Smith, and John Kratus, eds**. 2019. "Special Issue: Popular Music Education: A Call to Action." *Music Educators Journal* 106(1): 1–66. ISSN: 0027-4321.

The third issue of the *Music Educators Journal* to address popular music education. Recognizes that "popular music" is a vague term that means different things to people. Essays provide an overview of popular music education since the previous special issues published in 1969 and 1991. Current essays engage with popular music from a cultural standpoint that frames popular music education within amateurism, pedagogical approaches for teaching popular music, teaching popular music in choral music classes, and using technology in popular music education.

718.   **Powers, Devon, and Tom Perchard, eds**. 2017. "Special Issue: The Critical Imperative." *Popular Music* 36(1): 1–156. ISSN: 0261-1430.

Focuses on writing about popular music that places primacy on sounds as made and heard and which is styled in a way that foregrounds not just academic rigor but also imaginative description, creative interpretation, and daring evaluation. Compiled essay topics include the X factor and reality television; post-identity and post-genre; listening while Muslim; dance-floor driven literature; mid-century modern jazz; making sense through Dawn of Midi's *Dysnomia*; Internet music and the brain; Kate Bush's temporal strategies and resistant consciousness; and musicians as workers.

719.   **Raine, Sarah, and Catherine Strong, eds**. 2018. "Special Issue: Gender Politics in the Music Industry." *IASPM Journal* 8(1): 1–153. ISSN: 2079-3871.

Focuses on gender and politics in the music, employing diverse case studies and research. Topics include the political economy of female club owners; negotiating the critique of gender inequality in the United Kingdom music industries; making women in jazz visible—negotiating discourses of unity and diversity in Sweden and the United States; gender ventriloquism in studio production; promoting women on the Senegalese rap scene; Girls Rock Regina—a feminist intervention; the genre barriers in the indie and dance music scene in Dublin (Ireland); and Amy Winehouse—back to black and the gothic.

720.   **Regev, Motti, ed**. 2006. "Special Issue: Canonization." *Popular Music* 25(1): 1–143. ISSN: 0261-1430.

A special issue that addresses some of the questions raised around the existence of a canon in popular music. Essay topics include popular music and canon formation; a canon of pop and rock albums from a sociological and aesthetic perspective; award ceremony as an arbiter of commerce in the popular music industry; resurrecting the anthology of American folk music; indie guitar rock, canonism, White masculinities; prestige and boundaries in popular music in Quebec; the enactment of the field of cultural and artistic production of popular music in Brazil; and review from the periphery—making music, making meaning.

721.   **Rennie, Tullis, ed**. 2021. "Special Issue: Socially Engaged Sound Practices, Part 2." *Organised Sound* 28(1): 1–146. ISSN: 1355-7718.

Part 2 of a special issue continuing research that builds and expands on the theme of "socially engaged sound practices," as well as moving into several key areas of binaries of professional/nonprofessional (or amateur), sound arts perspectives, and others. Essay topics include socially engaged sound process; creative agencies in participatory sound art; mediating space, sound, and experience; contemporary and future aesthetics in more than human worlds; manifesto for music and sound creation; politics of aesthetic preference in participatory music; creative action metaphors and timbral interaction; musical community in the information age; post-sonic perspectives or socially engaged compositional practices; participatory co-composition on YouTube and the Web; live electronics as a complex system; sine wave in music and sound art—a typology of artistic approaches; and sound and video examples.

722.   **Rennie, Tullis, ed**. 2021. "Special Issue: Socially Engaged Sound Practices, Part 1." *Organised Sound* 26(2): 163–301. ISSN: 1355-7718.

A special issue that contributes to the growing area of research in socially engaged sound practices and features scholarly accounts by those doing socially engaged sound practices with such efforts moving towards more inherently (self) critical sound practices and study of such works. Includes a diversity of interpretations in sociality and addresses distinct areas and eras of sound practices when doing so. Compiled essay topics include silence, listening, and undoing; sound and more-than-human sociality; localizing acoustic ecology; amplifying social justice and aural counter publics through field recordings; sonic politics and careers; challenges of designing with physically disabled musicians during a global pandemic; dialogic listening; collaborative composition as social participation; developing public engagement in sound mapping; sonic methodology for diaspora studies; exploring the intersections of oral history and sonic art; entanglement in the sociopolitical context of place; listening to *Green Ways* (an album by Áine O'Dwyer and Graham Lambkin); and sound and video examples.

723.   **Rieveld, Hillegonda C., ed**. 2011. "Special Issue: State of the Union: Review(s) of Popular Music Studies." *IASPM Journal* 2(1–2): 1–95. ISSN: 2079-3871.

A special issue that reflects a range of scholarly discourses on popular music studies' differentiated geographically located perspectives that correspond to each other through a shared involvement with transnational networks. Topics include review of popular music studies—caught on the back foot—epistemic inertia and visible music (position paper by Philip Tagg); how did popular music come to mean *música popular*? (a focus on Spanish-speaking Latin America and examines what popular music and *música popular* have meant in some of their respective sociolinguistic spaces); the introduction of popular music studies in Ghanian universities; German-language popular music studies in Germany, Austria, and Switzerland; and reflections of popular music studies in Turkey.

724.   **Root, Deane L., ed**. 1984. "Special Issue: Music of the American Theater." *American Music* 2(4): 1–112. ISSN: 1945-2349.

A special issue of *American Music* journal that focus on the impact of music in the theater in American life. Essay topics include music in eighteenth-century American theater; Pocahontas—her life and time; action music in American pantomime and melodrama, 1730–1913; music as social history; American Yiddish theater music, 1882–1920; *Oklahoma!*—its origin and influence; Black theater 1870–1930 research problems and resources; and conflicting views of American musical theater history.

725. **Sanjek, Dave, ed**. 2012. "Special Issue: Copyright." *Popular Music and Society* 35(5): 601–709. ISSN: 0300-7766.

Focuses on issues concerning copyright. Essay topics include sound law and the scholar; copyright and some twenty-first century developments; copyright in sound recordings; Irish traditional music and the Irish music rights organization, 1995–2000; and the association for recorded sound collections and the movement to reform copyright in the United States.

726. **Schoop, Monika E., and Federico Spinetti, and Ana Hofman, eds**. 2021. "Special Issue: Music and the Politics of Memory: Resounding Antifascism Across Borders." *Popular Music and Society* 44(2): 119–240. ISSN: 0300-7766.

A special issue that grew out of the field research project between the University of Cologne, Germany, and the Slovenian Academy of Sciences and Arts in Ljubljana, regarding a common interest in the sounding memories of anti-fascism. Inquiries concern musical memories of the World War II anti-fascist resistances. Essay topics include Catalan antifascist song; anti-fascism and post-Yugoslav singing; "new" Nueva Canción Movement in post-authoritarian Chile; musical memories of Cologne's anti-Hitler youth; and punk rock anti-fascist resistance in contemporary Italy.

727. **Sernoe, Jim, ed**. 2007. "Special Issue: Record Charts." *Popular Music and Society* 30(2): 135–304. ISSN: 0300-7766.

Reflects research and the ways that record charts interact with popular music and society and interact with each other. Essays come into play as an important aspect of popular music studies. Essay topics include a political economic analysis of rap *Billboard* toppers; an examination of the Top 100 from 1997 to 2005 (North America); multi-stage markets in the recording industry; chart performance of hard rock and heavy metal groups, 1990–1992; and international influences on American popular recordings, 1945–63 (before the Beatles).

728. **Simonett, Helena, *et al*.** 2000. "Special Issue: Popular Music and National/Ethnic Identity." *Popular Music and Society* 24(2): 1–177. ISSN: 0300-7766.

Concerns scholarly research on popular music and national and ethnic identity in regional and case studies. Essay topics include popular music and the politics of identity; the empowering sound of technobanda; bhangra music and South Asian presence in Toronto (Canada); geopolitics and identity in Australian Indigenous rock music; consumerism reconsidered in the case of Elvis Presley fans; conjecture and conviction in the myth of Kennedy, America, and the Beatles, Double (Bob) Dylan; and Velour 100 and Christian rock.

729.   **Sloop, John, Andrew Herman, and Thomas Swiss, eds**. 1997. "Special Issue: Cartographies of Sound, Noise, and Music at Century' End." *Popular Music and Society* 21(3): 1–171. ISSN: 0300-7766.

Informed by Jacques Attali's concern with a specialized politics of sound, noise, and music. Compiled essays are concerned with sound as a spatial topography as well as a cultural technology, examining relationships of power as located in the shifting boundary between noise and music, and so forth. Essay topics include music and noise in hegemony and resistance; making noise—notes from the 1980s; exploring Jacques Attali's concept of composition from a queer perspective; tropes of hybrid, crossovers, and critical dialogue through music; a cartography of the Christchurch (New Zealand) music scene; representations of the African American female body in urban rap videos; the corporate annexation of Black popular music; projective sociology extrapolates a (hopefully mistaken) trend in popular music; and popular music on British television, 1960–1985.

730.   **Stahl, Geoff, and Shane Homan, eds**. 2013. "Special Issue: The Digital Nation: Copyright, Technology, and Politics." *IASPM Journal* 3(1): 1–104. ISSN: 2079-3871.

Explores the nature of copyright and international property in national and international popular music contexts and how they intersect in a shifting mediascapes. Essay topics include Brazilian popular music economy aspects—the baile funk circuit; digital culture between Creative Commons and moral economy; radical monetization of the music industry; copyright management and its effect on the sampling practice of United Kingdom dance music production; copyright, piracy, and the politics of culture in postcolonial Mali; and Turkey and the copyright music production.

731.   **Stein, Daniel, and Martin Butler, eds**. 2015. "Special Issue: Musical Autobiography." *Popular Music and Society* 38(2): 115–278. ISSN: 0300-7766.

Focuses on musical autobiography. Many of the essays focus on American musical biographies. Essay topics include W. C. Handy, Abbe Niles, and autobiographical positioning in the Whiteman era; jazz autobiography and the Cold War; the singing sixties, autobiography, and the other Beatle; Jack White and the unsolvable problem blues autobiography; why Nirvana, the true story could never be told; paratext in popular musician's autobiography; strategic visuals in hip-hop life writing; and musical autobiography as national counter-story.

732.   **Strong, Catherine, ed**. 2021. "Special Issue: Music History and the COVID-19 Pandemic." *Popular Music History* 14(1): 5–91. ISSN: 1740-7133.

A special issue of essays that deal with aspects of the relationship between popular music history or heritage and the COVID-19 pandemic. Essays cover an array of perspectives and geographical regions, giving a glimpse into the diverse impacts of the pandemic and the multitude of understandings of what it meant for popular music's history's past and the music scenes and industries around different places in world that began to feel the impact of the rapid spreading of COVID-19. Essay topics include the sound of Düsseldorf city walk-authenticity in real life and virtual implementation of music heritage tourism; Chinese rap and the main melody at the outset of the COVID-19 pandemic; trauma and hope during the COVID-19 crisis; and considering COVID-prompted loss of ephemerality in live music's dichotomy between labor and time and capital income.

733. **Taylor, Ian A., ed**. 2023. "Special Issue: Popular Music Materiality." *Riffs: Experimental Writing in Popular Music* 6(2): 4–81. ISSN: 2513-8537.

A special issue that frames *Riffs* as a place where several goings on become entwined across the journal's existence—its materiality has been the core aspect of its projects. The debates and issues contained in this special issue explore the materiality of music and culture contained in the issue and act as a reflection upon the ongoing change to the form, format, and materiality of *Riff*. Topics covered include Japanese jazu-kissa-inspired communal listening experience in the heart of East Belfast (Ireland); hip-hop sampling and material memory; Suede's singles and psychogeography in Madrid (Spain); affective materiality and vinyl records as boundary objects; and evidential heritage values of grassroots music venues.

734. **Tahiroğlu, Koray, and Thor Magnusson, eds**. 2021. "Special Issue: Socio-Cultural Role of Technology in Digital Musical Instruments." *Journal of New Music Research* 50(2): 117–198. ISSN: 0929-8215.

A special issue that stems from a symposium in Helsinki, Finland, in 2019 that represents a diverse group of scholars and practitioners in presenting a broad range of approaches in the making, thinking, and writing about digital musical instruments and considers the sociocultural role of technology in current and emerging digital music practices with changing social roles, historical, and critical reflections. Essay topics include co-regulated timing in music ensembles; embodiment through digital intangibility; ever-shifting roles in building, composing, and performing with digital musical instruments; migration of musical instruments and socio-technological conditions of musical evolution; composition as cultural technology; and digital anthropology meets multisensory listening.

735. **Tecun, Arcia, Kirsten Zemke, and Raquel C. Valverde, eds**. 2021. "Special Issue: Popular Music, Decolonization, and Indigenous Studies." *IASPM Journal* 11(2): 1–122. ISSN: 2079-3871.

Aims to contribute to an ongoing process of colonization through the lens and practice of popular music by highlighting Indigenous academics, theorists, and musical explorations. Essay topics compiled in this special issue include musical festivals and Indigenous popular music; Indigenous musical discourse in the history of Kurdish Baghdad; the colonial attitude in Chilean psychedelic rock; Tanya Taqap covers Nirvana—"Rape Me" and a history of settler colonial violence; resistance in Maxida Märak's album *Utopi*; and *Canto Livre de Nara Leão* (Brazil).

736.   **Tessler, Holly, ed**. 2020. "Special Issue: Popular Music and Curation." *Popular Music History* 13(1–2): 5–208. ISSN: 1740-7133.

A series of essays that make up a special issue examining how the work of music curation illustrates a form of community and belonging either through participation and engagement with some type of activity or in acknowledgment of how others are either liminal or overtly excluded from it. Essays are intended to demonstrate that the ultimate value of curation in both popular culture and popular music is its power to communicate stories that foster new forms of community, identity, and collectivity in an increasingly disaggregated and isolating work. Essay topics include examining the work, popular music curation; collecting the Dunedin sound; exhibiting the musical past in Liverpool; negotiating the co-curation of an online community music archive; learning from George Harrison and Indian music; curation and independent record shops; a case study of We Buy White Albums; psychedelic trace, Internet curation, and free music distribution; Billboard's Hot Country songs' chart and the curation of country music culture; and curatorship in the production of garage rock resistance compilation albums.

737.   **Till, Rupert, ed**. 2017. "Special Issue: Practice-Led and Practice-Based Popular Music Studies." *IASPM Journal* 7(2): 1–68. ISSN: 2079-3871.

Focuses on practice-based and -led research that was inspired by Phillip Tagg's keynote speech at the IASPM 2011 conference in Grahamstown, South Africa. Essays published in this special issue are intended to provide new examples to expand the research in practice-based and -led research. Essay topics include fully automated luxury composition; spatio-temporal suspension and imagery in popular music recordings; responding to place through song; impact of remote music collaboration software on music production and process; and practice-based study into the evolving role of party mixers.

738.   **Till, Rupert, eds**. 2013. "Special Issue: Popular Music Studies in the Twenty-First Century." *IASPM Journal* 3(2): 1–132. ISSN: 2079-3871.

A special issue inspired by the International Association for the Study of Popular Music (IASPM) 2011 conference in Grahamstown, South Africa, and Philip Tagg's keynote address that discussed the state of popular music studies where Tagg also concluded that musicologists working in this area have failed to make inroads into conventional musicology so that popular music and art music are treated equally. Tagg's address also questioned why researchers from nonmusical backgrounds still struggle to address the music of popular music studies and offer solutions. Compiled essays in this issue include topics of popular music studies—the problems of sound, society, and method; popular music studies and ethnomusicology in Australia; IASPM and the provision of popular music studies; degrees in the United Kingdom; popular music, gender, and sexualities; a student's response to Philip Tagg's "Caught on the Back Foot"—epistemic inertia and visible music; and popular music and its mediations.

739. **Toner, P. G., and Stephen A. Wild, eds**. 2004. "Special Issue: World Music: Politics, Production, and Pedagogy." *The Asia Pacific Journal of Anthropology* 5(2): 95–199. ISSN: 1444-2213.

Focuses on world music and the kinds of aesthetic and musical decisions made by non-Western musicians as they produce music for the global market as both producers and consumers of global music, musicians labeled by the term "world music" must consider both local and global audiences when they take the stage or enter the recording studio. Topics include how some Torres Strait Islander songwriters incorporate traditional dance chants with contemporary songs; music and digital media across the Lao diaspora; globalization and Cook Islands popular music; and music education in remote Aboriginal communities.

740. **Valiquet, Patrick, ed**. 2020. "Special Issue: Contemporaneities." *Contemporary Music Review* 39(2): 187–292. ISSN: 0749-4467.

A special issue that implies a special relationship with music history rather than foregrounds genres, idiom, location, period, or technique. Suggests that the adjective "contemporary," seems to stake out boundaries at the edge of time. Essays describe a series of obstacles to the normal run of contemporary musical practice and contemporary music scholarship. Essay topics include contemporary in Indigeneity—the musical practices of Cris Derksen and Jeremy Dutcher; categorizing electronic music; challenges in reconnecting bodies with instruments of the future; and contemporary music, gender, and reproduction.

741. **Van Deen, Tobias C., and Hillegonda C. Rietveld, eds**. 2015. "Special Issue: Echoes from the Dub Diaspora." *Dancecult: Journal of Electronic Dance Music and Culture* 7(2): 1–130. ISSN: 1947-5403.

A special issue that concentrates on the on the dub diaspora. Defines "dub" as a term that resonates in multiple aspects of electronic dance music culture. Compiled essays offer inquiries into how research has been conducted around the critical dimension of dub in its cross-genre and transnational influence upon dub techno and how scholars that attend dub as a sonic, cultural, and Black Atlantic formation might coordinate various perspectives on what might be called the "dub diaspora." Essay topics include dub and transnational dynamics in Jamaican music; Finnish reggae sound system culture; the complexities of an Afrofuturist reading of dub; dub techno's hauntological politics of acoustic ecology; sensory language and bass fiction of the Space Age; dubs dark legacy in drum 'n' bass culture; encountering Jah Shaka; the dub riddim revival in Kingston (Jamaica); and dub diaspora DJ mix.

742. **Van Deen, Tobias C., ed**. 2013. "Special Issue: Afrofuturism." *Dancecult: Journal of Electronic Dance Music and Culture* 5(3): 1–166. ISSN: 1947-5403.

Establishes an initial foray into addressing Afrofuturism within both what has been shaped as electronic dance music culture studies and its borders. Essays are structured to test the limits of what has previously theorized about Afrofuturism.

Essay topics include transmission from the afterworlds of Afrofuturism; allegories of Afrofuturism in Jeff Mills and Janelle Monaé; Afrofuturism and hauntology; aliens, Afropsychedelia, and pysculture; Afrofuturism industry-based research in the Sydney (Australia) EDMC scene; performing cosmopolitanism in an Athens (Greece) festival; Afrofuturism's unbound MC culture in the United Kingdom; and Sylvester James, Black queer Afrofuturism, and the Black fantastic.

743.   **Van Hoose, Matthew, and Shane Greene, eds**. 2016. "Special Issue: The Worlds of Popular Music." *Popular Music and Society* 39(3): 283–392. ISSN: 0030-7766.

A special issue that focuses on a critique of world popular music and draws inspiration from some of its core theoretical and methodological propositions. Compiled essays focus on how music produces worlds that are neither coterminous nor contemporaneous with the globalized "world" of music. Essay topics include Peruvian punk and globalization; infrastructure and voice on Uruguayan FM radio; labor, materiality, and nonrepresentational music; space and language from Cape Verdean rappers; ethnography, Afro-Asian, and Jamaican music in Japan; and Indigenous Day of the Dead music.

744.   **Velasco-Pufleau, Luis, ed**. 2020. "Special Issue: Son, Musique et Violence (Sound, Music, and Violence)." *Transpositions-Musiques et Sciences Sociales* 2: Electronic Resource at https://doi.org/10.4000/transposition.3213. French and English texts. ISSN: 2110-6134.

Explores the questions of how listening can become a tool for exploration of engagement with a sensorial knowledge of the world, and how the study of sound and music can help one to understand collective violence and war. Compiled essays demonstrate how music can be a desire for projecting, framing, and preparing for confrontation with the enemy, and the authors provide analysis of links between sound, music, and violence.

745.   **Waterman, Stanley, and Stanley D. Brun, eds**. 2006. "Special Issue: Geography and Music." *GeoJournal* 65(1–2): 1–135. ISSN: 0343-2521.

A special issue that is grounded on paradigms of globalization in music in several geographic areas. Essay topics include reflections on national musical heritage; the English art of change ringing; geographies of the orchestra; the folk music of Appalachia; searching for silenced voices in Appalachian music; contemporary Aboriginal music and NCI-FM broadcasting in Manitoba, Canada; government regulation in the Australian popular music industry; music and moral geographies—constructions of "nation" and identity in Singapore; the politics of art music in Israel; and celebrating a nation's heritage on music stamps—constructing an international community.

746.   **Watt, Paul, ed**. 2016. "Special Issue: Street Music: Ethnography, Performance, Theory." *Journal of Musicological Research* 35(2): 69–157. ISSN: 0141-1896.

Provides case studies of street music, which comes in all shapes and sizes and is played, danced, sung, acted, or expressed in a combination of these forms.

In addition, this issue also considers street music within paradigms of protest, commercial issues, entertainment, and at times nationalist expressions where the street occupies a powerful force in the formation of musical identity, genre, and practice. Topics of the essays in this special issue include street music in Iran; sonic production as commercial enterprise in urban Japan; understanding of street performance of Cantonese opera (*Jie Dang*) in Hong Kong; street music and the law in Australia; political action and resistance in Melbourne (Australia): and busking in musical thought—value, affect, and becoming.

747.   **Waxman, Steve, ed**. 2003. "Special Issue: Reading the Instrument." *Popular Music and Society* 26(3): 251–418. ISSN: 0300-7766.

Focuses on the musical instrument in critical and analytical perspectives of genre, region, and culture in popular music. Essay topics include studying musical instruments in the Cretan musical language; Black tradition, White novelty (jamming on the gum leaves) in the Bush (Australia); the diatonic button accordion in ethnic content idiom and style in Cajun dance music; the guitar as artifact and symbol; the appearance of the electronic bass guitar—a rockabilly perspective; early microphone singers, 1925–1939, American pop singing; and accordions, banjos, cornets and zithers—sound recording archives and musical instruments.

748.   **Weisbard, Eric, ed**. 2005. "Special Issue: These Magic Moments." *Popular Music* 24(3): 307–465. ISSN: 0261-1430.

A special issue intended to suggest what might be gained with a shift and focus from movements to moments from the representative to the sublime and from the categorical to the quizzical. Also encourages other crossings between academia and the rest of the writerly world. Essay topics include these magic moments—pop writing and the little stuff; mechanics and mysteries of the pop market; listening to the B-side of history; the story of ORCH5, or the classical ghost in the hip-hop machine; Elvis Costello, the empire of the E-chord, and a magic moment or two; Teena Maria and Lewis Taylor; accidents, hooks, and theory; popular music performance in journalism and in academic discourse; writing about music is writing first; critical karaoke; land of a thousand dances—an R&B fable; and classical puts me to sleep.

749.   **Zubillaga, Igor C., ed**. 2013. "Special Issue: Musique et Théorie Queer (Music and Queer Theory)." *Transpositions-Musiques et Sciences Sociales* 3: Electronic Resource at https://doi.org/10.4000/transposition.79. French and English text. ISSN: 2110-6134.

Focuses on case studies on queer theories to analyze different fields and aspects of the musical world of creation, listening, vocal typology, and the musical representation of genre. Compiled essay topics include classical concert music and queer listening; understanding music and sexuality through ethnography—dialogue between queer studies and music; rejection and anger in queer-feminist punk rock; boy bands, drag kings, and the performance of (queer) masculinities; baro/

queer; female-to-male (FTM) singing and its interaction with queer theory; and Rufus Wainwright as opera queen musicality, essentialism, and closet.

II. GEOGRAPHICAL AND REGIONAL STUDIES

750.   **Aterianus-Owanga, Alice, and Pauline Guedj, eds**. 2014. "Special Issue: Musique dans l'Atlantique Noir [Music in the Black Atlantic]." *Cahiers d'Études Africaines* 54(216): 865–1136. French and English texts. ISSN: 0008-0055.

Establishes and links music and globalization on the relevance of the Black Atlantic tool for empirically observing the various circulations of musical practices, their various appropriations, and the identity process they convey. Compiled essays are part of research that focuses on the plurality of cultural construction and relations of solidarity developed from the Black populations of the Americas, Africa, and Europe. Essay topics include Afro-Caribbean music in the state of Quintana Roo, Mexico; neo-soul and the making of diasporan identities; circulation, creation, and transformation of identity categories in Gabonese hip-hop; Moroccan multiplicities and performing transnationalism; jazz, initiation societies, and Afrocentrism; urban bachata and Dominican racial identity in New York; national musical heritage from the Black Atlantic in contemporary Ethiopia; Black art, music, and dance and cultural nationalism in the United States; and the role of new and social media in Tanzanian hip-hop production.

751.   **Bader, Sandra, and Sean Martin-Iverson, eds**. 2014. "Special Issue: Creative Intersubjectivity in Performance: Perspectives for the Asia-Pacific." *Ethnomusicology Forum* 23(2): 147–281. ISSN: 1741-1912.

Explores the dynamics of creative intersubjectivity in diverse contexts from Indonesia and the Asia-Pacific. Compiled essays integrate research into a range of music and dance from the Asia-Pacific including modern, hybrid, and movement traditions. Essay topics include Dangdut and Nyawer encounters in West Java, Indonesia; hardcore punk scene in Bandung, Indonesia; relationships between sound and movement in West Sumatran plate dancing; Hindu epic Ramayana performance of an Indonesian community in Perth Australia; and Polynesia youth hip-hop in Australia.

752.   **Becker, Heike, and Dorothea Schultz, eds**. 2017. "Special Issue: Un/Making Difference Through Performance and Mediation in Contemporary Africa." *Journal of African Cultural Studies* 29(2): 149–259. ISSN: 1369-6815.

Examines how performance facilitates sensorial and embodied experiences of difference or sharing and unmaking of difference, and how performance makes people feel difference and its opposite, similarity, to be true, authentic, and real. Compiled essay topics include nostalgia, urban critique, and generational difference in Kinshasa's TV music shows; jali pop in Paris; Obama K'Ogelo cultural festivals in Siaya County, Kenya; performative ethnography in Bellvillle (Cape

Town); performing identity of a professional choreographer; and hip-hopera in Cape Town and aesthetics and politics of performing Afrikaaps.

753. **Bradley, Barbara, Jan Fairley, and Patria Roman-Velazquez, eds**. 2011. "Special Issue: Crossing Borders: Music in Latin America." *Popular Music* 30(2): 171–296. ISSN: 0261-1430.

Investigates musical routes and social links between Latin America, Spain, Portugal, and other parts of the world and challenges conventional musicological and geographical categorizations. Compiled essays offer dialogues in Latin American music that break with conventional ideas of geographical bounded music but examine music "at the borders," both aesthetically and culturally. Essay topics include emergent collaborations between Brazilian and Angolan music makers; Latin American migrant musicians in Australia and New Zealand; carnival, creativity, and Indigenous music video production in the Bolivian Andes; reflections on global popular music; musical categories, place, and identity in a transnational listening community; and the routes and roots of *danzón*—a critique of the history of a genre.

754. **Brunt, Shelley**. 2011. "Special Issue: New Perspectives on Popular Music in Asia." *Perfect Beat* 12(2): 103–197. ISSN: 1038-2909.

A special issue on popular music in Asia that observes how, for more than a decade, academics have developed an increasing fascination for Asian popular music as a subject for research. Argues that this has arisen during a time when popular music studies have gained momentum as a fruitful field of scholarly inquiry and coincided with a firm shift away from the privileging of Anglophone-centric popular music from North America or the United Kingdom as the popular music norm. Notes that the growth in interest has been supported by several key publications on popular music forms coming out of Asia.

755. **Brunt, Shelley, and Oli Wilson, eds**. 2021. "Special Issue: COVID-19, Music, and the Asia-Pacific (Part 2)." *Perfect Beat* 21(2): 91–188.

Part 2 of a special issue that deals with the influences and effects of the COVID-19 pandemic on the music, musicians, music industries, and audiences in the Asia-Pacific region. Topics covered include K-pop beyond the lockdown, fandom, participation, and experiencing community online (South Korea); the role of communication technologies between choreographer and composer during the Aotearoa/New Zealand COVID response; social media, music propaganda, and public health in Vietnam; the embodiment of Chinese struggle cultural collectives in the lyrics of epidemic songs; the Hong Kong experimental music scene in the COVID-19 pandemic; fieldwork in Hong Kong through protest and pandemic; the impact of COVID-19 on Australian live music and arts entertainment industries; jazz performance during COVID-19; struggles of punk and metal bands on Instagram in Melbourne; using splice studio and audio movers to enhance online music outcomes; and pandemic pedagogy and facilitating connection.

756.   **Brunt, Shelley, and Oli Wilson, eds**. 2021. "Special Issue: COVID-19, Music, and the Asia-Pacific (Part 1)." *Perfect Beat* 21(1): 5–86. ISSN: 1038-2909.

Part 1 of a special issue that deals with the influences and effects of COVID-19 pandemic on the music, musicians, music industries, and audiences in the Asia-Pacific region. Essay topics include precarity, creative justice, and the impact of the COVID-19 pandemic on the Victorian (Australia) music industries; the impact of COVID-19 on music venues in regional South Australia; Filipino immigrant musicians in Australia during the COVID-19 pandemic; Keri Nuttall on life as a songwriter in the pandemic; being a DJ—tales from a locked-down India; platformication of Tencent's TME Live in post-pandemic China; leveraging pedagogy for teaching music online; devising an interdisciplinary radio playing in a pandemic; experiencing the COVID-19 pandemic as a post-graduate music student; and Shakuhachi learning during the pandemic.

757.   **Carr, Paul, ed**. 2022. "Special Issue: The Impacts of COVID-19 on the Music Industries of the Global North." *Journal of World Popular Music* 9(1–2): 5–268. ISSN: 2052-4900.

Focuses on the impact of COVID-19 on the music industries in the Global North. Essay topics include Birmingham (England) and the international business of live music in times of COVID-19; tourism-dependent local music ecosystems under COVID-19 (Portugal); planning for music careers in the Victorian music industries and during COVID-19 (Australia); how German music venues can survive the lockdown; the impact of COVID-19 on the Welsh music industry (Wales); music venues, COVID-19, and the handling of the crisis (Germany); COVID-19 British jazz musicians; ethnographic explorations of the impacts of COVID-19 on sociality and spatiality in a Swiss live music scene (Switzerland); and the impact of COVID-19 on virtual guitar music communities.

758.   **Cooper, B. Lee**. 2008. "Special Issue: New Orleans Music: Legacy and Survival." *Popular Music and Society* 31(2): 149–268. ISSN: 0300-7766.

A special issue that concentrates on the richness of popular music in New Orleans. Compiled essay topics include discovery, dominance, and decline of Crescent City popular music influence, 1946–2006; the Boswell Sisters; the panorama jazz band and Zyde punks; Katrina: the dynamic of disaster and inspiration; New Orleans sound, 1946–2006—a bio-bibliography and discography.

759.   **Creutzenberg, Jan, and Anna Yates-Lu, eds**. 2022. "Special Issue: Korean Traditional Music on the Global Stage." *The World of Music (New Series)* 11(1): 1–175. ISSN: 0043-8774.

A special issue that focuses on live performances of traditional Korean music (*kugak*) outside of Korea, mainly in the Western world, and lays out reasons for its relevance. Compiled essay topics are varied and include nationalist construction and global representation of traditional performing arts in South Korea; cultural ambassadors and global impact; localization, globalization, and Korean community arts in New York City; traditional Korean music today in the Korean diaspora in London; the pansori experience in Europe; and experiences of *kugak* in Europe and beyond.

760. **Fugellie, Daniela, ed**. 2020. "Special Issue: Musical Trajectories Between Latin America and Europe, 1970–2000." *Twentieth-Century Music* 17(3): 283–444. ISSN: 1478-5722.

A special issue that grew out of a dialogue that relates to issues of transnational biographies or musical genres that have tended to stay invisible or were even regarded as problematic objects for a nation-centered categorization. Essay topics include art music and transterritoriality reflections on Cuban migrations to Europe during the 1990s; Argentine composers in the contemporary French music scene; European professors at the Cursos Latinoamericanos de musica contemporánea—two experiences—Piriápolis 1974 and Buenos Aires 1977; cultural exchange and competing systems; art music from the Chilean exile in Anacrusa Festivals at the Goethe Institute Santiago; avatars of the Andean sound and their reception by Italian music groups (1973–1996); Latin American songs in the GDR and the East German singer-songwriter repertoire (1970–2000); and transatlantic myth—the 1994 Arica Eclipse Rave as an example of the history and historiography of electronic dance music between Chile and Germany.

761. **Gunner, Liz, ed**. 2015. "Special Issue: Performance and Social Meaning." *Journal of African Cultural Studies* 3: 247–369. ISSN: 1369-6815.

Engages directly with different kinds of performance by focusing on the countries of Zimbabwe, South Africa, Cote d'Ivoire (Ivory Coast), and Tanzania. Compiled essays engage with the spectrum of expressive practices on the continent from both live performance and electronic media. Essay topics include poetics, aesthetics of HIV/AIDS on Tanzania; Tanzanian nation building with guitar music, sung Swahili, poems, and healing; the quest of nationalism; performance culture in 1980s South Africa; song, identity, and the state; reggae musicians as political actors in the Ivorian crisis; and the performative state and the nature of power in a post-colony.

762. **Lewis, George E., ed**. 2008. "Special Issue: Technology and Black Music in the Americas." *Journal of the Society for American Music* 2(2): 139–293. ISSN: 1752-1963.

Integrates a series of essays that explore the relatively unchartered current in the overall flow of Black music technology. Essay topics include telepresence and biopolitics in post-Timbaland rap production; the retrofuture tabulations of Kora Lynch; Anthony Braxton's speculative musics; and Black music and the Afro-technological in the science fiction of Henry Dumas and Samuel R. Delany.

763. **Matsue, Jennifer M., ed**. 2008. "Special Issue: Popular Music in Changing Asia." *Asian Music* 39(1): 1–150. ISSN: 0044-9202.

A special issue whose publication is motivated by a need for both teaching and research sources on Asia's popular music. Discusses how popular music studies in general have exploded, with increasing interest in popular musics throughout Asia keeping pace. Essay topics include Hanoi rock, rock and roll in Vietnam; popular music in Cambodia after the Khmer Rouge; tradition and modernity in Yaeyaman popular music; Jay Chou's rap and hip-hop in China; new technologies, industrial structure, and consumption of music in Japan; and Filipino diasporas and postcolonial hip-hop.

764.   **Moore, Robin D., Laura Putman, Matthew B. Karush, *et al*.** 2016. "Special Issue: Latin America, the Caribbean, and New Jazz Studies." *Journal of Latin American Cultural Studies* 25(3): 321–483. ISSN: 1356-9325.

A special issue that focuses on different aspects and new trends that Latin America and the Caribbean have contributed to the body of jazz. Essay topics include danzón, North American radical discourses and reflections on early jazz; Panama and Harlem as Caribbean crossroads circa 1910–1940; jazz and the samba debate and vice versa; reinventing the Latin in Latin jazz—the music of Gato Barbieri; recent histories and economies of Afro-Latin jazz; and others.

765.   **Oliver, Paul, and John Bailey, eds**. 1988. "Special Issue: Aspects of the South Asia/West Crossover & Essays." *Popular Music* 7(2): 119–246. ISSN: 0261-1430.

Commentary and compiled scholarly essays that focus on popular music, musicians, and musical instruments in South Asia. Compiled essay topics are varied and include popular expression of religious syncretism of the Bauls of Bengal; Ain-e-Diwaneh, the musician as madmen; a concise history of the phonograph industry in India; popular music in India, 1901–1986; popular film song in India; the use of elements from Indian music in popular music and jazz; ghazals to bhangra in Britain; Indian cinema; musico-ethnological approaches to musical instruments; Tagore collection of Indian musical instruments; Raja Sir Sourindro Mohun Tagore; Sufi music of Indian and Pakistan; and phonogram and cultural communication in India.

766.   **Rijven, Stan, ed**. 1989. "Special Issue: African Popular Music." *Popular Music* 8(3): 216–318. ISSN: 0261-1430.

A special issue comprised of several scholarly essays on African popular music. Compiled essays are diverse and topics include early history of West African juju highlife music; diachronic study of change in juju music; songs of Remmy Ongala and Orchestra Super Matimila; domestication of ingoma dancing in South Africa, 1929–39; key to N'Dour—roots of the Senegalese star; Black music, Afro-American music, and European music; Graceland revisited; brief history of South African popular music; selected discography; and books on popular music in Africa.

767.   **Sakata, Lorraine H., ed**. 2005. "Special Issue: Music and Identity in Central Asia." *Ethnomusicology Forum* 14(2): 127–233. ISSN: 1741-1912.

Focuses on the music of Central Asia as a cultural/geographic area, known as Transoxiana, Tartary, Turkestan, and more recently Central or Inner Asia, whose names and geographical reach have fluctuated throughout recent history. Compiled essays are varied and include music and identity in Central Asia; power, authority, and music in the cultures of Inner Asia; musical heritage and national identity in Uzbekistan; open borders, tradition, Tajik popular music; and Kabul's music in exile.

768. **Shin, Hyunjoon, Yoshitaka Mōri, and Tung-Hung Ho, eds**. 2013. "Special Issue: East Asian Popular Music and Its (Dis)Contents." *Popular Music* 32(1): 1–123. ISSN: 0261-1430.

A special issue that seeks to address the gap in scholarly research concerning popular music in East Asia. Essays covers a broad range of topics that include gender independence in East Asian popular music; national styles among Japanese hip-hop DJs; Korean hip-hop and cultural reterritorialization; covers, localization, the waning hybridity of cantopop; the new wave of Chinese pop's Chris Li; Taiwanese American independent rock music; and Shibuya-kei as transnational soundscape.

769. **Spicer, Richard, et al**. 2001. "Special Issue: Nineteenth Century American Popular Music." *Popular Music and Society* 25(1–2): 1–249. ISSN: 0300-7766.

Focuses on nineteenth-century American popular music. Essay topics include popular song for celebration in federal Portsmouth, New Hampshire; William Bradbury's mountain songs, 1847–52; The Fisk Jubilee Singers' civil rights tours of 1879–1882; history of bluegrass and the segregation of popular music in the United States; Lilith Fair, resisting anger, celebrating, contradictions; nationality, race, and gender on the American popular charts; and alternative countrymen: origins, music, and worldview.

770. **Steinholdt, Yngvar B., and David-Emil Wickström, eds**. 2016. "Special Issue: Popular Music in Post-Soviet Space: Trends, Movements, and Social Contexts." *Popular Music and Society* 32(3): 307–424. ISSN: 0300-7766.

A special issue that delves into the vulnerable status of popular music studies at the institutional level within the former Soviet republics. Essay topics include motherland in contemporary Russian popular music; nostalgia, patriotism, religion, and *Russkii rok*; the packaging and repackaging of Soviet rock; female singers and gay male fans in Russian popular music; performing *maqom* and Uzbek National *estrada* in the twenty-first century; historical nostalgia and modern nationalism in contemporary Kazah popular music videos; and the poetics of pop polyphony and translating Georgian song for the world.

771. **Stone, Ruth, ed**. 2017. "Special Issue: Mobilizing Musical Performance and Expressive Culture in the Ebola 2014 Pandemic." *Africa Today* 63(3): 3–123. ISSN: 1527-1978.

Considers the role of the arts in addressing the 2014 Ebola pandemic and how the arts were employed at both grassroots and formal levels to reach large populations of people with critical health information. Essay topics include Ebola as African American discourses of panic and otherization; music, the ecology of fear—Kanyeleng women performers and Ebola prevention in The Gambia; fundraising and the impact of Ebola music and dance tourism in Guinea; music, media, and the ethnopoetics of two songs in Liberia; and creating musical connections in Liberian communities during the 2014 crisis in West Africa.

772. **Sweers, Britta, ed**. 2019. "Special Issue: Music, Climate Change, and the North." *European Journal of Musicology* 18(1): 1–159. ISSN: 2504-1916.

A special issue that is intended to enhance discourses on global warming and climate change in Europe and especially its Nordic countries and the United States, to open musicology to studies in global climate through music, and to contribute to the newly emerging field within cultural theory, musicology, ethnomusicology, and sustainability studies. Topics covered include climate crisis and the North, ecomusicology and academic discourse; Arctic Arcadia and modern adaptations of an antique idea; representation of Iceland and Icelanders in the film *Heima* by Sigur Rós; Meredith Monk's facing north and the art of natural voice; structure and improvisation in Björk's "Mouth Cradle"; Libby Larsen's "Up Where the Air Gets Thin"; music and northern forest cultures; towards a theory of remix; and alpine song and sound impressions.

773. **Taylor, Timothy, and Kristy Gillespie, eds**. 2009. "Special Issue: On Identity— Contemporary Music Research in the Asia-Pacific Region." *Asia-Pacific Journal of Anthropology* 10(2): 75–142. ISSN: 1444-2213.

A special issue that focuses on different theoretical aspects that surround the contemporary music of the Asia-Pacific region. Essay topics include Indonesians and Australians playing Javanese gamelan in Perth, Western Australian; Australian Aboriginal desert musicians on tour; Easter Island fusion of cultural performance; and transnational relationships transforming selves.

774. **Whyton, Tony, and George McKay, eds**. 2020. "Special Issue: The Cultural Heritage of Jazz Festivals." *International Journal of Cultural Heritage* 26(6): 543–618. ISSN: 1352-7258.

Charts and interrogates key questions relating to heritage research on jazz festivals and provides specific case studies from contrasting heritage locations. Topics covered include European jazz festivals as cultural heritage sites; Dutch landscape experienced through SummerJazzCycleTour; heritage of slavery in British jazz festivals; production and politics of heritage on a Dutch Caribbean island; and festivals as integrative sites for sustainable urban development.

775. **Zhang, Qian, and Anthony Fung**. "Special Issue: Asian Popular Music: Transnationality and Globalization." *China Media and Culture* 4(4): 399–514. ISSN: 2059-4364.

Focuses on Asian popular music as an influential form of contemporary media cultural studies through a unique mixture of theoretical analysis and multidimensional methodologies. Aims to contribute to broadening the field of global media studies by opening a variety of music-related disciplines and debates. Essay topics include transnational corporations and cosmopolitans in the global popular music economy; historicizing pop formations in China; and United Kingdom–Asia music business collaborations, transnational, and transregional production of modernity in 1980s Chinese disco (Ali Baba and Genghis Kahn).

776. **Zemke, Kirsten, ed**. 2020. "Special Issue: Music and Politics." *Perfect Beat* 20(2): 113–187. ISSN: 1038-2909.

A special issue that deals with concerns of music and politics and explores case studies in the Asia-Pacific area. Topics covered in this special issue include understanding the mode of resistance among young DIY Indonesian musicians; kava artists and rebellious music in Tonga; role of green music in Australia in climate change activism; and Pasifika climate activist music in New Zealand, queered and disabled.

III. MUSICAL GENRES AND STYLES

777. **Anderton, Chris, Chris Anton, Andrei Sora, *et al***. 2020. "Special Issue: Progressive Rock." *Rock Music Studies* 7(1): 1–99. ISSN: 1949-1159.

Informs about the growth of academic research clusters and networks dedicated to studying specific genres including punk, reggae, heavy metal, electronic dance music, and jazz. Also is informed by the *Progect* network dedicated to the study of progressive rock in all its forms. Compiled essays stem from research presented at the Edinburgh and Lund conferences. Topics include the absent presence of progressive rock in the British music press, 1968–1978; Transylvania Phoenix, Romanian ethno-rock, and the politics of folk music; the impact of Chris Cutler and rock in opposition on Czech rock music in the Communist era; politics, authenticity, and identity conflicts in Spanish progressive rock, 1970–1981; the world's first flamenco rock band—Anglo-American progressive rock, politics, and national identity in Spain around Carmen's *Fandangos in Space*; and utopian and spiritual experiences, encountering *The Dark Side of the Moon*.

778. **Bolden, Tony, ed**. 2013. "Special Issue: The Funk Issue." *American Studies Journal* 45(4): 1–261. ISSN: 0026-3079.

Focuses on how funk music contributed to three global forms of music: hip-hop, Afrobeat, and jazz. Compiled essays examine the artistry and ethos of funk as well as its impact on related Black musical forms and Black expressive culture. Essay topics include groove theory; rediscovering the musical career of Betty Mabry Davis; the feminist funk of Betty Davis and Renee Stout; (Patti)

Labelle, funk, feminism, and politics; Fela Kuti, James Brown, and the invention of Afrobeat; the blues/funk futurism of Roger Troutman; "Chameleon" meets Soul Train; Herbie, James, Michael, Damita Jo, and jazz-funk; intertextuality and cosmic philosophy in Funkadelic's album covers; belief in lyrics; Meshell Ndegeocello and the expanding definition of funk in post-soul America; Outkast, the funk connection, and Afrofuturism; and Janelle Monáe's neo-Afrofuturism.

779. **Bridge, Simone K., and Nicholas Tochka, eds**. 2018. "Special Issue: Hip-Hop Activism and Representational Politics, Part 2." *Journal of World Popular Music* 5(2): 143–283. ISSN: 0252-4900.

Part 2 of a special issue series that contributes to understandings of the diversification of global hip-hop. Hip-hop activism and representation are explored through a series of compiled essays that focus on Ireland, Denmark, France, South Africa, Canada, and the United States.

780. **Bridge, Simone K., Nicholas Tochka, and Raphael Nowak, eds**. 2018. "Special Issue: Hip-Hop Activism and Representational Politics, Part 1." *Journal of World Popular Music* 5(1): 5–138. ISSN: 0252-4900.

Part 1 of a special issue series that explores hip-hop activism and representational politics in selected countries from the Global North and South. Topics include multilingual activism in South African hip-hop; global and local in Mozambique; hip-hop and marginal speakers' hip-hop activism beyond acts of artistic performance into education; the Moroccan political context and hip-hop artists; hip-hop activism and representation and the ways that Sister Souljah employs her art and activism to seize political and artistic agency.

781. **Claus-Bachman, Martina**. 2000. "Special Issue: Gothic, Metal, Rap, and Rave-Youth Culture and its Educational Dimensions." *The World of Music* 42(1): 1–173. ISSN: 0043-8774.

A special issue that stems from a conference on the topic "Gothic, Metal, Rap, and Rave: Youth Subcultures and Their Cultural Pedagogical Possibilities," which was held at the University of Bemberg in 1999, bringing together scholars and cultural educators throughout Germany. The papers, now published essays, are intended to contribute new approaches and recommendations to be made on the educational system. Essay topics covered in this special issue include cultural identity and educational possibilities in humanistic studies; gothic and dark music—forms and background; hip-hop origins—characteristics and creative processes; techno music—its special forces of unification and fragmentation within a musical subculture; fan-specific involvement with music; dimensions of aesthetic intensity in music—related expressive forms of youth culture; cultural logic of "Generation Z" and the consequences for music educational concepts; and dramatic expression of the gothic subculture in school.

782. **Covach, John, and Walter Everett, eds**. 2000. "Special Issue: Traditions, Institutions, and American Popular Music." *Contemporary Music Review* 19(1): 1–166. ISSN: 0749-4467.

A companion volume to the previous special issue titled "American Rock and the Classical Music Tradition" (2000). Issue further suggests that the interaction of popular and art music in American culture not only raises highly charged questions but also has a rich history dating back to the nineteenth century. Essays compiled in this companion issue include American pop harmonies (1925–1950) and their European kin; performances in early Hollywood sound film—source, background music, and the integrated sound track; analyzing third stream (jazz); vernacular music and the American Academy; redrawing boundaries—The Kronos Quartet; and can music reweave the fabric of our fragmented culture?

783. **Covach, John, and Walter Everett, eds**. 2000. "Special Issue: American Rock and the Classical Music Tradition." *Contemporary Music Review* 18(4): 1–169. ISSN: 0749-4467.

A special issue that explores the relationship between rock and classical music and focuses on the composers, performers, theorists, historians, critics, and listeners who welcome the potentially difficult intercourse between "classical" and "popular" styles and techniques in American music and culture. Topics include facing rock reality (1988); Echolyn and American progressive rock; listening to Zappa; and the learned vs. the vernacular in the songs of Billy Joel.

784. **DeVeaux, Scott**. 1989. "Special Issue: Jazz." *American Music* 7(1): 1–122. ISSN: 1945-2349.

A special issue of *American Music* journal that enhances scholarly research in jazz. Essay topics include the emergence of the jazz concert, 1935–1945; the reception and institution of American jazz during the Weimar Republic; James Reese Europe and the prehistory of jazz; and the seven jazz preludes of Gershwin, a historical narrative.

785. **Evans, David, ed**. 1996. "Special Issue: New Perspectives on the Blues." *American Music* 14(4): 397–526. ISSN: 1945-2349.

Focuses on theoretical, historical, and cultural perspectives of the blues. Essay topics include sheet music, Southern vaudeville, and the communal ascendancy of the blues; the hands of blues guitarists; and Houston Creoles and zydeco and the emergence of an African American urban popular music.

786. **Fagge, Roger, and Nicholas Gebhardt, eds**. 2020. "Special Issue: Jazz and Everyday Aesthetics." *Jazz Research Journal* 13(1–2): 5–282. ISSN: 1753-8637.

A special double issue that emerged from a two-year project on jazz and everyday aesthetics, funded by the Arts and Humanities Council in the United Kingdom, that involved a series of seminars, musical performances, and workshops examining different claims about jazz's aesthetic value in the context of everyday practices of living. Compiled essays continued this exploration from a range of perspectives. Essay topics include politics, aesthetics, and dissonance of music in everyday life: jazz and the American mundane in Jean-Michel Basquiat's writing; what can everyday aesthetics teach us?; Russia and the creation of jazz in the British everyday imaginary; Christian Scott aTunde Adjuah's critique of Danziger Bridge shootings; jazz, space, and labor; Rhythm Clubs, record series, and everyday connoisseurship of the "hot rhythm" records in interwar Britain; how international radio broadcasts affected the experience of jazz in 1920s–1930s New Zealand; contemporary jazz violin pedagogy and the legacy of gypsy (Roma) jazz; songwriting, identity, and everyday aesthetics in African American tradition; towards an understanding of distraction, advertising, and newspaper coverage of the Kansas City jazz scene in the 1950s; a photographic project on contemporary jazz musicians' lives in Birmingham (United Kingdom); a history of listenings; and departures and returns among early New Orleans jazz musicians.

787. **Gamble, Steven, and Raquel C. Valverde, eds**. 2021. "Special Issue: Its Where You're @: Hip-Hop and the Internet." *Global Hip-Hop Studies* 2: 1–248. ISSN: 2632-6825.

Focuses on hip-hop in different global manifestations. Essays are intended to draw attention to the complex interactions of the hip-hop phenomenon between online and offline, physical, digital dominant, and marginalized. Topics include digital feminisms in Palestine; exploring the emotional and relational labor of Black women rappers in sexual dance economies on OnlyFans; pirate Internet infrastructure and the ephemeral hip-hop archive in South Africa; and navigating the online music platform for royalty-free samples.

788. **Guibert, Gérôme, ed**. 2019. "Special Issue: Paradoxal Metal: Entre pratiques ori-dinaires ét représentations transgressives (Paradoxical Metal: Ordinary Practices and Transgressive Representatives)." *Volume! La revue des musiques popularies— The French Journal of Popular Music Studies* 15(2): 7–176. French and English texts. ISSN: 1634-5495.

Explores the tensions between the negative myths surrounding metal music and the norms of its fans via a series of essays that deal with the reception of NOW BHW, shrieking and growing in French metal music, the live metal music industry, metal worlds according to the Encyclopedia Metallum, black metal, and contemporary art. Essay topics include reception of new wave of British heavy metal; live music industry in France; short history of French metal through the prism of growling language; metal world according to the Encyclopedia Metallum (a collective database dedicated to the metal scene assessable since 2002); and others.

789. **Guibert, Gérôme, and Emmanuel Parent, eds**. 2004. "Special Issue: Hip-Hop Sounds: Global and French Dynamics." *Volume! La revue des musiques*

populares—The French Journal of Popular Music Studies 3(2): 1–176. French and English texts. ISSN: 1634-5495.

Focuses on French rap, the interactions between music DJing, dance, video clips, and the movies, and discussions about a recent book dedicated to hip-hop studies talking about the genre's globalization. Compiled essay topics include hip-hop social–global French logics; crossing the Atlantic; the musical analysis of rap; violence in rap as catharsis—towards a political consciousness; hip-hop music and dance—a technical musical practice in the social arena; Jim Jarmusch's aesthetics of sampling in *Ghost Dog*; and intermediality, intertextuality, and nonmusical factors in the evolution of pop music.

790.   **Harris, Travis, ed.** 2021. "Special Issue: Funk What You Heard: Hip-Hop Is a Field of Study." *Journal of Hip-Hop Studies* 9(1): 1–131. ISBN: 2331-5563.

A special issue that intended to be emblematic and a call to all scholars who engage with hip-hop studies and offers ways in which the field should properly respond to the wave of oppression in the world. Compiled essays chart paths forward for the future of hip-hop studies. Topics covered include hip-hop as a field of study; critical analysis of hip-hop beingness—Kendrick Lamar's 2016 Grammy Award performance; hip-hop entrepreneurialism in Houston (Texas); Nipsey Hussle, community health, and care ethics; 2Pac, sociopolitical realities, and hip-hop nation language; and its hip hop not hip-hop (explains two hip-hop scholars' discourse on official academic spelling of the field).

791.   **Harris, Travis, ed.** 2020. "Special Issue: Twenty-First Century B.I.T.C.H. Frameworks: Hip-Hop Feminism Comes of Age." *Journal of Hip-Hop Studies* 7(1): 4–118. ISBN: 2331-5563.

Charts the course of the field of hip-hop feminisms and provides highlights of the importance of Black women and girls and what it means to reclaim power over representations and images. Essay topics include mapping contemporary hip-hop feminism; the City Girls: the Cardi B–Beyoncé complex; stylized and gendered performativity in trap music; Black hip-hop feminist art community on the United States; how scamming aesthetics utilized by Black female rappers undermine existing institutions of gender; and hip-hop feminism starter kit.

792.   **Harris, Travis, Daniel W. Hodge, and Siram Singh, eds.** 2019. "Special Issue: If I Ruled the World: Putting Hip-Hop on the Atlas." *Journal of Hip-Hop Studies* 6(2): 1–250. ISSN: 2331-5563.

A special issue that is both dedicatory to the Nigerian poet Ikeogu Oke (1967–2018), recognized for publishing his work on Tupac Shakur posthumously, and comprised of research from scholars around the world and with an inclusion of an extensive bibliography on global hip-hop studies. Essay topics include using hip-hop as a form of decolonizing public pedagogy; generation hip-hop and the universal hip-hop museum; negotiating French Muslim identities through hip-hop; configurations of space and identity in hip-hop; performing Global South: the rise of Aboriginal Australian hip-hop; and so forth.

793. **Harris, Travis, and Cassandra D. Chaney, eds**. 2018. "Special Issue: Hip-Hop and Religion And . . ." *Journal of Hip-Hop Studies* 5(1): 4–178. ISSN: 2331-5563.

Addresses how religion and hip-hop highlight the experiences of marginalized Black and Brown people within and outside the United States. Essay topics include hip-hop perspective of religion; hip-hop, spirituality, and heaven; hip-hop hermeneutics and how the culture influences preachers; hip-hop, religion, and the youth of Romania; radical aesthetics in Black cultural production of Kendrick Lamar's collapsing hip-hop realness and Christian identity; and existential theology between God, Blackness, and being.

794. **Hoad, Catherine**. 2022. "Special Issue: Metal, Punk, and Hardcore in Aotearoa/ New Zealand." *Perfect Beat* 22(1): 1–86. ISSN: 1038-2909.

Focuses on heavy metal, punk, and hardcore music scenes, practices, and cultures in Aotearoa/New Zealand. Compiled essays demonstrate how metal, punk, and hardcore have a long-nuanced history in Aotearoa where all three genres have interfaced with localized aesthetics and colonial histories and responded to deindustrialization in complex and multifaceted ways.

795. **Horn, David, ed**. 2007. "Special Issue: The Blues in Honor of Paul Oliver." *Popular Music* 16(1): 1–193. ISSN: 0261-1430.

A special issue produced in honor of Paul Oliver in recognition of his outstanding contribution to popular music scholarship. Essay topics include an interview with Paul Oliver; Paul Oliver's contribution to ethnomusicology; country music on location—field recordings before Bristol; folklore, commercialism, and exploitation—copyright in the blues; loss, nostalgia, and the blues; aesthetics and Robert Johnson's blues style as a product of recorded culture; the idea of Oklahoma in early recordings; Bessie Smith's "Back Water Blues": the story behind the song; Bessie Smith's "Down Hearted Blues" and Gulf Coast Blues" revisited; African American topical songs on the 1928 Florida hurricanes and floods; why British blues; and Paul Oliver—a selective bibliography.

796. **Hyunkim, Kyung, and Cedar B. Saeji, eds**. 2020. "Special Issue: Korean Hip-Hop and New Explorations of Afro-Asian Identity." *Journal of World Popular Music* 7(2): 115–270. ISSN: 0252-4900.

A special issue based on papers that were presented at a conference on hip-hop and new explorations of Afro-Asian identity held at the University of California Irvine, October 7, 2019. The conference and papers were conceived to stimulate a conversation to understand Korean hip-hop's debt to African American hip-hop. Essay topics include identity and de-blacking rap music in South Korea; Korean hip-hoppers' identity; regional hip-hop in Seoul and underground hip-hop in Gwangja; and Korean hip-hop songs by female rappers.

797. **Jipson, Art, ed**. 2007. "Special Issue: Hate Rock." *Popular Music and Society* 30(4): 449–547. ISSN: 0300-7766.

Concentrates on hate rock, which highlights a departure in the study of popular music. Compiled essays further the understanding of White racial extremist music also called hate music or hate rock by analyzing the various manifestations of hate-based music. Essays demonstrate how the term "hate rock" can be applied to individual groups and organizations in various segments of White racial extremist movements worldwide. Essay topics make clear that hate rock has a long history as demonstrated in the work of various racist musicians and promoters such as Ku Klux Klan–sponsored recordings of the 1940s and Johnny Rebel in the 1960s. Other topics include German hip-hop from the Right; musical performance and the Cajun roots of right-wing rock; social analysis of country hate music; and popular music and the 2002 Bali bombings.

798. **Johnson, Ann, Mike Stax, *et al***. 2006. "Special Issue: Garage Rock." *Popular Music and Society* 29(4): 411–503. ISSN: 0300-7766.

Focuses on garage rock music and musicians presented in scholarly discourse. Essay topics include the appropriation of garage rock in the Clash's "Garageland"; Sir Douglas Sahm and the garage as big Texas; and the ethos of '60s garage punk. Also includes miscellaneous essays relating to New Orleans and Katrina, and whether pop music journals have any impact.

799. **Johnson, Bruce, and Adam Havas, eds**. 2022. "Special Issue: Jazz Diasporas." *Popular Music and Society* 45(4): 371–529. ISSN: 0300-7766.

A special issue that is concerned with jazz outside the United States. Essays focus on jazz studies in Australia, the Caribbean, Estonia, the Philippines, Portugal, South Africa, and Sweden with a historical span from forerunners of jazz with world music since the late twentieth century and continuing reinvention of the music in its global negotiations with the local.

800. **Kastin, David, *et al***. 2006. "Special Issue: Jazz." *Popular Music and Society* 29(3): 279–409. ISSN: 0300-7766.

Presents discourse on various aspects of jazz history, autobiography, jazz creativity and musicianship, and improvisation. Essay topics include the life and legend of the jazz baroness; New Orleans and the creation of early jazz; rethinking oral tradition in the learning of jazz improvisation; the South-Grappelli recordings of the Bach Double Concerto; in the movies, 1931–1969; and narrating the jazz life—three approaches to jazz autobiography.

801. **Land, Roderic R., and David O. Stovall, eds**. 2009. "Special Issue: Hip-Hop and Social Justice." *Equity & Excellence in Education* 42(1): 1–94. ISSN: 1066-5684.

A special issue with the purpose of providing educational administrators, faculty, students, and practitioners with a series of essays intended to facilitate conversations and raise awareness of how hip-hop can serve as a useful tool to bring students into the classroom and to inform and influence curriculum, pedagogical practices, and the construction of knowledge. Essay topics include a brief introduction to hip-hop and social justice; education, social justice, and the curriculum of hip-hop culture; dialoguing, cultural capital, and student engagement—toward a hip-hop pedagogy in the high school and university classroom; recruiting hip-hop as curriculum at a school for pregnant and parenting teens; critical hip-hop pedagogy as a form of liberatory praxis; Latinas'/Latinos' use of hip-hop as pedagogy and interpretative framework to negotiate and challenge racism; and hip-hop educational resources.

802.   **Littlejohn, John T., ed**. 2009. "Special Issue: Krautrock." *Popular Music and Society* 32(5): 577–653. ISSN: 0030-7766.

Focuses on Krautrock, the single most important strand of popular music outside the United States and England. Compiled essay topics are diverse and include Faust and the politics of the unpolitical; music as a weapon—reactions and responses to RAF terrorism in the music of Ton Steine Scherben; James Brown, Kraftwerk, and the practice of musical timekeeping before techno; NEU!—(Walter) Benjamin meets (Michael) Rother and (Klaus) Dinger; and Kraftwerk, language, lucre, and loss of identity.

803.   **Maloney, Liam, and Nicolas Pillai, eds**. 2022. "Special Issue: What If . . .? Speculative Histories of Jazz." *Jazz Research Journal* 15(1–2): 5–167. ISSN: 1753-8637.

Interrogates the conjectural mode as a new beginning for the understanding of jazz and its culture and contends that despite the destabilizing intentions of new jazz studies, discourse has remained centered on ahistorical canon formation and radicalized conceptions of genius and on the status of jazz. Essay topics covered include without making a song and dance out of it; dystopian lateness and speculation in Nina Simone's Afrofuturism; Sun Ra and Karlheinz Stockhausen as intergalactic collaborators; sex, dance, and gender in the world of the pre–World War II "Chorus Girl"; Marvel Comic's greatest jazz musician; imaginary collaborations of Miles Davis; John Coltrane, the sonic philosopher of opposition; the two Simones at Montreux; free jazz; and Albert Ayler's *Ghost*—a one-act play.

804.   **Pillai, Nicholas, ed**. 2019. "Special Issue: Jazz in Television." *Jazz Research Journal* 12(1): 5–162. ISSN: 1753-8637.

A special issue that challenges scholars to address the variety of jazz in film and television and its place within wider cultural movements. Essay topics include television, performance, and the modern jazz canon; an interpretation of the semiotics of "self" with the Modern Jazz Quartet on Jazz 625 as a case study; jazz music in children's television; the politics of gender, sexuality, and jazz in *The Golden Girls*; material and expositional frames in BBC Arena's visual jazz jukebox; and jazz and the politics of representation in three dramedies.

805. **Pittleman, Karen, ed**. 2020. "Special Issue: Uncharted Country: New Voices and Perspectives in Country Music Studies." *Journal of Popular Music Studies* 32(2): 1–240. ISSN: 1533-1598.

A winner of the American Musicological Society's 2021 Ruth A. Solie Award, this special issue reflects how country music's sounds and meaning of shifting change in relation to queer, Indigenous, of-color artists, themes, and audiences in growing numbers are claiming the music as their own. The issue aims to capture the moment of change and to amplify its generative potential and to suggest country music's constitutive entanglements in key elements of the American story, including racial, religion, sex-gender, and class relations and to make it a potential vehicle for scholarly inquiry. Essays include You're My Country Music; Following the Ache of Americana and Decoding the Queer Paul Clayton; Me, Hank Williams, and My Dad; Ragtime Country—Rhythmically Recovering Country's Black Heritage; Migration Narratives, Cultural Resonances, and Latinx Experiences in Appalachian Music; Freddy Fender's Blackbrown Country Ecologies; Country Music and Radical Community Organizing in Uptown Chicago; Radical Limitations of Country-Soul Crossover in Bobby Womack's *BW Goes C&W*, 1976; Race and the Country Music Industry in the 1970s; Rhiannon Gidden's Powerful Reclamation of Country Culture; Country Music and Masculinities in Post-War Japan, 1945–56; Listening to Simone Schmidt's *Audible Songs From Rockwood*; The Presence and Perseverance of Jews, Judaism, and Jewishness in Country Music and Bluegrass; and "Tennessee Whiskey" and the Politics of Harmony.

806. **Quinn, Eithne, Joy White, and John Street**. 2022. "Special Issue: Prosecuting and Policing Rap." *Popular Music* 41(4): 1–526. ISSN: 0261-1430.

A special issue that examines how the state's coercing engagement with Black youth expressive culture and rap music has become a topic of public and scholarly concern. Compiled essays examine how rap lyrics and videos made by defendants and co-defendants are regularly used as evidence in court cases in ways that incite bias against young people in the dock. Essays include prosecuting rap and case law; the role of YouTube videos in the criminalization of United Kingdom drill music; censorship and racialized public morality in grim and drill music; the role(s) of the expert witness when rap is on trial; the marginalization of Black rap musicians in Manchester's live music scene; and schoolhouse rap.

807. **Raine, Sarah, and Emily Jones, eds**. 2021. "Special Issue: Diversity and Inclusion at Jazz Festivals." *Jazz Research Journal* 14(2): 101–229. ISSN: 1753-8637.

Presents scholarly discourse relating diversity and inclusion in the current jazz scene and offers a playlist inspired by different people, places, and problems of jazz. Topics include programming, diversity, and inclusion in a jazz festival; a case study on gender (im)balance in Portuguese jazz; diversity of programming for audiences in Australian jazz festivals; gender and politics in United Kingdom festivals and COVID-19; sidestepping race for inclusion at the New Orleans

Jazz Festival; and further thoughts, and a ManiFESTo, on jazz (festivals) and the decolonization of music.

808.   **Smith, Gareth, and Bryan Powell, eds**. 2018. "Special Issue: Hip-Hop, or How Not to Other the Other." *Journal of Popular Music Education* 2(1–2): 3–187. ISSN: 2397-6721.

Focuses on various topics on hip-hop music education. Essay topics include hip-hop and music education and race; hip-hop culture and hip-hop theology as challenges to oppression; conscious hip-hop—Lupe Fiasco's critical teachings on raced and gendered representations; hip-hop pedagogy as production practice; holistic educational ideals and pedagogy of trust with popular music education in civil society; racism and resilience in hip-hop; reharmonization and recontextualization in Kanye West's "Famous"; B-girls, gender identities, and hip-hop education; using the tradition of knowledge and education in hip-hop to transform classroom outcomes; hip-hop authenticity and music education; United Kingdom rap and music education.

IV. ARTISTS, BANDS, AND MUSICAL GROUPS

809.   **Attias, Bernardo, *et al***. 2016. "Special Issue: The Velvet Underground." *Rock Music Studies* 3(2): 131–232. ISSN: 1940-1159.

Focuses on the Velvet Underground, an American rock band that contributed greatly to popular music in global perspectives. Essays offers scholarly and theoretical arguments about the band, its members, discourses about authenticity in popular music, and others. Essay topics include authenticity and artifice in rock and roll; Lou Reed's "Ostrich" tuning as an aesthetic point of articulation; Velvet Underground—an interview with Walter Powers; "Loop" (one of the Velvet Underground's earliest tracks); theoretical perspectives that examine Lou Reed's wide-ranging humor; and an interview with Doug Yule.

810.   **Borshuk, Michael, Kevin Fellezs, *et al***. 2022. "Special Issue: Steely Dan at 50." *Rock Music Studies* 9(3): 249–387. ISSN: 1949-1159.

Focuses on Steely Dan in scholarly discourse and in popular music studies. Topics covered in this special issue include Steely Dan at 50; Steely Dan's grumpy old White guy's blues; the Odyssean masculinities of Steely Dan's *Aja*; the interplay of lyrics and music in Steely Dan's compositions; intimacy, alienation, and Donald Fagen's voice; groove voice and mystery reflections on Steely Dan's cool; and an interview with Kenny Weissberg.

811.   **Carter, Dale, Thomas Smucker, and Philip Lambert, *et al***. 2021. "Special Issue: The Beach Boys." *Rock Music Studies* 8(3): 187–295. ISSN: 1949-1159.

Commemorates the popular music of the Beach Boys addressing scholarly research that ties in issues such as associations in music; themes; and social, political, and ideological inquiries that inform popular music studies research focusing on this legendary musical group. Topics include the Beach Boys as an American national interest; tracing the consecrated technical anima from the Beach Boys to Janelle Monaé; Brian Wilson's song cycles; the Beach Boys and the Beatles in the mid-1990s; an interview with Bobby Figueroa; and an interview with Peter Hammill.

812.   **Costa, Jacopo, Mariana Vujnovic, *et al*.** 2020. "Special Issue: The Beatles." *Rock Music Studies* 7(3): 175–282. ISSN: 1949-1159.

Offers a special issue focusing on the Beatles, in terms of their legacy and impact on global popular music history. Topics include 1968—The Beatles, Frank Zappa, the Soft Machine, Pink Floyd, and establishing dialogues between experimentalism and tradition in rock music; the rise of the ex-Yu 1960s progressive rock music scenes, indie, and the influence of the Beatles; John Lennon's out and in: "Revolution"; the Beatles and the movies in 1968; sexual honesty of the Beatles' *White Album*; playing with *The White Album*; George Harrison's dialect shifting in his late 1960s songs; and recreating *The White Album*.

813.   **Danielsen, Anne, and Stan Hawkins, eds**. 2020. "Special Issue: The Quest of Princian Research." *Popular Music and Society* 43(3): 231–353. ISSN: 0300-7766.

Focuses on the popular musician Prince. The essays in this volume draw together numerous perspectives and provide occasion to reflect on Prince's standing as a pop phenomenon and the importance of his music. The essays demonstrate how Prince bridged Black popular music traditions and White mainstream pop and rock with his music and opened discussions of pop music's function in terms of pleasure, political engagement, and cultural resistance. The essays include Pop Life: Prince in the Recording Studio; Prince's Rhythm Programming: 1980s Music Production and the Esthetics of LM-Drum Machine; "The Right Amount of Odd": Vocal Compulsion, Structure, and Groove in Two Love Songs From *Around the World in a Day*; Rapping Done Let Us Down: Prince's Hip-Hop Ambivalence; Prince as the Post-Civil Rights Archetype: Navigating Between Assimilation and Self-Determination; From Prince's "Party Up" to "Baltimore": Three Decades of Social Protest and Social Awareness; and Some Stick Around 4 the Aftershow: Reproducing Prince During Public Mourning.

814.   **Dougan, John, *et al*.** 2015. "Special Issue: Sex Pistols." *Popular Music and Society* 38(4): 413–544. ISSN: 0300-7766.

Offers scholarly research on the legacy of the Sex Pistols and to recognize that the band occupies a crucial role in any historiography of punk, a role that at times is viewed as problematic. Essays seek not only to reiterate a punk orthodoxy but also to broaden and challenge an understanding of the Sex Pistols' impact and legacy. Topics include messianism in Sex Pistols historiography; Sex Pistols, school kids, and 1979; reading the feminine approach to the Sex Pistols; a tech-processual analysis; the Sex Pistols at the seaside; and legacy and authenticity in Portugal.

815.   **Fogarty, Mary, and Gina Arnold, eds**. 2021. "Special Issue: Taking Taylor Seriously." *Contemporary Music Review* 37(3): 189–271. ISSN: 0749-4467.

Offers a special issue on Taylor Swift, emphasizing that just as Bob Dylan's early works encapsulate much of the 1960s, Swift's work is envisioned as symptomatic of some of the more vexing aspects about the twenty-first century and can provide a lens through which to consider issues of race, class, gender, and the rise of neoliberalism in America. Essays approach the topics of Swift's stardom, songwriting, and business from frameworks that seek to center the musical phenomenon that is "Taylor Swift." Essay topics include Taylor Swift and the work of songwriting; Taylor Swift, Beyoncé Knowles, and performance; Taylor Swift as celebrity, businesswoman, and advocate; embodiment and flourishing with Taylor Swift; specific technocultural discourse in response to Taylor Swift's LGBTQ and allyship in "You Need to Calm Down"; and Taylor Swift and rainbow capitalism.

816.   **Hawkins, Stan, ed**. 2018. "Special Issue: David Bowie." *Contemporary Music Review* 37(3): 189–271. ISSN: 0749-4467.

A commentary and special issue David Bowie that offers a range of methodologies that orients scholars towards an understanding of what makes contemporary popular music meaningful and builds on an existing scholarship by offering interpretations and opinions within a broad-based hermeneutic project surrounding the artist. Essay topics include David Bowie's critical sexualities; David Bowie's vocal personae; Bowie remembered at the Grammys and the Brit Awards; and a critical reading of "Love Is Lost."

817.   **Hawkins, Stan, ed**. 2012. "Special Issue: Michael Jackson: Musical Subjectivities." *Popular Music and Society* 35(2): 145–319. ISSN: 0300-7766.

A special issue that focuses on the popular music legacy of Michael Jackson. Compiled essays place Michael Jackson's music under a spotlight and help reveal the wealth of markers that inscribe the richness of the artistic expression. Contributors to this special issue celebrate Jackson for his virtuosity as an all-around performer as much as for the features that defined his acts. Essayists united and extended a compilation that engages in debates from one essay to the next in logical succession: exploration of issues of crossover and race; a focus on dance; discourses on race through postmodern subjectivity; theorization of Orientalism in Jackson's "Liberian Girl"; studies of vocality that take on debates on the voice and singing; and a debate on Jackson's sexuality alongside his musical virtuosity.

818.   **Jezinski, Marek, and Thomas Grochowski, eds**. 2021. "Special Issue: The Residents." *Rock Music Studies* 8(2): 97–185. ISSN: 1949-1159.

A special issue that focuses on the Residents, one of the most important bands in avant-garde/alternative music who, with their first albums in the 1970s, quickly established themselves as fierce critics of popular culture and visionaries of new technologies and multimedia esthetics. Essays commemorate and sum up approximately fifty years of the Residents and the band's place in the history of popular music. Topics include the Residents, visionaries, satirists, and mythmakers; avant-garde and activism in the songs of the Residents; the Residents and popular music; the Residents' *Eskimo* and the electronic (re)construction of ethnic music; the Residents meets the world; and on freaks, voyeurs, and the cultural uses of the freak show in the Residents' art and CD-ROM project.

819. **Kitts, Thomas M., ed**. 2006. "Special Issue: The Kinks." *Popular Music and Society* 29(2): 141–278. ISSN: 0300-7766.

Focuses on the Kinks, the English rock band often regarded as one of the most influential rock bands of the 1960s. Essay topics include identity, social class, and the nostalgic Englishness of Ray Davies and the Kinks; relations in the Kinks—familiar but not fully familiar; postwar British urban planning in *The Kinks Are the Village Green Preservation Society*; Ray Davies, romanticism, and the art of being English; Ray Davies and the rise and fall and rise of Japanese rock and roll; Ray Davies's spiritual journey from the 1960s to the present—content analysis; and the Kinks and the music industry.

820. **Laing, Dave, and Norman Josephs, eds**. 1987. "Special Issue: The Beatles." *Popular Music* 6(3): 257–408. ISSN: 0261-1430.

A special issue that marks the twenty-fifth anniversary of the Beatles' first recordings with producer George Martin and the first recording, which made the group the most well-known artists in popular music history. Offers a practical reason for the special issue, arguing that without the advent of the Beatles, a journal such as *Popular Music* would not have been possible. Compiled essays are not intended to summarize all aspects of the Beatles' career but to illustrate the value of the multidisciplinary status of popular music studies. Essay topics include notes on the Beatles' achievements; the search for Sweet Georgia Brown—a case of discographical detection; the impact of the Beatles on popular music in Australia, 1963–66; photographs, early Beatles, Beatles v. Jesus Christ; Beatles record burning; Paul and Linda McCartney with dancers; the Beatles and the religious far right; Paul, John, and Broad Street, troubles at the house; the future of Folkways; and the Charlie Parker archive.

821. **Lyndon, Michael, Werner Bies, Thomas Collins, *et al*.** 2019. "Special Issue: Chuck Berry." *Rock Music Studies* 6(1): 1–79. ISSN: 1949-1159.

A special issue that reflects rock and roll icon Chuck Berry and his legendary status and impact on popular music and popular music studies. Topics include Chuck Berry as a rock and roll trailblazer; the magic of Chuck Berry in German life and literature; Chuck Berry—not so much a poet as a storyteller; whether Chuck Berry had a co-writer; and how artifacts narrate the story of Chuck Berry at the National Museum of African American History and Culture.

822.   **Mazzarella, Sharon R., and Jan Muto, eds**. 1995. "Special Issue: Grunge, Youth, and Communities of Alienation." *Popular Music and Society* 19(2): 1–133. ISSN: 0300-7766.

Offers a focus on Kurt Cobain and a scholarly discourse on grunge. Essay topics include Kurt Cobain, Generation X, and the press; the politics of grunge; media coverage of the suicide of Kurt Cobain; identity, gender, and Kurt Cobain; an analysis of the music of Kurt Cobain; and narrative patterns in journalism and rock criticism.

823.   **Nehring, Neil, *et al*.** 2015. "The Rolling Stones." *Rock Music Studies* 2(3): 221–336. ISSN: 1940-1159.

Celebrates the fiftieth anniversary of the Rolling Stones with scholarly discourse on the impact and influence of the band on popular music and popular music studies. Topics include the Rolling Stones and the commodification of rock; Googling with the Stones—the greatest rock and roll corporation in the world; the mainstreaming of bootleg recordings; the reception of the Rolling Stones in communist Czechoslovakia; the Stones' "Gimme Shelter": Martin Scorsese's musical signature in context; and the Rolling Stones and the myth of decline.

824.   **Ray, Timothy D., and Julie DeLong, Anna Cohen Miller, eds**. 2022. "Special Issue: Teaching and Learning With the Grateful Dead." *Dialogue: The Interdisciplinary Journal of Popular Culture and Pedagogy* 9(1–2): [Electronic Resource online atjournaldialogue.org]. OCLC Number: 8-9205-006-3.

A compilation of essays that provide answers to two questions: why teach about the music of the Grateful Dead and how to teach about it? Compiled essays examine the ways that the Grateful Dead provide a rich and unique study toward a deeper understanding of American music. Essay topics include teaching and studying the music of the Grateful Dead; collaborative pedagogy—teaching with the Grateful Dead—on tour, on campus, and online; teaching the Grateful Dead phenomenon and cultural communication; teaching the Grateful Dead, happenings, and spontaneous pedagogy; teaching the Grateful Dead with Friedrich Nietzsche's *Birth of Tragedy*; the discourse communities of the Grateful Dead; teaching the Dead; remembrances; and reflections on teaching the Grateful Dead.

825.   **Smith, Marquita R**. 2019. "Special Issue: Beyoncé." *Popular Music and Society* 42(1): 1–117. ISSN: 0300-7766.

Scholarly discourse that concentrates on the musical and cultural impact of Beyoncé. Offers scholarly context for the issue and its contents that details Beyoncé's career shift from her early girl group beginning toward the global stardom and outlines the scope of the issue's included articles. Essay topics include Beyoncé as Black diva; remixing Beyoncé's "*** Flawless" in the YouTube Archive; Beyoncé, "Blue" and the politics of Black motherhood; viral techniques and the visual album; queer resonances in Beyoncé's *Lemonade*; and Beyoncé, Serena, and hegemonic hierarchies in *Lemonade*.

826. **Steinholdt, Yngvar B., and David-Emil Wickström, eds**. 2016. "Special Issue: Pussy Riot." *Popular Music and Society* 39(4): 393–464. ISSN: 0300-7766.

A special issue that focuses on different issues relating to the musical group known as Pussy Riot. Essay topics on Pussy Riot include a new stage of academic research; content analysis of the Russian media coverage; punk music production of similarity and difference; recalcitrant incorporeality; and precursors, the National Bolshevik Party Band, 1994–2007.

4

Annotated Bibliographies, Companions, Dictionaries, Encyclopedias, Handbooks, and Other Reference Works

827. **Abjorensen, Norman**. 2017. *Historical Dictionary of Popular Music*. Series: *Historical Dictionaries of Literature and the Arts*. Lanham: Lexington Books. xi, 653 p. Appendix and Bibliography. ISBN: 9-781-53810-214-5.

A reference source that seeks to trace the rise of popular music, identify key figures, and track the origins and development of its multiple genres and styles. Contains a chronology, an introduction, an appendix, and an extensive music bibliography, as well as cross-referenced entries on major figures across genres, definitions of genres, technical innovation, and surveys of countries and regions.

828. **Ashley, Richard, and Renee Timmers, eds**. 2019. *The Routledge Companion to Music Cognition*. Series: *Routledge Music Companions*. New York: Routledge. xxiii, 561 p. Bibliography and Index. ISBN: 9-780-36787-655-5.

A collection of essays that address fundamental questions about the nature of music from a psychological perspective. Information on music cognition is presented as the field that investigates the psychological and physical processes that allow music to take place, seeking to explain how and why music has such a powerful and mysterious effect on people.

829. **Baker, Sarah, Catherine Strong, Lauren Istvandity, and Zelmarie Cantillon, eds**. 2018. *The Routledge Companion to Popular Music History and Heritage*. Series: *Routledge Music Companions*. Abingdon, Oxon & New York: Routledge. xv, 415 p. Bibliography and Index. ISBN: 9-781-31529-931-0.

Examines the social, cultural, political, and economic value of popular music as history and heritage. Incorporates a cross-disciplinary approach and explores the relationship between popular music and the past and how interpretations of

DOI: 10.4324/9781003507345-4

the changing nature of the past in post-industrial societies play out in the field of popular music. Each chapter covers key themes around historiography, heritage, memory, and institutions alongside case studies from around the world, including the United Kingdom, Australia, South Africa, and India, exploring popular music's connection to culture both past and present.

830. **Bartinetto, Alessandro, and Marcello Ruta, eds**. 2021. *The Routledge Handbook of Philosophy and Improvisation in the Arts*. Series: *Routledge Handbooks in Philosophy*. New York: Routledge. xviii, 737 p. Illustrations, Bibliography, and Index. ISBN: 9-781-03201-649-8.

A collection of essays that focus on the philosophy of improvisation, synthesizing, and explaining various subjects and issues from the expansive wave of journal articles and monographs in the field. Essays are divided into four parts: Part I: Art and Improvisation: Theoretical Perspectives; Part II: Art and Improvisation: Aesthetical, Ethical, and Political Perspectives; Part III: Improvisation in Musical Practices; and Part IV: Improvisation in the Visual, Narrative, Dramatic, and Interactive Arts.

831. **Baxter-Moore, Nicolas, and Thomas M. Kitts, eds**. 2019. *The Routledge Companion to Popular Music and Humor*. Series: *Routledge Music Companions*. Abingdon, Oxon, & New York: Routledge. xii, 421 p. Illustrations, Bibliography, and Index. ISBN: 9-780-36772-990-5.

A compilation of essays that draws together scholarship exploring how the element of humor interacts with the artistic and social aspects of the musical experience. Discusses humor in popular music across eras from Tin Pan Alley to the present and examines the role of music in different musical genres, provides case studies of artists, and describes its media forms. Compiled essays are varied and structured into eight parts and sections that explore topics such as parody and satire; humor in rock and global music; gender, sexuality, and politics; the music of mockumentary; and novelty songs. Topics covered on specific geographical areas include English psychedelia; kaiso in Trinidad calypso and soca music; kwaito music of South Africa; Ugandan pop music; K-pop; French rural spaces; British invasion, Rolling Stones, and others; British bands; and much more.

832. **Beech, Mark R**. 2009. *A Dictionary of Rock and Pop Names: The Rock and Pop Names Encyclopedia From Aaliyah to ZZ Top*. Barnsley, South Yorkshire: Penn & Sword. 319 p. Illustrations, Portraits, Facsimiles, and Index. ISBN: 9-781-84415-807-2.

An A–Z encyclopedia that covers entries and the names in rock generated from radio interviews, articles, and features in nationals and serializations. Covers music genres other than just rock and pop, including punk, indie, reggae, soul, country, blues, folk, jazz, heavy metal, grunge, and rap artists and bands.

833. **Bennett, Andy, ed**. 2022. *The Bloomsbury Handbook of Popular Music and Youth Culture*. New York: Bloomsbury. 704 p. Bibliography and Index. ISBN: 9-781-50133-370-5.

A compilation of essays that provide a comprehensive overview of key themes and debates relating to the academic study of popular music and youth culture. Essays cover a range of topics that include theory, method, historical perspectives, genres, audiences, media, globalization, aging, and generation.

834.   **Bennett, Andy, and Steve Waksman**. 2015. *The SAGE Handbook of Popular Music*. Los Angeles & London: SAGE Publications. 664 p. Illustrations, Bibliography, and Index. ISBN: 9-781-44621-085-7.

A comprehensive reference in popular music. Chapters and texts are divided into several sections that include Theory and Method; The Business of Popular Music; Popular Music Studies; The Global and the Local; The Star System; Body and Identity; Media; Technology; and Digital Economics. Each section has been chosen to reflect both established aspects of popular music studies as well as more broadly emerging subfields.

835.   **Billig, Michael**. 2001. *Rock 'n' Roll and Jews*. Previously published, Nottingham: Five Leaves, 2000. Series: *Judaic Tradition in Literature, Music, and Art*. Syracuse: Syracuse University Press. 170 p. Bibliography. ISBN: 0-90712-353-8.

Examines the roles and contributions of the most celebrated popular musicians of Jewish heritage. Discusses the contributions of Lieber and Stoller, Paul Simon, Bob Dylan, Carole King, and Lou Reed.

836.   **Bithell, Caroline, and Juniper Hill, eds**. 2014. *The Oxford Handbook of Music Revival*. Series: *Oxford Handbooks*. New York: Oxford University Press. x, 701 p. Discography, Bibliography, and Index. ISBN: 9-780-19976-503-4.

An edited volume that focuses on why music from the past is significant today and how it has been transformed to suit new values and agendas. Compiled essays examine globally recurrent and cultural processes of revival, resurgence, restoration, and renewal. Some of the topics covered include popular music and dance, string bands, jazz, bossa nova, and others.

837.   **Bogdanov, Vladimir, ed**. 2001. *All Music Guide to Electronics: The Definitive Guide to Electronic Music*. San Francisco: Backbeat Book xiv, 688 p. Illustration, Discography, and Index. ISBN: 0-87930-628-9.

Explains the sounds and styles of electronic and experimental dance music and provides ratings of works by the large number of artists contained within the umbrella of "electronic music." Highlights how electronic encompasses an immense range of musical styles and artists from disco and centric house to producers such as Armand Van Helden to experimental electronic crews like Finland's Pan Sonic. Covers areas such as house, techno, trance, jungle/drum 'n' bass, trip-hop, and much more.

838.   **Bogdanov, Vladimir, Chris Woodstra, and Thomas Erlewine, eds**. 2001. *All Music Guide: The Definitive Guide to Popular Music, 4th ed*. Series: *AMG All Music Guides*. San Francisco: Backbeat Books. viii, 1491 p. Index. ISBN: 0-87930-627-0.

Arranged in several different musical categories that provide entries of releases from numerous artists. Also includes a history of each musical genre. Musical genres covered include rock, rap, blues, country, world music, reggae, easy listening, avant-garde, and jazz.

839. **Bourdon, Andrew, and Simon Zagorski-Thomas, eds**. 2020. *The Bloomsbury Handbook of Music Production*. Series: *Bloomsbury Handbooks*. New York: Bloomsbury. xvii, 413 p. Bibliography and Index. ISBN: 9-781-50133-402-3.

Provides essays on current research on the production of stereo and mono recorded music. Divided into several sections: background record music; technologies from tubes to transistors: developments in recording technology up to 1970; place/recording studios in the first half of the twentieth century; organizing the production process; creating recorded music/songwriting in the studio; creating desktop music; post-production/audio processing; distribution/producer consumption in the digital age, and so forth.

840. **Brennan, Matt, Joseph M. Pignato, and Daniel A. Stadnicki, eds**. 2021. *The Cambridge Companion to the Drumkit*. Series: *Cambridge Companions to Music*. Cambridge & New York: Cambridge University Press. xviii, 264 p. Bibliography and Index. ISBN: 9-781-10877-951-7.

Highlights the scholarship on the drumkit, drummers, and key debates related to the instrument and its players. Interdisciplinary in scope, the volume provides research from across the humanities and social sciences. Topics covered include histories of the drumkit; historically informed jazz performance on the drumkit; Colombia's Música Tropical Sabanera; drumkit in Brazil; complex meters and irregular grooves; electronic drumkit technology; jazz drumming across generations; performing gender and popular feminism, and others.

841. **Bridge, Simone K., ed**. 2021. *The Oxford Handbook of Global Popular Music*. Series: *Oxford Handbooks Online*. New York: Oxford University Press. ISBN: 9-780-19008-138-6 and 9-780-19008-137-9.

Currently in development with individual essays published online in advance of print publication. Contents for this reference source will continue to grow as additional essays are peer-reviewed and published. The editor indicates that the online publication for this handbook is the date that the first essay was published online.

842. **Buckley, Peter**. 2003. *The Rough Guide to Rock, 3rd ed*. London & New York: Rough Guides. 1225 p. Illustrations, Portraits, Discography, and Index. ISBN: 9-781-84353-105-0.

Features album reviews covering all areas of rock music. Also touches on dance, hip-hop, blues, country, and soul. Also contains entries of biographies, original images, a selection of classic album covers, and so forth.

843. **Bull, Michael, and Marcel Cobussen, eds**. 2021. *The Bloomsbury Handbook of Sonic Methodologies*. Series: *Bloomsbury Handbooks*. New York: Bloomsbury. xx, 828 p. Bibliography and Index. ISBN: 9-781-50133-878-6.

Provides essays on current research of sonic methodologies. Topics covered that relate to research in sonic methodologies include time, space, and cognition; anthropology; deconstruction; environmental biology; psychoacoustics; noise management; Salomé Voegelin; arts, music, and spaces; auditory spaces; interdisciplinary research; autoethnography; centrifugal sound, sound recordings; film and sonic art; urban studies; materialism; philosophy; science technology studies; urban planning; and so forth.

844. **Burns, Lori, and Stan Hawkins, eds**. 2019. *The Bloomsbury Handbook of Popular Music Video Analysis*. Series: *Bloomsbury Handbooks*. New York: Bloomsbury. xvi, 445 p. Bibliography and Index. ISBN: 9-781-50134-233-2.

Covers a wide range of current research on music video and audiovisual elements in popular music. Topics covered are varied and include music video analysis; changing dynamics and diversity in music video production and distribution; the work of Steve Hanft and Danny Perez; research creation perspectives on music video; animated videos of Radiohead, Chris Hopewell, and Gastón Vinãs; framing personae in music videos; the politics of representation in early British punk music videos; the variety show in the mid-1960s; indie rock; nostalgia, digitization, and technological materiality; Katy Perry and lyric video as genre; multimodality and transmedia practice in popular music; palimpsestic pop music video; Laurie Anderson's transformative repetition; analysis of music videos—Beyoncé and Melinda Matsouka's "Pretty Hurts"; rural-urban imagery in country music videos; Justin Timberlake's "Man of the Woods"; God in hip-hop narratives; Nicki Minaj's "Anaconda" intersectional feminist studies; and representations of violence against men in Pink's "Please Don't Leave Me."

845. **Burns, Robert G. H**. 2018. *Experiencing Progressive Rock: A Listener's Companion*. Series: *Listener's Companions*. Lanham: Rowman & Littlefield. xxxiv, 182 p. Bibliography and Index. ISBN: 9-781-44226-602-5.

A reference source that integrates the many strands that define the progressive rock movement of the late 1960s and early 1970s to chart the evolution of this rock tradition over the decades. Discusses the contribution of acts such as Yes, Pink Floyd, King Crimson, the Who, Jethro Tull, Genesis, Moody Blues, and many others. Draws on personal experiences and interviews with members of progressive rock acts and much more.

846. **Butt, John, Nicholas Cook, Anthony Poole, and Tim Carter, eds**. 2008. *The Cambridge History of Twentieth-Century Music*. Series: *Cambridge History of Music*. Cambridge: Cambridge University Press. xviii, 676 p. Bibliography and Index. ISBN: 9-780-51146-913-8.

Surveys the Western twentieth-century art tradition alongside the developments in jazz, popular music, and world music. Traces the progressive fragmentation of European art tradition and its relocation as tradition among many at the turn of the century's end. While the focus is on Western music traditions in both art and popular music, these are studied within the context of world music, including a case history of the interaction of art and traditional music in post-colonial Africa. Aims throughout to set musical developments in the context of social, ideological, and technological change to understand reception and consumption as integral to the history of music.

847. **Bynoe, Yvonne**. 2006. *Encyclopedia of Rap and Hip-Hop*. Westport: Greenwood Press. xxviii, 449 p. Illustrations, Bibliography, an Index. ISBN: 0-31333-058-1.

Contains entries that examine the four elements of hip-hop culture: MCing or rapping; B-boying or breakdancing; deejaying (music), and graffiti art (visual art). Traces the early roots from Black dances in the 1970s and the scratching and sampling to the founding of Def Jam production. Also examines the current East Coast–West Coast rivalry and superstars such as Eminem and 50 Cent. Includes selections of photographs, discographies after each entry, a further reading listing section, and much more.

848. **Campbell, Christopher, ed**. 2017. *The Routledge Companion to Media and Race*. Series: *Routledge Companions*. New York: Routledge. xi, 326 p. Bibliography and Index. ISBN: 9-781-31769-583-7.

A comprehensive guide for scholars, students, and media professionals who seek to understand the key debates about the impact of media messages on racial attitudes. Essays are compiled into three sections that include summaries of theoretical approaches that scholars have adopted to analyze the complexities or race and ethnicity; reviews of studies related to a variety of media including film, television, print media, social media, music, and video games; and issues relating to specific races and ethnicities and so forth. On the topic of popular music is an essay titled "Popular Music: Translating Races and Genre From Ethnic to Epic" (by Paul Linden).

849. **Cenciarelli, Carlo, ed**. 2021. *The Oxford Handbook of Cinematic Listening*. Series: *Oxford Handbooks*. New York: Oxford University Press. xii, 774 p. Bibliography and Index. ISBN: 9-780-19085-362-4.

Explores the genealogies of cinema's audiovisual practices, the listening relationship between film aesthetics and listening, protocols, and the extension of cinematic modes of listening into other media and everyday situations. Offers a series of case studies and perspectives that show how listening is constantly being redefined in relation to shifting, historical, spatial, textual, and theoretical frameworks.

850. **Clauhs, Matthew, Bryan Powell, and Ann C. Clements, eds**. 2021. *Popular Music Pedagogies: A Practical Guide for Music Teachers*. New York: Routledge. xviii, 197 p. Illustrations, Bibliography, and Index. ISBN: 9-780-42929-444-0.

Provides a solid foundation of playing and teaching a variety of instruments and technologies. Examines how these elements work together in a comprehensive school music program. Chapters are designed to stand independently, and instructors can adapt this guide to a wide range of learning by combining the pedagogies and methodologies presented.

851.   **Cleland, Kent, and Paul Kleet, eds**. 2021. *The Routledge Companion to Aural Skills Pedagogy: Before, In, and After Higher Education*. Series: *Routledge Music Companions*. New York: Routledge. xxi, 494 p. Illustrations, Bibliography, and Index. ISBN: 9-780-36771-589-2.

Offers a comprehensive survey of issues, practices, and current developments in the teaching of aural skills. Regards aural training as a lifelong skill that is engaged with before, during, and after university or conservatoire studies in music, central to the holistic training of the contemporary musician. Addresses key new developments such as the use of technology for aural training and the use of popular music.

852.   **Coelho, Victor, and John Covach, eds**. 2019. *The Cambridge Companion to the Rolling Stones*. Series: *Cambridge Companions to Music*. Cambridge & New York: Cambridge University Press. xxii, 223 p. Illustration, Bibliography, and Index. ISBN: 9-781-10703-026-8.

Provides an overview of the music, career, influences, history, and cultural impact of the Rolling Stones. Compiles a series of essays by musicologists, ethnomusicologists, players, film scholars, and filmmakers that stimulate thinking about the Rolling Stones as they vault well over the mid-century point of their career. Compiled essays are album and song oriented and provide discussions of the landmark recordings of the group and their influences, new insights about sound, culture, media representation, the influence of world music, fan communities, group personnel, and the importance of their revival after 1989.

853.   **Coelho, Victor, ed**. 2011. *The Cambridge Companion to the Guitar*. Series: *Cambridge Collections Online; Cambridge Companions to Music; Cambridge Companions Complete Collection*. Cambridge: Cambridge University Press. xiii, 264 p. Illustrations, Facsimiles, Maps, Music Examples, Portraits, Bibliography, and Index. ISBN: 9-781-13900-202-8.

Covers research on the guitar in terms of different traditions, styles, and instruments. Topics include flamenco guitar: history, style, status; the Celtic guitar: cultural boundaries in the twentieth century; African reinvention of the guitar; the guitar in jazz; a century of blues guitar; rock guitar from the 1950s to the 1970s; rock guitar since 1976; and the guitar in country music. Also include topics on baroque and classical guitar.

854.   **Cogan, Brian, ed**. 2010. *The Encyclopedia of Punk*. Originally published, *The Encyclopedia of Punk and Culture*, Westport: Greenwood Press, 2006. New York: Sterling Lewes: GMC Distribution. 390 p. Illustrations, Discography, Bibliography, and Index. ISBN: 9-781-40277-937-3.

An A–Z encyclopedia that provides information on the history and culture of punk music. Entries profile many punk musicians, such as the Clash, the Sex

Pistols, the Ramones, Patti Smith, David Bowie, Johnny Rotten, Sid Vicious, straight edge, and Vivienne Westwood, as well as topics as CBGB's, the DIY movement, gender and punk, hardcore, anarchy, drugs, flyers, and punk movements in geographic areas of London and New York.

855. **Cohen, Selma J., ed**. 1998. *International Encyclopedia of Dance: A Project of Dance Perspectives Foundation, Inc.* Six Volumes. Illustrations, Bibliography, and Index. ISBN: 9-780-19517-588-2.

A reference source that can provide research on popular music and dance. Volumes cover the full spectrum of dance—theatrical, ritual, drama, folk, traditional, ethnic, and social. Incorporates cultural and national overviews that are accompanied by entries on dance forms, music, costumes, performances, and biographies of dancers and choreographers.

856. **Collins, Nick, and Julio D'Escrivan, eds**. 2017. *The Cambridge Companion to Electronic Music*. Series: *Cambridge Companions to Music*. Cambridge: Cambridge University Press. xxi, 287 p. Illustrations, Music Examples, Bibliography, and Index. ISBN: 9-780-52186-861-7.

Covers historical movements in electronic music such as musique concrète and elektronische musik, and contemporary trends such as electronic dance music and electronica as well as composers and inventors who have contributed to a diverse set of technologies, practices, and music. Incorporates viewpoints of researchers at the forefront of the sonic explorations empowered by electronic technology and information on recent activity such as audiovisuals, live electronic music, interactivity, and network music.

857. **Cook, Nicholas, Monique M. Ingalls, and David Trippett, eds**. 2019. *The Cambridge Companion to Music in Digital Culture*. Series: *Cambridge Companions to Music*. Cambridge & New York: Cambridge University Press. xiv, 332 p. Illustrations, Bibliography, and Index. ISBN: 9-781-10716-178-8.

Focuses on how the impact of digital technologies on music has been overwhelming since the commercialization of these technologies in the early 1980s, both the practice of music and thinking about it have changed almost beyond recognition. Integrates research that brings the relationship between technology and musical culture by considering both theory and practice. Provides a comprehensive introduction to the place of music within digital culture. Themes and topics include music and the Internet; social networking and participatory culture; music recommendation systems; posthumanism; surveillance; copyright; and new business models for music production.

858. **Cook, Nicholas, ed**. 2011. *The Cambridge Companion to Recorded Music*. Series: *Cambridge Collections Online; Cambridge Companions to Music; Cambridge Companions Complete Collection*. Cambridge: Cambridge University Press. xvii, 359 p. Illustrations, Bibliography, and Index. ISBN: 9-781-13900-268-4.

Provides an overview of the transformation encompassing both classical and popular music. Topics addressed include the history of recording technology and the business built on it, the impact of recording on performance style, studio practices viewed from the perspective of performers, producers and engineers, approaches to the study of recordings, and so forth.

859.   **Cooke, Mervyn, and Fiona Ford, eds**. 2016. *The Cambridge Companion to Film Music*. Series: *Cambridge Companions to Music*. Cambridge: Cambridge University Press. xxi, 411 p. Illustrations, Music Examples, Bibliography, and Index. ISBN: 9-781-10709-451-2.

A compilation of essays that provide a comprehensive overview of the many and various ways in which music functions in film soundtracks. Examples are provided from a variety of historical periods, genres, and film industries including those in the United States, France, Italy, India, and Japan. Incorporates research and interpretative perspectives from genres such as animation, the screen musical, film noir, Hollywood melodrama, popular music and jazz films, documentary, period drama, horror, science fiction, and Westerns.

860.   **Cooke, Mervyn, and David Horn, eds**. 2011. *The Cambridge Companion to Jazz*. Series: *Cambridge Companions to Music*. Cambridge & New York: Cambridge University Press. xxii, 403 p. Illustrations, Bibliography, and Index. ISBN: 9-781-13900-223-3.

Compiles a volume of research that provides information on the world of jazz from many perspectives from social and cultural history, musical analysis, economics, and ethnography. Compiled essays consider what kind of identity jazz has acquired, current practices that define jazz, specific moments of historical change, important issues for jazz study, and so forth.

861.   **Cooper, B. Lee**. 2010. "Rock Journalists and Music Critics: A Selected Bibliography." *Popular Music and Society* 33(1): 75–141. ISSN: 0261-1430.

A bibliographic study that lists numerous articles and books that address rock journalism and popular music criticism. Covers general studies on rock journalism, key music, commentators, venues for journalistic reports (newspapers, magazines, fanzines, and academic journals), and subjects of critical commentaries (recordings, concerts, books, interviews, biographies, and historical perspectives). Illustrates the breadth of critical commentary available on contemporary music and recording artists.

862.   **Cooper, B. Lee, and Rebecca A. Condon, eds**. 2004. *The Teaching of Popular Music Handbook: An Educator's Guide to Music-Related Print Resources*. Westport: Greenwood. xi, 371 p. Bibliography and Indexes. ISBN: 1-59158-039-0.

Provides lists and reports dealing with popular music resources as classroom teaching materials. **Chapters include** Interdisciplinary applications of popular music for classroom teaching activities and student research projects; Biographical Studies, Oral History, and Popular Music Personality Profiles for Classroom

Investigation; Popular Music Styles and Dance trends as topics for classroom discussion and student research projects; and Popular Music Reference Resources for Teachers, Librarians, Media Specialists, and Students. Also includes artists, authors, and topical indexes.

863. **Correa, Delia de Sousa**. 2020. *The Edinburgh Companion to Literature and Music*. Series: *Edinburgh Companions to Literature and the Humanities*. Edinburgh: Edinburgh University Press. xvi, 726 p. Illustrations, Music Examples, Bibliography, and Index. ISBN: 9-780-74869-312-2.

Provides an interdisciplinary focus of literature and music of nine centuries. Compiled essays represent a multiplicity of approaches: theoretical, contextual, and close reading. Incorporates case studies that reach beyond literature and music to engage with related fields including philosophy, history of science, theater, broadcast media, and popular culture.

864. **Deaville, James, Siu-Lan Lam, and Ron Rodman, eds**. 2021. *The Oxford Handbook of Music and Advertising*. Series: *Oxford Handbooks*. New York: Oxford University Press. xxviii, 925 p. Illustrations, Tables, Bibliography, and Index. ISBN: 9-780-19069-124-0.

A compilation of essays that focus on the production, texts, and reception of advertising through music. Compiled essays draw from traditional music theory and implementation of research methods to examine how the presence of music may influence people's attitudes, emotions, thoughts, and behaviors in the context of advertisements within service environments such as stores, restaurants, and banks.

865. **Dingle, Christopher P., ed**. 2019. *The Cambridge History of Music Criticism*. Series: *Cambridge History of Music*. Cambridge: Cambridge University Press. xv, 826 p. Bibliography and Index. ISBN: 9-781-10703-789-2.

Reaches back to the medieval period and expands the geographical reach both within and beyond Europe, including key issues such as women, criticism of recordings, and the study of criticism in jazz, popular music, and world music. Draws on a mixture of scholarship that presents a substantial historical survey of music.

866. **Doffman, Mark, Emily Payne, and Toby Young, eds**. 2021. *The Oxford Handbook of Time in Music*. Series: *Oxford Handbooks*. New York: Oxford University Press. 468 p. Bibliography and Index. ISBN: 9-780-19094-730-9.

A compilation of essays that focus on the centrality of time to our understanding of music and music making. Essays offer perspectives on time in music, particularly though not exclusively to contemporary forms of musical work. Essays draw from philosophy, ethnomusicology, psychology of performance, and cultural studies and articulate a range of understandings on the metrics, politics, and socialities woven into musical time.

867. **Emmerson, Simon, ed**. 2018. *The Routledge Research Companion to Electronic Music: Reaching Out With Technology*. Series: *Routledge Music Companions*.

Abingdon, Oxon: Routledge. 374 p. Bibliography and Index. ISBN: 9-780-36713-457-2.

A series of essays with the themes of connectivity and the global reach of electro-acoustic music and sonic arts made with technology. Essays focus on the trends of the field in the last thirty years, highlighting how the definition of the field has broadened, blurring the clear boundaries between electronic music and "sound art." The distinction between "art" and "popular" practices has become less straightforward or has been facilitated, contributing to a rich and diverse stream of practices with numerous histories, including traditions from world music.

868. **Epstein, Jonathan S., Simon Firth, Howard Horne, *et al*.** 2016. *Popular Music.* Series: *Routledge Library Editions.* London: Routledge. 4888 p. Index. ISBN: 9-781-13819-432-8.

Compiles a set of reissues of previously out-of-print books that focus on the phenomenon of popular music. Includes *Adolescents and Their Music: If It's Too Loud You're Too Old* (Jonathan S. Epstein, ed.); *Art Into Pop* (Simon Firth and Howard Horne); *Cross-Overs: Art Into Pop/Pop Into Art* (John A. Walker); *Jazz and Blues* (Graham Vulliamy); *Lost in Music: Culture, Style and the Musical Event* (Aaron Levine White, ed.); *Popular Music: A Reference Guide* (Roman Iwaschkin); *Popular Music: A Teacher's Guide* (Graham Vulliamy and Edward Lee, eds.); *Rock 'n' Roll* (Dave Rogers); *Rock Around This Clock: Music Television, Post Modernism, and Consumer Culture* (E. Anne Kaplan); and *Tin Pan Alley* (John Shepherd).

869. **Europa Publications, eds.** 2024. *International Who's Who in Popular Music, 26th ed.* Series: *Europa Biographical Reference Series.* London: Routledge. 822 p. Appendices. ISBN: 9-781-03274-224-3.

Provides biographical information and contact details from some of the most talented and influential artists and individuals from the world of popular music. Compiles over seven thousand biographies, charting careers and achievements of artists in pop, rock, folk, jazz, dance world, country music, and much more. Entries include biographical information, principal career details, recordings and compositions, honors, and contact information where available.

870. **Europa Publications, eds.** 2024. *International Who's Who in Classical Music, 40th ed.* Series: *Europa Biographical Reference Series.* New York: Routledge. 1100 p. Appendices. ISBN: 9-781-03274-224-3.

Provides biographical and contact information for thousands of singers, instru-mentalists, composers, conductors, managers, and others. Each entry con-tains personal information, principal career details, repertoire, recordings and compositions, and full details when available. Appendices provide for national orchestras, opera companies, music festivals, music organizations, and major competition and awards.

871.   **Everett, William, and Paul R. Laird, eds**. 2017. *The Cambridge Companion to the Musical, 3rd ed.* Series: *Cambridge Companions to Music*. Cambridge: Cambridge University Press. xvii, 310 p. Illustrations, Bibliography, and Index. ISBN: 9-781-10753-529-9.

A companion that provides an accessible and broadly based survey of one of the most popular forms of musical performance. Contexts range from the American musical of the nineteenth century to the most recent productions on Broadway, in London's West End, and in many other venues. Includes key information on singers, audiences, critical reception, and traditions. Contributors approach the subject from a wide variety of perspectives including historical concerns, artistic aspects, important trends, various genres, the importance of stars, the influence of race, changes in technology, and others. Also includes chapters on the television musical and the British musical since the 1970s.

872.   **Firth, Simon, Will Straw, and John Street, eds**. 2011. *The Cambridge Companion to Pop and Rock*. Series: *Cambridge Collections Online; Cambridge Companions to Music; Cambridge Companions Complete Collection*. Cambridge: Cambridge University Press. xvii, 303 p. Portraits, Bibliography, and Index. ISBN: 9-781-13900-224-0.

An edited volume of essays that map the world of pop and rock. Pinpoints the most significant moments in its history and presents the key issues involved in understanding popular culture's most vital art form. Topics covered include technology and popular music; the pop music industry; consumption; popular music; reconsidering rock; dance music; world music; interpretation of pop and rock; popular music, gender, and sexuality; race in pop and rock; and local and global perspectives in popular music.

873.   **Firth, Simon, ed**. 2004. *Popular Music: Critical Concepts in Media and Cultural Studies*. Series: *Critical Concepts in Media and Cultural Studies*. London: SAGE Publications. Four Volumes. Illustrations, Music Examples, Bibliography, and Index. ISBN: 9-780-41529-905-3.

A multi-volume set of essays that focus on popular music studies as a rapidly expanding field with changing emphasis and agenda. Compiled essays are divided into four volumes as follows: Volume I—Music and Society; Volume II—The Rock Era; Volume III—Popular Music Analysis; and Volume IV—Music and Identity.

874.   **Fritsch, Melanie, and Tim Summers, eds**. 2021. *The Cambridge Companion to Video Game Music*. Series: *Cambridge Companions to Music*. Cambridge & New York: Cambridge University Press. xxxvi, 446 p. Illustrations, Bibliography, and Index. ISBN: 9-781-10867-028-9.

Focuses on how video game music has been permeating popular culture for over forty years. Provides a comprehensive up-to-date survey of game music.

Features research and essays by diverse scholars and industry professionals. Topics include globalization, localization, and video game music; pop music, economics, and marketing; producing game music concerts; game music and identity; semiotics in game music; and others.

875.   **Gammond, Peter, ed**. 1991. *The Oxford Companion to Popular Music*. Oxford & New York: Oxford University Press. vii, 739 p. Bibliography and Index. ISBN: 0-19311-323-6.

An encyclopedic reference source that covers popular music areas in jazz, reggae, blues, calypso, Broadway musicals, rock music, and country western. Provides biographical profiles of a range of diverse artists who have influenced global perspectives in popular music, such as John Philip Sousa, Ma Rainey, Fred Astaire, Joan Baez, Bob Dylan, Otis Redding, Prince, Cole Porter, Duke Ellington, Miles Davis, and many others.

876.   **Garcia-Mispireta, Luis Manuel, and Robin James, eds**. 2021. *The Oxford Handbook of Electronic Dance Music*. Series: *Oxford Handbooks*. New York: Oxford University Press. ISBN: 9-780-19009-372-3 and 9-780-19009-373-0.

Currently in development with individual essays published online in advance of print publication. Contents for this reference source will continue to grow as additional essays are peer-reviewed and published. The editor indicates that the online publication for this handbook is that date that the first essay was published online.

877.   **Gebhardt, Nicholas, Nicole Rustin-Paschal, and Tony Whyton, eds**. 2019. *The Routledge Companion to Jazz Studies*. Series: *Routledge Music Companions*. New York: Routledge. xxxi, 481 p. Illustrations, Bibliography, and Index. ISBN: 9-781-13823-116-0.

A collection of essays from international scholars that highlight the strengths of current jazz scholarship in cross-disciplinary and global perspectives. Compiled essays reflect the developments within jazz studies over the last twenty-five years. The essays also offer surveys and provide new insights into the major perspectives and approaches to jazz research in terms of historical perspectives, methodologies, core issues, communities, politics, and others.

878.   **Goldsmith, Melissa G. D., and Anthony J. Fonesca, eds**. 2019. *Hip-Hop Around the World: An Encyclopedia*. Santa Barbara: Greenwood. Two Volumes [Volume 1: A-L & Volume 2: M-Z]. xliii, 984 p. Illustrations. ISBN: 9-780-031335-758-9.

Includes entries on global hip-hop culture as it focuses on music, art, fashion, dance, social and cultural movements, organizations, and styles of hip-hop. Includes hip-hop information on virtually every country with a focus on music styles and notable musicians. Provides discussions of the sound of various hip-hop styles and musical artists, lyrical content, vocal delivery, vocal ranges, and much more. Additional entries deal with dance styles such as breakdancing or B-boying/B-girling, popping/locking, clowning, krumping, and cultural movements such as Black Nationalism, Nation of Islam, Five Percent Nation, Universal Zulu Nation, and others.

879. **Gopinath, Sumanth, and Jason Stanyek, eds**. 2014. *The Oxford Handbook of Mobile Music Studies*. Series: *Oxford Handbooks*. New York: Oxford University Press. Two Volumes. Illustrations, Bibliography, and Index. ISBN: 9-780-19537-572-5.

A compilation of essays that examines how electrical technologies and their corresponding economies of scale have rendered music and sound increasingly mobile—portable, fungible, and ubiquitous. Compiled essays are interdisciplinary in scope and consider devices, markets, theories of mobile music, and its aesthetics and forms of performance.

880. **Gouk, Penelope, James Kennaway, Jacomien Prins, and Wiebke Thormahlen, eds**. 2019. *The Routledge Companion to Music, Mind, and Well-Being*. Series: *Routledge Music Companions*. New York: Routledge. xvii, 329 p. Bibliography and Index. ISBN: 9-780-36765-967-7.

Seeks to foster interdisciplinary approaches to key questions about the nature of musical experience and to determine the importance of the conceptual ideological framework underlying research in the field. Essays are divided into two sections: the Part II: Historical section considers the ways in which music, the emotions, wellbeing, and their interactions have been understood in the past from antiquity to the twentieth century; and the Part II: Contemporary section offers a variety of scientific perspectives on these topics and engages wider philosophical problems.

881. **Grant, Jane, John Matthias, and Dave Prior, eds**. 2021. *The Oxford Handbook of Sound Art*. Series: *Oxford Handbooks*. New York: Oxford University Press. xxv, 597 p. Illustrations, Music Examples, Bibliography, and Index. ISBN: 9-780-19027-405-4.

Defines sound art as spaces between music, fine art, and performances. Surveys the practices, politics, and emerging frameworks that now defines the study of sound art. Comprised of essays authored by artists and scholars that explore the use of sound in contemporary arts practices, imbued with global perspectives in music, fine arts, and performance. Essays are presented in several themes: Space, Time, Things, Fabrics, Senses, and Relationality.

882. **Gray, John**. 2019. *Creative Improvised Music: AnInternational Bibliography of the Jazz Avant-Garde, 1959–Present*. Series: *Black Music Reference Series*. Nyack: African Diaspora Press. xv, 639. Bibliography and Indexes. ISBN: 9-780-98441-348-5.

An annotated bibliography that offers a sequel to the author's early publication of *Fire Music: A Bibliography of the New Jazz, 1959–1990* (1991, Greenwood Press) that chronicles approximately three decades of American free jazz and European improvisation that document writings on expressive culture in Africa and the

African diaspora. Covers topics underrepresented in the earlier publication, such as free jazz's intersection with civil rights and the Black arts movement of the 1960s, the rise of Asian improv arts, the contributions of women with waves of feminism in jazz music, and the impact of politics and spirituality on free jazz. Annotated entries include materials from books, book chapters, dissertations, theses, electronic resources, journals, discographies, and biographical dictionaries and encyclopedias.

883.   **Gray, John**. 2016. *Hip-Hop Studies: An International Bibliography and Research Guide*. Series: *Black Music Reference Series*. Nyack: African Diaspora Press. xviii, 1116 p. Indexes. ISBN: 9-780-98441-346-1.

Provides a comprehensive overview of the burgeoning field of hip-hop studies and its vast amount of literature. Incorporates more than seven thousand annotated entries from both early journalistic and popular writing on hip-hop as well as a wealth of scholarship that has emerged since the mid-1990s. Offers a focus on three of hip-hop's most important facets: MCing, DJing, and dance, along with variety of related dance music styles such as house, techno, and reggaeton.

884.   **Gray, John**. 1991. *Fire Music: A Bibliography of the New Jazz, 1959–1990*. Series: *Music Reference Collection*. New York: Greenwood Press. 536 p. Appendices and Indexes. ISBN: 9-780-31327-892-1.

An annotated bibliography that is concerned with the music of jazz avant-gardists such a John Coltrane, Ornette Coleman, Cecil Taylor, and Sun Ra. Makes accessible extensive scholarship in the new jazz beginning in the 1950s. Incorporates approximately seventy-one hundred entries with materials from books, journals, videos, dissertations, and other sources on topics such as jazz collectives and the New York loft scene, as well as jazz in specific countries and regions and an extensive section of biographical ad critical studies on more than four hundred artists and ensembles from around the world.

885.   **Grayck, Theodore, and Andrew Kania, eds**. 2011. *The Routledge Companion to Philosophy and Music*. Series: *Routledge Philosophy Companions*. New York: Routledge. xxiv, 654 p. Illustrations, Music Examples, Bibliography, and Index. ISBN: 9-780-20383-037-6.

A resource to key subjects, topics, thinkers, and debates in philosophy and music. Divided into five parts that include Part I: General Issues—includes essays on topics such as silence, sound, noise, music, music and imagination, music and language, and others; Part II: Emotion—includes essays on topics such as expression theories, and others; Part III: History—incudes essays on topics such as continental philosophy and music, analytical philosophy and music, and others; Part IV: Figures—includes essays on philosophy; Part V: Kinds of Music—includes essays on topics such as popular music, rock, jazz, and others; and Part VI: Music, Philosophy, and Related Disciplines—includes essays on topics such as musicology, ethnomusicology, music and politics, music and gender, and others.

886. **Groth, Sanne, and Holger Schulze, eds**. 2020. *The Bloomsbury Handbook of Sound Art*. Series: *Bloomsbury Handbooks*. London: Bloomsbury. 474 p. Bibliography and Index. ISBN: 9-781-50133-879-3.

An edited volume that explores and delineates what sound art is in the twenty-first century and sound artwork that embodies contemporary and traditional trends. Compiled essays are integrated into areas of musicology, art history, and sound studies and demonstrate how sound art has evolved since the 1980s into a field of academic critique and aesthetic analysis.

887. **Gulla, Bob**. 2009. *Guitar Gods: The 25 Players Who Made Rock History*. Westport: Greenwood & Santa Barbara: ABC-CLIO. ix, 280 p. Illustrations, Bibliography, and Index. ISBN: 9-780-31335-806-7.

Provides profiles on the most prominent guitarists in rock music history. Includes information on Darrell Abbott, Duane Allman, Chuck Berry, Eric Clapton, Kurt Cobain, The Edge, John Frusciante, Jerry Garcia, David Gilmour, Kirk Hammett and James Hetfield, George Harrison, Jimi Hendrix, Tony Iommi, Yngwie Malmsteen, Jimmy Page, Randy Rhoads, Keith Richards, Carlos Santana, Slash, Pete Townsend, Eddie Van Halen, Stevie Ray Vaughan, Neil Young, and Frank Zappa.

888. **Halbscheffel, Bernwald**. 2013. *Sachlexikon Rockmusik: Instrumente, Technik, Industrie (Sachlexikon on Rock Music: Instruments, Technology, Industry)*. Series: *Musik (Leipzig, Germany); 6*. Leipzig: Halbscheffel Verlag. German text. Two Volumes. x, 432 p. & 821 p. Bibliography. ISBN: 9-783-94348-303-1.

Contains a series of articles on the terminology and topics of rock music and its performance—musical instruments ranging from electric guitar to the theremin, the equipment necessary for concerts and studios, including microphones, amplifiers, and mixing boards, small record companies, and so forth. Incorporates discographies bibliographies, and Web references. Boundaries of rock music are often crossed into pop and jazz with references that provide an extended overview of a topic to help to better understand its context.

889. **Halbscheffel, Bernwald**. 2013. *Lexikon Progressive Rock: Musiker, Bands, Instrumente, Begriffe (Encyclopedia of Progressive Rock: Musicians, Bands, Instruments, Terms) revised ed*. Series: *Musik (Leipzig, Germany)*. German text. Leipzig: Halbscheffel Verlag. iii, 560 p. Bibliography. ISBN: 9-783-94348-301-7.

Provides entries that feature not only classics of pop rock such as Procol Harum, the Nice, Yes, Emerson, Lake & Palmer, Genesis, and King Crimson, but also more recent groups like Dream Theater, Gazpacho, Glass Hammer, Porcupine Tree, Shining, Spock's Beard, Grand General, and many others. Although many of the entries focus on British and American bands, some articles include information on obscure bands. Some articles also address current trends in progressive rock, such as retroprog, neoprog, and new artrock, and foundational musical terms such as polyrhythmics and much more.

890.   **Hall, Patricia, ed**. 2018. *The Oxford Handbook of Music Censorship*. Series: *Oxford Handbooks*. New York: Oxford University Press. xii, 709 p. Bibliography and Index. ISBN: 9-780-19973-316-3.

Offers a series of scholarly essays that focus on centuries of music censorship across the globe from the medieval era to the modern day. Essays offer case studies that address several instances both well and lesser known, including the tumultuous history of Richard Wagner in Israel; rap music in the United States; silencing women composers; and music in post-revolutionary Iran. Compiled essays are integrated into sections organized by nature of censorship, religious, racial and sexual, and types of government enforcement—democratic, totalitarian, and transitional, and they also focus on individual composers, artists, and eras within single countries.

891.   **Hamer, Laura, ed**. 2021. *The Cambridge Companion to Women in Music Since 1900*. Series: *Cambridge Companions to Music*. New York: Cambridge University Press. xxx, 325 p. Illustrations, Bibliography, and Index. ISBN: 9-781-10855-649-1.

Focuses on the roles and images of women at the start of the twentieth century and continuing to contemporary times. Offers diverse topics about women in music that include women in composition before World War II; women in compositions after the Cold War; female composers in the Soviet Bloc; women in popular music; women in the progression of jazz; girl groups in the 1960s; women and rock; women in songwriting; the British Folk Festival and women; MTV idols; survival in popular music from 1981 to the present; women in music and technology; women and music education; women in the music industry; and so forth.

892.   **Handel, Leigh Van, ed**. 2020. *The Routledge Companion to Music Theory Pedagogy*. Series: *Routledge Music Companions*. New York: Routledge. xv, 498 p. Illustrations, Music Examples, Bibliography, and Index. ISBN: 9-781-03217-413-6.

A collection of essays that takes a unique approach to resources for both the conceptual and pragmatic sides of music theory pedagogy. Essays focus on core elements of music theory curriculum that include fundamentals; rhythm and meter; core curriculum; aural skills; post-tonal theory; form; popular music; and who, what, and how to teach.

893.   **Harris, Travis**. 2019. "(Global) Hip-Hop Studies Bibliography." *Journal of Hip-Hop Studies* 6(2): 71–121, 244, & 71A. ISSN: 2331-5563.

Documents hip-hop scholarship outside of America, including scholarly works that may be centered in the United States but expand the analysis to other parts of the world. Also demonstrates how hip-hop studies outside the United States stretches as far and wide as hip-hop itself. Includes the variety of scholarly works in the first wave of scholarship in 1984 and beyond.

894.   **Hartenberger, Russell, and Ryan McClelland, eds**. 2020. *The Cambridge Companion to Rhythm*. Series: *Cambridge Companions to Music*. Cambridge & New

York: Cambridge University Press. xxvi, 343 p. Illustrations, Bibliography, and Index. ISBN: 9-781-10863-173-0.

Explores the richness of musical time through a variety of perspectives, surveys writings on the topic, and incorporates the perspectives of listeners, analysts, composers, and performers. Includes chapters on music perception, visualizing rhythmic notation, composers writing on rhythm, rhythm in jazz, rock, and hip-hop. Provides a global approach and explores rhythmic style in the music of India, Africa, Bali, Latin America, and the Caribbean, as well as Indigenous music of North and South America.

895.   **Hawkins, Stan, ed**. 2017. *The Routledge Companion to Popular Music and Gender*. Abingdon, Oxon & New York: Routledge. xvii, 382 p. Illustrations, Music Examples, Bibliography, and Index. ISBN: 9-781-47245-683-0.

An edited volume that develops and present new theories and methods in the analysis of popular music and gender. Contributions are drawn from a range of disciplines, including musicology, sociology, anthropology, gender studies, philosophy, and media studies. Topics addressed inquire into why gender is inseparable from pop songs, what gender represents in musical performances, and why there are strong links between gender, sexuality, and popular music. Includes innovative approaches to queer performativity, gender theory, gay and lesbian agency, the female pop celebrity, masculinities, transculturalism, queering, transgenderism, and androgyny. The volume also covers musicians such as Justin Bieber, Ludacris, Tanya Tagaq, Johnny Cash, Beyoncé, Lady Gaga, Jenny Lind, Missy Elliott, Jesse Jones (Norwegian rapper), Erykah Badu, Marit Larsen, Kanye West, and Mina Caputo.

896.   **Heesch, Florian**. 2016. "Voicing the Technological Body: Some Methodological Reflections on Combinations of Voice and Technology in Popular Music." *Journal for Religion, Film and Media* 2(1): 49–69. ISSN: 2414-0201.

Deals with intersections of voice, body, and technology in popular music from a methodological perspective to outline a systematic approach to the history of music technology and aesthetic aspects of a popular song. Examines several relations between voice, body, and technology to musical representations of identity, gender, and race.

897.   **Heile, Björn, and Charles Wilson, eds.** *The Routledge Research Companion to Modernism in Music*. Series: *Routledge Music Companions*. London: Routledge. 534 p. Bibliography and Index. ISBN: 9-780-36773-303-2.

A series of essays contributed by scholars associated with "new musicology," that address issues in modernist studies such as aesthetics, history, institutions, place, diaspora, cosmopolitanism production, performance, communication technologies, and the interface with postmodernism. Essays also explore topics less established such as modernism and affect; modernism and comedy; modernism versus the contemporary; and the crucial distinction between modernism in popular culture and popular music. Essays also seek to define modernism in music by probing its margins as much as by restating its supposed essence.

898. **Henderson, Lol, and Lee Stacey**. 2013. *Encyclopedia of Music in the 20th Century*. Previously published London & Chicago: Fitzroy Dearborn, 1999. Abingdon: Routledge. 801 p. Illustrations, Portraits, Bibliography, and Index. ISBN: 9-781-13592-953-4.

Covers all aspects of twentieth-century music from around the world, ranging from classical to popular music genres with entries devoted to composers, performers, genres, and styles of music, countries, and regions. Provides biographical and historical content, but many articles also contain suggestions for further readings and listening and cross-references to other relevant entries. Also features a biographical digest with descriptions of performers, composers, a glossary, and so forth.

899. **Henry, Clarence B**. 2022. *Global Jazz: A Research and Information Guide*. Series: *Routledge Music Bibliographies*. New York: Routledge. x, 378 p. Bibliography and Indexes. ISBN: 9-780-36772-483-2.

An annotated bibliography that defines the field of global jazz and introduces scholars, researchers, practitioners, performers, and the public to the vastness of global jazz research and jazz experiences from around the world. This book is comprised of annotated essays that explore the global impact of jazz, detailing the evolution of the African American tradition as it has been absorbed, transformed, and expanded cross the world's historical, political, and social landscapes. Covers a broad range of subjects, people, and geographic regions as they relate to interdisciplinary research in jazz studies. The volume presents jazz as a common language in a global landscape of diverse artistic expression and is divided into several chapters that include North America: United States and Canada; South America/Latin America and Caribbean; Europe; Africa and Middle East; Asia; and Australia, New Zealand, and Oceania.

900. **Hoffman, Frank W., and Howard Ferstler**. 2006. *Encyclopedia of Recorded Sound 2nd ed*. New York: Routledge. Two Volumes. xxi, 1289 p. Illustrations, Bibliography, and Index. ISBN: 9-780-20348-427-2.

An encyclopedia that covers technical concepts such as oversampling; music genres such as rock music recordings; key figures in the development of recorded sound, recording groups, and artists; equipment manufacturers; and even practical matters such as cleaning. Topics focus mainly on developments in the United States but also include contributions to the nation's musical life from other countries. Also incorporates updated new content including information from the 1990s and early 2000s, such as the merger of AOL and Time Warner.

901. **Homan, Shane, ed**. 2022. *The Bloomsbury Handbook of Popular Music Policy*. New York: Bloomsbury. 496 p. Bibliography and Index. ISBN: 9-781-50134-534-0.

Offers analysis of how policy frames the behaviors of audiences, industries, and governments in the production and consumption of popular music. Covers a range of industrial and national contexts and assesses how music policy has become an important arm of government and a contentious arena of global debates across areas of cultural trade, intellectual property, and media cultural contents, and much more.

902.   **Ingham, Richard, ed**. 2011. *The Cambridge Companion to the Saxophone*. Series: *Cambridge Collections Online; Cambridge Companions to Music; Cambridge Companions Complete Collection*. Cambridge: Cambridge University Press. xvi, 226 p. Illustrations, Facsimiles, Music Examples, Portraits, Bibliography, and Index. ISBN: 9-781-13900-204-2.

Provides a history, technical development, and repertoire of the saxophone. Incorporates a vast amount of information that details the developments in classical, jazz, rock music, pop studios, and electronic age with midi wind instruments. Also provides information on the saxophone in terms of a practical performance guide and teaching the instrument.

903.   **Iwaschin, Roman, ed**. 2017. *Popular Music: A Reference Guide*. Originally published, New York: Garland, 1986. Series: *Routledge Library Editions*. New York: Routledge. xiii, 658 p. Index. ISBN: 9-781-13865 529 4.

A comprehensive guide to popular music literature. Focus is on American and British works but also includes works from other countries. The guide is divided into several sections: The Music—Folk Music, Country Music, Cajun Music, Black Music, General Works, Sacred Music, Ragtime, Blues, Rhythm and Blues, Soul, Rap and Hip Hop, Caribbean Music, African Pop, Jazz, Stage and Screen, Minstrelsy, Music Hall, Vaudeville to Cabaret, Musicals and Revue, Venues, and Dance; Biography; Technical; The Music Business; Product; Literary Works; and Periodicals.

904.   **Jeffries, Stan, ed**. 2003. *Encyclopedia of World Pop Music 1980–2001*. Westport: Greenwood Press. xiii, 277 p. Illustrations, Appendices, Bibliography, and Index. ISBN: 9-780-31309-120-9.

An encyclopedia that chronicles the careers of over one hundred musical artists from thirty-seven different countries. Entries include biographical information. Traces artists' musical development and recounts performers' critical and popular reception. Includes photographs, an index by nation, appendices of music industry awards, and standards for gold and platinum certification by country.

905.   **Kim, Suk-Young, ed**. 2023. *The Cambridge Companion to K-Pop*. Series: *Cambridge Companions to Music*. Cambridge: Cambridge University Press. 296 p. Bibliography and Index. ISBN: 9-781-10893-807-5.

A companion that probes into the complexities of K-pop as both a music industry and a transnational cultural scene. Compiled chapters investigate the ascent of K-pop within the context of growing global connectivity, highlighting iconic groups such as BTS. They examine how a distinctive model of production and consumption is closely associated with creativity and futurity. Chapters are divided into six parts: Part I—Genealogies; Part II—Sounding Out K-Pop; Part III—Dancing to K-Pop; Part IV—The Making of Idols; Part V—The Band That Surprised the World; and Part VI—Circuits of K-Pop Flow.

906.   **Kostelanetz, Richard**. 2019. *A Dictionary of Avant-Gardes, 3rd ed*. Abingdon: Routledge. xxii, 735 p. Bibliography and Index. ISBN: 9-781-35126-712-0.

Provides information on aesthetic innovation in the arts including music, film, literature, visual arts, dance, and theater. Covers artists mainly active in the twentieth century such as Charles Ives, John Lennon, Igor Stravinsky, Edgard Varese, Laurie Anderson, and many others. Entry sections include Kinetic Art, Serial Musk, Mixed-Means Theater, Zaum (poetry), SoHo, and Something Else Press.

907.   **Kureishi, Hanif, and Jon Savage, eds**. 1995. *The Faber Book of Pop*. London: Faber & Faber. xxxiii, 862 p. Illustrations, Bibliography, and Index. ISBN: 0-57116-992-9.

Charts the course of popular music from its underground origins through its low- and high-art phases out to the mainstream. Incorporates fiction, reportage, fashion, art, and fantasy as filtered through popular music.

908.   **Larkin, Colin**. 2006. *Encyclopedia of Popular Music, 4th ed*. New York: MUZE & Oxford University Press. Revised edition of *The Guinness Encyclopedia of Popular Music*, 1995. Ten Volumes. Bibliography and Index. ISBN: 9-780-19531-373-4.

Contain entries that cover all genres and periods of popular music from 1900 to the present day, including jazz, country, folk, rap, reggae, techno, musicals, and world music. Includes thousands of new entries on trends, styles, record labels, venues, and music festivals. Includes key dates, biographies, and further readings for artists covered along with discographies, release dates, and a five-star album rating system.

909.   **Lesaffre, Micheline, Pieter-Jan Maes, and Marc Leman, eds**. 2017. *The Routledge Companion to Embodied Music Interaction*. Series: *Routledge Music Companions*. New York: Routledge. 484 p. Bibliography and Index. ISBN: 9-780-36787-684-5.

A compilation of essays that offer both empirical and theoretical perspectives and focus on the role of the human body in musical experiences. Essays explore all aspects of understanding how we interact with music. They also address the issues that have stimulated the curiosities of scientists to understand the complex multifaceted way in which music manifests itself not just as sound but also as a variety of cultural styles and experiences.

910.   **Lewis, George, and Benjamin Piekut, eds**. 2018. *The Oxford Handbook of Critical Improvisation Studies*. Series: *Oxford Handbooks*. New York: Oxford University Press. Two Volumes. Illustrations, Bibliography, and Index. ISBN: 9-780-19537-093-5 and 9-780-19760-251-5.

A reference source that focuses on how improvisation forms a vast array of human activity from creative practices in art, dance, music, and literature to everyday conversation and relationships to natural and built environments. Compiled essays stem from scholars in architecture, anthropology, art history, computer science, cognitive sciences, cultural studies, musicology, popular music studies, performance studies, and many others.

911. **Lindgren, Mia, and Jason Loviglio, eds**. 2022. *The Routledge Companion to Radio and Podcast Studies*. Series: *Routledge Media and Cultural Studies Companions*. Abingdon, Oxon: Routledge. 502 p. Illustrations, Bibliography, and Index. ISBN: 9-780-36743-263-8.

Offers a comprehensive companion to the field of radio, audio, and podcast study, integrating a range of essays that examine the core questions and key debates surrounding radio practices, technologies, industries, policies, resources, histories, and relationships with audiences. Compiled essays draw upon multidisciplinary scholarship and offer global perspectives on radio's enduring affinity to the local historical relationship to the national and its unpredictably transnational reach.

912. **MacDonald, Raymond, David J. Hargreaves, and Dorothy Miell, eds**. 2017. *Handbook of Musical Identities*. Oxford: Oxford University Press. xix, 876 p. Illustrations, Maps, Bibliography, and Index. ISBN: 9-780-19967-948-5.

An edited compilation that examines and discusses how music is used to communicate emotions, thoughts, political statements, social relations, and physical expression. Essays consider how music can have a profound influence on our developing sense of identity, values, and beliefs, be it from rock music, classical music, or jazz. Compiled essays are featured in several sections: current psychological approaches to musical identities; context in which musical identities have been investigated; concerns about definition, development, individual difference, global intertextual musical arena, and so forth.

913. **Mantie, Roger, and Gareth D. Smith, eds**. 2017. *The Oxford Handbook of Music-Making and Leisure*. Series: *Oxford Handbooks*. New York: Oxford University Press. 696 p. Illustrations, Bibliography, and Index. ISBN: 9-780-19024-470-5.

A reference source that presents ways for reconsidering and refocusing in which people of all ages make time for making music. Topics discussed are broadly Western, including a diversity of voices from scholars across fields and disciplines, framing complex and multifaceted phenomena that may be viewed as an attempt to reclaim music making and leisure as a serious concern for policy makers, scholars, and educators.

914. **Mathias, Rhiannon, ed**. 2022. *The Routledge Handbook of Women's Work in Music*. Series: *Routledge Music Handbooks*. London & New York: Routledge. xxi, 465 p. Illustrations, Bibliography, and Index. ISBN: 9-780-36719-209-9.

Provides a collection of essays by academics and music practitioners from around the world that engages with a wide range of topics on women's contributions to

Western and Eastern art music, popular music, world music, music education, and ethnomusicology, as well as in the music industry. Essays are divided into several sections: Challenging Gender Inequalities; (Re)Discoveries: Aesthetics and Music Creation; Performance and Reception; Opportunities and Leadership in the Music Profession; and New Perspectives on Women's Work in Music.

915.	**Matzke, Peter, Tobias Seeliger, Volkmar Kuhnle, and Conny Bruckbauer, eds**. 2003. *Das Gothic und Dark Wave-Lexikon die Schwarzen Szene von A–Z (The Gothic and Dark Wave Lexicon from A–Z)*. Berlin: Schwarkopf & Schwarzkopf. German text. 614 p. Illustrations, [64 p.] of plates, Portraits, Discography, and Index. ISBN: 9-783-89602-522-7.

A reference source that includes fourteen hundred entries that link music and cultural studies through topics such as esotericism and vampirism, role play, and death. Entries focus on how goth music and culture are commonly buried in reference works on youth culture and counterculture. Covers the subject in depth and considers performers, styles, and concepts.

916.	**Maus, Fred E., Shelia Whiteley, Tavia Nyong'o, and Zoe Sherinian, eds**. 2010. *The Oxford Handbook of Music and Queerness*. New York: Oxford University Press. xiii, 676 p. Illustrations, Bibliography, and Index. ISBN: 9-780-19979-352-5.

Contributors of this edited volume explore their relationship with music and queerness to their work within and outside the academic community. Compiled essays offer a decisive departure from a Western and Eurocentric approach to music and reflect different rhetoric of queer musicology. Essays examine music and queerness experiences across a range of venues and approaches from gospel to electronic dance music and from Hong Kong public music to Ukrainian pop. Compiled essays illustrate the potential of queer methodologies in the musical realm and where we go from here.

917.	**McLean, Alex, and Roger T. Dean, eds**. 2021. *The Oxford Handbook of Algorithmic Music*. Series: *Oxford Handbooks*. New York: Oxford University Press. xi, 694 p. Bibliography and Index. ISBN: 9-780-19022-699-2.

A compilation of essays that features research on emerging and established scholarship. Compiled essays describe the state of algorithmic composition and set the agenda for critical research and analysis of algorithmic music. Topics include history, philosophy, psychology, algorithmic development in music, music makers, the role of algorithms, culture at large, and others.

918.	**Meadows, Eddie S**. 2010. *Blues, Funk, Rhythm and Blues, Soul, Hip Hop, and Rap: A Research and Information Guide*. Series: *Routledge Music Bibliographies*. New York: Routledge. xxviii, 388 p. Bibliography and Index. ISBN: 9-780-20385-472-3.

An annotated bibliography that offers a wealth of information on numerous examples of African American popular music. In compiling this resource, the author notes that despite the influence of African American music and study as a worldwide phenomenon, no comprehensive and fully annotated reference tool currently exist that covers the wide range of genres. This annotated bibliography is constructed to fill an important gap and will prove indispensable resource of librarians and scholars studying African American music and society.

919. **Midgelow, Vida, ed**. 2019. *The Oxford Handbook of Improvisation and Dance.* Series: *Oxford Handbook*. New York: Oxford University Press. xxvi, 805 p. Illustrations, Bibliography, and Index. ISBN: 9-780-19939-698-6.

Provides a reference source on dance improvisation in all its facets. Examines the ways dance improvisation practices reflect the ability to adapt, communicate, and respond to the environment. Provides case studies from a variety of disciplines and demonstrates the role of individual agency and collective relationships in improvisation not just to dancers but to all people of all backgrounds and abilities.

920. **Moir, Zack, Bryan Powell, and Gareth D. Smith, eds**. 2019. *The Bloomsbury Handbook of Popular Music Education: Perspectives and Practices.* Series: *Bloomsbury Handbooks*. New York: Bloomsbury. xix, 484 p. Illustrations, Bibliography, and Index. ISBN: 9-781-35004-941-3.

Draws on current research regarding thinking and practice on popular music education from empirical, ethnographic, sociological, and philosophical perspectives. Explores the ways in which international groups of music educators approach popular music education. Discusses pedagogies from across the spectrum of formal to informal learning including "outside" and "other" perspectives that provide insight into the myriad ways in which popular music education is developed and implemented. Compiled essays are organized into several sections: Conceptualizing Popular Music Education; Musical, Creative and Professional Development; Originating Popular Music; Popular Music Education in Schools; Identity, Meaning and Value in Popular Music Education; Formal Education; and Creativities and Assessment.

921. **Moore, Allan, and Paul Carr, eds**. 2020. *The Bloomsbury Handbook of Rock Music Research.* Series: *Bloomsbury Handbooks*. New York: Bloomsbury. xvii, 636 p. Illustrations, Bibliography, and Index. ISBN: 9-781-50133-045-2.

A compilation of scholarly essays that examine more than fifty years of rock music. Essays inquire into what rock music is; why it is studied; and how it works both as music and cultural activity. Draws on scholarly investigation on rock music to provide answers to these inquiries and much more. The compilation is divided into four sections: practice of rock (analysis, performance, and recording); theories; business of rock; and social and cultural issues. It also combines approaches that include providing a summary of current knowledge of the area, consequences of the research, and suggestions for subsequent directions in rock music.

922. **Moore, Allan, ed**. 2011. *The Cambridge Companion to Blues and Gospel Music.* Series: *Cambridge Collections Online; Cambridge Companions to Music; Cambridge Companions Complete Collection*. Cambridge & New York: Cambridge

University Press. xviii, 208 p. Illustrations, [8 p.] of plates, Music Examples, Bibliography, and Index. ISBN: 9-780-51199-871-3.

Covers musicians such as Robert Johnson, Aretha Franklin, Mahalia Jackson, John Lee Hooker, and others and how blues and gospel artists have played significant roles in twentieth-century culture. Provides an overview of histories, song and lyrical imagery analysis, so forth. Presents perspectives on artists from the standpoint of voice, guitar, piano, and as working musicians. Also includes discussions on the impact that blues and gospel has had on mainstream culture.

923.   **Musiker, Naomi, and Rueben Musiker, eds**. 2013. *Conductors and Composers of Popular Orchestral Music: A Biographical and Discographical Sourcebook*. First published in 1998. New York: Routledge. xxiv, 335 p. Bibliography and Index. ISBN: 9-781-13591-770-8.

A sourcebook that provides biographical and discographical information for approximately five hundred individuals who have written popular and mood music for film, shows, and theater. Delves into the recent history of popular orchestral music and covers the latter half of the twentieth century. The sourcebook focuses on music from the 1940s through the 1960s. Includes information on composers from the United States and Britain and classical conductors as well. However, those who composed for military brass bands, dance bands, and jazz are for the most art excluded.

924.   **Navas, Eduardo, Owen Gallagher, and xtine Burrough, eds**. 2015. *The Routledge Companion to Remix Studies*. Series: *Routledge Companions*. New York: Routledge. xxiii, 532 p. Illustrations, Bibliography, and Index. ISBN: 9-781-13474-874-7.

Comprises essays by authors and artists who are active in the emerging field of remix studies. Compiled essays inform on the art of remix as an organic international movement—a remix culture that originated in the popular music culture of the 1970s and has grown into a rich cultural activity encompassing numerous forms of media. Essays integrate discussion centering on issues such as the act of recombining existing material and questions of authenticity, reception, authorship, copyright, and the techno politics of media activism. Essays also approach remix studies from various angles and include sections on history.

925.   **Partridge, Christopher, and Marcus Moberg**. 2017. *The Bloomsbury Handbook of Religion and Popular Music*. Series: *Bloomsbury Handbooks in Religion*. London & New York: Bloomsbury. xiv, 425 p. Bibliography and Index. ISBN: 9-781-47423-733-8.

Provides a systematic analysis of the most important themes and concepts in the field, combining religious studies, theology, critical musicology, and sociology. Comprises thirty-three essays that explore the principal areas of inquiry as well as suggest new directions for scholarship. Religious traditions covered include Christianity, Islam, Judaism, Hinduism, Buddhism, Paganism, and occultism.

Coverage of popular music genres range from heavy metal and hip-hop to country music and film and television music.

926. **Peddie, Ian, ed**. 2020. *The Bloomsbury Handbook of Popular Music and Social Class*. Series: *Bloomsbury Handbooks*. New York: Bloomsbury. xviii, 598 p. Bibliography and Index. ISBN: 9-781-50134-538-8.

Incorporates research in ethnomusicology, sociology, cultural studies, history, and race studies. Explores the interactions between music and class and how the meanings of class are asserted and denied, confused, and clarified through popular music. Topics covered include methodologies; theoretical approaches; genres; punk rock; jazz, Argentine, and British rock; neo-folk music in socialist Yugoslavia; rhythm and blues and soul music; hip-hop in Cape Town, South Africa; country music; blues and the development of the African American working class before World War II; lesbian hip-hop; Norwegian black metal; globalization in African and Middle Eastern world music; popular music in Britain; California indie rock; music scene; and much more.

927. **Pendle, Karin, and Melinda Boyd**. 2015. *Women in Music: A Research and Information Guide*. Originally published in 2010. Series: *Routledge Music Bibliographies*. London & New York: Routledge. xxi, 846 p. Bibliography and Index. ISBN: 9-781-13887-043-7.

An annotated bibliography that reflects feminist scholarship and music. Provides extensive bibliographic information on many topics that relate to women in music. Provides country and regional information, as well as extensive sections that include the topical headings of Women in Rock and Pop; Women in Blues and Jazz; and Women in Country, Folk, and Gospel.

928. **Phillips, William, and Brian Cogan, eds**. 2012. *Encyclopedia of Heavy Metal and Culture*. Westport: Greenwood Press & Santa Barbara: ABC-CLIO. xxi, 285 p. Discography, Bibliography, and Index. ISBN: 9-780-31334-800-6.

An encyclopedia of A–Z entries that provides an extensive overview of the music, musicians, fashion, films, and philosophies behind the heavy metal movement. Chronicles the history and development of heavy metal including sub-movements of death metal, speed metal, grindcore, and hair metal. Biographical profiles include many of the bands and musicians that have defined heavy metal such as Led Zeppelin, Black Sabbath, Motley Crue, Metallica, and many others.

929. **Potter, John, ed**. 2001. *The Cambridge Companion to Singing*. Series: *Cambridge Companions to Music*. Cambridge: Cambridge University Press. x, 286 p. Illustrations, Bibliography, and Index. ISBN: 9-780-52162-225-7.

A companion on singing that ranges from medieval music to Madonna and beyond. Covers details on many aspects of the voice. Divided into four broad sections: Popular Traditions, which begins with an overview of singing traditions in world music and continues with aspects of rock, rap, and jazz; Voice in

Theatre, which includes opera singing to the present day and twentieth-century stage and screen entertainers; Choral Music and Song, which features a history of the art song, choir, the English cathedral traditions, and the choral movement in the United States; and a final section that focuses on performance practices, contemporary vocal techniques, ensemble singing, and others.

930. **Reddan, James, Monika Herzig, and Michael Kahr, eds**. 2022. *The Routledge Companion to Jazz and Gender.* Series: *Routledge Music Companions.* New York: Routledge. xv, 498 p. Illustrations, Bibliography, and Index. ISBN: 9-780-36753-414-1.

A compilation of essays that defines and examines the construct of gender in all forms of jazz, jazz culture, and jazz education, shaping and transforming the discourse in response to changing cultural and societal norms across the globe. Essays are divided into four parts: Part I: Historical Perspectives; Part II: Identity and Culture; Part III: Society and Education; and Part IV: Policy and Advocacy.

931. **Reily Suzel A., and Katherine Brucher, eds**. 2018. *The Routledge Companion to the Studies of Local Musicking.* Series: *Routledge Music Companions.* New York: Routledge. 548 p. Bibliography and Index. ISBN: 9-780-36757-055-2.

A compilation of essays that provide a reference to how cross-culturally musicking constructs locality, how locality is constructed by the musicking that takes place within, and how people engage with ideas of community and place through music. Essays offer insights into which musical practices and discourses interact with people's everyday life experience and understandings of their immediate environment, their connections and commitment to that locality, and the people who exist within it. Essays also explore what makes local musicking "local."

932. **Rodrigues, Eva M., and Inja Stanovic, eds**. 2023. *Early Sound Recordings: Academic Research and Practice.* Abingdon, Oxon: Routledge. ix, 268 p. Illustrations, Music Examples, Bibliography, and Index. ISBN: 9-781-03204-751-5.

Offers a wide range of contemporary research of performance practice and performance histories. Compiled essays employ the use of early recordings as a primary source to research performance in its broadest sense in a wide range of repertoires within the margins of the classical canon from the analysis of specific performing practices, notation, compositions, and others.

933. **Rojek, Chris, ed**. 2011. *Popular Music.* Series: *SAGE Benchmarks in Culture and Society.* London: SAGE Publications. Four Volumes. Illustrations, Bibliography, and Index. ISBN: 9-781-84920-758-4.

A multi-volume of essays that focus on social science perspectives of popular music since the late 1970s. Compiled essays are divided into four volumes as follows: Volume I—History and Theoretical Traditions; Volume II—Mode of Production; Volume III—Institutions of Popular Music; and Volume IV—Cultures and Subcultures of Popular Music.

934. **Sadie, Stanley, and John Tyrell, eds**. 2001. *The New Grove Dictionary of Music and Musicians, 2nd ed.* New York: Grove's Dictionary of Music, Oxford Music

Online/Grove Music Online. Twenty-Nine Volumes. Illustrations, Maps, Photographs, Music Examples, and Bibliography. ISBN: 9-781-56159-239-5.

Researchers of popular music studies will find this multi-volume resource helpful in that it incorporates in-depth coverage of art music, traditional music, regions, and popular music. Also includes topics such as gendered-related, multicultural, and interdisciplinary issues and notions about the ways music is being studied in contemporary times. This source can be accessed through *Oxford Music Online/Grove Music Online*, which offers music research of over fifty-two thousand entries written by approximately nine thousand scholars charting diverse history, theory, and culture of music from around the world.

935. **Schulze, Holger, ed**. 2020. *The Bloomsbury Handbook of the Anthropology of Sound*. Series: *Bloomsbury Handbooks*. New York: Bloomsbury. 486 p. Bibliography and Index. ISBN: 9-781-50133-539-6.

Presents the key subjects and approaches of anthropological research in sound culture. Essays are organized into six sections: Artifacts; Sound and the Body; Habitat and Sound; Sonic Desires; Sounds and Machines; and Overarching Sensologies. They explore research, methodological approaches, historical predecessors, research practices, and contemporary research gaps.

936. **Schwartz, Jeff**. 2018. *Free Jazz: A Research and Information Guide*. Series: *Routledge Music Bibliographies*. New York: Routledge. xx, 388 p. Index. ISBN: 9-781-13823-267-9.

Selected and annotated sources on free jazz and jazz musicians of published works that include English-language academic books, journal articles, dissertations, and others. Coverage includes selected annotations of free jazz and jazz musicians from many parts of the world including the United States, Argentina, Australia, Belgium, Canada, Eastern Europe, England, France, Germany, Italy, Japan, The Netherlands, Russia/The Soviet Union, and South Africa.

937. **Scott, Derek B., ed**. 2016. *The Ashgate Companion to Popular Musicology*. Previously published, Farnham, Surrey & Burlington: Ashgate, 2009. Series: *Ashgate Research Companions*. London: Routledge. xvii, 557 p. Illustrations, Music Examples, Bibliography, and Index. ISBN: 9-780-75466-476-5.

A compilation of essays that consider rethinking popular musicology and its purpose, aims, and methods. Geared to assist graduate students with research methodology and the applications of relevant theoretical models. Compiled essays are based on several themes: Film, Video and Multimedia; Technology and Studio Production; Gender and Sexuality; Identity and Ethnicity; Performance and Gesture; Reception and Scenes; and The Music Industry and Globalization.

938. **Scotto, Ciro, Kenneth M. Smith, and John Brackett, eds. 2019.***The Routledge Companion to Popular Music Analysis: Expanding Approaches*. Series: *Routledge Music Companions*. Abingdon, Oxon & New York: Routledge. xviii, 441 p. Bibliography and Index. ISBN: 9-780-36757-054-5.

A resource that widens the scope of analytical approaches for popular music by incorporating methods developed for analyzing contemporary art music. Approaches for popular music analysis is broadly defined by exploring the pitch-class structure, form, timbre, rhythm, or aesthetics of various forms of popular music in a conceptual space not limited to the domain of common practice tonality but broadened to include any applicable compositional, analytical, or theoretical concepts illuminates the music. Essays investigate a variety of topics, styles, and genres from rock and pop to hip-hop, rap, dance, and electronica, from the 1930s to the present day. The compilation is divided into five parts: Establishing and Expanding; Analytical Frameworks; Technology and Timbre; Rhythm, Pitch and Harmony; Form and Structure; and Critical Frameworks: Analytical, Formal, Structural and Political.

939. **Sheinberg, Esti, and William P. Dougherty, eds**. 2020. *The Routledge Handbook of Music Signification*. New York: Routledge. 428 p. Illustrations, Bibliography, and Index. ISBN: 9-781-03217-279-8.

Essays capture the complexity of music signification by incorporating a vast array of methodologies that seek to explore essential components in thinking about music. Essays embrace concepts and practices from semiotics, literary criticism, linguistics, the visual arts, philosophy, sociology, history, psychology, and others. Essays also cover various contexts in which music is created and experienced.

940. **Shepherd, John, David Horn, Dave Laing, Paul Oliver, and Peter Wicke, eds**. 2003. *Bloomsbury Encyclopedia of Popular Music of the World, Volume 1—Music, Industry, Society*. Imprint of *Continuum Encyclopedia of Popular Music of the World, Volume 1—Music, Industry, Society*. London & New York: Bloomsbury. 832 p. Discographies, Filmographies, Bibliographies, and Indexes. ISBN: 9-780-82646-321-0.

Provides an overview of media, industry, and technology and its relation to popular music. Combines entries authored by contributors from around the world. Explores the topic in two parts: Part I: Social and Cultural Dimensions, which covers the social phenomena of relevance to the practice of popular music. Topics include documentation, popular music studies, social phenomena, stylistic and textual dimensions, and venues; and Part II: The Industry, which covers all aspects of the popular music industry. Topics include audio technical terms, broadcasting, copyright, deals and contracts, the film industry, popular music, instrument manufacture, management and marketing, publishing, recording: record corporations, recording studios, record labels/companies, and unions.

941. **Shepherd, John, David Horn, Dave Laing, Paul Oliver, and Peter Wicke, eds**. 2003. *Bloomsbury Encyclopedia of Popular Music of the World, Volume 2—Performance and Production*. Imprint of *Continuum Encyclopedia of Popular Music of the World, Volume 2—Performance and Production*. London & New York: Bloomsbury. 712 p. Discographies, Filmographies, Bibliographies, and Indexes. ISBN: 9-780-82646-322-7.

Explores elements of production and performance and their relationship to popular music. Comprised of entries by contributors from around the world and is arranged in four parts: Part I: Performers and Performing Groups, Individuals, Performance Techniques; Part II: Musical Production and Transmission Personnel, Processes: Interpretative, Technological, Technologies; Part III: Musical Instruments—Found Instruments, Guitars, Keyboard Instruments, Mechanical Instruments, Percussion Instruments, Stringed Instruments, Voice, Wind Instruments; Part IV: Musical Form and Practice—Form, Harmony, Melody, Rhythm, the Piece, Timbre, Words, Images, and Movement.

942. **Shuker, Roy**. 2017. *Popular Music Culture: The Key Concepts, 4th ed.* Series: *Routledge Key Guides*. Abingdon, Oxon & New York: Routledge. xiv, 366 p. Bibliography and Index. ISBN: 9-781-13868-092-0.

An A–Z student handbook that provides a comprehensive survey of key ideas and concepts in popular music. With new and expanded entries on genres and sub-genres it offers a text that comprehensively examines the social and cultural aspects of popular music considering the digital music revolution and changes in the way that music is manufactured, marketed, and delivered. Examples of the entries include Age and Youth; Black Music; Digital Music Culture; K-Pop; Mash-Ups; Soul; Pub Music; Religion and Spirtiualty; Remix; Southern Soul; Streaming; and Vinyl.

943. **Smith, Gareth D., Zack Moir, Matt Brennan, Shara Rambarran, and Phil Kirkman, eds**. 2017. *The Routledge Research Companion to Popular Music Education.* London & New York: Routledge. xix, 490 p. Illustrations, Bibliography, and Index. ISBN: 9-781-47246-498-9.

A companion and reference work that integrates popular music as a growing presence in education, formal or otherwise, from primary school to postgraduate study. Deals with research on programs, courses, and modules in popular music studies, popular music performance, songwriting and areas of music technology, and others. Integrates a diverse range of research and scholarship in the emerging field of popular music education with perspective in the historical, sociological, pedagogical, musicological, axiological, reflexive, and other aspects of concern in popular music education.

944. **Stahl, Geoff, and J. Mark Percival, eds**. 2022. *The Bloomsbury Handbook of Popular Music, Space, and Place.* Series: *Bloomsbury Handbooks*. New York: Bloomsbury. xvii, 413 p. Bibliography and Index. ISBN: 9-781-50133-402-3. 380 p. Bibliography and Index. ISBN: 9-781-50133-631-7.

Integrates scholarship to introduce researchers to concepts and theories used to explore the relationships between place and music. Draws from interdisciplinary perspectives of sociology, geography, ethnomusicology, media, cultural, and communication studies and covers a wide range of topics related to the production and consumption of place in popular music. Considers the changes in technology and the mediascape that have shaped the experience of popular music (e.g., vinyl, iPod, social media), the role of social difference and how it shapes sociomusical encounters (queer spaces, gendered and racialized spaces), as well as the construction and representations of place (musical tourism, city branding, urban mythologies), and so forth.

945.   **Sturman Janet**. 2019. *The Sage International Encyclopedia of Music and Culture*. Thousand Oaks: Sage. Five Volumes, 2585 p. Appendix, Illustrations, Maps, Bibliography, and Index. Bibliography. ISBN: 9-781-48331-775-5.

A five-volume encyclopedia that covers music and culture in its cultural contexts and introduces the discipline of ethnomusicology, its methods, concerns, and contribution to knowledge and understanding of the world's musical cultures, genres, styles, and practices. Contains over seven hundred thirty entries, many of which are scholarly discourses on popular music genres from around the world. Also includes sections such as Further Readings and Cross References and a Reader's Guide that organize entries by broad topical and thematic areas.

946.   **Sullivan, Steve**. 2013. *Encyclopedia of Great Popular Song Recordings*. Lanham: Scarecrow Press. Two Volumes. 1030 p. ISBN: 9-780-81088-295-9.

Covers artists from John Philip Sousa to Green Day, Scott Joplin to Kanye West, Stephen Foster to Coldplay, and many others in the vast scope of great popular sound recordings. Contains approximately one thousand key song recordings from 1889 to the present time and explores the full narratives behind the songs, recordings, performers, and songwriters. Extends the coverage to genres neglected in popular music histories, from ethnic and world music, the gospel recordings of both Black and White artists, and lesser-known traditional folk tunes that extend back hundreds of years. Offers a resource for popular music scholars as well as fans of recording history and much more.

947.   **Thompson, Clifford**. 1999. *Contemporary World Musicians*. New York: Routledge. 600 p. Illustrations, Photographs, and Index. ISBN: 9-781-31506-241-9.

Traces the personal and artistic influences behind music makers from Elton John to Leontyne Price. Provides individual entries on over four hundred of the world's most renowned and accomplished living performers, composers, conductors, and band leaders in music genres from opera to hip-hop. Also includes an in-depth index covering musicians of all eras so researchers can discern which artists, alive or dead, influenced the work of today's most important figures in the music industry.

948.   **Tröndale, Martin, ed., and Erik Dorset, translator**. 2021. *Classical Concert Studies: A Companion to Contemporary Research and Performance*. New York: Routledge. xviii, 362 p. Illustrations, Bibliography, and Index. ISBN: 9-780-36753-126-3.

Based on two earlier volumes titled *Das Konzert* (*The Concert*), with a selection of new essays written for the English edition. Maps out a new interdisciplinary field of concert studies concerning new ways of understanding the classical music concert in the twenty-first century. Compiled essays integrate research articles and case studies and draw approaches from sociology, ethnology, musicology, cultural studies, and other disciplines to create a portrait of classical concert's past, present, and future.

949. **Vulliamy, Graham, and Edward Lee, eds**. 2016. *Popular Music: A Teacher's Guide*. Series: *Routledge Library Editions; Popular Music*. New York: Routledge. viii, 127 p. Illustrations, Music Examples, and Bibliography. ISBN: 9-780-71000-895-4.

Provides instructional and study material for teaching popular music. Divided into three sections: Why This Series?; Guidance for Teaching and Classroom Projects; and Further Resources.

950. **Warner, Jay**. 2004. *On This Day in Music History: Over 2000 Popular Music Facts for Every Day of the Year*. New York: Rowman & Littlefield & Hal Leonard. v, 369 p. Illustrations. ISBN: 9-780-63406-693-1.

Provides information and profiles on over two thousand entries that are listed in chronological order. Covers every day of the year and combines calendar format with photos and illustrations and includes elevated trivia about selected popular music songs.

951. **Whiteley, Shelia, and Shara Rambarran, eds**. 2016. *The Oxford Handbook of Music and Virtuality*. Series: *Oxford Handbooks*. New York: Oxford University Press. 720 p. Figures and Tables, Companion Website, Glossary, Bibliography, and Index. ISBN: 9-780-19932-128-5.

An edited volume in which contributors survey the terrain of music and virtuality and examine how the virtual environment has also allowed musicians to connect directly with their audiences and fans. Essays address the complex issues of what it means to listen to and engage in an age of illusion on the role of performers and musician, and what technologies such as looped performance animations and streamed music mean for an understanding of liveness and virtuality. Essays question whether and how Internet-mediated and face-to-face virtual practices give rise to an expanded conception of what it means to be a musician.

952. **Williams, Justin A**. 2015. *The Cambridge Companion to Hip-Hop*. Series: *Cambridge Companions to Music*. London: Cambridge University Press. xv, 349 p. Illustrations, Music Examples, Bibliography, and Index. ISBN: 9-781-10703-746-5.

Covers expansive materials on the hip-hop elements, methods of study, hip-hop and case studies from Nerdcore to Turkish-German, Japanese hip-hop, Senegal, Germany, Cuba, the United Kingdom, and other geographical areas. Compiled essays are written by scholars and industry professionals. Chapters provide an overview of the four elements of hip-hop: MCing, DJing, breakdancing (or breakin'), and graffiti. In addition, includes key topics such as religion, theater, film, gender, politics, and music.

953.   **Williams, Katherine, and Justin A. Williams, eds**. 2016. *The Cambridge Companion to the Beatles*. Series: *Cambridge Companions to Music*. Cambridge: Cambridge University Press. xvi, 366 p. Illustrations, Music Examples, Bibliography, and Index. ISBN: 9-781-31656-920-7.

Explores how the tradition of singer-songwriter has been expressed around the world and throughout its history. Topics are varied and include the emergence of the singer-songwriter, the German lied, Bill Monroe and bluegrass, the Brill Building, Los Angeles Troubadours, professional songwriters in the 1970s, Leadbelly, Thomas D'Urfey, and regional identity in Dolly Parton's songwriting. Topics also focus on the singer-songwriter roles of Elton John, Billy Joel, Adele, Kanye West, James Blake, and Joni Mitchell, female singer-songwriters, Greek entechno, global perspectives, and others.

954.   **Womack, Kenneth, ed**. 2011. *The Cambridge Companion to the Beatles*. Series: *Cambridge Collections Online; Cambridge Companions to Music; Cambridge Companions Complete Collection*. Cambridge: Cambridge University Press. xxiii, 316 p. Illustrations, Music Examples, Discography, Bibliography, and Index. ISBN: 9-780-52186-965-2.

From *Please Please Me* to *Abbey Road*, this collection of essays conveys the story of the Beatles. In scope, the essays focus on the creation of the band, their musical influences, and their cultural significance. Emphasis is placed on the Beatles in terms of genres and practices as musicians, songwriters, and recording artists. Some of the essay topics include the forefront years of 1950–1962, psychedelic years, free rhythms, and much more.

955.   **Wright, Ruth, Geir Johansen, Panagiotis A. Kanellopoulos, and Patrick Schmidt, eds**. 2021. *The Routledge Handbook to Sociology of Music Education*. Abingdon, Oxon & New York: Routledge. 538 p. Illustrations, Bibliography, and Index. ISBN: 9-781-13858-636-9.

A reference source appropriate for popular music studies, cultural studies, and others that provides the exclusive and explicit application of sociological constructs and theories to issues such as globalization, immigration, post-colonialism, intergenerational musicking, socialization, inclusion, exclusion, hegemony, symbolic violence, and pop culture. Contexts range from formal compulsory schooling to non-formal communal environments to informal music making and listening.

Note on the Indexes

For easy access and cross-referencing, complete and comprehensive sets of indexes for all the entries included in *Global Popular Music: A Research and Information Guide, Volumes 1 and 2* are compiled in each volume. These include: Index of Global Popular Music Genres, Index of Continents, Countries, Cities, Regions, and Localities, Index of Names, and Index of Subjects.

Index of Global Popular Music Genres

Dhrupad 3075
Diablada 1551
Dialect Pop 1864
Digital 300, 310, 312, 465, 860, 913, 934, 977, 983, 1550. 2251, 2270, 2397, 2412, 2414, 2739, 2786, 2856, 2937, 3002, 3003, 3048, 3056, 3093, 3131, 3263, 3452
Digital Cumbia 1769
Digital Reggae 1669
Digital Underground 934, 952, 983
Dikir 2866
Dimotiki Mousiki 934
Dirèk Konpa 1550
Dirge 934
Disco 41, 65, 260, 303, 312, 354, 369, 388, 399, 429, 477, 860, 916, 926, 934, 937, 945, 951, 977, 980, 983, 994, 999, 1027, 1085, 1178, 1274, 1280, 1411, 1591, 1592, 1806, 1885, 2106, 2200, 2249, 2275, 2307, 2335, 2403, 2410, 2411, 2437, 2459, 2608, 2838, 2866, 2961, 3003, 3120, 3123, 3035, 3191
Disco-Bhangra 3152
Disco-Funk 860
Discolypso 2446
Disco-Polo 1864
Disco-Pop 2275
Disco-Punk 476
Disney Music 977
Divertimento 934
Dixieland Jazz 38, 934, 977, 983
DIY 20, 22, 37, 38, 137, 214, 259, 310, 398, 607, 630, 634, 654, 678, 776, 834, 913, 926, 1574, 1858, 2030, 2159, 2200, 2275, 2411, 2860, 3191
Dobrado 1551
Doina 1864
Dominican-American Music 983
Đón ca tài tù 931, 3091
Dondang Sayang 934, 2866
Doom Metal 74, 926, 2430
Doo-Wop 922, 929, 934, 937, 983, 994, 1020, 1044, 1157, 1398, 1575, 2307, 2461
Dōtonbori Jazz 899
Downhouse Blues 922
Dream Pop 1887
Drill Music 1949, 2092
Drinking Songs 945
Drone Metal 74, 102
Drum 'n' Bass 110, 303, 354, 410, 834, 837, 934, 983, 1828, 1864, 1884, 1887, 1890, 2275
Drum Corps 983

Drūphād 2866
Du ca 2866
Dub 399, 410, 899, 834, 951, 1547, 1550, 1551, 1560, 1569, 1573, 1685, 1708, 1710, 1713, 1884, 1887
Dub-Electronic 1670
Dub-Poetry 1573, 1685
Dub-Reggae 115, 834
Dubsmash 1077
Dubstep 934, 945, 983, 1864, 2043, 2105
Duduk Music 2449
Duet 934, 1575
Dūlāb 2449
Dumka 934
Dunedin Sound 3356, 3376, 3398
Dupla 1591
Dupla Caipira 1591
Duplo 2866
Duranquense 934, 994
Dutar 2866
Dutch-Turkish Arabesk Rap 860
Dziriyyat 354

E

Early Computer Music 917
Early Country-Western Music 934
Early Music 929
Early Visual Music 917
Eartone Music 917
East Coast Hip-Hop 968, 991, 1244, 1483
East Coast Jazz 899, 934, 983, 994
East Coast Jazz 934
East Coast Rap 968, 991, 1244, 1483
East Coast Swing 983
Eastern European-American Music 999
Easy Listening 464, 838, 846, 983, 994
ECM Jazz 1864
Ecossaise 934
Eisterddfod 1864
Electric Blues 978, 981, 998, 1020, 1024
Electric Body Music 1864
Electric Boogaloo 980, 1228
Electric Jazz 1858
Electric Music 2866
Electric Percussion 934
Electric Rhythm and Blues 2030
Electric-Pop (Polynesian) 2866
Electro (Europe) 1864
Electro 934, 2411

2089, 2090, 2105, 2184, 2200, 2249, 2317,
2317, 2411, 2415, 2429, 2430, 2437, 2446,
2450, 2514, 2574, 2637, 2657, 2665, 2678,
2698, 2722, 2859, 2939, 2939, 2955, 2956,
3035, 3089, 3145, 3154, 3191, 3209, 3253,
3290, 3291, 3340, 3346, 3356, 3364, 3377,
3393–3395, 3407, 3442
Reggae (Malawi) 2446
Reggae (South Africa) 2446
Reggae (Sub-Saharan Africa) 2446
Reggae and Rap 966
Reggae en Español 1551
Reggae-Dub 1550, 3384
Reggae-Rock 934
Reggaeton 399, 648, 883, 931, 934, 945, 983, 1550,
    1551, 1568, 1569, 1572, 1573, 1575, 1580,
    1591, 1599, 1627, 1646, 1651, 1702, 1703, 1873
Regional Language Songs 3152
Regional Mexican Music 983
Regular Singing 983
Religious Music 999
Re-Mix 306, 834, 846, 917, 951, 966, 983, 1887
Renaissance 934
Requiem 934
Requinto Jarocho 1591
Resistance Music 983
Retro-Rock 74, 934
Reverse Stimulation Music 917
Revue 983, 994, 1864, 2411
Rhapsody 934
Rhumba 1558, 1568, 1569, 1591
Rhythm and Blues (International) 41, 119, 152,
    194, 274, 354, 370, 399, 410, 860, 903, 918,
    922, 926, 934, 945, 977, 983, 988, 994, 999,
    1027, 1031, 1139, 1072, 1082, 1083, 1096,
    1114, 1127, 1134, 1139, 1149, 1164, 1165,
    1176–1178, 1182, 1210, 1236, 1239, 1245,
    1270, 1287, 1290, 1291, 1313, 1329, 1385,
    1433, 1467, 1485, 1503, 1637, 1660, 1674,
    1864, 1869, 1884, 1921, 2010, 2022, 2067,
    2184, 2200, 2226, 2307, 2411, 2430, 2437,
    2459, 2692, 2698, 2899, 2919, 2980, 2982,
    3003, 3035, 3122, 3255
Ricercar 934
Rigaudon 934
Rigsar 3054
Rímur 1864, 2293
Ring Shout 312, 983
Ringbang 1551, 1559
Riot Grrrl 38, 345, 403, 994, 1931

Ritmo Orquidea 1551
Ritual Black Metal 926
Roadmarch 1637
Rock (Belarus) 1864
Rock (Europe) 1864
Rock (Georgia) 1864
Rock (German Democratic Republic) 1864
Rock (International) 41, 45, 47, 74, 88, 92,
    98, 112, 131, 133, 136, 146, 147, 198, 207,
    258, 264, 265, 270, 271, 301, 310, 312, 345,
    354, 399, 359, 370, 381, 383, 403, 404, 407,
    410, 412, 420, 435, 460, 465, 473, 480, 483,
    491, 497, 511, 513, 560, 567, 573, 592, 601,
    831, 832, 838, 844–846, 853, 860, 861, 869,
    872, 873, 885, 888, 889, 894, 899, 902, 917,
    921, 926, 927, 929, 931, 934, 937, 945, 951,
    957, 959, 963, 967, 968, 971, 972, 978, 983,
    986, 999, 1003, 1008, 1020, 1027, 1034,
    1041, 1046, 1047, 1062, 1063, 1065, 1068,
    1080, 1089, 1090, 1098, 1107, 1110, 1111,
    1115, 1119, 1123, 1130, 1136, 1151, 1153,
    1159, 1163, 1179, 1180, 1197, 1198, 1223,
    1241, 1255, 1275, 1282, 1288, 1296, 1297,
    1324, 1334, 1340, 1352, 1353, 1357, 1362,
    1367, 1370–1372, 1383, 1387, 1413, 1442,
    1457, 1464, 1488, 1494, 1495, 1500–1502,
    1514–1516, 1524, 1540, 1542, 1544, 1550,
    1560, 1566, 1568, 1572, 1574, 1575, 1578,
    1586, 1591, 1592, 1609, 1617, 1625, 1627,
    1637, 1643, 1664, 1704, 1715, 1720, 1724,
    1742, 1761, 1773, 1775–1777, 1784, 1785,
    1804, 1806, 1807, 1816, 1827, 1840, 1848,
    1849, 1864, 1865, 1885, 1886, 1900, 1901,
    1905, 1907, 1913–1917, 1922–1928, 1931,
    1937–1939, 1944, 1945, 1953, 1956–1963,
    1970, 1971, 1975–1977, 1982, 1983, 1988,
    1990, 1991, 1995, 2000, 2002–2005, 2007,
    2018, 2022, 2027, 2028, 2030, 2032, 2033,
    2049, 2056, 2067, 2071, 2103, 2104, 2005,
    2021, 2024, 2064, 2067, 2070, 2082, 2114,
    2116, 2124, 2126, 2132, 2133, 2134, 2152,
    2155, 2163, 2169, 2178, 2187, 2199, 2205,
    2215, 2224, 2227, 2230, 2234, 2238, 2239,
    2243, 2249, 2250, 2262, 2284, 2293, 2294,
    2299, 2307, 2309, 2320, 2324, 2335, 2345,
    2347, 2348, 2349, 2352, 2359, 2384, 2387,
    2388, 2391, 2403, 2405, 2410, 2415, 2417,
    2420, 2422, 2430, 2437, 2459, 2467, 2589,
    2711, 2715, 2720, 2722, 2733, 2734, 2744,
    2748, 2753, 2755, 2757, 2770, 2773, 2774,

West Coast Rap 968, 991, 1244, 1483
Western Folk Music 1145
Western Swing 7, 934, 957, 983, 994, 1020
White Metal 1828
White-Power Music 2249
Wienerlied 1864
Wind Band Music 2332
Wind Pop Music 3025
Wizard Rock (Wrock) 934, 983
Womyn's Music 38
Work Songs 931, 945, 983, 1020, 1700
Workout Music 312
World Beat 154, 270, 274, 338, 354, 435, 465, 664, 945, 999, 1547, 1564, 1664, 2240, 2633
World Fusion 934
World Jazz 899, 934
World Music 14, 52, 53, 55, 65, 109, 113, 124, 125, 154, 196, 200, 274, 279, 284, 289, 290, 294, 338, 347, 353–355, 399, 403, 410, 422, 429, 435, 441, 465, 536, 551, 616, 620, 664, 670, 694, 714, 739, 743, 799, 839, 846, 852, 860, 865, 867, 872, 908, 909, 914, 917, 926, 929, 931, 934, 945–947, 977, 983, 999, 1246, 1331, 1382, 1548, 1550, 1553, 1560, 1564, 1569, 1579, 1592, 1611, 1643, 1663, 1733, 1734, 1751, 1784, 1806, 1811, 1828, 1843, 1850, 1851, 1868, 1872, 1873, 1884, 1995, 2023, 2030, 2130, 2154, 2158, 2249, 2270, 2275, 2303, 2311, 2349, 2403, 2411, 2437, 2447, 2456, 2459, 2467, 2470, 2497, 2507, 2539, 2610, 2614, 2626, 2629, 2629, 2659, 2712, 2742, 2794, 2800, 2847, 2863, 2871, 2923, 2935, 2938, 3076, 3085, 3086, 3113, 3133, 3156, 3158, 3191, 3211, 3226, 3238, 3240, 3279, 3303, 3319, 3321, 3326, 3399, 3423
World Pop 354
Worship and Praise Music 983
Wylers 1667
Wyrd Folk 926

X

Xaxado 1551
Xinyao Pop 2866
Xote 1591, 1773

Y

Yahaengga (Fashionable Songs) 3003
Yambú 1573, 1575

Yangge 934
Yanvalou 1573
Yaravi 1551
Yéla 2446
Yenyengo 2446
Yeşil Pop (Islamic Pop Music) 2800
Yéyé 1560, 1573, 1864, 2200
Yé-Yé Québécois 994
Yiddish Popular Songs 834, 983, 1421
Yodeling 983
Yoreme Music 1628
Yugoslav-American Music 983
Yuhaengga 2866
Yumbo 1551

Z

Zabavna Muzika 1864, 2410
Zabavna-Pop 2410
Zabumba 934, 1591, 1592, 1755, 1784
Zagal 354
Zajal 2449, 2734
Zamacueca 1551
Zamba 1591
Zamrock 2430, 2446
Zapateado 399
Zapateo 301, 1551, 1573
Zār 2449
Zarabanda 1569, 1573
Zarb 399
Zarzuela 574, 934, 983, 1591, 1864
Zeitoper Jazz 846
Zemer Mizrahi 354
Zenji Flava 2446
Zenli 2446
Zikir 934
Zikiri 2446
Zilizopendwa 2446
Ziuta 2871
Zoblazo 2446
Zouglou 2446, 2662
Zouk 301, 399, 410, 934, 1547, 1550, 1551, 1557, 1560, 1568, 1569, 1573, 1575, 1591, 1806, 1884, 2437, 2459
Zouk-Soca 1674
Zumba 58, 1551, 1575
Zwiefacher 1864
Zydeco 399, 934, 945, 977, 983, 994, 1003, 1029, 1496

Index of Continents, Countries, Cities, Regions, and Localities

Index of Names

Sarno, Guilia 2
Sarrazin, Natalie 3032, 3076
Sartre, Jean-Paul 1254
Sasabe 2949
Satie, Erik 358, 694
Saunders, Tanya L. 1658
Saunderson, Kevin 1416
Savage, Jon 907
Savvopoulos, Kostas 2267
Scales, Christopher 1536
Scanlan, John 393
Scannell, John 1404
Scarlatti, Domenico 2399
Scarparo, Susana 2317
Schaap, Julian 345, 1878
Schade-Poulsen, Marc 2503
Schafer, Raymond Murray 2252
Schaub, Christoph 1405
Schedel, Margaret 666
Scheibling, Casey 1258
Schembari, Andrea 1300
Schenker, Frederick 1406, 3129
Scherben, Ton Steine 802
Schicker, Juliane 2243
Schifrin, Lalo 1761
Schiller, Melanie 2244, 2245
Schleifer, Ronald 394
Schlicher, Monika 3130
Schloss, Joseph G. 395, 1407
Schmidt, Cynthia 2455
Schmidt, Eric J. 2456, 2693
Schmidt, Joshua I. 2776
Schmidt, Patrick 955
Schmidt, Simone 805
Schmutz, Vaughn 153
Schneider, Britta 1891
Schoenebeck, Mechthild von 2246
Scholz, Arno 1825
Schoon, Aletta 2624
Schoop, Monika E. 726, 2247
Schreffler, Gibb 3077
Schulenberg, Ulf 679
Schulz, Dorothea 2694
Schulze, Holger 886, 935
Schumann, Anne 2662
Schwartz, Jeff 936
Schwartz, Jessica 3417
Schwartz, Roberta F. 2095
Schwartz, Stephen 1262

Schwarze, Tilman 2092
Scientists 3332, 3334
Scorpio Rising 393
Scorsese, Martin 239, 393, 823
Scott, Bon 3163, 3333
Scott, Derek B. 937, 2096
Scott, Jo Collinson 1920
Scott, Little Jimmy 1134
Scott, Michael 3388–3391
Scott, Michelle R. 1408
Scott, Niall 74, 606
Scott-Maxwell, Aline 3303, 3304, 3341, 3342, 3387
Scotto, Ciro 938
Screaming Trees 1371
Scribe 3368
Scrivanti-Tidd, Lisa 1020
Scruggs, Earl 127, 1039
Scruggs, T. M. 1626, 1627
Sculthorpe, Peter 3248
Seabear 2294
Seago, Alex 396, 2248
Sebald, Brigita 2386
Sebastian, Guy 3276
Sebiane, Maho 2827
Sedano, Livia J. 2357
Seeger, Anthony 14
Seeger, Pete 1024
Seeliger, Tobias 915
Seeman, Sonia T. 2828
Seibt, Oliver 2249
Seilstad, Brian 2504
Selby, Hilary S. 992
Selena 601, 1326, 1341, 1462
Sellers, Julie A. 1409, 1659
Sellheim, Nikolas 397
Selman, Brianne 1509
Sels, Liselotte 2829
Sem Terra Movement (Brazil) 1749
Seman, Pablo 1789
Sendioh, Ben 2479
Sengupta, Anita 2879
Seoul City Traditional Music Orchestra 2976
Seppälä, Henkka 27
Sepultura 1196, 1757
Serduchka, Verka 1873
Sernoe, Jim 727
Seroff, Doug 1035
Seroussi, Edwin 398, 2773

Westwood, Vivienne 854
Wetzel, Richard D. 462
Wexler, Jerry 1484
Whannel, Paddy 2714
Whatley, Jodie 1178
Wheaton, R. J. 463
Wheeler, Deborah 2840
Whelan, Andrew 464
Whidden, Lynn 1544
Whiskey 1998
White, Aaron Levine 868
White, Barry 1178
White, Bob 465
White, Bob W. 2482
White, Bukka 1469
White, Cameron 3340
White, Forrest 1485
White, Jack 731
White, Joy 806, 2123
White, Maurice 1091, 1121
White, Verdine 1091
Whiteaok, John 3341–3345
Whitehead, Alfred North 180
Whitehead, Peter 2038
Whiteley, Shelia 466–470, 916, 951
Whiteman-Charles, Nadia 1715
Whitener, John L. 2979
Whiticker, Alan J. 2124
Whiting, Samuel 3300
Whitmore, Aleysia K. 1662
Whitney, Karl 2125
Whitt, David 613
Who 304, 365, 571, 845, 2005, 2021, 2067, 2124
Whorf, Michael 1032
Whyton, Tony 774, 877, 1210
Wiatrowski, Myc 471
Wicke, Peter 472, 473, 940, 941, 2150
Wickström, David-Emil 770, 826, 2249, 2391
Widdess, Richard 3075
Wierzchwoska, Justyna 1364
Wiggins, Ella May 1471
Wikström, Patrik 2412
Wilcken, Lois 1045
Wilco 346, 658, 1024
Wilcox, Felicity 474
Wild, Stephen 739, 3346
Wilde, Kim 1183
Wilde, Oscar 1993
Wilkins, Jack 593

Wilkinson, Carlton J. 2126
Wilkman, Jon 1486
Williams, Hank 505, 564, 805, 962, 1360, 1401
Williams, Harry 3331
Williams, James 614
Williams, John 1050, 1051
Williams, Joseph 2127
Williams, Justin A. 475, 615, 952, 953, 2128, 2129
Williams, Katherine 953
Williams, Matthew 616
Williams, Oswald "Count Ossie" 1713
Williams, Pharrell 1114
Williams, Quentin 2632
Williams, Richard D. 2841
Williams, Robbie 1993
Williams, Sean 2130
Williams, Tony 1159
Williams, Wilga 3331
Williamson, John 647, 1962–1965
Willoughby, Bart 346
Willoughby, Heather S. 3028
Wills, Bob 1360
Wilson, Brian 811, 1108, 1130, 1265, 1266, 1301, 1420
Wilson, Charles 897
Wilson, Dave 373, 2360, 2361
Wilson, Gretchen 1470
Wilson, Jackie 988
Wilson, James A. 1487
Wilson, Oli 229, 755, 756, 3347, 3370, 3398, 3448–3452
Wilson, Rachel B. 2842
Wilson, Scott 2131
Wilson, Tony 2198
Wilson-Bokowiec, Julie 299
Winans, Priscila Marie "CeCe" 1332
Winans, Robert B. 2636
Winehouse, Amy 429, 719
Winkle Keller, Kate Van 1002
Winnicott, D. W. 487
Winningham, Mare 1087
Winter, Chris 3348, 3349
Winter, Rainer 1062
Winter, Robert 2230
Winzenburg, John 2967
Wire MC 3192, 3340
Wirrinyga Band 346
Wisnick, José M. 1804

Index of Subjects

World Music: Roots and Routes 714, Youth
Music: A Special Report 681

T

Theory, Methodology, and Musicianship Studies
7, 19, 35, 47, 60, 64, 68, 70, 97, 99, 104,
105, 115, 123, 133, 134, 138, 147, 149, 157,
166, 172, 173, 183, 196, 202, 205, 208, 213,
214, 240, 248, 258, 266, 270, 275, 287, 288,
290, 293, 294, 298, 307, 320, 330, 332, 337,
353, 356, 366, 369, 371, 374, 376, 377, 380,
396, 415, 419, 423, 442, 446, 462, 475, 479,
485–617, 633, 637, 638, 650, 655, 678, 681,
693, 699, 701, 702, 705, 706, 707, 708, 735,
742, 743, 746, 748, 749, 772, 773, 775, 778,
783, 785, 817, 830, 833, 834, 848, 849, 857,
863, 864, 879, 885, 892, 895, 909, 921, 926,
933, 937, 938, 944, 955, 980, 1036, 1063,
1064, 1100, 1115, 1137, 1215, 1230, 1240,
1250, 1253, 1270, 1281, 1288, 1298 1302,
1311, 1312, 1222, 1323, 1326, 1366, 1380,
1419, 1424, 1426, 1454, 1497, 1508, 1511,
1512, 1516, 1531, 1567, 1574, 1578, 1625,
1630, 1652, 1667, 1719, 1726, 1780, 1811,
1818, 1821, 1828, 1851, 1855, 1876, 1878,
1890, 1896, 1905, 1912, 1926, 1950, 1952,
1973, 1994, 2007, 2012, 2015, 2026, 2034,
2045, 2049, 2059, 2086, 2093, 2098, 2119,
2134, 2135, 2161, 2182, 2211, 2212, 2232,
2241, 2263, 2277, 2282, 2325, 2339, 2393,
2427, 2444, 2448, 2450, 2458, 2468, 2482,
2490, 2526, 2578, 2593, 2601, 2602, 2609,
2612, 2630, 2648, 2668, 2682, 2684, 2730,
2731, 2744, 2747, 2779, 2780, 2783, 2789,
2804, 2834, 2838, 2842, 2855, 2856, 2880,
2903, 2916, 2943, 2969, 2970, 2996, 3009,
3013, 3021, 3030, 3039, 3044, 3066, 3091,
3106, 3111, 3139, 3158, 3160, 3182,3192,
3232, 3249, 3263, 3270, 3292, 3298, 3330,
3340, 3372, 3395, 3404, 4307, 3442
Transmusical, Transcultural, Transnational,
Cross-Cultural Studies 30, 35, 53, 57, 136, 143,
172, 173, 175, 186, 206, 218, 223, 251, 286,
292, 336, 352, 354, 371, 379, 385, 392, 410,
415, 465, 475, 477, 501, 542, 556, 580, 590,
600, 631, 634, 648, 664, 679, 683, 707, 708,
723, 741, 750, 753, 760, 768, 773, 775, 905,
911, 931, 1062, 1111, 1172, 1231, 1245, 1277,
1293, 1294, 1306, 1307, 1318, 1333, 1356,

1382, 1405, 1409, 1507, 1525, 1534, 1546,
1547, 1565, 1573, 1574, 1582, 1589, 1598,
1601, 1602, 1630, 1642, 1662, 1687, 1697,
1747, 1750, 1761, 1806, 1828, 1832, 1838,
1839, 1843, 1846, 1849, 1850, 1851, 1856,
1857, 1858, 1861, 1873–1875, 1879, 1884,
1885, 1891, 1903, 1923, 1924, 1937, 1950,
1973, 2097, 2115, 2136, 2145, 2147, 2158,
2159, 2166, 2172, 2177, 2186, 2201, 2208,
2209, 2218, 2225, 2240, 2241, 2281, 2282,
2313, 2314, 2330, 2329, 2351, 2358, 2396,
2398, 2404, 2407, 2409, 2413, 2416, 2426,
2441, 2443, 2444, 2495, 2496, 2515, 2535,
2559, 2630, 2639, 2645, 2649, 2664, 2673,
2690, 2702, 2707, 2710, 2714, 2740, 2761,
2775, 2778, 2786, 2791, 2813, 2822, 2836,
2849, 2856, 2868, 2919, 2928, 2945, 2950,
2958, 2961, 2983, 2989, 3017, 3018, 3040,
3041, 3056, 3093, 3099, 3136, 3160, 3194,
3198, 3362, 3384, 3408, 3415, 3424, 3430

W

Women Studies 33, 47, 68, 82, 96, 111, 129,
135, 141, 143, 151, 152, 156, 165, 170,
171, 182, 188, 224, 228, 241, 249, 286,
287, 334, 339, 341, 345, 347, 381, 382,
386, 408, 443, 460, 470, 474, 478, 499,
612, 630, 637, 644, 647, 653, 655, 656,
664, 665, 703, 712, 719, 771, 787, 791,
865, 882, 890, 891, 914, 927, 956, 986,
987, 989, 1033, 1072, 1130, 1144, 1158,
1206, 1214, 1222, 1223, 1225, 1237, 1243,
1246, 1250, 1259, 1297, 1307, 1323, 1332,
1334, 1338, 1339, 1341, 1401, 1436, 1456,
1461, 1462, 1472, 1474, 1475, 1476, 1477,
1521, 1530, 1538, 1552, 1566, 1583, 1641,
1665, 1682, 1695, 1696, 1719, 1736, 1779,
1821, 1824, 1904, 1961, 2013, 2050, 2072,
2078, 2079, 2100, 2121, 2157, 2186, 2324,
2333, 2336, 2362, 2388, 2463, 2483, 2490,
2498, 2543, 2549, 2550, 2551, 2560, 2567,
2584, 2611, 2612, 2615, 2657, 2668, 2671,
2694, 2702, 2703, 2710, 2719, 2736, 2748,
2762, 2764, 2765, 2783, 2820, 2873, 2874,
2998, 3042, 3059, 3073, 3074, 3096, 3142,
3171, 3207, 3212, 3266, 3293, 3295, 3313,
3316, 3321, 3322, 3343, 3387, 3405
World Music 14, 52, 53, 55, 65, 109, 113, 124,
125, 154, 196, 200, 274, 279, 284, 289, 290,